Sources for
Western Society

Since 1300

Sources for
Western Society

Since 1300

Thirteenth Edition

THE COMPANION READER FOR
A HISTORY OF WESTERN SOCIETY

THIRTEENTH EDITION

Merry E. Wiesner-Hanks
Clare Haru Crowston
Joe Perry
John P. McKay

bedford/st.martin's
Macmillan Learning
Boston | New York

For Bedford/St. Martin's

Vice President, Editorial, Macmillan Learning Humanities: Edwin Hill
Senior Executive Program Director for History: Michael Rosenberg
Senior Program Manager for History: William J. Lombardo
History Marketing Manager: Melissa Rodriguez
Director of Content Development, Humanities: Jane Knetzger
Associate Development Editor: Stephanie Sosa
Senior Content Project Manager: Christina M. Horn
Assistant Content Project Manager: Natalie Jones
Senior Workflow Project Manager: Jennifer Wetzel
Production Coordinator: Brianna Lester
Advanced Media Project Manager: Sarah O'Connor Kepes
Media Editor: Mary P. Starowicz
Editorial Services: Lumina Datamatics, Inc.
Composition: Lumina Datamatics, Inc.
Text Permissions Manager: Kalina Ingham
Text Permissions Editor: Michael McCarty
Executive Permissions Editor: Robin Fadool
Director of Design, Content Management: Diana Blume
Text Design: Lumina Datamatics, Inc.
Cover Design: William Boardman
Cover Image: Madrazo y Garreta, Raimundo de (1841–1920)/Prado, Madrid, Spain/
   Bridgeman Images
Printing and Binding: LSC Communications

Manufactured in the United States of America.

2   3   4   5   6   25   24   23   22   21

For information, write: Bedford/St. Martin's, 75 Arlington Street, Boston, MA 02116

ISBN 978-1-319-26587-8

Acknowledgments
Text acknowledgments and copyrights appear at the back of the book on pages 502–503, which constitute an extension of the copyright page. Art acknowledgments and copyrights appear on the same page as the art selections they cover.

PREFACE

This updated edition of *Sources for Western Society* gathers a diverse array of primary sources from Western history that brings the past to life for students. Recognizing that history is shaped by the many as much as it is shaped by the few, *Sources for Western Society* includes the voices of men and women from across the social spectrum offering their own unique perspective on the events and developments of their times. Designed specifically to be used with all versions of *A History of Western Society*, Thirteenth Edition, the collection mirrors and complements each chapter of the parent textbooks, encouraging students to place the viewpoints of individual authors and artists in the context of the changing world in which they lived.

With input from current instructors of the Western civilization survey course, these documents have been compiled with one goal in mind: to make history's most compelling voices accessible to students, from the most well-known thinkers of their times to the most put-upon commoner. This emphasis on accessibility is crucial, since the reader is designed to challenge students to put aside their own preconceptions and to see history from the point of view of the people of the past. In Chapter 15, for example, students have the opportunity to read Jean Domat's 1689 argument supporting absolute monarchy in France and compare it to the English Bill of Rights from the same year, which limited the king's power. Written from different perspectives, these documents help students to develop a nuanced, multisided picture of this seminal development in Western history.

To allow instructors flexibility in assigning individual sources while providing opportunities for students to focus on a document-based issue through analysis of multiple sources, each chapter provides a selection of individual documents that illuminate the variety of major developments and themes from the textbook, as well as a "Sources in Conversation" feature that allows students to examine an issue from multiple perspectives. Selections range widely in length to allow for a range of class assignments.

This companion reader steps back from drawing conclusions and instead provides just enough background to facilitate students' own analyses of the sources at hand. Chapter introductions set the context of the documents that follow within the framework of the corresponding textbook chapter. A concise headnote for each document provides key information about the author and the circumstances surrounding the document's creation, while helpful gloss notes aid comprehension of unfamiliar terms and references. Each document is followed by Reading Questions that promote understanding and critical analysis of the material. In addition, new Read and Compare questions in the "Sources in Conversation" feature guide students in their comparison of the sources provided. Finally, chapter-concluding Comparative and Discussion Questions encourage students to contemplate the harmony and discord among the sources within and across the chapters.

New to This Edition

More than thirty new documents — including several compelling images — have been added to the Thirteenth Edition of *Sources*, offering increased representation of women and minority, particularly Muslim, perspectives. For example, Chapter 4 includes a new source describing the Jewish response to being ruled by the Greeks during the Hellenistic era; Chapter 9 now includes a Muslim account comparing two sieges of Jerusalem during the Crusades, one by the Catholics in 1099 and the other by the Muslims in 1187; Chapter 22 features an excerpt from Emmeline Pankhurst's speech made when she was sentenced to prison for having fought for voting rights for women; and Chapter 30 provides an excerpt of writings from Abdolkarim Soroush, an Iranian Muslim reformist scholar, who addresses militant secularism and the role it plays in contemporary society.

One of the most significant changes in the new edition is the addition of Read and Compare questions to the "Sources in Conversation" feature. Placed before the collected sources, these questions help students read the sources with purpose and consider their similarities and differences. For example, "Assyrian, Persian, and Hebrew Perceptions of Monarchy" in Chapter 2 asks students to think about the different expectations of kingship in three different societies, as well as the tone of the documents themselves; and "Debating the 'Iron Curtain'" in Chapter 28 invites students to compare Winston Churchill's and Joseph Stalin's speeches discussing the division of eastern and western Europe, specifically asking about their methods of addressing the audience and the ways in which their speeches reflect their positions of power.

Affordability Option

Sources for Western Society, Thirteenth Edition, is now offered in two low-cost e-books, and also as part of our Bedford Select for History affordability program, alongside the Value edition of *A History of Western Society*, Thirteenth Edition. Bedford Select lets you put together the ideal set of print materials for your course by allowing you to choose the chapters, readings, skills-based tutorials, and document projects you want — and even add your own resources as well. Instructors with enrollments as low as twenty-five students can take advantage of the options within Bedford Select to save students money. Visit macmillan-learning.com/bedfordselect to learn more.

Acknowledgments

Thanks to the instructors whose insightful comments and thoughtful suggestions helped shape the Thirteenth Edition: William Wantland, Mount Vernon Nazarene University; Ginette Aley, Kansas State University; Jennifer Foray, Purdue University; Kelley Obernuefemann, Lewis and Clark Community College; James Kabala, Community College of Rhode Island; Gesche Peters, Dawson College; Jeffrey Michael Long, Front Range Community College; Robert Janda, Cameron University; Jonathan Hall, Union County College; Laura Wertheimer, Cleveland State University; and George Gerdow, Northeastern Illinois University.

Special thanks go to Jeffrey Michael Long from Front Range Community College for his excellent and substantive contributions to this reader. Many thanks also to development editor Stephanie Sosa, William Lombardo, Heidi Hood, and Natalie Jones.

CONTENTS

CHAPTER 25   **War and Revolution**   1914–1919

SOURCES IN CONVERSATION
World War I in the Trenches and in the Air

CHAPTER 26   **The Age of Anxiety**   1880–1940

CHAPTER 30   Life in an Age of Globalization

Sources for
Western Society

Since 1300

The Later Middle Ages

1300–1450

Calamity followed calamity over the course of the fourteenth century. The High Middle Ages had been a period of slow but sustained population growth. That trend began to reverse itself at the beginning of the fourteenth century, when Europe's climate took a turn for the worse. As Europe grew colder and wetter, crop yields fell and famine followed. Thus, Europe's population was already weakened by malnutrition when plague struck in 1347, introduced into Europe through the same trade routes that had fueled the prosperity of the previous century. In the wake of the plague, peasant uprisings were frequent, as were uprisings of the urban poor. Between 1337 and 1453, the Hundred Years' War—in actuality a series of wars and civil wars—wreaked havoc on France. Finally, the papacy experienced a period of sharp decline in prestige and power, as the political rivalries of secular rulers led to schism within the church. The documents included in this chapter examine these catastrophes and their consequences. As you read the documents, think about the impact of war, disease, and religious strife on medieval social, religious, and political institutions. What changes in European society were made possible by the destruction of the fourteenth century?

11-1 | The Psychological and Emotional Impact of the Plague

GIOVANNI BOCCACCIO, *The Decameron: The Plague Hits Florence* (ca. 1350)

The first wave of the Black Death began in the late 1340s. The disease spread rapidly, and contemporaries understood very little about it, although they did associate it with rats. The only effective countermeasures were quarantine and isolation. The infection, which

From *The Decameron, or Ten Days' Entertainment of Boccaccio* (Chicago: Stewart & Kidd Company, 1920), pp. xix–xxii.

spread along trade routes from Central Asia, killed some 75 million people. Even after the first incidence receded, plague returned to Europe in many subsequent outbreaks until the 1700s, with varying mortality rates. In this document, excerpted from his famous collection of novellas, the Italian writer Giovanni Boccaccio (JEE-oh-VAH-nee buh-CAH-chee-oh) details the chaos unleashed in Florence as a result of the plague.

In the year then of our Lord 1348, there happened at Florence, the finest city in all Italy, a most terrible plague; which, whether owing to the influence of the planets, or that it was sent from God as a just punishment for our sins, had broken out some years before in the Levant;[1] and after passing from place to place, and making incredible havoc all the way, had now reached the west; where, in spite of all the means that art and human foresight could suggest, such as keeping the city clear from filth, and excluding all suspected persons, notwithstanding frequent consultations what else was to be done; nor omitting prayers to God in frequent processions: in the spring of the forgoing year, it began to show itself in a sad and wonderful[2] manner; and, different from what it had been in the east, where bleeding from the nose is the fatal prognostic, here there appeared certain tumors in the groin, or under the armpits, some as big as a small apple, others as an egg; and afterwards purple spots in most parts of the body; in some cases large and but few in number, in others smaller and more numerous, both sorts the usual messengers of death. . . .

These accidents, and others of the like sort, occasioned various fears and devices amongst those people who survived, all tending to the same uncharitable and cruel end; which was to avoid the sick, and everything that had been near them, expecting by that means to save themselves. And some holding it best to live temperately, and to avoid excesses of all kinds, made parties, and shut themselves up from the rest of the world; eating and drinking moderately of the best, and diverting themselves with music, and such other entertainments as they might have within doors; never listening to anything from without, to make them uneasy. Others maintained free living to be a better preservative, and would balk no passion or appetite they wished to gratify, drinking and revelling incessantly from tavern to tavern, or in private houses; which were frequently found deserted by the owners, and therefore common to every one, yet avoiding, with all this irregularity, to come near the infected. And such at that time was the public distress, that the laws, human and divine, were not regarded; for the officers, to put them in force, being either dead, sick, or in want of persons to assist them, every one did just as he pleased. A third sort of people chose a method between these two: not confining themselves to rules of diet like the former, and yet avoiding the intemperance of the latter; but eating and drinking what their appetites required, they walked everywhere with odors and nosegays[3] to smell to; as holding it best to corroborate the brain: for they supposed the

---

[1]**the Levant**: The eastern Mediterranean.
[2]**wonderful**: Astonishing.
[3]**odors and nosegays**: Perfumes and small bunches of flowers.

whole atmosphere to be tainted with the stink of dead bodies, arising partly from the distemper itself, and partly from the fermenting of the medicines within them. Others of a more cruel disposition, as perhaps the more safe to themselves, declared that the only remedy was to avoid it: persuaded, therefore, of this, and taking care for themselves only, men and women in great numbers left the city, their houses, relations, and effects, and fled into the country; as if the wrath of God had been restrained to visit those only within the walls of the city. . . . I pass over the little regard that citizens and relations showed to each other; for their terror was such that a brother even fled from his brother, a wife from her husband, and, what is more uncommon, a parent from its own child.

READING QUESTIONS

1. According to this account, how did civil order break down during the plague?
2. How does the narrator try to explain why the plague happened?
3. What are some of the things people thought might save them from the plague?

11-2 | A Town Chronicler Describes the Black Death

AGNOLO DI TURA, *Sienese Chronicle* (1348–1351)

Densely populated and closely connected to the Mediterranean trade routes that brought the plague to Europe, Italian cities were among the hardest hit communities. Agnolo di Tura was the town chronicler for the Tuscan town of Siena when the Black Death struck in the spring of 1348. According to di Tura, more people died in Siena in the first few months following the arrival of plague than had died in the previous twenty years. As you read his account of the devastation, reflect on the impact of the plague on the town's ability to function. With more than half the population wiped out, how did the Sienese community keep from falling into anarchy?

The mortality, which was a thing horrible and cruel, began in Siena in the month of May [1348]. I do not know from where came this cruelty or these pitiless ways, which were painful to see and stupefied everyone. There are not words to describe how horrible these events have been and, in fact, whoever can say that they have not lived in utterly horrid conditions can truly consider themselves lucky. The infected die almost immediately. They swell beneath the armpits and in the groin, and fall over while talking. Fathers abandon their sons, wives their husbands, and one brother the other. In the end, everyone escapes and abandons anyone who might be infected. Moreover, it appears that this plague can be communicated through bad breath and even by just seeing one of the infected.

From John Aberth, *The Black Death: The Great Mortality of 1348–1350: A Brief History with Documents* (Boston: Bedford/St. Martin's, 2005), pp. 81–82.

In these ways, they die and no one can be found who would want to bury them, not even for money or in the name of friendship. Those who get infected in their own house, they remove them the best way they can and they bury them without the supervision of a priest. No one controls anything and they do not even ring the church bells anymore. Throughout Siena, giant pits are being excavated for the multitudes of the dead and the hundreds that die every night. The bodies are thrown into these mass graves and are covered bit by bit. When those ditches are full, new ditches are dug. So many have died that new pits have to be made every day.

And I, Agnolo di Tura, called the Fat, have buried five of my sons with my own hands. Yet still I do not steal from those who were poorly buried like the dogs that eat them and litter them about the city. There is no one who weeps for any of the dead, for instead everyone awaits their own impending death. So many have died that everyone believes it is the end of the world. Medicine and other cures do not work. In fact, the more medicine people are given the quicker they die. The leaders of the city have elected three citizens that have been given 1,000 florins for the expense of taking care of the homeless and for burying them. These conditions have been so horrible that I do not reflect as often as I used to about the situation. I have thought so much about these events that I cannot tell the stories any longer. This is how the people lived until September [1348], and it would be too much for me to write the whole story. One would find that in this period of time more people died than in twenty years or more. In Siena alone, 36,000 people have died. If you count the elderly and others, the number could be 52,000 in total. In all of the boroughs, the number could be as high as 30,000 more. So it can be seen that in total the death toll may be as high as 80,000. There are only about 10,000 people left in the city and those that live on are hopeless and in utter despair. They leave their homes and other things. Gold, silver, and copper lay scattered about. In the countryside, even more died, so many that farms and agricultural lands are left without people to work them. I cannot write about the cruelties that existed in the countryside: that wolves and other wild beasts eat the improperly buried and other horrors that are too difficult for anyone who would read this account. . . .

The city of Siena appeared uninhabited because almost no one was found there. The pestilence remained and everyone who survived celebrated his or her fate. Of the monks, priests, nuns, women, and others from the secular community, they didn't worry about their expenses or games. Everyone appeared to be rich because they had survived and regained value in life. Now, no one knows how to put their life back in order.

READING QUESTIONS

1. How would you characterize di Tura's reaction to the plague?
2. What explanation, if any, did di Tura offer for the terrible events he described?
3. What signs of social breakdown did he note? What do they suggest about the full impact of the plague on late medieval life?

11-3 | Social and Economic Unrest in England

The Anonimalle Chronicle: The English Peasants' Revolt (1381)

Agricultural labor was traditionally carried out by serfs, who were bound by tradition to fulfill their obligations to their lords. The high mortality rate of the plague, however, resulted in a labor shortage across Europe. Some peasants tried to act on this advantage and force the lords to end their serfdom. When their demands were not satisfied, peasants often rose up against their lords. In England in 1381, an unpopular tax on all adult males prompted thousands of peasants to revolt. As you read this account of the revolt, pay particular attention to the targets of the peasants' anger. What distinction did the rebels make between the nobility and the king?

And on that Thursday, the said feast of Corpus Christi, the King, being in the Tower [of London] very sad and sorry, mounted up into a little turret towards St. Catherine's, where were lying a great number of the commons, and had proclamation made to them that they all should go peaceably to their homes, and he would pardon them all manner of their trespasses. But all cried with one voice that they would not go before they had captured the traitors who lay in the Tower, nor until they had got charters to free them from all manner of serfdom, and had got certain other points which they wished to demand. And the King benevolently granted all, and made a clerk write a bill in their presence in these terms: "Richard, King of England and France, gives great thanks to his good commons, for that they have so great a desire to see and to keep their king, and grants them pardon for all manner of trespasses and misprisions and felonies done up to this hour, and wills and commands that every one should now return to his own home, and wills and commands that each should put his grievances in writing, and have them sent to him; and he will provide, with the aid of his loyal lords and his good council, such remedy as shall be profitable both to him and to them, and to all the kingdom." On this document he sealed his signet in presence of them all, and sent out the said bill by the hands of two of his knights to the folks before St. Catherine's. And he caused it to be read to them, and the knight who read it stood up on an old chair before the others so that all could hear. All this time the King was in the Tower in great distress of mind. And when the commons had heard the Bill, they said that this was nothing but trifles and mockery. Therefore they returned to London and had it cried around the City that all lawyers, and all the clerks of the Chancery and the Exchequer and every man who could write a brief or a letter should be beheaded, whenever they could be found. At this time they burnt several more houses in the City, and the King himself ascended to a high garret of the Tower and watched the fires. Then he came down again, and sent for the lords to have

From Charles Oman, *The Great Revolt of 1381* (Oxford: Clarendon Press, 1906), pp. 196–203.

their counsel, but they knew not how they should counsel him, and all were wondrous abashed. . . .

And by seven o'clock the King [went to meet the peasants]. And when he was come the commons all knelt down to him, saying "Welcome our Lord King Richard, if it pleases you, and we will not have any other king but you." And Wat Tighler [Wat Tyler], their leader and chief, prayed in the name of the commons that he would suffer them to take and deal with all the traitors against him and the law, and the King granted that they should have at their disposition all who were traitors, and could be proved to be traitors by process of law. The said Walter and the commons were carrying two banners, and many pennons and pennoncels,[1] while they made their petition to the King. And they required that for the future no man should be in serfdom, nor make any manner of homage or suit to any lord, but should give a rent of 4d. an acre for his land. They asked also that no one should serve any man except by his own good will, and on terms of regular covenant.

And at this time the King made the commons draw themselves out in two lines, and proclaimed to them that he would confirm and grant it that they should be free, and generally should have their will, and that they might go through all the realm of England and catch all traitors and bring them to him in safety, and then he would deal with them as the law demanded.

[Meanwhile, fighting between the nobles and peasants continues, and many lords lose their heads to the commoners.]

And when he was summoned, . . . Wat Tighler of Maidstone, he came to the King with great confidence, mounted on a little horse, that the commons might see him. And he dismounted, holding in his hand a dagger which he had taken from another man, and when he had dismounted he half bent his knee, and then took the King by the hand, and shook his arm forcibly and roughly, saying to him, "Brother, be of good comfort and joyful, for you shall have, in the fortnight that is to come, praise from the commons even more than you have yet had, and we shall be good companions." And the King said to Walter, "Why will you not go back to your own country?" But the other answered, with a great oath, that neither he nor his fellows would depart until they had got their charter such as they wished to have it, and had certain points rehearsed, and added to their charter which they wished to demand. And he said in a threatening fashion that the lords of the realm would rue it bitterly if these points were not settled to their pleasure. Then the King asked him what were the points which he wished to have

---

[1]**pennons and pennoncels**: Small banners attached to lances.

revised, and he should have them freely, without contradiction, written out and sealed. Thereupon the said Walter rehearsed the points which were to be demanded; and he asked that . . . there should be equality among all people save only the King, and that the goods of Holy Church should not remain in the hands of the religious, nor of parsons and vicars, and other churchmen; but that clergy already in possession should have a sufficient sustenance from the endowments, and the rest of the goods should be divided among the people of the parish.

[The king agrees to these terms, and after he leaves, the mayor of London captures Wat Tyler and kills him.]

READING QUESTIONS

1. Who did the peasants blame for their troubles? Why?

2. What demands did the peasants make? What do these demands reveal about their social and political beliefs?

3. Is it plausible that the mayor of London would have Wat Tyler killed without the king's consent? What does this tell you about the king's true attitude toward the rebellion?

11-4 | Popular Religious Responses to the Plague

Flagellants in the Netherlands Town of Tournai (1349)

Because European people and institutions were not equipped to prevent or treat the plague of the fourteenth century, and the Catholic Church itself could offer little solace or assistance to commoners, many people took matters into their own hands and attempted to do penance for the perceived sins of humanity by ritually whipping themselves to seek God's forgiveness. This extreme form of popular religion was memorialized in some of the artwork of the period, including this mid-fourteenth-century piece from the Netherlands.

acubiq anno predicto q̃ m die accũpṫonis uirginis glori ose uenerunt a uilla brugen fi arater. cc̃. hominꝭ:. quasi hora ceperuũt com pãti persouis en penitenne coudolere eci deo gra tias redoere fup̃ tãnta peni tencia quam grauiffimam re

Ann Ronan Pictures/Print Collector/Hulton Archive/Getty Images.

READING QUESTIONS

1. How did the flagellants' mode of dress aid their message and mission as they traveled around?

2. What were the broad social consequences of this expression of popular religion for Catholics and people of other faiths? How did the flagellants' actions challenge traditional power structures and institutions in Europe, and how did the Catholic Church respond to their movement?

SOURCES IN CONVERSATION

Women and Power

Power politics in the late Middle Ages was a man's game. The medieval vision of government and society was profoundly patriarchal, and assumptions of male superiority shaped almost every aspect of medieval life. There were, however, women who were exceptions to the rule. For the most part, such women enjoyed the advantages of wealth and status. Less common were women, such as Catherine of Siena (1347–1380) and

Joan of Arc (ca. 1412–1431), who gained power through their reputation for holiness. Catherine, a nun of humble background who claimed to have experienced mystical visions, was an important participant in the religious and political debates of her day. Joan of Arc, a young woman from a small farming community, convinced many of France's leaders that God had chosen her to guide the French to victory in the Hundred Years' War.

READ AND COMPARE

1. What made it possible for these two women to play such powerful roles?

2. What precedents helped legitimize their actions in male-dominated arenas?

3. What made their claims to divine authority more dangerous than they would have been for men?

11-5 | CATHERINE OF SIENA, *Letter to Gregory XI* (1372)

In the early 1300s, the papacy moved its capital to Avignon, inside French territory. Because the pope was the bishop of Rome, it seemed wrong to move the head of the church away from his rightful home—and to a place where he could be easily influenced by the French king. Many people blamed the Avignon papacy for the plague and warfare across Europe. Still more linked the Avignon papacy to a general decline in the reputation and prestige of the church. In the 1370s, Catherine joined the effort to persuade Pope Gregory XI to return to Rome. As you read her letter to the pope, consider how her gender and spiritual reputation might have influenced the pope's reaction to her message.

Alas, what confusion is this, to see those who ought to be a mirror of voluntary poverty, meek as lambs, distributing the possessions of Holy Church to the poor: and they appear in such luxury and state and pomp and worldly vanity, more than if they had turned them to the world a thousand times! Nay, many seculars put them to shame who live a good and holy life. . . . For ever since [the Church] has aimed more at temporal than at spiritual, things have gone from bad to worse. See therefore that God, in judgment, has allowed much persecution and tribulation to befall her. But comfort you, father, and fear not for anything that could happen, which God does to make her state perfect once more, in order that lambs may feed in that garden, and not wolves who devour the honor that should belong to God, which they steal and give to themselves. Comfort you in Christ sweet Jesus; for I hope that His aid will be near you, plenitude[1] of divine grace, aid and support divine in the way that I said before. Out of war you will attain greatest peace; out of persecution, greatest unity; not by human power, but by holy virtue, you will discomfit those visible demons, wicked men, and those invisible demons who never sleep around us.

From Vida D. Scudder, trans. and ed., *Catherine of Siena as Seen in Her Lives and Letters* (London: J. M. Dent, 1906), pp. 131–132.

[1]**plenitude:** Full supply.

But reflect, sweet father, that you could not do this easily unless you accomplished the other two things which precede the completion of the other: that is, your return to Rome and uplifting of the standard of the most holy Cross. Let not your holy desire fail on account of any scandal or rebellion of cities which you might see or hear; nay, let the flame of holy desire be more kindled to wish to do swiftly. Do not delay, then, your coming.

READING QUESTIONS

1. What did Catherine want the pope to do, and why did she want him to do it?

2. According to Catherine, what happened to the church when the pope left Rome for Avignon?

3. What authority did Catherine have to make demands of the pope? How would you explain her prominence in the effort to persuade the pope to return to Rome?

11-6 | *The Debate over Joan of Arc's Clothes* (1429)

The public debate over Joan of Arc's status began almost as soon as she presented herself to the French court. Even after Joan had been accepted by the dauphin and joined the French in battle, supporters and opponents clashed over her claims to divine inspiration. In the spring of 1429, one of Joan's supporters circulated a treatise entitled *De mirabili victoria*. Later that same year, an anonymous member of the University of Paris countered with *De bono et malo spiritu*. One important point of contention between the two authors was Joan's decision to wear men's clothing. As you read the excerpts from these treatises, think about how female models and stereotypes shaped each author's argument.

De mirabili victoria

Here follow three truths in justification of the wearing of male clothing by the Pucelle,[1] chosen while following her sheep.

I. The old law [of the Old Testament], prohibiting the woman from using the clothing of a man and the man from the clothing of a woman [Deuteronomy 22: 5], is purely judicial and does not carry any obligation under the new law [of the New Testament]. [This is] because it is a constant and necessary truth for salvation that the judicial precepts of the ancient law [Old Testament] are quashed and, as such, do not bind the new one, unless they have been instituted again and confirmed by superiors.

From Craig Taylor, trans. and ed., *Joan of Arc: La Pucelle* (Manchester, U.K.: Manchester University Press, 2006), pp. 82–83, 125–127.

[1]**the Pucelle**: The maid.

II. This law [of the Old Testament] included a moral dimension that must remain in all law. It can be expressed as a prohibition on indecent clothing both for the man and for the woman, [as this is] contrary to the requirement of virtue. This should affect all circumstances bound by law, so that the wise person will judge when, where, to whom and how it is appropriate, and in this way the rest. This [law of the Old Testament] on these things is not confined to that one situation.

III. This law [of the Old Testament], whether judicial or moral, does not condemn the wearing of the clothing of a man and a warrior by our Pucelle, manly and a warrior, whom God in heaven has chosen through certain signs as his standard-bearer for those fighting the enemies of justice and to raise up his friends, so that he might overthrow by the hand of a woman, a young girl [*puellaris*] and a virgin, the powerful weapons of iniquity, with the help of the angels. By her virginity, she is loved and known, according to St. Jerome; and this frequently appears in the histories of saints, such as Cecilia,[2] visibly with a crown of roses and lilies. On the other hand, through this she is safeguarded from the [consequences of the] cutting of her hair, which the Apostle prohibits from being seen on a woman.

Therefore may the iniquitious [*sic*] talk be put to an end and cease. For, when divine virtue operates, it establishes the means according to its aim; hence, it is not safe to disparage or to find fault, out of rash bravado, with those things which are from God, according to the Apostle.

Finally many details and examples from sacred and secular history could be added; for example those of Camilla and the Amazons,[3] and moreover in cases either of necessity or evident utility, or where approved by custom, or by the authority and dispensation of superiors. But these are sufficient for brevity and for the truth. The party having just cause should be on close guard unless, through disbelief and ingratitude, or some injustices, they might render the divine help useless, that has begun so patiently and miraculously; just as [happened] for Moses and the sons of Israel, after having received such divine promises, as we read contained [in the Scriptures]. For even if God does not change His advice, He does change his opinion according to what people deserve.

De bono et malo spiritu

Regarding the preceding, I mean to deduce from canon law a small number of issues, in praise of all-mighty God, and in exaltation of the holy catholic faith.

And first, we have a duty to adhere firmly to the catholic faith, following the chapter Firmiter of the title *De Summa Trinitate*, without giving in any manner our approval to superstitious innovations, seeing that they engender discords, as one reads in the chapter Cum consuetudinis of the title *De consuetudine*.

Item, to give his support so easily to a young girl that was not known, without the support of a miracle or on the testimony of the holy scriptures, is to undermine this truth and this unchanging force of the catholic faith: wise men and canonists would not have any doubt about this. The proof is in the chapter Cum ex injuncto of the title *De hæreticis.*

---

[2]**Cecilia:** Catholic saint, martyred by the Romans in the second century C.E.
[3]**Camilla and the Amazons:** Examples of female warriors from classical mythology.

Item, if those who approve of the matter of this Pucelle say that she has been sent by God in an invisible, and in some sense inspired way, and that such an invisible mission is much more worthy than a visible mission, just as a divine mission is more worthy than a human mission, it is reasonable to reply to them that as this entirely inner mission escapes observation, it is not enough that someone claims purely and simply to be sent from God — this is the claim of all heretics — but it is necessary that he proves this invisible mission to us through a miraculous work or by a precise testimony drawn from the holy scripture. All this is demonstrated in the chapter cited above, Cum ex injuncto.

Item, as this Pucelle has not proved in any of these ways that she has been sent from God, there is no room to believe in her on her word, but there is room to proceed against her as if suspected of heresy.

Added to this, if she has really been sent from God, she would not take clothing prohibited by God and forbidden for women by canon law under penalty of anathema, according to the chapter Si qua mulier. . . .

Moreover, in the case where those who let themselves be deceived by this Pucelle attempt to excuse and to justify her clothing in consideration of the matter for which she was supposedly sent, such niceties are useless; these are rather those excuses of which the Psalmist speaks, that one searches for to excuse sins (Psalm 140: 4), and they accuse more than they excuse, as it says in chapter Quanto of the title *De consuetudine*. In this case, one might do lots of evil things under the appearance of good. And yet it is necessary to refrain not only from evil, but from all appearance of evil, as one reads in the chapter Cum ab omni of the title *De vita et honestate clericorum*.

Item, if a women [sic] could put on male clothing as she liked with impunity, women would have unrestrained opportunities to fornicate and to practice manly acts which are legally forbidden for them according to doctrine, etc., [as this is] against the canonical teaching contained in the chapter Nova quædam of the title *De pœnitentiis et remissionibus*.

Item, in general, all masculine duties are forbidden to women, for example, to preach, to teach, to bear arms, to absolve, to excommunicate, etc., as one sees in that chapter Nova quædam and in the Digest, in the [second] law of the title *De regulis juris*.

READING QUESTIONS

1. On what grounds did the author of *De mirabili victoria* support Joan's insistence on wearing men's clothing?

2. Why did the author of *De bono et malo spiritu* believe that Joan's clothes supported his position that she was, in all likelihood, a heretic?

3. What do these treatises tell you about late medieval ideas about women's nature and their proper role in society?

■ COMPARATIVE AND DISCUSSION QUESTIONS ■

1. Consider the account of the English Peasants' Revolt and *Flagellants in the Netherlands Town of Tournai*. What light do they shed on disruption and challenges to institutions in late medieval Europe, as well as the eventual outcomes of those challenges?

2. What do the writings of Boccaccio and di Tura reveal about the range of reactions to the devastation produced by the Black Death?

3. What do Catherine and Joan have in common? What kind of power did they have, and how did they use it?

European Society in the Age of the Renaissance

1350–1550

The Renaissance began in the Italian city-states in the fourteenth century and spread throughout Europe. Renaissance scholars, artists, and philosophers articulated a new vision of human possibility inspired by the classical past. Standing on the shoulders of the giants of Greco-Roman culture, they believed that their own society could match, or even exceed, the achievements of their ancestors. The commercial and political dynamism of the Italian city-states played a key role in fostering the Renaissance. Italian cities were primary beneficiaries of the commercial revival of the High Middle Ages, and competition, both within and between cities, spurred individuals and communities to pour their resources into cultural activity. Competition between city-states had a darker side, however, and often escalated into conflict; endemic warfare left Italy weak and divided. As you explore the sources, consider what the Renaissance meant to these authors and artists. How would they describe the movement in which they were participants? What hopes and fears did they have for their own society?

12-1 | An Italian Admirer of the Classical Past

PETRARCH, *Letter to Livy* (1350)

Around 1350, Italian scholar and poet Francesco Petrarca, or Petrarch (1304–1374), proposed a new kind of education that centered on the study and emulation of the works of ancient Roman authors. In his view, this program would produce a generation

---

From Marco Emilio Cosenza, trans., *Petrarch's Letters to Classical Authors* (Chicago: University of Chicago Press, 1910), pp. 100–103.

of young men capable of achievements unmatched in Europe for a thousand years. Petrarch and his followers came to be known as humanists, and their intellectual agenda had a profound influence on the art and ideas of their age. We can sense the intensity of Petrarch's regard for classical culture in a letter addressed to the ancient Roman historian Livy. As you read it, consider what it tells you about the aspirations of Petrarch and his fellow humanists.

I should wish (if it were permitted from on high) either that I had been born in thine age or thou in ours; in the latter case our age itself, and in the former I personally should have been the better for it. I should surely have been one of those pilgrims who visited thee. For the sake of seeing thee I should have gone not merely to Rome, but indeed, from either Gaul or Spain I should have found my way to thee as far as India. . . . We know that thou didst write one hundred and forty-two books on Roman affairs. With what fervor, with what unflagging zeal must thou have labored; and of that entire number there are now extant scarcely thirty. . . . It is over these small remains that I toil whenever I wish to forget these regions, these times, and these customs. Often I am filled with bitter indignation against the morals of today, when men value nothing except gold and silver, and desire nothing except sensual, physical pleasures. If these are to be considered the goal of mankind, then not only the dumb beasts of the field, but even insensible and inert matter has a richer, a higher goal than that proposed to itself by thinking man. But of this elsewhere.

It is now fitter that I should render thee thanks, for many reasons indeed, but for this in especial: that thou didst so frequently cause me to forget the present evils, and transfer me to happier times. . . .

Pray greet in my behalf thy predecessors Polybius and Quintus Claudius and Valerius Antias, and all those whose glory thine own greater light has dimmed; and of the later historians, give greeting to Pliny the Younger, of Verona, a neighbor of thine, and also to thy former rival Crispus Sallustius. . . . Farewell forever, thou matchless historian!

Written in the land of the living, in that part of Italy and in that city in which I am now living and where thou were once born and buried, . . . and in view of thy very tombstone; on the twenty-second of February, in the thirteen hundred and fiftieth year from the birth of Him whom thou wouldst have seen, or of whose birth thou couldst have heard, hadst thou lived a little longer.

READING QUESTIONS

1. Why did Petrarch admire Livy?

2. What implicit contrast did Petrarch draw between Livy's time and his own?

3. In what ways does Petrarch's wish to bring Livy into his world encapsulate the humanist program?

12-2 | Power Politics During the Italian Renaissance
NICCOLÒ MACHIAVELLI, *The Prince* (1513)

Niccolò Machiavelli (nee-koh-LOH mah-key-ah-VEL-ee) (1469–1527) was a political philosopher and diplomat who had represented the Italian republic of Florence on numerous diplomatic missions. In 1512, when the powerful Medici family regained control of Florence, the anti-Medici Machiavelli was arrested and tortured. In 1513, he wrote *The Prince*, a guide to gaining and consolidating political power, and dedicated it to Lorenzo de Medici, perhaps as a way to curry favor with the new rulers. The cynicism of *The Prince* stands in stark contrast to the idealism exhibited in the excerpt from Petrarch included in this chapter. Here, Machiavelli argues that a willingness to engage in deception and violence is critical to a ruler's success.

Every one understands how praiseworthy it is in a prince to keep faith, and to live uprightly and not craftily. Nevertheless we see, from what has taken place in our own days, that princes who have set little store by their word, but have known how to overreach men by their cunning, have accomplished great things, and in the end got the better of those who trusted to honest dealing.

Be it known, then, that there are two ways of contending,—one in accordance with the laws, the other by force; the first of which is proper to men, the second to beasts. But since the first method is often ineffectual, it becomes necessary to resort to the second. A prince should, therefore, understand how to use well both the man and the beast. . . . But inasmuch as a prince should know how to use the beast's nature wisely, he ought of beasts to choose both the lion and the fox; for the lion cannot guard himself from the toils, nor the fox from wolves. He must therefore be a fox to discern toils, and a lion to drive off wolves.

To rely wholly on the lion is unwise; and for this reason a prudent prince neither can nor ought to keep his word when to keep it is hurtful to him and the causes which led him to pledge it are removed. If all men were good, this would not be good advice, but since they are dishonest and do not keep faith with you, you in return need not keep faith with them; and no prince was ever at a loss for plausible reasons to cloak a breach of faith. Of this numberless recent instances could be given, and it might be shown how many solemn treaties and engagements have been rendered inoperative and idle through want of faith among princes, and that he who has best known how to play the fox has had the best success.

It is necessary, indeed, to put a good color on this nature, and to be skilled in simulating and dissembling. But men are so simple, and governed so absolutely by their present needs, that he who wishes to deceive will never fail in finding willing dupes. One recent example I will not omit. Pope Alexander VI had no care or thought but how to deceive, and always found material to work on.

From Niccolò Machiavelli, *The Prince*, trans. N. H. Thomson, in James Harvey Robinson, ed., *Readings in European History*, vol. 2 (Boston: Ginn, 1906), pp. 10–13.

No man ever had a more effective manner of asseverating, or made promises with more solemn protestations, or observed them less. And yet, because he understood this side of human nature, his frauds always succeeded. . . .

In his efforts to aggrandize his son the duke [Cesare Borgia], Alexander VI had to face many difficulties, both immediate and remote. In the first place, he saw no way to make him ruler of any state which did not belong to the Church. Yet, if he sought to take for him a state of the Church, he knew that the duke of Milan and the Venetians would withhold their consent, Faenza and Rimini [towns in the province of Romagna] being already under the protection of the latter. Further, he saw that the forces of Italy, and those more especially of which he might have availed himself, were in the hands of men who had reason to fear his aggrandizement, — that is, of the Orsini, the Colonnesi [Roman noble families] and their followers. These, therefore, he could not trust. . . .

And since this part of his [Cesare Borgia's] conduct merits both attention and imitation, I shall not pass it over in silence. After the duke had taken Romagna, finding that it had been ruled by feeble lords, who thought more of plundering than of governing their subjects, — which gave them more cause for division than for union, so that the country was overrun with robbery, tumult, and every kind of outrage, — he judged it necessary, with a view to rendering it peaceful, and obedient to his authority, to provide it with a good government. Accordingly he set over it Messer Remiro d'Orco, a stern and prompt ruler, who, being entrusted with the fullest powers, in a very short time, and with much credit to himself, restored it to tranquility and order. But afterwards the duke, apprehending that such unlimited authority might become odious, decided that it was no longer needed, and established [at] the center of the province a civil tribunal, with an excellent president, in which every town was represented by its advocate. And knowing that past severities had generated ill feeling against himself, in order to purge the minds of the people and gain their good will, he sought to show them that any cruelty which had been done had not originated with him, but in the harsh disposition of this minister. Availing himself of the pretext which this afforded, he one morning caused Remiro to be beheaded, and exposed in the market place of Cesena with a block and bloody ax by his side. The barbarity of this spectacle at once astounded and satisfied the populace.

READING QUESTIONS

1. Why must a prince be both a lion and a fox? What qualities do these animals represent?

2. What light does *The Prince* shed on the realities of Italian politics?

3. How might a Renaissance critic of Machiavelli have responded to his work? What objections might such a person have raised to *The Prince*? How might Machiavelli have countered his critics' arguments?

12-3 | A Description of the Ideal Courtier

BALDASSARE CASTIGLIONE, *The Book of the Courtier* (1528)

Baldassare Castiglione (ball-duh-SAH-ray kahs-teel-YOH-nay) (1478–1529) was an Italian diplomat who spent many years traveling through the courts of Europe. Based on his experiences, he wrote *The Book of the Courtier* as a manual on the proper education, manners, dress, and skills of a companion to and defender of royalty. The book was written in the form of a conversation among some of the leading nobility in Italy and was a bestseller in its time. As you read this excerpt, think about the models upon which Castiglione might have drawn. To what extent does his courtier resemble the ideal medieval knight? To what extent does he seem to be a product of humanist education and training?

I wish then, that this Courtier of ours should be nobly born. I am of the opinion that the principal and true profession of the courtier ought to be that of arms;[1] which I would have him follow actively above all else, and be known among others as bold and strong, and loyal to whomsoever he serves. . . .

Therefore let the man we are seeking be very bold, stern, and always among the first, where the enemy are to be seen; and in every other place, gentle, modest, reserved, above all things avoiding ostentation and that impudent self-praise by which men ever excite hatred and disgust in all who hear him. . . .

And so I would have him well built and shapely of limb, and would have him show strength and lightness and suppleness, and know all bodily exercises that befit a man of war: whereof I think the first should be to handle every sort of weapon well on foot and on horse. . . .

There are also many other exercises, which although not immediately dependent upon arms, yet are closely connected therewith, and greatly foster manly sturdiness; and one of the chief among these seems to me to be the chase,[2] because it bears a certain likeness to war; and truly it is an amusement for great lords and befitting a man at court, and furthermore it is seen to have been much cultivated among the ancients. It is fitting also to know how to swim, to leap, to run, to throw stones, for besides the use that may be made of this in war, a man often has occasion to show what he can do in such matters; whence good esteem is to be won, especially with the multitude, who must be taken into account withal. Another admirable exercise, and one fitting a man at court, is the game of tennis, in which are well shown the disposition of the body. . . .

I think that the conversation, which the Courtier ought most to try in every way to make acceptable, is that which he holds with his prince; and although this word "conversation" implies a certain equality that seems impossible between a lord and his inferior, yet we will call it so for the moment. Therefore, besides

From Baldassare Castiglione, *The Book of the Courtier*, trans. Leonard Opdycke (New York: Charles Scribner's Sons, 1903), pp. 22, 26, 29, 31, 93–94.

[1] **arms:** Weaponry.
[2] **chase:** Hunting.

daily showing everyone that he possesses the worth we have already described, I would have the Courtier strive, with all the thoughts and forces of his mind, to love and almost adore the prince whom he serves, above every other thing, and mold his ways to his prince's liking. . . .

Moreover it is possible without flattery to obey and further the wishes of him we serve, for I am speaking of those wishes that are reasonable and right, or of those that in themselves are neither good nor evil, such as would be a liking for a play or devotion to one kind of exercise above another. And I would have the Courtier bend himself to this even if he be by nature alien to it, so that on seeing him his lord shall always feel that he will have something agreeable to say. . . . He will not be an idle or untruthful tattler, nor a boaster nor pointless flatterer, but modest and reserved, always and especially in public showing the reverence and respect which befit the servant towards the master.

READING QUESTIONS

1. What are the characteristics of a good courtier? How would you explain the stress Castiglione places on military aptitude and training?

2. What role does the courtier play in royal government? How does he facilitate his master's success?

3. Would you describe Castiglione's courtier as a medieval or a Renaissance figure? Why?

12-4 | A Humanist Prescription for the Education of Princes

DESIDERIUS ERASMUS, *The Education of a Christian Prince* (1516)

Desiderius Erasmus (1462–1536) of Rotterdam was the foremost northern humanist. A priest, theologian, and teacher, Erasmus placed humanist scholarship in the service of religious reform. His work combines a humanist's respect for reason and the value of the individual with an equally profound commitment to his faith. In this excerpt from *The Education of a Christian Prince*, Erasmus begins by discussing a classical metaphor for the relationship of the ruler to the state, and then uses this as a starting point for exploring the relationship between a Christian prince, his subjects, and God. As you read it, pay particular attention to the way in which he mixes classical and Christian concepts.

[R]emember this idea also, which was known and handed down by the pagan philosophers, that the rule of a prince over his people is no different from that of the mind over the body. The mind dominates the body because it knows more than the physical body, but it does so to the great advantage

From Desiderius Erasmus, *The Education of a Christian Prince*, trans. Lester K. Born (New York: Columbia University Press, 1936), pp. 175–178.

of the latter rather than to itself. The blessed fortune of the physical form is this rule of the mind. What the heart is in the body of a living creature, that the prince is in the state. If the heart is sound, it imparts life to the whole body, since it is the fountain of the blood and life spirit; but if it has been infected, it brings utter collapse to every part of the body. The heart is the last part of a living body to be broken down, and the very last traces of life are thought to survive in it. Consequently the prince should keep himself clean and undefiled from all corrupting folly whenever any such disease lays hold of the people. In a man it is the finely organized part (namely, the mind) that exercises the control. Likewise, in the mind it is its finest element, reason, that asserts itself. And God, who rules the universe, is the very essence of all things. Therefore, whosoever assumes the functions of rule in a state, as in a sort of great body, should excel all others in goodness, wisdom, and watch-fulness. The prince should be superior to his officers in the same degree that they are to the common people. If there is any evil in the mind it springs from infection, and contact with the body, which is subject to the passions. Any good that the body possesses is drawn from the mind as from a foun-tain. How unbelievable it would be and how contrary to nature, if ills should spread from the mind down into the body, and the health of the body be corrupted by the vicious habits of the mind. It would be just as absurd for wars, seditious uprisings, profligate morals, debased laws, corrupt officials, and every similar curse to a state, to spring from the prince whose wisdom should lay the storms stirred up by the folly of the common folk. But we often see states (*civitates*), well established and flourishing under the diligent activity of the people, overthrown by mismanagement of the princes. How unlike a Christian it is to take pleasure in the title "Master," which many who were not in the fold of Christ have shunned; that which in their ambition they desire to be but do not want to be called because of the odium attached to the name. Yet will a Christian prince think it just in the eyes of God for him to be the same [sort of man] and be called "The Magnificent"? The emperor Augustus, even though he had gained the imperial throne through foul intrigue, considered it an insult to be called "Master;" and when this title was used by an actor before all the people, he showed his disapproval by his facial expression and his remarks, as if it were a term of reproach applied to tyrants. And shall the Christian prince not imitate this propriety of the pagan? If you are master of all your subjects, they must of necessity be your slaves. Then have a care that you do not fulfill the ancient proverb: "You have as many enemies as you have slaves."

Nature created all men equal, and slavery was superimposed on nature, which fact the laws of even the pagans recognized. Now stop and think how out of proportion it is for a Christian to usurp full power over other Christians, whom the laws did not design to be slaves, and whom Christ redeemed from all slavery. Recall the instance when Paul called Onesimus (who was born a slave) the brother of his former master Philemon, from the time of his baptism. How incongruous it is to consider them slaves whom Christ redeemed with the same blood [as He did you]; whom He declared free along with all others; whom He fostered with the same sacraments as He did you; whom He calls to the same heritage of immortality! And over them, who have the same Master as you, the Prince, Jesus Christ, will you impose the yoke of slavery?

There is only one Master of Christian men. Why, then, do those who assume His functions, prefer to take their pattern of government from anyone except Him, who alone is in all ways to be imitated? It is proper enough to gather from others whatever virtues they have; but in Him is the perfect example of all virtue and wisdom. This seems the [essence of] foolishness to those outside the faith, but to us, if we are really faithful, He is the goodness of God and the wisdom of God. Now I do not want you to think that this means that you should be a slave, not a ruler. On the contrary, it illustrates the finest way to rule, unless, of course, you think God is only a bondsman because He governs the whole universe without recompense, because everyone and everything has felt His kindness, although they give Him nothing in return, and unless the mind seems a slave because it looks out so zealously for the welfare of the body, which it does not need, or unless you think the eye is a slave to all the other parts of the body because it sees for them all. You may well consider this: if someone should turn all these men whom you call your own into swine and asses by the art of Circe,[1] would you not say your ruling power had been reduced to a lower level? I think you would. And yet you may exercise more authority over swine and asses than over men. You may treat them as you please, divide them off as you will, and even kill them. Surely he who has reduced his free subjects to slaves has put his power on a meaner level. The loftier the ideal to which you fashion your authority, the more magnificently and splendidly will you rule. Whoever protects the liberty and standing of your subjects is the one that helps your sovereign power. God gave the angels and men free will so that He would not be ruling over bondsmen, and so that He might glorify and add further grandeur to His kingdom. And who, now, would swell with pride because he rules over men cowed down by fear, like so many cattle?

READING QUESTIONS

1. What metaphors does Erasmus use to describe the relationship of a prince to his people?

2. In Erasmus's view, what qualities should a Christian prince embody? Why?

3. Erasmus argues that the ideal Christian prince rules over a "free" people. How might he have explained this apparent contradiction? What similarities and differences do you see between his understanding of the meaning of freedom and your own?

---

[1]**Circe**: An enchantress who turned the legendary Greek hero Odysseus and his men into pigs.

12-5 | A Female Author Argues for the Education of Women

CHRISTINE DE PIZAN, *The Book of the City of Ladies: Against Those Men Who Claim It Is Not Good for Women to Be Educated* (1404)

Christine de Pizan (ca. 1363–1434) may have been the first European woman to earn her living as a writer. The daughter of a Venetian nobleman and scholar, de Pizan grew up in the court of Charles V of France, where her father had accepted a position as royal astrologer and physician. There, de Pizan was given the opportunity to develop her intellectual interests and abilities. In 1390, when her husband died in an epidemic and left her with three children, de Pizan began her literary career. Her works were popular among the French nobility, and she even enjoyed the financial support of the French queen. At this time, humanists were divided in their opinions on the education of women. Some thought women were simply not capable of learning. Others thought a limited form of education in good morals was sufficient. De Pizan challenged both of these ideas, and some scholars now regard her as one of the first Western feminists.

I realize that women have accomplished many good things and that even if evil women have done evil, it seems to me, nevertheless, that the benefits accrued and still accruing because of good women—particularly the wise and literary ones and those educated in the natural sciences whom I mentioned above—outweigh the evil. Therefore, I am amazed by the opinion of some men who claim that they do not want their daughters, wives, or kinswomen to be educated because their mores would be ruined as a result.

Here you can clearly see that not all opinions of men are based on reason and that these men are wrong. For it must not be presumed that mores necessarily grow worse from knowing the moral sciences, which teach the virtues, indeed, there is not the slightest doubt that moral education amends and ennobles them. How could anyone think or believe that whoever follows good teaching or doctrine is the worse for it? Such an opinion cannot be expressed or maintained. I do not mean that it would be good for a man or a woman to study the art of divination or those fields of learning which are forbidden—for the holy Church did not remove them from common use without good reason—but it should not be believed that women are the worse for knowing what is good.

Quintus Hortensius, a great rhetorician and consummately skilled orator in Rome, did not share this opinion. He had a daughter, named Hortensia, whom he greatly loved for the subtlety of her wit. He had her learn letters and study the science of rhetoric, which she mastered so thoroughly that she resembled her father Hortensius not only in wit and lively memory but also in her excellent delivery and order of speech—in fact, he surpassed her in nothing. . . . That is, during the time when Rome was governed by three men, this Hortensia began to support the cause of women and to undertake what no man dared to undertake. There was a question whether certain taxes should be levied on women and on their jewelry during a needy period in Rome. This woman's eloquence was so compelling that she was listened to, no less readily than her father would have been, and she won her case.

From Christine de Pizan, *The Book of the City of Ladies*, trans. Earl Jeffrey Richards (New York: Persea Books, 1982), pp. 153–155.

Similarly, to speak of more recent times, without searching for examples in ancient history, Giovanni Andrea, a solemn law professor in Bologna not quite sixty years ago, was not of the opinion that it was bad for women to be educated. He had a fair and good daughter, named Novella, who was educated in the law to such an advanced degree that when he was occupied by some task and not at leisure to present his lectures to his students, he would send Novella, his daughter, in his place to lecture to the students from his chair. And to prevent her beauty from distracting the concentration of her audience, she had a little curtain drawn in front of her. In this manner she could on occasion supplement and lighten her father's occupation. . . .

Thus, not all men (and especially the wisest) share the opinion that it is bad for women to be educated. But it is very true that many foolish men have claimed this because it displeased them that women knew more than they did. [My] father, who was a great scientist and philosopher, did not believe that women were worth less by knowing science; rather, as you know, he took great pleasure from seeing your inclination to learning.

READING QUESTIONS

1. How does de Pizan defend a woman's ability to learn?

2. According to de Pizan, why do some men not want to see women educated? What other reasons might have motivated them?

3. How and why does Pizan couch her arguments that women should be educated within accepted moral norms of the fifteenth century?

SOURCES IN CONVERSATION

A Female Painter Tells Stories About Women

Renaissance and early modern artists drew heavily for their inspiration on Christianity and the classical past, but this does not mean that they were uninterested in the present. In the hands of a skilled artist, the past became a vehicle for commenting on what was important to the artist, his or her patron, and the community to which they both belonged. The work of the Roman painter Artemisia Gentileschi (1593–ca. 1656) is a case in point. The daughter of painter Orazio Gentileschi, Artemisia was perhaps the most successful female artist of her day. Her paintings *Susannah and the Elders* and *Judith and Holofernes*, both depicting scenes from the Old Testament, demonstrate how deeply personal such works could be. *Susannah and the Elders*, Artemisia's first work, was completed in 1610 when she was seventeen. Between that time and the completion of *Judith and Holofernes* in 1612, Artemisia was raped by one of her father's colleagues, Agostino Tassi. As you examine these two works, consider the connections between the content and themes of the paintings and Gentileschi's own experiences.

How did she use these paintings to comment on the power dynamics that shaped women's lives?

READ AND COMPARE

1. Compare the power relationships being portrayed in the two paintings. How are they different?

2. How do you think seventeenth-century Europeans would have reacted to the stories being told in the two paintings? If the reactions would have been different, why would they have differed?

12-6 | ARTEMISIA GENTILESCHI, *Susannah and the Elders* (1610)

Taken from the book of Daniel, the story of *Susannah and the Elders* centers on a false accusation of adultery. As Susannah, a young wife, bathes in her garden, two elders of her community watch secretly. Filled with lust, the two men threaten to denounce her as an adulteress if she refuses to have sex with them. When she resists their attempts at blackmail, they follow through on their threat. Only the intervention of Daniel, who exposes inconsistencies in their story, saves Susannah from execution. As you examine the painting, pay particular attention to the way Gentileschi composed it. How does the placement of the three figures amplify its message?

Fine Art Images/Superstock.

READING QUESTIONS

1. How would you describe Gentileschi's Susannah? How does the position of her arms and head help to convey her reaction to the unwanted advances of the elders?

2. How would you characterize the two elders? How does their placement in the painting reflect their power? What might explain Gentileschi's decision to depict them whispering to one another at the very moment they accost Susannah?

12-7 | ARTEMISIA GENTILESCHI, *Judith and Holofernes* (1612)

Like *Susannah and the Elders*, *Judith and Holofernes* depicts a scene from the Old Testament, this time from the book of Judith. In order to save Israel from Assyrian domination, Judith seduces the Assyrian general Holofernes. After he falls asleep drunk, Judith and her maidservant cut off his head. The personal importance of the story to Gentileschi is underscored by the fact that she chose to depict herself as Judith and Agostino Tassi, her rapist, as Holofernes.

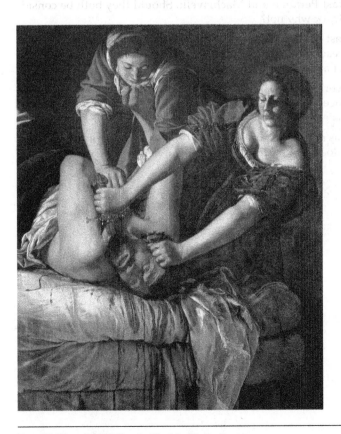

Fratelli Alinari IDEA S.p.A./Corbis/Getty Images.

READING QUESTIONS

1. How would you describe Gentileschi's Judith? How would you characterize her facial expression?

2. What might explain Gentileschi's decision to focus attention on Judith's arms and those of her maid?

3. Compare this work to *Susannah and the Elders*. Taken together, what do the two paintings tell us about the connections Gentileschi made between gender, power, and violence?

▪ COMPARATIVE AND DISCUSSION QUESTIONS ▪

1. Compare and contrast Petrarch and Machiavelli. Should they both be considered humanists? Why or why not?

2. Compare and contrast Erasmus's depiction of the successful prince with Machiavelli's. How does each one envision the Renaissance state? What does each think is necessary for a government to function well?

3. What light do the works of Christine de Pizan and Artemisia Gentileschi shed on the challenges faced by women of their day? How would you explain the success of each in male-dominated fields?

4. What marks Erasmus's *Education of a Christian Prince* as a work of the northern Renaissance? How does it differ from some of the other works included in this chapter?

13

Reformations and Religious Wars

1500–1600

Even before Martin Luther posted his "Ninety-five Theses on the Power of Indulgences," numerous Catholic practices had come under widespread criticism. The specific political situation in the Holy Roman Empire enabled Luther and other reformers to spread their ideas. Strong local governments and high nobles, who exercised more power in their territories than did the central government of the Holy Roman Empire, welcomed Lutheran ideas and offered safe havens to the Protestants. Protestant reform extended to social thought as well—for example, priests were no longer required to remain celibate in the Protestant tradition. Some reformers adopted beliefs that were far more radical than those of Luther or other reformers and were condemned by Protestants and Catholics alike. Meanwhile, the Catholic Church developed its own plans for reform, both to counter Protestant attacks and to revitalize the church. The age of reformation was also an age of religious violence, as religious and political conflicts merged and overlapped, fueling war, riots, and the persecution of dissenters and outsiders.

13-1 | Martin Luther Takes a Stand

MARTIN LUTHER, *Ninety-five Theses on the Power of Indulgences* (1517)

Martin Luther (1483–1546) composed his "Ninety-five Theses" in response to Pope Leo X's decision to raise funds for the construction of a new cathedral in Rome through the sale of indulgences in Germany. An indulgence was a document issued by the Catholic Church lessening a person's penance or time in purgatory. Many believed that the purchase of an indulgence was an effective substitute for genuine repentance, a belief that papal agents did little or nothing to discourage. Luther's attack on this practice went far beyond a simple accusation of papal corruption. Instead, it struck directly at the power of the church, suggesting that priests had no necessary role in salvation.

1. Our Lord and Master Jesus Christ in saying "Repent ye" etc., intended that the whole life of believers should be penitence.
2. This word cannot be understood as sacramental penance, that is, of the confession and satisfaction which are performed under the ministry of priests.
3. It does not, however, refer solely to inward penitence; nay such inward penitence is naught, unless it outwardly produces various mortifications of the flesh.
4. The penalty thus continues as long as the hatred of self (that is, true inward penitence); namely, till our entrance into the kingdom of heaven.
5. The pope has neither the will nor the power to remit any penalties except those which he has imposed by his own authority, or by that of the canons.
6. The pope has no power to remit any guilt, except by declaring and warranting it to have been remitted by God; or at most by remitting cases reserved for himself; in which cases, if his power were despised, guilt would certainly remain.
7. Certainly God remits no man's guilt without at the same time subjecting him, humbled in all things, to the authority of his representative the priest. . . .
20. Therefore the pope, when he speaks of the plenary remission of all penalties, does not mean really of all, but only of those imposed by himself.
21. Thus those preachers of indulgences are in error who say that by the indulgences of the pope a man is freed and saved from all punishment.
22. For in fact he remits to souls in purgatory no penalty which they would have had to pay in this life according to the canons.
23. If any entire remission of all penalties can be granted to any one it is certain that it is granted to none but the most perfect, that is to very few.

From Martin Luther, "Ninety-five Theses," in *Translations and Reprints from the Original Sources of European History* (Philadelphia: University of Pennsylvania Press, 1898), 2/6:12–18.

24. Hence, the greater part of the people must needs be deceived by this indiscriminate and high-sounding promise of release from penalties. . . .

26. The pope acts most rightly in granting remission to souls not by the power of the keys (which is of no avail in this case) but by the way of intercession.[1]

27. They preach man [rather than God] who say that the soul flies out of Purgatory as soon as the money thrown into the chest rattles.[2]

28. It is certain that, when the money rattles in the chest, avarice and gain may be increased, but the effect of the intercession of the Church depends on the will of God alone. . . .

30. No man is sure of the reality of his own contrition, much less of the attainment of plenary remission. . . .

35. They preach no Christian doctrine who teach that contrition is not necessary for those who buy souls [out of purgatory] or buy confessional licenses.

36. Every Christian who feels true compunction has of right plenary remission of punishment and guilt even without letters of pardon.

37. Every true Christian, whether living or dead, has a share in all the benefits of Christ and of the Church, given him by God, even without letters of pardon. . . .

38. The remission, however, imparted by the pope is by no means to be despised, since it is, as I have said, a declaration of the divine remission.

39. It is a most difficult thing, even for the most learned theologians, to exalt at the same time in the eyes of the people the ample effect of pardons and the necessity of true contrition.

40. True contrition seeks and loves punishment; while the ampleness of pardons relaxes it, and causes men to hate it, or at least gives occasion for them to do so. . . .

43. Christians should be taught that he who gives to a poor man, or lends to a needy man, does better than if he bought pardons.

44. Because by works of charity, charity increases, and the man becomes better; while by means of pardons, he does not become better, but only freer from punishment. . . .

49. Christians should be taught that the pope's pardons are useful if they do not put their trust in them, but most hurtful if through them they lose the fear of God. . . .

54. Wrong is done to the Word of God when, in the same sermon, an equal or longer time is spent on pardons than on it.

55. The mind of the pope necessarily is that, if pardons, which are a very small matter, are celebrated with single bells, single processions, and single ceremonies, the Gospel, which is a very great matter, should be preached with a hundred bells, a hundred processions, and a hundred ceremonies.

---

[1]**intercession:** Prayer to God on another's behalf.

[2]**They preach . . . rattles:** This was the claim being made by the indulgence seller Tetzel in Luther's Saxony.

56. The treasures of the Church, whence the pope grants indulgences, are neither sufficiently named nor known among the people of Christ.

57. It is clear that they are at least not temporal treasures, for these are not so readily lavished, but only accumulated, by many of the preachers. . . .

67. Those indulgences, which the preachers loudly proclaim to be the greatest graces, are seen to be truly such as regards the promotion of gain.

68. Yet they are in reality most insignificant when compared to the grace of God and the piety of the cross. . . .

75. To think that the papal pardons have such power that they could absolve a man even if — by an impossibility — he had violated the Mother of God, is madness.

76. We affirm on the contrary that papal pardons cannot take away even the least of venial sins, as regards its guilt. . . .

79. To say that the cross set up among the insignia of the papal arms is of equal power with the cross of Christ, is blasphemy.

80. Those bishops, priests, and theologians who allow such discourses to have currency among the people will have to render an account. . . .

82. As for instance: Why does not the pope empty purgatory for the sake of most holy charity and of the supreme necessity of souls — this being the most just of all reasons — if he redeems an infinite number of souls for the sake of that most fatal thing, money, to be spent on building a basilica — this being a very slight reason?

83. Again; why do funeral masses and anniversary masses for the deceased continue, and why does not the pope return, or permit the withdrawal of, the funds bequeathed for this purpose, since it is a wrong to pray for those who are already redeemed?

84. Again; what is this new kindness of God and the pope, in that, for money's sake, they permit an impious man and an enemy of God to redeem a pious soul which loves God, and yet do not redeem that same pious and beloved soul out of free charity on account of its own need?

85. Again; why is it that the penitential canons, long since abrogated and dead in themselves, in very fact and not only by usage, are yet still redeemed with money, through the granting of indulgences, as if they were full of life?

86. Again; why does not the pope, whose riches are at this day more ample than those of the wealthiest of the wealthy, build the single Basilica of St. Peter with his own money rather than with that of poor believers? . . .

89. Since it is the salvation of souls, rather than money, that the pope seeks by his pardons, why does he suspend the letters and pardons granted long ago, since they are equally efficacious? . . .

91. If all these pardons were preached according to the spirit and mind of the pope, all these questions would be resolved with ease; nay, would not exist.

READING QUESTIONS

1. In Thesis 36, Luther writes, "Every Christian who feels true compunction has of right plenary remission of punishment and guilt even without letters of pardon." Why would many interpret this as an attack on the papacy?

2. According to the theses, in what ways have the leaders of the church failed to teach true Christian doctrine?

3. Based on your reading of Theses 82–91, how would you classify the sorts of reform that Luther would like to see within the church?

13-2 | Reformation Propaganda

HANS HOLBEIN THE YOUNGER, *Luther as the German Hercules* (ca. 1519)

One of Martin Luther's greatest assets was the printing press. Print technology facilitated the rapid dissemination of Lutheran ideas to a wide variety of audiences. The propaganda campaign waged by Luther's supporters included inexpensive print versions of his tracts, pamphlets, and treatises. It also included images aimed at the illiterate and semi-literate. A majority of sixteenth-century Europeans could not read, and woodcuts like this one, created by Hans Holbein the Younger (1498–1543), helped common people take part in the religious debates that dominated much of the century. Here, Luther is depicted as the Greek hero Hercules, who killed the hydra, a beast with nine heads. The artist has replaced the hydra with nine churchmen, including the theologian Thomas Aquinas (see Document 10-6), monks, and priests. The strangled pope, identifiable by his triple crown, dangles from the rope in Luther's mouth.

De Agostini Picture Library/Getty Images.

READING QUESTIONS

1. How would you describe the way Luther is depicted here? What about the church leaders?

2. How would you sum up the intended message of this image in a single sentence? What group or groups might it have been meant to influence?

3. What light does this image shed on the nature of religious conflict during the Reformation? What room, if any, did such images leave for compromise between Protestants and Catholics?

SOURCES IN CONVERSATION

The War on Witches

Starting around 1560, prosecutions of alleged witches rose dramatically. The next century would see between 100,000 and 200,000 people tried for witchcraft, which resulted in 40,000 to 60,000 executions. Seventy-five to eighty percent of the accused witches of the early modern period were women, suggesting the role of deep-seated biases against females in European society and medieval Christianity in particular. Possible explanations for this phenomenon include changes in legal procedures, the religious upheaval of the Reformation, the social and economic dislocation created by a changing agricultural economy, the efforts of early modern states to assert greater control over their subjects, and new definitions of witchcraft. It should be stressed, however, that each witchcraft trial was different and that a different combination of factors was in play in each case. While shaped by larger social and cultural trends, witchcraft trials were, in the end, local events, and the relationships and personal histories of the individuals involved were at the heart of each outbreak of accusations.

READ AND COMPARE

1. What do these two documents reveal about aspects of human nature that society and church officials feared most?

2. Why do you suppose women were overwhelmingly the majority of accused witches? Are there any clues you can detect in these documents? What aspects of the Judeo-Christian tradition might have contributed to targeting women as suspected witches?

13-3 | HEINRICH KRAMER, *Malleus Maleficarum* (*The Hammer of Witches*) (1487)

Roughly thirty years before Martin Luther wrote his "Ninety-five Theses" and started the Protestant Reformation, a clergy member named Heinrich Kramer tried to start persecuting people for witchcraft in Tyrol, but he failed and was discredited by the local bishop. He then successfully appealed to the pope Innocent VIII, who wrote a papal bull in 1484 that gave the Inquisition, a church organization created to root out heresy, the authority to try people accused of witchcraft. Kramer then wrote his famous and hugely influential treatise that defined the practices of witchcraft, identified the practices as criminal heresy, and offered instructions for determining the guilt or innocence of accused witches.

The method of beginning an examination by torture is as follows: First, the jailers prepare the implements of torture, then they strip the prisoner (if it be a woman, she has already been stripped by other women, upright and of good report). This stripping is lest some means of witchcraft may have been sewed into the clothing — such as often, taught by the Devil, they prepare from the bodies of unbaptized infants, [murdered] that they may forfeit salvation. And when the implements of torture have been prepared, the judge, both in person and through other good men zealous in the faith, tries to persuade the prisoner to confess the truth freely; but, if he will not confess, he bid attendants make the prisoner fast to the strappado or some other implement of torture. The attendants obey forthwith, yet with feigned agitation. Then, at the prayer of some of those present, the prisoner is loosed again and is taken aside and once more persuaded to confess, being led to believe that he will in that case not be put to death.

Here it may be asked whether the judge, in the case of a prisoner much defamed, convicted both by witnesses and by proofs, nothing being lacking but his own confession, can properly lead him to hope that his life will be spared when, even if he confess his crime, he will be punished with death.

It must be answered that opinions vary. Some hold that even a witch of ill repute, against whom the evidence justifies violent suspicion, and who, as a ringleader of the witches, is accounted very dangerous, may be assured her life, and condemned instead to perpetual imprisonment on bread and water, in case she will give sure and convincing testimony against other witches; yet this penalty of perpetual imprisonment must not be announced to her, but only that her life will be spared, and that she will be punished in some other fashion, perhaps by exile. And doubtless such notorious witches, especially those who prepare witch-potions or who by magical methods cure those bewitched, would be peculiarly suited to be thus preserved, in order to aid the bewitched or to accuse other witches, were it not that their accusations

From George L. Burr, ed., *Translations and Reprints from the Original Sources of European History*, vol. 3, part 4 (Philadelphia: University of Pennsylvania Press, 1897), pp. 11–13.

cannot be trusted, since the Devil is a liar, unless confirmed by proofs and witnesses.

Others hold, as to this point, that for a time the promise made to the witch sentenced to imprisonment is to be kept, but that after a time she should be burned.

A third view is, that the judge may safely promise witches to spare their lives, if only he will later excuse himself from pronouncing the sentence and will let another do this in his place. . . .

But if, neither by threats nor by promises such as these, the witch can be induced to speak the truth, then the jailers must carry out the sentence, and torture the prisoner according to the accepted methods, with more or less of severity as the delinquent's crime may demand. And, while he is being tortured, he must be questioned on the articles of accusation, and this frequently and persistently, beginning with the lighter charges—for he will more readily confess the lighter than the heavier. And, while this is being done, the notary must write down everything in his record of the trial—how the prisoner is tortured, on what points he is questioned and how he answers.

And note that, if he confesses under the torture, he must afterward be conducted to another place, that he may confirm it and certify that it was not due alone to the force of the torture.

But, if the prisoner will not confess the truth satisfactorily, other sorts of tortures must be placed before him, with the statement that unless he will confess the truth, he must endure these also. But, if not even thus he can be brought into terror and to the truth, then the next day or the next but one is to be set for a continuation of the tortures—not a repetition, for it must not be repeated unless new evidences produced.

The judge must then address to the prisoners the following sentence: We, the judge, etc., do assign to you, such and such a day for the continuation of the tortures, that from your own mouth the truth may be heard, and that the whole may be recorded by the notary.

And during the interval, before the day assigned, the judge, in person or through approved men, must in the manner above described try to persuade the prisoner to confess, promising her (if there is aught to be gained by this promise) that her life shall be spared. The judge shall see to it, moreover, that throughout this interval guards are constantly with the prisoner, so that she may not be alone; because she will be visited by the Devil and tempted into suicide.

READING QUESTIONS

1. Setting aside that these people are being interrogated for the crime of suspected witchcraft, how likely would it be that this process of questioning could result in an honest confession for any crime? Why do you think so?

2. What do you think was the most important societal factor that moved witchcraft trials from the status of marginalized and discredited phenomena to mainstream, widespread occurrences?

13-4 | JEAN BODIN, *On the Demon-Mania of Witches* (1580)

Jean Bodin (1529/30–1596) was one of the foremost political theorists of his time. A professor of law and adviser to kings, he is best known for his *Six livres de la République* (1576), in which he developed a case for royal absolutism that rested on a belief in the divine right of kings. It might be surprising that a man of such erudition and international status was also a leading proponent of aggressive efforts to detect and punish witchcraft. For Bodin, however, concern about witchcraft was a natural extension of his interest in politics and government. As he saw it, the "status and greatness of the state" depended on the "punishment of the bad," and there was no greater evil than witchcraft.

Now if ever there was a way to appease the anger of God, to obtain His blessing, to dismay some by the punishment of others, to preserve some from the infection of others, to reduce the number of the wicked, to secure the safety of the good, and to punish the most despicable wickednesses that the human mind can imagine, it is to chastise witches with the utmost rigour. However, the word "rigour" is a misnomer, since there is no penalty cruel enough to punish the evils of witches, since all their wickednesses, blasphemies, and all their designs rise up against the majesty of God to vex and offend Him in a thousand ways. . . . Some people raise objections to burning witches, even witches who have a formal pact with Satan. For it is principally against those witches that one must seek vengeance with the greatest diligence and utmost rigour, in order to bring an end to the wrath of God, and His vengeance upon us. And especially since those who have written on it interpret a magic spell as heresy, and nothing more—although true heresy is the crime of treason against God, and punishable by the fire. It is necessary, however, to note the difference between this crime and simple heresy. For we showed initially that the first occupation of witches is to deny God and all religion. The law of God condemns that person who has left the true God for another to be stoned, which all the Hebrew commentators say is the most terrible form of execution. This point is very significant. For the witch whom I have described does not just deny God in order to change and take up another religion, but he renounces all religion, either true or superstitious, which can keep men in the fear of committing offence.

The second crime of witches is, after having renounced God, to curse, blaspheme and scorn Him, and any other god or idol which he feared. Now the law of God declares as follows, "Whoever curses his God shall bear his sin. He who blasphemes the name of the Lord shall be put to death." . . .

For it seems that God wants to show that those who blaspheme what they think is God, do blaspheme God, with respect to their intention, which is the foundation of the hearts and minds of men: like the witches described above who broke the arms and legs on crucifixes, which they thought were gods. They also offered toads the host[1] to feed on. One sees then a double outrage of impiety

---

Excerpt (pp. 208–213) from Jean Bodin, *On the Demon-Mania of Witches*, translated by Randy A. Scott, with an introduction by Jonathan L. Pearl. Reprinted by permission of the Centre for Reformation & Renaissance Studies, Victoria University.

[1]**the host:** The sanctified bread that signifies the body of Christ.

with witches who blaspheme the true God, and anything they think has some divinity, so as to uproot all pious conviction and fear of offence.

The third crime is even more abominable. Namely, they do homage to the Devil, worship him, offer sacrifice, and the most despicable make a trench and put their face in the ground praying and worshiping him with all their heart. . . . This abomination surpasses any penalty that man can conceive, considering the formal text of the law of God, which requires that one who only bows down to pay honour to images, which the Greeks call "idols," be put to death. . . . Now witches are not content to worship, or only to bow down before Satan, but they offer themselves to Satan, pray to him and invoke him.

The fourth crime is even greater: many witches have been convicted, and have confessed to promising their children to Satan. The fifth is even worse; that is, that witches are frequently convicted by their confession of having sacrificed to the Devil their infant children before they are baptised. They raise them in the air, and then insert a large pin into their head, which causes them to die and is a crime more bizarre than the one before. In fact Sprenger[2] relates that he had one burned who had killed forty-one of them in this way.

The sixth crime is even more horrible. For witches are not satisfied to offer their own children to the Devil and burn them as a sacrifice . . . but they even dedicate them right from the mother's womb . . . which is a double parricide with the most abominable idolatry imaginable.

The seventh and the most common is that witches make an oath and promise the Devil to lure as many as they can into his service, which they customarily do, as we showed earlier. Now the law of God states that that person who is called this way, must stone the one who tried to entice him.

The eighth crime is to call upon and swear by the name of the Devil as a mark of honour, as witches do having it always on their lips, and swearing only by him, except when they renounce God. This is directly against the law of God, which forbids swearing by anything other than the name of God. This, Scripture says, gives glory to God. Thus judges said in taking the oath of parties or witnesses, "Glory be to God."

The ninth is that witches are incestuous, which is the crime they have been charged with and convicted of from earliest times. For Satan gives them to understand that there was never a perfect sorcerer or enchanter who was not born from father and daughter, or mother and son. . . . All these impieties are directly against God and His honour, which judges must avenge with the utmost rigour, and bring an end to God's wrath against us. As for the other crimes of witches, they concern injuries done to men, which they will avenge whenever they can. Now there is nothing so displeasing to God as to see judges avenge the smallest offences committed against themselves or others, but dissemble the horrible blasphemies against the majesty of God, such as those I have cited about witches.

---

[2]**Sprenger:** Jacob Sprenger (1436–1495). A Dominican inquisitor and coauthor with Heinrich Kramer of the *Malleus Maleficarum,* or *The Hammer of Witches* (1487), an influential handbook for the investigation of witchcraft.

Let us continue then with the other crimes. The tenth is that witches make a profession of killing people, and worse of murdering little children, then boiling them to render their humours and flesh drinkable, which Sprenger says he learned from their confessions; and the Neopolitan Battista della Porta[3] writes about it in his book on magic. And still another fact to underline, is that they put children to death before they are baptised. These are four circumstances which make the murder very much worse.

The eleventh crime is that witches eat human flesh, especially of little children, and of course drink their blood. . . . But one sees that it is a vile belief the Devil puts into the hearts of men in order to make them kill and devour each other, and destroy the human race. Again it must be noted that all witches customarily make poisons, which is enough to justify the death sentence. . . .

Now murder, according to the law of God and the laws of men, merits death. And those who eat human flesh, or have others eat it, also deserve death: as for example, a baker in Paris who made a business of making pies from the flesh of people hanged. He was burned, and his house razed to the ground. . . .

The twelfth is particular, killing with poisons or spells, which is distinct from simple homicide. . . . For it is a much more serious offence to kill with poison than with overt violence, as we shall presently point out; and even more serious to cause death by sorcery than by poison. . . .

The thirteenth crime of witches is to kill livestock, something which is customary. . . . The fourteenth is common, and recognised by law, namely, killing crops and causing famine and sterility in an entire region. The fifteenth is that witches have carnal copulation with the Devil, (and very often near their husbands, as I remarked earlier), a wickedness they all confess to.

There then are fifteen detestable crimes, the least of which merits a painful death. This does not mean that all witches are guilty of such evils, but it has been well established that witches who have a formal compact with the Devil are normally guilty of all or of most of these evil deeds.

READING QUESTIONS

1. What crimes does Bodin attribute to witches?

2. Why does Bodin believe that it was essential for the state to aggressively pursue witchcraft allegations?

3. What does Bodin's discussion of witchcraft tell us about his religious views? What about his political views?

---

[3]**Battista della Porta**: Giambattista della Porta (1535–1615). Italian natural philosopher and author of *Magiae Naturalis*, or *Natural Magic* (1558).

13-5 | Calvin Defines His Protestant Vision

JOHN CALVIN, *The Institutes of Christian Religion* (1559)

Martin Luther may have initiated the Protestant Reformation, but once it began it quickly moved beyond his control. Over the course of the sixteenth century, Protestantism splintered into numerous sects, some largely conforming to Luther's views, others deviating from them in important ways. The most important alternative to Lutheranism was developed by the French theologian John Calvin (1509–1564). At the core of Calvin's theology was a belief in the omnipotence of God and the utter powerlessness of human beings. It was on this foundation that he built the principle of predestination, the idea that the salvation or damnation of every person is foreordained by God and there is nothing any individual can do to alter his or her ultimate fate. In this excerpt from *The Institutes of Christian Religion*, Calvin defines predestination and offers the history of the Jews as evidence of its veracity.

When we attribute foreknowledge to God, we mean that all things always were, and perpetually remain, under His eyes, so that to His knowledge there is nothing future or past, but all things are present. And they are present in such a way that He not only conceives them through ideas, as we have before us those things which our minds remember, but He truly looks upon them and discerns them as things placed before Him. And this foreknowledge is extended throughout the universe to every creature. We call predestination God's eternal decree, by which He determined with Himself what He willed to become of each man. For all are not created in equal condition; rather, eternal life is foreordained for some, eternal damnation for others. Therefore, as any man has been created to one or the other of these ends, we speak of him as predestined to life or to death.

God has attested this not only in individual persons but has given us an example of it in the whole offspring of Abraham, to make it clear that in His choice rests the future condition of each nation. "When the Most High divided the nations, and separated the sons of Adam . . . the people of Israel were His portion, . . . the cord of His inheritance" [Deut. 32:8–9]. The separation is apparent to all men: in the person of Abraham, as in a dry tree trunk, one people is peculiarly chosen, while the others are rejected; but the cause does not appear except that Moses, to cut off from posterity any occasion to boast, teaches that they excel solely by God's freely given love. For he declares this the cause of their deliverance: that God loved the patriarchs, "and chose their seed after them" [Deut. 4:37].

More explicitly, in another chapter: "Not because you surpassed all other peoples in number did He take pleasure in you to choose you, . . . but because He loved you" [Deut. 7:7–8]. . . . Believers also proclaim this with one voice: "He chooses our heritage for us, the glory of Jacob, whom He has loved" [Psalms 47:4]. For all who have been adorned with gifts by God credit them to His freely given love because they knew not only that they had not merited them but that even the holy patriarch himself was not endowed with such virtue as to acquire such a high honor for himself and his descendants. And in order more effectively to crush all pride,

From Hans J. Hillerbrand, *The Protestant Reformation* (New York: Harper and Row, 1968), pp. 184–185.

he reproaches them as deserving no such thing, since they were a stubborn and stiff-necked people [Ex. 32:9; cf. Deut. 9:6]. Also, the prophets often confront the Jews with this election, to the latters' displeasure and by way of reproach, since they had shamefully fallen away from it [cf. Amos 3:2].

Be this as it may, let those now come forward who would bind God's election either to the worthiness of men or to the merit of works. Since they see one nation preferred above all others, and hear that God was not for any reason moved to be more favorably inclined to a few, ignoble—indeed, even wicked and stubborn—men, will they quarrel with Him because He chose to give such evidence of His mercy? But they shall neither hinder His work with their clamorous voices nor strike and hurt His righteousness by hurling the stones of their insults toward heaven. Rather, these will fall back on their own heads!

READING QUESTIONS

1. How did Calvin define predestination? What about foreknowledge?
2. Why did Calvin believe that the history of the Jews provided evidence in support of predestination?
3. Why did Calvin believe it was a mistake to "bind God's election either to the worthiness of men or to the merit of works"?
4. How could the principle of predestination be used for political purposes, or to reinforce social hierarchy or inequality?

13-6 | Training the Soldiers of Christ

IGNATIUS OF LOYOLA, *Rules for Right Thinking* (1548)

While recovering from an injury, the Spanish soldier Ignatius (ig-NAY-shus) of Loyola (1491–1556) had a religious experience that inspired him to found a new monastic order unlike most others. Conceived as frontline troops in the battle against Protestantism, members of this order, which became known as the Society of Jesus, or the Jesuits, rejected monastic isolation and instead served as teachers and missionaries. Loyola's *Rules for Right Thinking* was designed to help individuals prepare to serve as Catholic soldiers in the Counter-Reformation. As you read this excerpt, consider what it reveals about how Loyola saw the conflict between Protestantism and Catholicism. Why did he believe that strict obedience to church teachings was critical to the ultimate triumph of Catholicism?

First Rule. The first: All judgment laid aside, we ought to have our mind ready and prompt to obey, in all, the true Spouse of Christ our Lord, which is our holy Mother the Church. . . .

Fifth Rule. The fifth: To praise vows of Religion, of obedience, of poverty, of chastity, and of other perfections. . . .

From Father Elder Mullen, S. J., trans., *The Spiritual Exercises of St. Ignatius of Loyola* (New York: P. J. Kennedy & Sons, 1914), p. 39. Christian Classics Ethereal Library, Web, February 24, 2010.

Sixth Rule. To praise relics of the Saints, giving veneration to them and praying to the Saints; and to praise . . . pilgrimages, indulgences, . . . and candles lighted in the churches. . . .

Eighth Rule. To praise the ornaments and the buildings of churches; likewise images, and to venerate them according to what they represent.

Ninth Rule. Finally, to praise all precepts of the Church, keeping the mind prompt to find reasons in their defense and in no manner against them.

Tenth Rule. We ought to be more prompt to find good and praise as well the . . . recommendations as the ways of our Superiors. Because, although some are not or have not been [upright], to speak against them, whether preaching in public or discoursing before the common people, would rather give rise to fault-finding and scandal than profit; and so the people would be incensed against their Superiors, whether temporal or spiritual. So that, as it does harm to speak evil to the common people of Superiors in their absence, so it can make profit to speak of the evil ways to the persons themselves who can remedy them. . . .

Twelfth Rule. We ought to be on our guard in making comparison of those of us who are alive to the blessed passed away, because error is committed not a little in this; that is to say, in saying, this one knows more than St. Augustine; he is another, or greater than, St. Francis; he is another St. Paul in goodness, holiness, etc.

Thirteenth Rule. To be right in everything, we ought always to hold that the white which I see, is black, if the Church so decides it, believing that between Christ our Lord, . . . and the Church, . . . there is the same Spirit which governs and directs us for the salvation of our souls. Because by the same Spirit and our Lord Who gave the ten Commandments, our holy Mother the Church is directed and governed.

Fourteenth Rule. Although there is much truth in the assertion that no one can save himself without being predestined and without having faith and grace; we must be very cautious in the manner of speaking and communicating with others about all these things.

Fifteenth Rule. We ought not, by way of custom, to speak much of predestination; but if in some way and at some times one speaks, let him so speak that the common people may not come into any error, as sometimes happens, saying: Whether I have to be saved or condemned is already determined, and no other thing can now be, through my doing well or ill; and with this, growing lazy, they become negligent in the works which lead to the salvation and the spiritual.

Sixteenth Rule. In the same way, we must be on our guard that by talking much and with much insistence of faith, without any distinction and explanation, occasion be not given to the people to be lazy and slothful in works, whether before faith is formed in charity or after.

READING QUESTIONS

1. What rules should the Jesuits follow to be faithful to the church?
2. What things should not be spoken of to the people? Why?

3. How do you think Ignatius's career as a soldier prepared him for founding this order?

4. Why might the methods and practices of the Jesuit order be more effective in fighting Protestantism than those of earlier, more insular monastic orders? Why would the papacy particularly value the Jesuits' actions?

5. What potential problems might the tactics of the Jesuit order cause that might undermine their goal to resist Protestantism?

▪ COMPARATIVE AND DISCUSSION QUESTIONS ▪

1. In what ways did Luther's and Calvin's versions of Protestantism differ? Which version might have seemed more threatening to secular rulers? Why?

2. Review Loyola's comments on predestination, as well as Calvin's explanation of the term. Why did Loyola consider it wise for Jesuits to remain silent on this subject?

3. What connections can you make between religious upheaval and the surge in witchcraft prosecutions that began in the mid-sixteenth century?

4. Compare and contrast the image of the pope in the woodcut (ca. 1519) with what Luther said of him in his "Ninety-five Theses" (1517). How would you explain the differences?

14

European Exploration and Conquest
1450–1650

In the mid-1400s, western Europe faced a rapidly expanding Muslim power in the east. The Ottoman Empire captured Constantinople in 1453 and over time came to rule, directly or indirectly, much of eastern Europe. Now cut off from direct access to Asian trade via the eastern Mediterranean, Europeans turned south and west in search of new trade routes to India and China. Portugal led the way in the fifteenth century, launching expeditions to explore the west coast of Africa and eventually rounding the tip of Africa and reaching India. After Columbus's voyages, Spain and Portugal began to explore and conquer the Americas. Portuguese exploration of Africa, combined with the establishment of colonial empires in the Americas, led to a new era of worldwide trade in African slaves. Through trade, travel, and missionary work, Europeans increasingly came into contact with peoples of whom they had previously had little or no knowledge. For many Europeans, this new experience only reinforced their sense of cultural and religious superiority. For others, it prompted a re-evaluation of basic assumptions about their own society and its place in the world.

14-1 | Columbus Sets the Context for His Voyage
CHRISTOPHER COLUMBUS, *Diario* (1492)

The year 1492 was a momentous one in Spanish history. With the fall of the Muslim state of Granada, Ferdinand of Aragon and Isabella of Castille completed the Christian *reconquista* (reconquest) of the Iberian Peninsula. Having driven the "infidel" from its last stronghold,

---

From *The Diario of Christopher Columbus's First Voyage to America*, trans. Oliver Dunn and James E. Kelly Jr. (Norman: University of Oklahoma Press, 1989), pp. 17, 19, 21.

they turned to the "enemy within," issuing a proclamation expelling all Jews from their lands. It was at this moment, fired with a crusading spirit and eager to gain access to the wealth of Asia, that Ferdinand and Isabella chose to sponsor the exploratory westward voyage of Christopher Columbus. As you read the introduction from Columbus's *Diario* (diary), compiled at the request of his sponsors, notice the connections Columbus makes between the events described above and his own voyage. What does his introduction suggest about the role of religion in sparking Spain's involvement in westward expansion?

Whereas, Most Christian and Very Noble and
Very Excellent and Very Powerful Princes, King
and Queen of the Spains and of the Islands of
the Sea, our Lords: This present year of 1492,
after Your Highnesses had brought to an end
the war with the Moors who ruled in Europe and
had concluded the war in the very great city
of Granada, where this present year on the
second day of the month of January I saw the
Royal Standards of Your Highnesses placed by
force of arms on the towers of the Alhambra,
which is the fortress of the said city; and I
saw the Moorish King come out to the gates of
the city and kiss the Royal Hands of Your
Highnesses and of the Prince my Lord; and
later in that same month, because of the
report that I had given to Your Highnesses about
the lands of India and about a prince who is
called "Grand Khan," which means in our
Spanish language "King of Kings"; how, many times,
he and his predecessors had sent to Rome to
ask for men learned in our Holy Faith in order
that they might instruct him in it and how the
Holy Father had never provided them; and thus
so many peoples were lost, falling into idolatry
and accepting false and harmful religions;
and Your Highnesses, as Catholic Christians
and Princes, lovers and promoters of the Holy
Christian Faith, and enemies of the false
doctrine of Mahomet and of all idolatries and
heresies, you thought of sending me, Christóbal
Colón, to the said regions of India to see
the said princes and the peoples and the lands,
and the characteristics of the lands and of
everything, and to see how their conversion to
our Holy Faith might be undertaken. And you
commanded that I should not go to the East by
land, by which way it is customary to go, but

by the route to the West, by which route we do
not know for certain that anyone previously
has passed. So, after having expelled all the
Jews from all of your Kingdoms and Dominions,
in the same month of January Your Highnesses
commanded me to go, with a suitable fleet, to
the said regions of India. And for that you
granted me great favors and ennobled me so
that from then on I might call myself "Don"
and would be Grand Admiral of the Ocean Sea
and Viceroy and perpetual Governor of all the
islands and lands that I might discover and
gain and [that] from now on might be discovered
and gained in the Ocean Sea; and likewise my
eldest son would succeed me and his son him,
from generation to generation forever. And I
left the city of Granada on the twelfth day of
May in the same year of 1492 on Saturday, and
I came to the town of Palos, which is a seaport,
where I fitted out three vessels very
well suited for such exploits; and I left the
said port, very well provided with supplies
and with many seamen, on the third day of
August of the said year, on a Friday, half an
hour before sunrise; and I took the route to
Your Highnesses' Canary Islands, which are in
the said Ocean Sea, in order from there to
take my course and sail so far that I would
reach the Indies and give Your Highnesses'
message to those princes and thus carry out
that which you had commanded me to do. And
for this purpose I thought of writing on this
whole voyage, very diligently, all that I
would do and see and experience, as will be
seen further along. Also, my Lord Princes,
besides writing down each night whatever I
experience during the day and each day what I
sail during the night, I intend to make a new
sailing chart. In it I will locate all of the
sea and the lands of the Ocean Sea in their
proper places under their compass bearings
and, moreover, compose a book and similarly
record all of the same in a drawing, by latitude
from the equinoctial line and by longitude
from the west; and above all it is very

important that I forget sleep and pay much
attention to navigation in order thus to carry
out these purposes, which will be great labor.

READING QUESTIONS

1. How did Columbus explain Ferdinand and Isabella's decision to sponsor his voyage?

2. What does the document suggest about the Spanish monarchs' motives for sponsoring Columbus? What does it suggest about Columbus's motives for conducting the expedition?

3. What might explain Columbus's decision to focus on the reconquista and the expulsion of the Jews in the introduction to the *Diario*?

14-2 | Cortés Describes the Conquest of the Aztecs
HERNÁN CORTÉS, *Two Letters to Charles V: On the Conquest of the Aztecs* (1521)

Hernán Cortés (1485–1547) described his conquest of the Aztec Empire of Mexico in a number of letters to his sovereign and king of Spain, the Holy Roman emperor Charles V. While Cortés was surprised, even impressed, by the advanced culture he encountered, his conquests were not without considerable violence. In one incident, one of his men ordered the massacre of thousands of unarmed members of the Aztec nobility who had assembled peaceably. Under examination, Cortés claimed that this act was done to instill fear and prevent future treachery. Some contemporaries speculated that Cortés embellished his accounts to retain the favor of the king.

[Second Letter]

This great city of Tenochtitlan is built on the salt lake. . . . It has four approaches by means of artificial causeways. . . . The city is as large as Seville or Cordoba. Its streets . . . are very broad and straight, some of these, and all the others, are one half land, and the other half water on which they go about in canoes. . . . There are bridges, very large, strong, and well constructed, so that, over many, ten horsemen can ride abreast. . . . The city has many squares where markets are held. . . . There is one square, twice as large as that of Salamanca, all surrounded by arcades, where there are daily more than sixty thousand souls, buying and selling . . . in the service and manners of its people, their fashion of living was almost the same as in Spain, with just as much harmony and order; and considering that these people were barbarous, so cut off from the knowledge of God

---

From *Letters of Cortés*, trans. Francis A. MacNutt (New York: G. P. Putnam's Sons, 1908), 1:256–257, 2:244.

and other civilized peoples, it is admirable to see to what they attained in every respect.

[Fifth Letter]

It happened . . . that a Spaniard saw an Indian . . . eating a piece of flesh taken from the body of an Indian who had been killed. . . . I had the culprit burned, explaining that the cause was his having killed that Indian and eaten him which was prohibited by Your Majesty, and by me in Your Royal name. I further made the chief understand that all the people . . . must abstain from this custom. . . . I came . . . to protect their lives as well as their property, and to teach them that they were to adore but one God . . . that they must turn from their idols, and the rites they had practiced until then, for these were lies and deceptions which the devil . . . had invented. . . . I, likewise, had come to teach them that Your Majesty, by the will of Divine Providence, rules the universe, and that they also must submit themselves to the imperial yoke, and do all that we who are Your Majesty's ministers here might order them.

READING QUESTIONS

1. Although Cortés described the people of Tenochtitlan as "barbarous" and lamented that they are "cut off from the knowledge of God and other civilized peoples," what positive qualities did he attribute to the city and its people?

2. Why do you think Cortés chose to describe an act of cannibalism? Why might he have believed that such an account would find favor with his royal reader?

3. What different images of Mexico was Cortés trying to impress upon Charles V?

SOURCES IN CONVERSATION

The Slave Trade in Africa

Slavery and the slave trade existed in West Africa long before the arrival of Europeans in the fifteenth and sixteenth centuries. For centuries, Africans had enslaved other Africans, both to use as slaves in Africa and to sell to Muslim merchants as part of the international trade that connected Africa to the Arab world. Nonetheless, European participation altered the African slave trade in profound ways. Most important, it resulted in a surge in demand for African slaves. As European empires in the New World grew, so, too, did the demand for slave labor. Over time, the combined efforts of Africans and Europeans to meet that demand would distort and destabilize African societies and economies.

1. What do these documents demonstrate about the competing interests and agendas of the Portuguese king and merchants interested in acquiring slaves, and King Affonso of Congo who provided them?

14-3 | ALVISE DA CA' DA MOSTO, *Description of Capo Bianco and the Islands Nearest to It: Fifteenth-Century Slave Trade in West Africa* (1455–1456)

Alvise da Ca' da Mosto (ca. 1428–1483) was an Italian trader and explorer. After his father was banished from Venice, Ca' da Mosto took up service with Prince Henry of Portugal, a key promoter of Portuguese exploration of the West African coast. In 1455, he traveled to the Canary and Madeira Islands and sailed past Cape Verde to the Gambia River. During another voyage in 1456, Ca' da Mosto discovered islands off Cape Verde and sailed sixty miles up the Gambia River. In the excerpt that follows, Ca' da Mosto describes the African Muslims who served as middlemen in the Atlantic slave trade. As you read it, notice both the details he chose to include and those he chose to leave out. What do these choices tell you about the nature of his interest in the communities he visited? What do they tell you about his readers' interests?

You should also know that behind this Cauo Bianco[1] on the land, is a place called Hoden,[2] which is about six days inland by camel. This place is not walled, but is frequented by Arabs, and is a market where the caravans arrive from Tanbutu [Timbuktu], and from other places in the land of the Blacks, on their way to our nearer Barbary. The food of the peoples of this place is dates, and barley, of which there is sufficient, for they grow in some of these places, but not abundantly. They drink the milk of camels and other animals, for they have no wine. They also have cows and goats, but not many, for the land is dry. Their oxen and cows, compared with ours, are small.

They are Muhammadans, and very hostile to Christians. They never remain settled, but are always wandering over these deserts. These are the men who go to the land of the Blacks, and also to our nearer Barbary. They are very numerous, and have many camels on which they carry brass and silver from Barbary and other things to Tanbutu and to the land of the Blacks. Thence they carry away gold and pepper, which they bring hither. They are brown complexioned, and wear white cloaks edged with a red stripe: their women also dress thus, without shifts. On their heads the men wear turbans in the Moorish fashion, and they always go barefooted. In these sandy districts there are many lions, leopards, and ostriches, the eggs of which I have often eaten and found good.

From Alvise da Ca' da Mosto, "Description of Capo Bianco and the Islands Nearest to It," in *European Reconnaissance: Selected Documents*, ed. J. H. Parry (New York: Walker, 1968), pp. 59–61.

[1]**Cauo Bianco**: West African port.

[2]**Hoden**: Wadan, an important desert market about 350 miles east of Arguim. Later, in 1487, when the Portuguese sought to penetrate the interior, they attempted to establish a trading factory at Wadan that acted as a feeder to Arguim, tapping the northbound caravan traffic and diverting some of it to the west coast.

You should know that the said Lord Infante of Portugal [the crown prince, Henry the Navigator] has leased this island of Argin to Christians [for ten years], so that no one can enter the bay to trade with the Arabs save those who hold the license. These have dwellings on the island and factories where they buy and sell with the said Arabs who come to the coast to trade for merchandise of various kinds, such as woollen cloths, cotton, silver, and "alchezeli," that is, cloaks, carpets, and similar articles and above all, corn, for they are always short of food. They give in exchange slaves whom the Arabs bring from the land of the Blacks, and gold tiber [gold dust]. The Lord Infante therefore caused a castle to be built on the island to protect this trade for ever. For this reason, Portuguese caravels are coming and going all the year to this island.

These Arabs also have many Berber horses, which they trade, and take to the land of the Blacks, exchanging them with the rulers for slaves. Ten or fifteen slaves are given for one of these horses, according to their quality. The Arabs likewise take articles of Moorish silk, made in Granata and in Tunis of Barbary, silver, and other goods, obtaining in exchange any number of these slaves, and some gold. These slaves are brought to the market and town of Hoden; there they are divided: some go to the mountains of Barcha, and thence to Sicily, [others to the said town of Tunis and to all the coasts of Barbary], and others again are taken to this place, Argin, and sold to the Portuguese leaseholders. As a result every year the Portuguese carry away from Argin a thousand slaves. Note that before this traffic was organized, the Portuguese caravels, sometimes four, sometimes more, were wont to come armed to the Golfo d'Argin, and descending on the land by night, would assail the fisher villages, and so ravage the land. Thus they took of these Arabs both men and women, and carried them to Portugal for sale: behaving in a like manner along all the rest of the coast, which stretches from Cauo Bianco to the Rio di Senega and even beyond.

READING QUESTIONS

1. Why do you think Ca' da Mosto wrote this account?
2. What were the principal patterns of commerce in northern Africa?
3. What groups were involved in the various facets of the slave trade?
4. In what ways did the arrival of the Portuguese change West African slavery and the slave trade?

14-4 | KING NZINGA MBEMBA AFFONSO OF CONGO,
Letters on the Slave Trade (1526)

In 1491, the Portuguese granted the right to send merchants and missionaries into the West African kingdom of Congo. King Affonso, the king of Congo, converted to Christianity, and the trading relationship between Portugal and Congo created many lucrative opportunities

From Basil Davidson, *The African Past: Chronicles from Antiquity to Modern Times* (Boston: Little, Brown, 1964), pp. 191–193; reissued by Africa World Press in 1990 as *African Civilization Revisited: From Antiquity to Modern Times*.

for merchants from both countries. By the 1520s, however, Affonso had grown increasingly concerned about the negative impact that the slave trade was having on his kingdom. The following selection contains two letters from Affonso to the king of Portugal, written in July and October 1526.

[First Letter]

Sir, Your Highness should know how our Kingdom is being lost in so many ways that it is convenient to provide for the necessary remedy, since this is caused by the excessive freedom given by your agents and officials to the men and merchants who are allowed to come to this Kingdom to set up shops with goods and many things which have been prohibited by us, and which they spread throughout our Kingdoms and Domains in such an abundance that many of our vassals, whom we had in obedience, do not comply because they have the things in greater abundance than we ourselves; and it was with these things that we had them content and subjected under our vassalage and jurisdiction, so it is doing a great harm not only to the service of God, but the security and peace of our Kingdoms and State as well.

And we cannot reckon how great the damage is, since the mentioned merchants are taking every day our natives, sons of the land and the sons of our noblemen and vassals and our relatives, because the thieves and men of bad conscience grab them wishing to have the things and wares of this Kingdom which they are ambitious of; they grab them and get them to be sold; and so great, Sir, is the corruption and licentiousness that our country is being completely depopulated, and Your Highness should not agree with this nor accept it as in your service. And to avoid it we need from those [your] Kingdoms no more than some priests and a few people to teach in schools, and no other goods except wine and flour for the holy sacrament. That is why we beg of Your Highness to help and assist us in this matter, commanding your factors that they should not send here either merchants or wares, because it is *our will that in these Kingdoms there should not be any trade of slaves nor outlet for them*. . . .

[Second Letter]

Moreover, Sir, in our Kingdoms there is another great inconvenience which is of little service to God, and this is that many of our people, keenly desirous as they are of the wares and things of your Kingdoms, which are brought here by your people, and in order to satisfy their voracious appetite, seize many of our people, freed and exempt men, and very often it happens that they kidnap even noblemen and the sons of noblemen, and our relatives, and take them to be sold to the white men who are in our Kingdoms; and for this purpose they have concealed them; and others are brought during the night so that they might not be recognized.

And as soon as they are taken by the white men they are immediately ironed and branded with fire, and when they are carried to be embarked, if they are caught by our guards' men the whites allege that they have bought them but they cannot say from whom, so that it is our duty to do justice and to restore to the freemen their freedom, but it cannot be done if your subjects feel offended, as they claim to be.

And to avoid such a great evil we passed a law so that any white man living in our Kingdoms and wanting to purchase goods in any way should first inform three of our noblemen and officials of our court whom we rely upon in this matter, and these are Dom Pedro Manipanza and Dom Manuel Manissaba, our chief usher, and Gonçalo Pires our chief freighter, who should investigate if the mentioned goods are captives or free men, and if cleared by them there will be no further doubt nor embargo for them to be taken and embarked. But if the white men do not comply with it they will lose the aforementioned goods. And if we do them this favor and concession it is for the part Your Highness has in it, since we know that it is in your service too that these goods are taken from our Kingdom, otherwise we should not consent to this.

READING QUESTIONS

1. What negative effects did King Affonso argue that the slave trade was having on his kingdom?

2. In the king's view, who profited from the slave trade? Who bore the social and economic costs of that trade?

3. What did King Affonso propose to do about the slave trade in the first letter? In the second letter? Why do you think he changed his plan?

14-5 | Circumnavigating the Globe

Navigation and Voyage Which Ferdinand Magellan Made from Seville to Maluco in the Year 1519 (1519–1522)

Ferdinand Magellan was a Portuguese explorer who sought to access the riches offered by the Spice Islands, as European markets were clamoring for spices that could flavor and preserve foods but that would not grow in the relatively cold, dry climate of Europe. After he was rejected by King Manuel of Portugal, he petitioned the young and ambitious King Charles I of Spain, who granted Magellan the support he needed. Magellan was successful in sailing around the globe, though he was killed in the Philippines in 1521, and his initial five ships and 270 crew members dwindled to one ship and 18 members when they limped back to Spain three years later in 1522.

[Magellan] sailed from Seville on the 10th day of August of the said year [1519], and remained at the bar until the 21st day of September . . . they entered the said Rio [de Janeiro] on the day of St. Lucy, which was the 13th December. . . .

. . .

From Oliver J. Thatcher, ed., *The Library of Original Sources*, vol. 5: *Ninth to Sixteenth Centuries* (Milwaukee, Wisc.: University Research Extension Co., 1907), pp. 41–55.

Thence they navigated along the said coast, and arrived on the last day of March of the year 1520 at the Port of St. Julian. . . .

In this port three of the ships rose up against the Captain-major, their captains saying that they intended to take him to Castile in arrest, as he was taking them all to destruction. Here, through the exertions of the said Captain-major, and the assistance and favor of the foreigners whom he carried with him, the Captain-major went to the said three ships which were already mentioned, and there the captain of one of them was killed, who was treasurer of the whole fleet, and named Luis de Mendoça; he was killed in his own ship by stabs with a dagger by the chief constable of the fleet, who was sent to do this by Fernando de Magelhaes [i.e., Magellan] in a boat with certain men. The said three ships having thus been recovered, five days later Fernando de Magelhaes ordered Gaspar de Queixada to be decapitated and quartered; he was captain of one of the ships, and was one of those who had mutinied.

. . .

They sailed on the 24th day of the month of August of the said year from this port of St. Julian . . . and they continued collecting the goods which had remained there during August and up to the 18th September, and there they took in water and much fish which they caught in this river; and in the other, where they wintered, there were people like savages, and the men are from nine to ten spans in height, very well made; they have not got houses, they only go about from one place to another with their flocks, and eat meat nearly raw: they are all of them archers and kill many animals with arrows, and with the skins they make clothes, that is to say, they make the skins very supple, and fashion them after the shape of the body, as well as they can, then they cover themselves with them, and fasten them by a belt round the waist. When they do not wish to be clothed from the waist upwards, they let that half fall which is above the waist, and the garment remains hanging down from the belt which they have girt round them. They wear shoes which cover them four inches above the ankle, full of straw inside to keep their feet warm. They do not possess any iron, nor any other ingenuity of weapons, only they make the points of their arrows of flints, and so also the knives with which they cut, and the adze and awls with which they cut and stitch their shoes and clothes. They are very agile people, and do no harm, and thus they follow their flocks: wherever night finds them there they sleep; they carry their wives along with them with all the chattels which they possess. The women are very small and carry heavy burdens on their backs; they wear shoes and clothes just like the men. Of these men they obtained three or four and brought them in the ships, and they all died except one, who went to Castile in a ship which went thither.

. . .

Fernan de Magalhaes would not make any further stay, and at once set sail, and ordered the course to be steered west, and a quarter south-west; and so they made land [i.e., in the Philippines], which is in barely eleven degrees.

. . .

This king conducted them thence a matter of thirty leagues to another island named Cabo, which is in ten degrees, and in this island Fernando de Magalhaes did what he pleased with the consent of the country, and in one day eight hundred people became Christian, on which account Fernan de Magalhaes desired that the other kings, neighbors to this one, should become subject to this who had become Christian: and these did not choose to yield such obedience. Fernan de Magalhaes seeing that, got ready one night with his boats, and burned the villages of those who would not yield the said obedience; and a matter of ten or twelve days after this was done he sent to a village about half a league from that which he had burned, which is named Matam, and which is also an island, and ordered them to send him at once three goats, three pigs, three loads of rice, and three loads of millet for provisions for the ships. . . . Because they did not choose to grant what he demanded of them, Fernan de Magalhaes ordered three boats to be equipped with a matter of fifty or sixty men, and went against the said place, which was on the 28th day of April, in the morning; there they found many people, who might well be as many as three thousand or four thousand men, who fought with such a good will that the said Fernan de Magalhaes was killed there, with six of his men, in the year 1521.

. . .

When Fernan de Magelhaes was dead the Christians got back to the ships, where they thought fit to make two captains and governors whom they should obey; and having done this, they took counsel and decided that the two captains should go ashore where the people had turned Christians to ask for pilots to take them to Borneo, and this was on the first day of May of the said year; when the two captains went, being agreed upon what had been said, the same people of the country who had become Christians, armed themselves against them, and whilst they reached the shore let them land in security as they had done before. Then they attacked them, and killed the two captains and twenty-six gentlemen, and the other people who remained got back to the boats, and returned to the ships, and finding themselves again without captains they agreed, inasmuch as the principal persons were killed, that one John Lopez, who was the chief treasurer, should be captain-major of the fleet, and the chief constable of the fleet should be captain of one of the ships; he was named Gonzalo Vaz Despinosa.

Having done this they set sail, and ran about twenty-five leagues with three ships, which they still possessed; they then mustered, and found that they were altogether one hundred and eight men in all these three ships, and many of them were wounded and sick, on which account they did not venture to navigate the three ships, and thought it would be well to burn one of them — the one that should be most suitable for that purpose — and to take into the two ships those that remained: this they did out at sea, out of sight of any land.

. . .

As soon as they arrived at the island of Tydor, which is in half a degree, the King thereof did them great honor, which could not be exceeded: there they treated with the King for their cargo, and the King engaged to give them a cargo and whatever there was in the country for their money . . . the inhabitants of the country gave them information that further on, in another island near, there was a Portuguese man. This island might be two leagues distant, and it was named

Targatell; this man was the chief person of Maluco; there we now have got a fortress. They then wrote letters to the said Portuguese, to come and speak with them, to which he answered that he did not dare, because the King of the country forbade it; that if they obtained permission from the King he would come at once; this permission they soon got, and the Portuguese came to speak with him. They gave him an account of the prices which they had settled, at which he was amazed, and said that on that account the King had ordered him not to come, as they did not know the truth about the prices of the country; and whilst they were thus taking in cargo there arrived the King of Baraham, which is near there, and said that he wished to be a vassal of the King of Castile, and also that he had got four hundred bahars of cloves, and that he had sold it to the King of Portugal, and that they had bought it, but that he had not yet delivered it, and if they wished for it, he would give it all to them; to which the captains answered that if he brought it to them, and came with it, they would buy it, but otherwise not. The King, seeing that they did not wish to take the cloves, asked them for a flag and a letter of safe conduct, which they gave him, signed by the captains of the ships.

While they were thus waiting for the cargo, it seemed to them, from the delay in the delivery, that the King was preparing some treachery against them, and the greater part of the ships' crews made an uproar and told the captains to go, as the delays which the King made were nothing else than treachery: as it seemed to them all that it might be so, they were abandoning everything, and were intending to depart; and being about to unfurl the sails, the King, who had made the agreement with them, came to the flagship and asked the captain why he wanted to go, because that which he had agreed upon with him he intended to fulfill it as had been settled. The captain replied that the ships' crews said they should go and not remain any longer, as it was only treachery that was being prepared against them. To this the King answered that it was not so, and on that account he at once sent for his Koran, upon which he wished to make oath that nothing such should be done to them. They at once brought him this Koran, and upon it he made oath, and told them to rest at ease with that. At this the crews were set at rest, and promised them that he would give them their cargo by the 1st December 1521, which he fulfilled within the said time without being wanting in anything.

READING QUESTIONS

1. How are the people of the Philippines and the "Moors" treated by Magellan's crew, and how are they described by the "Genoese pilot" that wrote this account?

2. What role do Christian and Muslim beliefs play in this account? What religious assumptions did Magellan make in the Philippines that ultimately got him killed?

3. How do you think this voyage might have changed the perceptions of Magellan's crew about the people they encountered? Why do you think so?

14-6 | A Critique of European "Superiority"

MICHEL DE MONTAIGNE, *Of Cannibals* (1580)

Michel de Montaigne (duh mahn-TAYN) (1533–1592), a French lawyer and government official, wrote about his personal experiences and travels in his *Essays* of 1580. Writing during a period of religious warfare in Europe and the expansion of the European presence around the world, Montaigne offered a critique of European assumptions of social and cultural superiority. In his essay "Of Cannibals," Montaigne pointed out the virtues of Native American society as he saw them. As you read this excerpt from the essay, consider how Montaigne's own assumptions and cultural commitments shaped his view of Native American society. How did Montaigne's diagnosis of the ills of his own society affect his perception of the peoples of the Americas?

When King Pyrrhus[1] invaded Italy, having viewed and considered the order of the army the Romans sent out to meet him; "I know not," said he, "what kind of barbarians" (for so the Greeks called all other nations) "these may be; but the disposition of this army that I see has nothing of barbarism in it." . . . By which it appears how cautious men ought to be of taking things upon trust from vulgar opinion, and that we are to judge by the eye of reason, and not from common report.

I long had a man in my house that lived ten or twelve years in the New World, discovered in these latter days, and in that part of it where Villegaignon landed, which he called Antarctic France.[2] This discovery of so vast a country seems to be of very great consideration. I cannot be sure, that hereafter there may not be another, so many wiser men than we having been deceived in this. I am afraid our eyes are bigger than our bellies, and that we have more curiosity than capacity; for we grasp at all, but catch nothing but wind. . . .

This man that I had was a plain ignorant fellow, and therefore the more likely to tell truth: for your better-bred sort of men are much more curious in their observation; . . . they never represent things to you simply as they are, but rather as they appeared to them, or as they would have them appear to you. . . . I would have every one write what he knows, and as much as he knows, but no more; and that not in this only but in all other subjects. . . .

Now, to return to my subject, I find that there is nothing barbarous and savage in this nation, by anything that I can gather, excepting, that every one gives

---

From *Essays of Montaigne*, trans. Charles Cotton, ed. William Carew Hazlitt, vol. 1 (London: Reeves and Turner, 1902), pp. 237–252.

[1]**Pyrrhus:** Greek king of Sicily (319–272 B.C.E.) who attempted to prevent Roman armies from advancing into southern Italy.

[2]**and in that part . . . Antarctic France:** Nicolas Durand de Villegaignon (1510–1571) was an officer in the French navy who in 1555 captured the region surrounding what is now Rio de Janeiro, Brazil, from the Portuguese. In addition to creating new trading opportunities, his goal was to build a refuge for the French Calvinists to escape religious persecution in France. Portugal retook the colony in 1567.

the title of barbarism to everything that is not in use in his own country. As, indeed, we have no other level of truth and reason than the example and idea of the opinions and customs of the place wherein we live: there is always the perfect religion, there the perfect government, there the most exact and accomplished usage of all things. . . .

These nations then seem to me to be so far barbarous, as having received but very little form and fashion from art and human invention, and consequently to be not much remote from their original simplicity. The laws of nature, however, govern them still, not as yet much [corrupted] with any mixture of ours: but 'tis in such purity, that I am sometimes troubled we were not sooner acquainted with these people, and that they were not discovered in those better times, when there were men much more able to judge of them than we are. . . . To my apprehension, what we now see in those nations, does not only surpass all the pictures with which the poets have adorned the golden age, and all their inventions in feigning a happy state of man, but, moreover, the fancy and even the wish and desire of philosophy itself; so native and so pure a simplicity, as we by experience see to be in them, could never enter into their imagination, nor could they ever believe that human society could have been maintained with so little artifice and human patchwork. I should tell Plato[3] that it is a nation wherein there is no manner of traffic, no knowledge of letters, no science of numbers, no name of magistrate or political superiority; no use of service, riches or poverty, no contracts, no successions, no dividends, no properties, no employments, but those of leisure, no respect of kindred, but common, no clothing, no agriculture, no metal, no use of corn or wine; the very words that signify lying, treachery, dissimulation, avarice, envy, detraction, pardon, never heard of. How much would he find his imaginary Republic short of his perfection? . . .

As to the rest, they live in a country very pleasant and temperate, so that, as my witnesses inform me, 'tis rare to hear of a sick person, and they moreover assure me, that they never saw any of the natives, either paralytic, bleary-eyed, toothless, or crooked with age. The situation of their country is along the sea-shore. . . . They have great store of fish and flesh that have no resemblance to those of ours: which they eat without any other cookery, than plain boiling, roasting, and broiling. The first that rode a horse thither, though in several other voyages he had contracted an acquaintance and familiarity with them, put them into so terrible a fright, with his centaur[4] appearance, that they killed him with their arrows before they could come to discover who he was. Their buildings are very long, and of capacity to hold two or three hundred people. . . . They have wood so hard, that they cut with it, and make their swords of it, and their grills of it to broil their meat. Their beds are of cotton, hung swinging from the roof, like our seamen's hammocks, every man his own, for the wives lie apart from their husbands. They rise with the sun, and so soon as they are up, eat for all day, for they have no more meals but that; they do not then drink, . . . but drink

---

[3]**Plato:** Greek philosopher (427–347 B.C.E.) and author of *The Republic*, who wrote about an ideal city in which people were ruled by philosophers.

[4]**centaur:** Half-human, half-horse creature from Greek mythology.

very often all day after, and sometimes to a rousing pitch. . . . The whole day is spent in dancing. Their young men go a-hunting after wild beasts with bows and arrows; one part of their women are employed in preparing their drink the while, which is their chief employment. One of their old men, in the morning before they fall to eating, preaches to the whole family, walking from the one end of the house to the other, and several times repeating the same sentence, till he has finished the round, for their houses are at least a hundred yards long. Valor towards their enemies and love towards their wives, are the two heads of his discourse. . . . They believe in the immortality of the soul, and that those who have merited well of the gods are lodged in that part of heaven where the sun rises, and the accursed in the west. . . .

They have continual war with the nations that live further within the mainland, beyond their mountains, to which they go naked, and without other arms than their bows and wooden swords, fashioned at one end like the head of our javelins. The obstinacy of their battles is wonderful, and they never end without great effusion of blood: for as to running away, they know not what it is. Every one for a trophy brings home the head of an enemy he has killed, which he fixes over the door of his house. After having a long time treated their prisoners very well, and given them all the regales they can think of, he to whom the prisoner belongs, invites a great assembly of his friends. They being come, he ties a rope to one of the arms of the prisoner, of which, at a distance, out of his reach, he holds the one end himself, and gives to the friend he loves best the other arm to hold after the same manner; which being done, they two, in the presence of all the assembly, dispatch him with their swords. After that, they roast him, eat him amongst them, and send some chops to their absent friends. They do not do this, as some think, for nourishment, . . . but as a representation of an extreme revenge; as will appear by this: that having observed the Portuguese, who were in league with their enemies, to inflict another sort of death upon any of them they took prisoners, which was . . . to shoot at [them] till [they were] stuck full of arrows, and then to hang them, they thought those people of the other world . . . did not exercise this sort of revenge without a meaning, and that it must needs be more painful than theirs, they began to leave their old way, and to follow this. I am not sorry that we should here take notice of the barbarous horror of so cruel an action, but that, seeing so clearly into their faults, we should be so blind to our own. I conceive there is more barbarity in eating a man alive, than when he is dead; in tearing a body limb from limb by racks and torments, that is yet in perfect sense; in roasting it by degrees; in causing it to be bitten and worried by dogs and swine (as we have not only read, but lately seen, not amongst inveterate and mortal enemies, but among neighbors and fellow-citizens, and, which is worse, under color of piety and religion), than to roast and eat him after he is dead. . . .

We may then call these people barbarous, in respect to the rules of reason: but not in respect to ourselves, who in all sorts of barbarity exceed them. Their wars are throughout noble and generous, and carry as much excuse and fair pretence, as that human malady is capable of; having with them no other foundation than the sole jealousy of valor. Their disputes are not for the conquest of new lands, for these they already possess are so fruitful by nature, as to supply them without labor or concern, with all things necessary, in such abundance that they have no need to enlarge their borders. And they are, moreover, happy in this, that they only covet so much as their natural necessities require: all beyond that is superfluous to them. . . . If their neighbors pass over the mountains to assault them, and obtain a victory, all the victors gain by it is glory only, and the advantage of having proved themselves the better in valor and virtue: for they never meddle with the goods of the conquered, but presently return into their own country, where they have no want of anything necessary, nor of this greatest of all goods, to know happily how to enjoy their condition and to be content. And those in turn do the same; they demand of their prisoners no other ransom, than acknowledgment that they are overcome. . . . There is not a man amongst them who had not rather be killed and eaten, than so much as to open his mouth to entreat he may not. They use them with all liberality and freedom, to the end their lives may be so much the dearer to them; but frequently entertain them with menaces of their approaching death, of the torments they are to suffer, of the preparations making in order to it, of the mangling of their limbs, and of the feast that is to be made, where their carcass is to be the only dish. All which they do, to no other end, but only to extort some gentle or submissive word from them, or to frighten them so as to make them run away, to obtain this advantage that they were terrified, and that their constancy was shaken; and indeed, if rightly taken, it is in this point only that a true victory consists. . . .

But to return to my story: these prisoners are so far from discovering the least weakness, for all the terrors that can be represented to them, that, on the contrary, during the two or three months they are kept, they always appear with a cheerful countenance; importune their masters to make haste to bring them to the test, defy, rail at them, and reproach them with cowardice, and the number of battles they have lost against those of their country. I have a song made by one of these prisoners, wherein he bids them "come all, and dine upon him, and welcome, for they shall withal eat their own fathers and grandfathers, whose flesh has served to feed and nourish him. These muscles," says he, "this flesh and these veins, are your own: poor silly souls as you are, you little think that the substance of your ancestors' limbs is here yet; notice what you eat, and you will find in it the taste of your own flesh": in which song there is to be observed an invention that nothing relishes of the barbarian. Those that paint these people dying after this manner, represent the prisoner spitting in the faces of his executioners and making wry mouths at them. And 'tis most certain, that to the very last gasp, they never cease to brave and defy them both in word and gesture. In plain truth, these men are very savage in comparison of us; of necessity, they must either be absolutely so or else we are savages; for there is a vast difference betwixt their manners and ours.

READING QUESTIONS

1. Why does Montaigne write that the words of a "plain ignorant fellow" are more reliable than the words of someone who has been educated? Why does he think it important that reason should be the guide to understanding?

2. How does Montaigne use the word *barbarian* in this essay? To him, what makes someone a barbarian, and why?

3. On what points does Montaigne compare and contrast Native American society with Portuguese society? In what ways does he find the Portuguese to be more barbarous than the cannibals? Why?

▪ COMPARATIVE AND DISCUSSION QUESTIONS ▪

1. What light do Cortés and Columbus shed on the motives behind Spanish exploration and colonization of the Americas?

2. Compare and contrast the two documents on the African slave trade (Documents 14-3 and 14-4). What do these documents reveal about the nature of Portuguese participation?

3. Based on your reading of the documents in these chapters, which distinctions among peoples seemed most important for Europeans of the fifteenth and sixteenth centuries?

4. How do Montaigne's impressions of non-Europeans contrast with those in other European accounts in this chapter? Why do you think they are different?

15

Absolutism and Constitutionalism
ca. 1589–1725

Sixteenth- and seventeenth-century Europe witnessed a prolonged struggle between monarchs seeking to consolidate and extend their power, and social groups and institutions opposing those efforts. Many factors — political, social, and economic — influenced the course of this struggle, and the outcome varied from country to country. France's kings managed to suppress some of the opposition to royal power and thus are termed "absolutist" monarchs, although even the greatest of them, Louis XIV, lacked the power and authority to exert his unchallenged will over all of his subjects, in particular the great nobles. Eastern European rulers in Prussia, Austria, and Russia also augmented their power and authority, although there were significant differences from state to state, and none matched Louis XIV's achievement. Still, all experienced greater success in expanding royal authority than did their counterparts in the Netherlands and England. Two English kings, Charles I and James II, lost their thrones as a consequence of political revolutions, and the former was also tried and executed for crimes against his subjects.

15-1 | A French King Establishes Limited Religious Toleration
HENRY IV, *Edict of Nantes* (1598)

Prince Henry of Navarre (1553–1610) was a Huguenot, or Protestant, in an overwhelmingly Roman Catholic country. He ascended to the French throne as Henry IV in 1589 in the midst of the French Wars of Religion. A pragmatist, Henry realized that the country's Catholic

---

From King Henry of Navarre, "Edict of Nantes," in *Readings in European History*, ed. James Harvey Robinson, vol. 2 (Boston: Ginn, 1906), pp. 183–185.

majority would never accept a Protestant as their legitimate ruler, so he converted to Catholicism. However, to protect the Huguenots against religiously motivated attacks, as well as to establish peace among the people he was determined to rule, he issued the Edict of Nantes. In so doing, Henry legally sanctioned a degree of religious tolerance in a Europe previously characterized by the formula "one king, one people, one faith."

Among the infinite benefits which it has pleased God to heap upon us, the most signal and precious is his granting us the strength and ability to withstand the fearful disorders and troubles which prevailed on our advent in this kingdom. The realm was so torn by innumerable factions and sects that the most legitimate of all the parties[1] was fewest in numbers. God has given us strength to stand out against this storm; we have finally surmounted the waves and made our port of safety,—peace for our state. For which his be the glory all in all, and ours a free recognition of his grace in making use of our instrumentality in the good work. . . . We implore and await from the Divine Goodness the same protection and favor which he has ever granted to this kingdom from the beginning. . . .

We have, by this perpetual and irrevocable edict, established and proclaimed and do establish and proclaim:

I. First, that the recollection of everything done by one party or the other between March, 1585, and our accession to the crown, and during all the preceding period of troubles, remain obliterated and forgotten, as if no such things had ever happened. . . .

III. We ordain that the Catholic Apostolic and Roman religion shall be restored and reestablished in all places and localities of this our kingdom and countries subject to our sway, where the exercise of the same has been interrupted, in order that it may be peaceably and freely exercised, without any trouble or hindrance; forbidding very expressly all persons, of whatsoever estate, quality, or condition, from troubling, molesting, or disturbing ecclesiastics in the celebration of divine service, in the enjoyment or collection of tithes, fruits, or revenues of their benefices, and all other rights and dues belonging to them; and that all those who during the troubles have taken possession of churches, houses, goods, or revenues, belonging to the said ecclesiastics, shall surrender to them entire possession and peaceable enjoyment of such rights, liberties, and sureties as they had before they were deprived of them. . . .

VI. And in order to leave no occasion for troubles or differences between our subjects, we have permitted, and herewith permit, those of the said religion called Reformed [Protestant] to live and abide in all the cities and places of this our kingdom and countries of our sway, without being annoyed,

---

[1]**the most legitimate of all the parties**: Faction supporting Valois king Henry III (r. 1574–1589) during the French Wars of Religion (1561–1598). Henry's subsequent reference to "one party or the other" refers to the three factions, two of them Catholic, one of them Protestant, that struggled for control of the French throne.

molested, or compelled to do anything in the matter of religion contrary to their consciences, . . . upon conditions that they comport themselves in other respects according to that which is contained in this our present edict.

VII. It is permitted to all lords, gentlemen, and other persons making profession of the said religion called Reformed, holding the right of high justice [or a certain feudal tenure], to exercise the said religion in their houses. . . .

IX. We also permit those of the said religion to make and continue the exercise of the same in all villages and places of our dominion where it was established by them and publicly enjoyed several and divers times in the year 1597, up to the end of the month of August, notwithstanding all decrees and judgments to the contrary. . . .

XIII. We very expressly forbid to all those of the said religion its exercise, either in respect to ministry, regulation, discipline, or the public instruction of children, or otherwise, in this our kingdom and lands of our dominion, otherwise than in the places permitted and granted by the present edict.

XIV. It is forbidden as well to perform any function of the said religion on our court or retinue, or in our lands and territories beyond the mountains, or in our city of Paris, or within five leagues of the said city. . . .

XVIII. We also forbid all our subjects, of whatever quality and condition, from carrying off by force or persuasion, against the will of their parents, the children of the said religion, in order to cause them to be baptized or confirmed in the Catholic Apostolic and Roman Church; and the same is forbidden to those of the said religion called Reformed, upon penalty of being punished with special severity. . . .

XXI. Books concerning the said religion called Reformed may not be printed and publicly sold, except in cities and places where the public exercise of the said religion is permitted.

XXII. We ordain that there shall be no difference or distinction made in respect to the said religion, in receiving pupils to be instructed in universities, colleges, and schools; or in receiving the sick and poor into hospitals, retreats and public charities.

XXIII. Those of the said religion called Reformed shall be obliged to respect the laws of the Catholic Apostolic and Roman Church, recognized in this our kingdom, for the consummation of marriages contracted, or to be contracted, as regards to the degrees of consanguinity and kinship.

READING QUESTIONS

1. Why was Henry so intent on "obliterating" the memory of "everything done by one party or the other" in the years immediately prior to his coronation as king of France?

2. Is the Edict of Nantes consistent with Henry's aim of increasing the monarchy's and the state's power? Why or why not?

3. Why might Henry's son, Louis XIII, have regarded the Huguenots as "a state within a state"?

4. Based on the details of the edict regarding ceremonies, property, literature, and education, what sorts of practices defined a religion before and during Henry's reign? What, if any, practices did he consider irreligious, or purely civil?

15-2 | An Argument for the Divine Right of Kings

JEAN DOMAT, *Of the Government and General Policy of a State* (1689)

Jean Domat was a French legal scholar who became one of the foremost experts on Roman law in seventeenth-century Europe. He compiled a massive and systematic guidebook for the French legal system that had enormous long-term influence, and in the process he defined and supported the basis of absolute monarchy, not surprisingly while in the service of the most successful absolute monarch of the period, the French Louis XIV. In these excerpts, he first lays out the rational roots of government in general, and then proceeds to explain why absolute monarchy was a legitimate form of political leadership.

There is nobody who does not appreciate the need for good order in a state, and who does not sincerely wish to see the state that he lives in well regulated. For everyone comprehends and feels within himself by experience and by reason, that the order of society concerns and affects him in many different ways. . . .

Everybody knows that every person is a member of society: and this Truth which the Scripture teaches us, and which the Light of Reason makes clear and evident, is the foundation of all the duties which respect the conduct of every member towards all the other members in particular, and towards the body in general. For a person's duties are nothing else but the functions which are proper to the relationships he has due to his rank in society.

It is from this principle that we draw all the rules of the duties of those who govern, and of those who are subject to the government. For it is by the rank that each person holds in society, that God, who determines the societal place of everyone, also determines their functions and duties. This includes the functions and duties between individual people and also between a person and society as a whole.

Because all men are equal by nature, simply because they are all human, nature does not allow for any person to dominate anyone else. . . . But within this natural equality, there are things that make people unequal, and create relationships and dependencies between them that determine the various duties of each toward the others, and make government necessary. . . .

The first distinction that makes some people able to dominate others is the relationship between parents and children. And this distinction lends itself to a sort of government in families, where children must obey their parents, who lead the family.

From Jean Domat, *The Civil Law in Its Natural Order Together with the Public Law*, trans. William Strahan (London: E. Bell et al., 1722), pp. 289–319.

The second distinction between people derives from the various jobs necessary to be done within a society, and which unite them all into a group that they all are part of. For just as God has made each person dependent upon others for certain things, He has varied their status and their occupations to meet all these needs, assigning people their roles and functions in society. And it is through these interdependent jobs and roles that the connections within human society are formed, as well as the ties among its people. This also makes it necessary to have a leader to unite and rule the society created by these various occupations, and to maintain the order of the relationships that give the public the benefit of the different duties of people that have various social ranks.

It also follows that, since not every person does their duties, and some actually commit injustices, in order to prevent societal chaos, injustices and anything that threatens the social order must be repressed: which was possible only by granting some people authority over others, and which made government necessary.

Causes of the Necessity of a Government

This necessity of government over people equal by their nature, distinguished from each other only by the differences that God established among them according to their stations and professions, makes it clear that government arises from His will; and because only He is the natural sovereign of men, it is from Him that all those who govern derive their power and all their authority, and it is God Himself Whom they represent in their functions.

The Duties of the Governed

Since government is necessary for the health of society, and God has established it, it is therefore also necessary that subjects of a government be submissive and obedient. For if they were not obedient they would resist God, and government, which should preserve societal peace and unity, would foster conflicts that would cause it to collapse.

The first duty of obedience to government is to obey those who have the most powerful roles, monarchs or others who lead society, and to obey them as the limbs of the human body obey the head of their body.

This obedience to the leader should be considered as obedience to the power of God, Who has installed [the leader] as His viceregent here on Earth.

. . .

Obedience to government includes observing the laws, not doing anything contrary to them, executing commands, avoiding things that are forbidden, bearing public burdens, whether they are performing occupations or paying taxes; and in general everyone is obliged not only not to disturb public order in any way, but to contribute everything that is necessary to maintain order.

Since this obedience is necessary to maintain the order and peace that should unite the sovereign and the members of society, it is a duty for all subjects in all cases to obey the orders of the prince, without passing judgment on the orders they should obey. For otherwise, the right to inquire what is just or not would make everyone a master, and it would encourage rebellions.

Thus each individual must obey even laws and orders that seem unjust and [even] to unjust orders, provided he can obey and follow them without being unjust in their own actions. And the only exception that where people could choose to disobey is limited to cases in which one could not obey without disobeying the divine law.

. . .

The Power, Rights, and Duties of Sovereigns

The sovereign power of government should be proportionate to its ministerial function, and in the rank he holds in a society that comprises a state, the sovereign should represent God. For since God is the only natural governor of men, their judge, their lawgiver, their king, no man can have lawful authority over others unless if comes from the hand of God. . . .

Since the power of sovereigns thus comes to them from God, and since He gives it to them only through His providence and His rule over the states whose government He delegates to them, it follows that they should use this power in alignment with the aims that divine providence and rule have established for them; and that the exercises of their authority should reflect the operation of the will of God. . . .

Among the rights of the sovereign, the first is the right to administer justice, the foundation of public order, whether he exercises it himself when necessary or whether he delegates others to exercise it. . . .

This same right to enforce the laws, and to maintain order in general by administering justice and exercising sovereign power, gives the prince the right to use his authority to enforce the laws of the Church, whose *protector, conservator, and defender* [sic] he should be; so that through his authority, religion rules all his subjects. . . .

Among the rights that the laws give the sovereign should be the ability to display all the signs of grandeur and majesty necessary to display his authority and power, and to make his subjects respect that power. . . .

The first and most essential of all the duties of God-appointed sovereigns is acceptance of this fact: that *it is from God that they hold all their power* [sic], that it is His authority they represent, that it is through Him they should reign, and that it is to Him they should look for the knowledge and wisdom needed to govern well. . . .

These general obligations . . . concern all the specific duties of sovereigns. For . . . everything that concerns administering justice, policing of the state, public order, the repose of subjects, peace of mind in families, vigilance over everything that can contribute to the common good, *the choice of able and just ministers,* the appointment of good men whom he knows to the dignities and offices, observing regulations for filling other offices with people that he cannot personally choose, using severity or mercy in those cases where the rigor of justice may be tempered, wisely distributing benefits, rewards, exemptions, privileges, and other favors; good administration of the public finances, wisdom in conducting relations with foreign states, and lastly everything that can make government favorable to good people, terrible to wicked people, and worthy in all respects of the divine mandate to govern men, and of the use of a power which, coming only from God, shares in His own Authority. . . .

We may add as a last duty of the sovereign, which follows from the first and includes all the others, that although his power seems to place him above the law, with no one able to make him accountable to the law, nevertheless he should follow the laws as they may apply to him. And he needs to do this not only to set a good example for his subjects and make them love their duty, but because his sovereign power does not free him from his own duty, and his station requires him to privilege the general good of the state above his personal interests, and it is a glory for him to look upon the general good as his own.

READING QUESTIONS

1. Why does Domat argue that government is necessary?

2. What is the basis for the power of monarchs, or where do they get their authority?

3. According to Domat, are there any limits to the absolute power of kings? If so, what are they? How likely is it that French kings would be hampered by those limits in practice?

4. How does this document differ from the parameters of monarchical power set in the English Bill of Rights (Document 15-3)?

5. What do you see as the benefits and drawbacks of the absolute authority that Domat describes?

15-3 | The English Place Limits on Monarchical Power
The Bill of Rights (1689)

Almost a century of struggle between the forces of constitutionalism and absolutism in England culminated in the Bill of Rights. The Bill of Rights was an unequivocal statement that Parliament, not the monarch, was the source of English law and that all Englishmen, including the monarch, were subject to the law. Acceptance of the Bill of Rights was a non-negotiable condition of the ascendency of William and Mary to the English throne. Thus, the very first act of the new monarchs was to acknowledge the limits of their power. As you read this excerpt, think about what it reveals about late-seventeenth-century notions of freedom and tyranny. What kinds of abuses of power did Parliament fear? What rights and liberties did it seek to protect?

Whereas the late King James the Second, by the assistance of divers evil counsellors, judges and ministers employed by him, did endeavour to subvert and extirpate the Protestant religion and the laws and liberties of this kingdom;

By assuming and exercising a power of dispensing with and suspending of laws and the execution of laws without consent of Parliament;

By committing and prosecuting divers worthy prelates for humbly petitioning to be excused from concurring to the said assumed power;

By issuing and causing to be executed a commission under the great seal for erecting a court called the Court of Commissioners for Ecclesiastical Causes;

http://avalon.law.yale.edu/17th_century/england.asp.

By levying money for and to the use of the Crown by pretence of prerogative for other time and in other manner than the same was granted by Parliament;

By raising and keeping a standing army within this kingdom in time of peace without consent of Parliament, and quartering soldiers contrary to law;

By causing several good subjects being Protestants to be disarmed at the same time when papists were both armed and employed contrary to law;

By violating the freedom of election of members to serve in Parliament;

By prosecutions in the Court of King's Bench for matters and causes cognizable only in Parliament, and by divers other arbitrary and illegal courses;

And whereas of late years partial corrupt and unqualified persons have been returned and served on juries in trials, and particularly divers jurors in trials for high treason which were not freeholders;

And excessive bail hath been required of persons committed in criminal cases to elude the benefit of the laws made for the liberty of the subjects;

And excessive fines have been imposed;

And illegal and cruel punishments inflicted;

And several grants and promises made of fines and forfeitures before any conviction or judgment against the persons upon whom the same were to be levied;

All which are utterly and directly contrary to the known laws and statutes and freedom of this realm;

And whereas the said late King James the Second having abdicated the government and the throne being thereby vacant, his Highness the prince of Orange (whom it hath pleased Almighty God to make the glorious instrument of delivering this kingdom from popery and arbitrary power) did (by the advice of the Lords Spiritual and Temporal and divers principal persons of the Commons) cause letters to be written to the Lords Spiritual and Temporal being Protestants, and other letters to the several counties, cities, universities, boroughs and cinque ports, for the choosing of such persons to represent them as were of right to be sent to Parliament, to meet and sit at Westminster upon the two and twentieth day of January in this year one thousand six hundred eighty and eight [old-style date], in order to such an establishment as that their religion, laws and liberties might not again be in danger of being subverted, upon which letters elections having been accordingly made;

And thereupon the said Lords Spiritual and Temporal and Commons, pursuant to their respective letters and elections, being now assembled in a full and free representative of this nation, taking into their most serious consideration the best means for attaining the ends aforesaid, do in the first place (as their ancestors in like case have usually done) for the vindicating and asserting their ancient rights and liberties declare

That the pretended power of suspending the laws or the execution of laws by regal authority without consent of Parliament is illegal;

That the pretended power of dispensing with laws or the execution of laws by regal authority, as it hath been assumed and exercised of late, is illegal;

That the commission for erecting the late Court of Commissioners for Ecclesiastical Causes, and all other commissions and courts of like nature, are illegal and pernicious;

That levying money for or to the use of the Crown by pretence of prerogative, without grant of Parliament, for longer time, or in other manner than the same is or shall be granted, is illegal;

That it is the right of the subjects to petition the king, and all commitments and prosecutions for such petitioning are illegal;

That the raising or keeping a standing army within the kingdom in time of peace, unless it be with consent of Parliament, is against law;

That the subjects which are Protestants may have arms for their defence suitable to their conditions and as allowed by law;

That election of members of Parliament ought to be free;

That the freedom of speech and debates or proceedings in Parliament ought not to be impeached or questioned in any court or place out of Parliament;

That excessive bail ought not to be required, nor excessive fines imposed, nor cruel and unusual punishments inflicted;

That jurors ought to be duly impanelled and returned, and jurors which pass upon men in trials for high treason ought to be freeholders;

That all grants and promises of fines and forfeitures of particular persons before conviction are illegal and void;

And that for redress of all grievances, and for the amending, strengthening and preserving of the laws, Parliaments ought to be held frequently.

READING QUESTIONS

1. According to the authors, in what ways did James II abuse his power?
2. What steps did the authors take to protect the power of Parliament? To ensure the impartial application of the law?
3. What restrictions did the Bill of Rights place on the rights of Catholics? How might the authors have justified their inclusion of discriminatory provisions in a law meant to protect the rights of the English people?

15-4 | A Tsar Imposes Western Styles on the Russians
PETER THE GREAT, *Edicts and Decrees* (1699–1723)

Peter the Great's reign (1682–1725) marked Russia's emergence as a major European power. Russia defeated Sweden in the grueling Great Northern War (1700–1721) and acquired a "window on Europe" at the head of the Gulf of Finland, where Peter built a new capital, St. Petersburg. In order to defeat the Swedes, who had routed his ill-trained army at Narva in 1700, Peter had reformed and modernized his military along western European lines. His enthusiasm for Western technology and tactics extended also to other realms, including

From Marthe Blinoff, *Life and Thought in Old Russia* (University Park: Pennsylvania State University Press, 1961), pp. 49–50; Eugene Schuyler, *Peter the Great*, vol. 2 (New York: Charles Scribner's Sons, 1884), pp. 176–177; L. Jay Oliva, *Peter the Great* (Englewood Cliffs, N.J.: Prentice-Hall, 1970), p. 50; George Vernadsky et al., *A Source Book for Russian History from Early Times to 1917*, vol. 2 (New Haven, Conn.: Yale University Press, 1972), pp. 329, 347, 357.

education, dress, and economic programs, as can be seen from the following excerpts. As you read them, ask yourself why the West was of such interest to Peter. What did he hope to accomplish through his program of "westernization"?

Decree on the New Calendar, 1699

It is known to His Majesty that not only many European Christian lands, but also Slavic nations which are in total accord with our Eastern Orthodox Church . . . agree to count their years from the eighth day after the birth of Christ, that is from the first day of January, and not from the creation of the world,[1] because of the many difficulties and discrepancies of this reckoning. It is now the year 1699 from the birth of Christ, and from the first of January will begin both the new year 1700 and a new century; and so His Majesty has ordered, as a good and useful measure, that from now on time will be reckoned in government offices and dates be noted on documents and property deeds, starting from the first of January 1700. And to celebrate this good undertaking and the new century . . . in the sovereign city of Moscow . . . let the reputable citizens arrange decorations of pine, fir, and juniper trees and boughs along the busiest main streets and by the houses of eminent church and lay persons of rank. . . . Poorer persons should place at least one shrub or bough on their gates or on their house. . . . Also . . . as a sign of rejoicing, wishes for the new year and century will be exchanged, and the following will be organized: when fire-works are lit and guns fired on the great Red Square, let the boyars [nobles], the Lords of the Palace, of the Chamber, and the Council, and the eminent personages of Court, Army, and Merchant ranks, each in his own grounds, fire three times from small guns, if they have any, or from muskets and other small arms, and shoot some rockets into the air.

Decree on the Invitation of Foreigners, 1702

Since our accession to the throne all our efforts and intentions have tended to govern this realm in such a way that all of our subjects should, through our care for the general good, become more and more prosperous. For this end we have always tried to maintain internal order, to defend the state against invasion, and in every possible way to improve and to extend trade. With this purpose we have been compelled to make some necessary and salutary changes in the administration, in order that our subjects might more easily gain a knowledge of matters of which they were before ignorant, and become more skillful in their commercial relations.

We have therefore given orders, made dispositions, and founded institutions indispensable for increasing our trade with foreigners, and shall do the same in the future. Nevertheless we fear that matters are not in such a good condition as we desire, and that our subjects cannot in perfect quietness enjoy

---

[1]**agree to count their years . . . world**: Before January 1, 1700, the Russian calendar started from the date of the creation of the world, which was reckoned at 5508 B.C.E. The year began on September 1.

the fruits of our labors, and we have therefore considered still other means to protect our frontier from the invasion of the enemy, and to preserve the rights and privileges of our State, and the general peace of all Christians. . . .

To attain these worthy aims, we have endeavored to improve our military forces, which are the protection of our State, so that our troops may consist of well-drilled men, maintained in perfect order and discipline. In order to obtain greater improvement in this respect, and to encourage foreigners, who are able to assist us in this way, as well as artisans profitable to the State, to come in numbers to our country, we have issued this manifesto, and have ordered printed copies of it to be sent throughout Europe. . . . And as in our residence of Moscow, the free exercise of religion of all other sects, although not agreeing with our church, is already allowed, so shall this be hereby confirmed anew in such manner that we, by the power granted to us by the Almighty, shall exercise no compulsion over the consciences of men, and shall gladly allow every Christian to care for his own salvation at his own risk.

An Instruction to Russian Students Abroad Studying Navigation, 1714

1. Learn how to draw plans and charts and how to use the compass and other naval indicators.

2. Learn how to navigate a vessel in battle as well as in a simple maneuver, and learn how to use all appropriate tools and instruments; namely, sails, ropes, and oars, and the like matters, on row boats and other vessels.

3. Discover . . . how to put ships to sea during a naval battle. . . . Obtain from foreign naval officers written statements, bearing their signatures and seals, of how adequately you are prepared for naval duties.

4. If, upon his return, anyone wishes to receive from the Tsar greater favors, he should learn, in addition to the above enumerated instructions, how to construct those vessels [aboard] which he would like to demonstrate his skills.

5. Upon his return to Moscow, every foreign-trained Russian should bring with him at his own expense, for which he will later be reimbursed, at least two experienced masters of naval science. They [the returnees] will be assigned soldiers, one soldier per returnee, to teach them what they have learned abroad. . . .

Decree on Western Dress, 1701

Western ["German"] dress shall be worn by all the boyars, okol'nichie,[2] members of our councils and of our court . . . gentry of Moscow, secretaries . . . provincial gentry, boiarskie,[3] gosti,[4] government officials, strel'tsy,[5] members of the guilds purveying for our household, citizens of Moscow of all ranks, and residents of provincial cities . . . excepting the clergy (priests, deacons, and church attendants) and peasant tillers of the soil. The upper dress shall

---

[2]**boyars, okol'nichie**: Nobles of the highest and second-highest rank, respectively.
[3]**boiarskie**: Sons of boyars.
[4]**gosti**: Merchants who often served the tsar in some capacity.
[5]**strel'tsy**: Members of the imperial guard stationed in Moscow.

be of French or Saxon cut, and the lower dress — [including] waistcoat, trousers, boots, shoes, and hats — shall be of the German type. They shall also ride German saddles. [Likewise] the womenfolk of all ranks, including the priests', deacons', and church attendants' wives, the wives of the dragoons, the soldiers, and the strel'tsy and their children, shall wear Western ["German"] dresses, hats, jackets, and underwear — undervests and petticoats — and shoes. From now on no one [of the abovementioned] is to wear Russian dress or Circassian coats,[6] sheepskin coats, or Russian peasant coats, trousers, boots, and shoes. It is also forbidden to ride Russian saddles, and the craftsmen shall not manufacture them or sell them at the marketplaces.

Decree on Shaving, 1705

A decree to be published in Moscow and in all the provincial cities: Henceforth, in accordance with this, His Majesty's decree, all court attendants . . . provincial service men, government officials of all ranks, military men, all the gosti, members of the wholesale merchants' guild, and members of the guilds purveying for our household must shave their beards and moustaches. But, if it happens that some of them do not wish to shave their beards and moustaches, let a yearly tax be collected from such persons. . . . Special badges shall be issued to them from the Administrator of Land Affairs [of Public Order] . . . which they must wear. . . . As for the peasants, let a toll of two half-copecks[7] per beard be collected at the town gates each time they enter or leave a town; and do not let the peasants pass the town gates, into or out of town, without paying this toll.

Decree on Promotion to Officer's Rank, 1714

Since there are many who promote to officer rank their relatives and friends — young men who do not know the fundamentals of soldiering, not having served in the lower ranks — and since even those who serve [in the ranks] do so for a few weeks or months only, as a formality; therefore . . . let a decree be promulgated that henceforth there shall be no promotion [to officer rank] of men of noble extraction or of any others who have not first served as privates in the Guards. This decree does not apply to soldiers of lowly origin who, after long service in the ranks, have received their commissions through honest service or to those who are promoted on the basis of merit, now or in the future; it applies exclusively to those who have remained in the ranks for a short time, only as a formality, as described above.

Statute for the College of Manufactures, 1723

His Imperial Majesty is diligently striving to establish and develop in the Russian Empire such manufacturing plants and factories as are found in other states, for the general welfare and prosperity of his subjects. He [therefore] most

---

[6]**Circassian coats:** Traditional outer garments worn by the people of Circassia, a Russian territory between the Caspian and Black Seas. The style was evidently adopted by the nobility.

[7]**half-copecks:** One-twentieth of a ruble, the basic unit of Russian money.

graciously charges the College of Manufactures[8] to exert itself in devising the means to introduce, with the least expense, and to spread in the Russian Empire these and other ingenious arts, and especially those for which materials can be found within the empire; [the College of Manufactures] must also consider the privileges that should be granted to those who might wish to found manufacturing plants and factories.

His Imperial Majesty gives permission to everyone, without distinction of rank or condition, to open factories wherever he may find suitable. . . .

Factory owners must be closely supervised, in order that they have at their plants good and experienced [foreign] master craftsmen, who are able to train Russians in such a way that these, in turn, may themselves become masters, so that their produce may bring glory to the Russian manufactures. . . .

By the former decrees of His Majesty commercial people were forbidden to buy villages [i.e., to own serfs], the reason being that they were not engaged in any other activity beneficial for the state save commerce; but since it is now clear to all that many of them have started to found manufacturing establishments and build plants, both in companies and individually, which tend to increase the welfare of the state . . . therefore permission is granted both to the gentry and to men of commerce to acquire villages for these factories without hindrance. . . .

In order to stimulate voluntary immigration of various craftsmen from other countries into the Russian Empire, and to encourage them to establish factories and manufacturing plants freely and at their own expense, the College of Manufactures must send appropriate announcements to the Russian envoys accredited at foreign courts. The envoys should then, in an appropriate way, bring these announcements to the attention of men of various professions, urge them to come to settle in Russia, and help them to move.

READING QUESTIONS

1. Why do you think Peter decreed that the nobles, merchants, and townspeople wear German, rather than French, clothes, seeing as the French kings and their palaces were objects of emulation throughout Europe?

2. What does Peter's decree encouraging foreign soldiers and artisans to emigrate to Russia and his Statute for the College of Manufactures suggest about the state of Russia's military forces and economy as of the early 1700s?

3. Why didn't Russia have a navy prior to 1700?

4. What, according to Peter, was wrong with the system of promotion in the Russian army, and how did he intend to redress it? What does his decree on promotion suggest about the power and benefits granted to the Russian nobility?

---

[8]**College of Manufactures**: One of several administrative boards created by Peter in 1717, modeled on Swedish practice.

The Commonwealth and the State of Nature

Over the course of the seventeenth century, England experienced two civil wars, the execution of a king, and the forced abdication of another. These dramatic events raised fundamental political questions: What limitations exist on monarchical authority? What rights do subjects enjoy, and under what conditions can those rights be abridged? What means of redress, if any, do subjects have if their leaders abuse their power? The political philosophers Thomas Hobbes and John Locke developed the two most important theoretical responses to these questions. While their answers differed, they framed their analyses in similar ways. Both addressed two overarching questions: How and why do governments form? And what do the origins of the state imply for contemporary political conflicts?

READ AND COMPARE

1. How do these two documents explain the reason that government exists, and how do those explanations differ? Why do you think they are different, based upon the identity of the authors?

2. Which people in society would benefit most from Hobbes's system on the one hand, and Locke's on the other?

15-5 | THOMAS HOBBES, *Leviathan* (1651)

Thomas Hobbes (1588–1679), the son of a Church of England clergyman, was educated at Oxford University and spent the years between 1608 and 1637 chiefly as a tutor to aristocratic families. Rising religious and political tensions in England drove Hobbes to flee to Paris in 1640, and there he remained until the publication of *Leviathan*, which aroused so much anger among English royalists that he was forced to seek protection from Cromwell's republican government. Leviathan originally referred to a biblical sea monster, but Hobbes used it as a synonym for the commonwealth; the frontispiece to his book depicts a gargantuan human figure made up of smaller people (members of the commonwealth) with the head of a monarch. *Leviathan* itself is based on the premise that without a sovereign authority invested with absolute power, human society is in a state of perpetual violence. Faced with such a prospect, he argued, individuals voluntarily relinquish their personal rights and liberties in return for protection.

Nature hath made men so equal, in the faculties of body and mind, as that though there be found one man sometimes manifestly stronger in body, or of quicker mind than another; yet when all is reckoned together, the difference between man and man is not so considerable, as that one man can thereupon claim to himself any benefit, to which another may not pretend, as well as he.

From Thomas Hobbes, *Leviathan, or the Matter, Form, and Power of a Commonwealth, Ecclesiastical and Civil* (London: George Routledge and Sons, 1886), pp. 64–66, 82, 84–85.

For as to the strength of body, the weakest has strength enough to kill the strongest, either by secret machination or by confederacy with others that are in the same danger with himself. . . .

From this equality of ability, ariseth equality of hope in the attaining of our ends. And therefore if any two men desire the same thing, which nevertheless they cannot both enjoy, they become enemies, and in the way to their end, . . . endeavor to destroy, or subdue one another. . . .

So that in the nature of man, we find three principal causes of quarrel. First, competition; secondly, diffidence; thirdly, glory.

The first maketh men invade for gain; the second, for safety; and the third, reputation. The first use violence to make themselves masters of other men's persons, wives, children, and cattle; the second, to defend them; the third, for trifles, as a word, a smile, a different opinion, and any other sign of undervalue, either direct in their persons, or by reflection in their kindred, their friends, their nation, their profession, or their name.

Hereby it is manifest, that during the time men live without a common power to keep them all in awe, they are in that condition which is called war; and such a war, as is of every man, against every man. . . .

[On "the state of nature":]

Whatsoever therefore is consequent to a time of war, where every man is enemy to every man; the same is consequent to the time wherein men live without other security, than what their own strength and their own invention shall furnish them withall. In such condition, there is no place for industry, because the fruit thereof is uncertain, and consequently no culture of the earth; no navigation, nor use of the commodities that may be imported by sea; no commodious building; no instruments of moving and removing such things as require much force; no knowledge of the face of the earth; no account of time; no arts; no letters; no society; and, which is worst of all, continual fear, and danger of violent death; and the life of man, solitary, poor, nasty, brutish, and short. . . .

The passions that incline men to peace, are fear of death; desire of such things as are necessary to commodious living; and a hope by their industry to obtain them. And reason suggesteth convenient articles of peace, upon which men may be drawn to agreement. . . .

And because the condition of man, as hath been declared in the precedent chapter, is a condition of war of everyone against everyone; in which case everyone is governed by his own reason, and there is nothing he can make use of, that may not be a help unto him, in preserving his life against his enemies; It followeth that, in such a condition, every man has a right to every thing, even to one another's body. And therefore, as long as this natural right of every man to everything endureth, there can be no security to any man, how strong or wise soever he be, of living out the time, which Nature ordinarily alloweth men to live. . . .

If there be no power erected, or not great enough for our security, every man will and may lawfully rely on his own strength and art, for caution against all other men. . . .

The only way to erect such a common power, as may be able to defend them from the invasion of foreigners, and the injuries of one another, and thereby to secure them in such sort as that by their own industry and by the fruits of the earth they may nourish themselves and live contentedly, is to confer all their power and strength upon one man, or upon one assembly of men, that may reduce all their wills, by plurality of voices, unto one will: which is as much as to say, to appoint one man, or assembly of men, to bear their person; and every one to own and acknowledge himself to be author of whatsoever he that so beareth their person shall act, or cause to be acted, in those things which concern the common peace and safety; and therein to submit their wills, every one to his will, and their judgments to his judgment. This is more than consent, or concord; it is a real unity of them all in one and the same person, made by covenant of every man with every man, in such manner as if every man should say to every man: "I authorize and give up my right of governing myself to this man, or to this assembly of men, on this condition, that thou give up thy right to him, and authorize all his actions in like manner." This done, the multitude so united in one person is called a "commonwealth," in Latin, *civitas*. This is the generation of that great "leviathan," or rather, to speak more reverently, of that "mortal god," to which we owe under the "immortal God," our peace and defense. For by this authority, given him by every particular man in the commonwealth, he hath the use of so much power and strength conferred on him that by terror thereof, he is enabled to perform the wills of them all, to peace at home, and mutual aid against their enemies abroad. And in him consisteth the essence of the commonwealth; which, to define it, is "one person, of whose acts a great multitude, by mutual covenants one with another, have made themselves every one the author, to the end he may use the strength and means of them all as he shall think expedient, for their peace and common defense."

And he that carryeth this person is called "sovereign," and said to have "sovereign power"; and every one besides, his "subject." . . .

They that have already instituted a commonwealth, being thereby bound by covenant to own the actions and judgments of one, cannot lawfully make a new covenant, amongst themselves, to be obedient to any other, in anything whatsoever, without his permission. And therefore, they that are subjects to a monarch cannot without his leave cast off monarchy, and return to the confusion of a disunited multitude; nor transfer their person from him that beareth it to another man, other assembly of men . . . [he] that already is their sovereign shall do and judge fit to be done: so that any one man dissenting, all the rest should break their covenant made to that man, which is injustice: and they have also every man given the sovereignty to him that beareth their person; and therefore if they depose him, they take from him that which is his own, and so again it is injustice. . . . And whereas some men have pretended for their disobedience to their sovereign, a new covenant, made not with men but with God; this also is unjust: for there is no covenant with God but by mediation of somebody that representeth God's person; which none doth but God's lieutenant, who hath the sovereignty under God. But this pretence of covenant with God is so evident a lie, even in the pretenders' own consciences, that it is not only an act of an unjust, but also of a vile and unmanly disposition. . . .

Consequently none of [the sovereign's] subjects, by any pretence of forfeiture, can be freed from his subjection.

READING QUESTIONS

1. How does Hobbes characterize human existence without the peace and order afforded by a ruler vested with absolute authority?

2. What is Hobbes's view of religious or divine justifications for absolute power?

3. Having placed themselves under the sovereign power of a ruler, what freedom of action do individuals have to govern their own affairs?

4. What options, according to Hobbes, do a sovereign's subjects have in the event that he abuses his power?

15-6 | JOHN LOCKE, *Second Treatise of Civil Government: Vindication for the Glorious Revolution* (1690)

John Locke (1632–1704) was, along with Thomas Hobbes, one of the two greatest English political theorists of the seventeenth century. Unlike Hobbes, however, who provided a justification for monarchical absolutism, Locke's *Second Treatise of Civil Government*, published anonymously in 1690, argued that government is an agreement between governors and the governed. The people submit to governmental authority in return for protection of their life, liberty, and property, and the governors' fundamental task is to provide those essential protections. According to Locke, a government that failed to do so or became tyrannical lost its claim to legitimacy, and could therefore be cast off by the governed.

87. Man being born, as has been proved, with a title to perfect freedom and an uncontrolled enjoyment of all the rights and privileges of the law of Nature, equally with any other man, or number of men in the world, hath by nature a power not only to preserve his property — that is, his life, liberty and estate against the injuries and attempts of other men; but to judge of and punish the breaches of that law in others, as he is persuaded the offense deserves, even with death itself, in crimes where the heinousness of the fact, in his opinion, requires it. But because no political society can be, nor subsist, without having in itself the power to preserve the property, and in order thereunto punish the offenses of all those of that society, there, and there only is political society where every one of the members hath quitted this natural power, resigned it up into the hands of the community in all cases that exclude him not from appealing for protection to the law established by it. And thus all private judgment of every particular member being excluded, the community comes to be umpire, and by understanding indifferent rules and men authorized by the community for their

From John Locke, *Two Treatises on Civil Government* (London: George Routledge and Sons, 1887), pp. 234–238.

execution, decides all the differences that may happen between any members of that society concerning any matter of right, and punishes those offenses which any member hath committed against the society with such penalties as the law has established; whereby it is easy to discern, who are, and are not, in political society together. Those who are united into one body, and have a common established law and judicature to appeal to, with authority to decide controversies between them and punish offenders, are in civil society one with another; but those who have no such common appeal, I mean on earth, are still in the state of Nature, each being where there is no other, judge for himself and executioner; which is, as I have before showed it, the perfect state of Nature.

88. And thus the commonwealth comes by a power to set down what punishment shall belong to the several transgressions they think worthy of it, committed amongst the members of that society (which is the power of making laws) as well as it has the power to punish any injury done unto any of its members by any one that is not of it (which is the power of war and peace); and all this for the preservation of the property of all the members of that society, as far as is possible. But though every man entered into society has quitted his power to punish offenses against the law of Nature in prosecution of his own private judgment, yet with the judgment of offenses which he has given up to the legislative, in all cases where he can appeal to the magistrate, he has given up a right to the commonwealth to employ his force, for the execution of the judgments of the commonwealth whenever he shall be called to it, which, indeed, are his own judgments, they being made by himself or his representative. And herein we have the original of the legislative and executive power of civil society, which is to judge by standing laws how far offenses are to be punished when committed within the commonwealth; and also by occasional judgments founded on the present circumstances of the fact, how far injuries from without are to be vindicated; and in both these to employ all the force of all the members when there shall be need.

89. Wherever, therefore, any number of men so unite into one society as to quit every one his executive power of the law of Nature, and to resign it to the public, there and there only is a political or civil society. And this is done wherever any number of men, in the state of nature, enter into society to make one people one body politic under one supreme government; or else when any one joins himself to, and incorporates with any government already made. For hereby he authorizes the society, or which is all one, the legislative thereof, to make laws for him as the public good of the society shall require; to the execution whereof his own assistance (as to his own decrees) is due. And this puts men out of a state of Nature into that of a commonwealth, by setting up a judge on earth with authority to determine all the controversies and redress the injuries that may happen to any member of the commonwealth; which judge is the legislative or magistrates appointed by it. And wherever there are any number of men, however associated, that have no such decisive power to appeal to, there they are still in the state of Nature.

90. And hence it is evident that absolute monarchy, which by some men is counted for the only government in the world, is indeed inconsistent with civil

society, and so can be no form of civil government at all. For the end of civil society being to avoid and remedy those inconveniencies of the state of nature which necessarily follow from every man's being judge in his own case by setting up a known authority to which every one of that society may appeal upon any injury received, or controversy that may arise, and which every one of the society ought to obey. Wherever any persons are who have not such an authority to appeal to, and decide any difference between them there, those persons are still in the state of Nature. And so is every absolute prince in respect of those who are under his dominion.

91. For he being supposed to have all, both legislative and executive, power in himself alone, there is no judge to be found, no appeal lies open to any one, who may fairly and indifferently, and with authority decide, and from whence relief and redress may be expected of any injury or inconveniency that may be suffered from him, or by his order. So that such a man, however entitled, Czar, or Grand Signior, or how you please, is as much in the state of Nature, with all under his dominion, as he is with the rest of mankind. For wherever any two men are, who have no standing rule and common judge to appeal to on earth, for the determination of controversies of right betwixt them, there they are still in the state of Nature, and under all the inconveniencies of it, with only this woeful difference to the subject, or rather slave of an absolute prince. That whereas, in the ordinary state of nature, he has a liberty to judge of his right, and according to the best of his power to maintain it; but whenever his property is invaded by the will and order of his monarch, he has not only no appeal, as those in society ought to have, but as if he were degraded from the common state of rational creatures, is denied a liberty to judge of, or to defend his right, and so is exposed to all the misery and inconveniencies that a man can fear from one, who being in the unrestrained state of Nature, is yet corrupted with flattery and armed with power.

92. For he that thinks absolute power purifies men's bloods, and corrects the baseness of human nature, need read but the history of this, or any other age, to be convinced of the contrary.

READING QUESTIONS

1. What, according to Locke, distinguishes "political, or civil society" from "a state of nature"?

2. What, in Locke's opinion, led to the creation of "political, or civil society"?

3. Why does he argue that "absolute monarchy, which by some men is counted for the only government in the world, is indeed inconsistent with civil society, and so can be no form of civil government at all"?

4. Why do you think Locke published this work anonymously, rather than publicly claiming credit for what is now generally regarded as one of the classics of Western political theory?

■ COMPARATIVE AND DISCUSSION QUESTIONS ■

1. What would Hobbes say of Domat's justification for absolute royal authority? What would Domat say of Hobbes's?

2. How does Hobbes's "social contract" theory differ from Locke's? How do Hobbes and Locke use "the state of nature" to further their arguments?

3. In what ways are Locke's views reflected in the English Bill of Rights?

4. What do Henry IV's and Peter the Great's edicts tell you about their attitudes toward monarchy and their roles in the lives of their subjects?

16

Toward a New Worldview
1540–1789

For the most part, medieval scholars turned to authoritative texts for information and ideas about the natural world. Placing their faith in the Bible and in the insights of ancient scholars, they forged a vision of the universe and its workings that infused classical models with Christian implications. Those models were first challenged and then overturned over the course of the sixteenth and seventeenth centuries, as direct observation and experiment combined with increasingly sophisticated mathematics to produce a revolution in the study of the natural world. This process culminated at the end of the seventeenth century in the discoveries of Isaac Newton, whose work would provide the fundamental framework for Western physics well into the twentieth century. By the eighteenth century, the spirit of this "scientific revolution" had spread to human affairs. Philosophers and scientists of the European Enlightenment, particularly in France, began to question traditional forms of social and political organization. Some thinkers rejected the legitimacy of absolutism and divine right. Others challenged the authority of the Roman Catholic Church. In the climate of the age, even absolutist monarchs saw advantages to embracing aspects of Enlightenment thought, though with varying degrees of enthusiasm and success.

16-1 | A New Model of the Solar System

NICOLAUS COPERNICUS, *On the Revolutions of the Heavenly Spheres* (1542)

There was nothing revolutionary about Polish cleric and astronomer Nicolaus Copernicus's (1473–1543) motives for developing a heliocentric (sun-centered) model of the universe. Frustrated by the cumbersome calculations and inaccuracies of the Ptolemaic model, Copernicus sought an alternative that overcame these limitations and, in his view, offered a better reflection of the perfection of God's creation. Moreover, he retained many elements of earlier systems. For example, Copernicus still imagined the stars embedded in crystalline spheres. For all the conservatism of his approach, however, Copernicus was well aware of the stir his work might produce. Fearful of the response of church authorities, he waited to publish his findings until 1542, more than a decade after his work was complete and shortly before his death. As you read this excerpt, consider its mix of traditional and revolutionary ideas. In what ways does Copernicus seem like a medieval scholar? In what ways does he seem closer to what we think of as a scientist?

That the Universe Is Spherical

First we must remark that the universe is globe-shaped, either because that is the most perfect shape of all, needing no joint, an integral whole; or because that it is the most capacious of shapes, which is most fitting because it is to contain and preserve all things; or because the most finished parts of the universe, I mean the Sun, Moon, and stars, are observed to have that shape, or because everything tends to take on this shape, which is evident in drops of water and other liquid bodies, when they take on their natural shape. There should therefore be no doubt that this shape is assigned to the heavenly bodies.

That the Earth Is Also Spherical

The Earth is also globe-shaped, because every part of it tends towards its center. Although it is not immediately apparent that it is a perfect sphere, because the mountains project so far and the valleys are so deep, they produce very little variation in the complete roundness of the Earth. That is evident from the fact that as one moves northward from any point that pole [the North Pole] of the diurnal [daily] rotation rises little by little, while the other pole on the contrary sinks to the same extent, and several stars round the North Pole seem not to set, while some in the South no longer rise. . . .

From Nicolaus Copernicus, *De Revolutionibus Orbium Celestium*, trans. A. M. Duncan (Newton Abbot, Devonshire: David and Charles, 1976), pp. 36, 37, 40–41, 43–44, 45–46.

Whether the Earth Has a Circular Motion, and Concerning the Location of the Earth

As it has now been shown that the Earth also has the shape of a globe, I believe we must consider whether its motion too follows its shape, and what place it holds in the universe, without which it is impossible to find a reliable explanation of celestial phenomena. Among the authorities it is generally agreed that the Earth is at rest in the middle of the universe, and they regard it as inconceivable and even ridiculous to hold the opposite opinion. However, if we consider it more closely the question will be seen to be still unsettled, and so decidedly not to be despised. For every apparent change in respect of position is due to motion of the object observed, or of the observer, or indeed to an unequal change of both. (Between objects which move equally in the same direction no motion is perceived, I mean between that which is observed and the observer.) Now the Earth is the point from which the rotation of the heavens is observed, and brought into our view. If therefore some motion is imputed to the Earth, the same motion will appear in all that is external to the Earth, but in the opposite direction, as if it were passing by. The first example of this is the diurnal rotation. This seems to whirl round the whole universe, except the Earth and the things on it. But if you grant that the heaven has no part in this motion, but that the Earth revolves from west to east, as far as the apparent rising and setting of the Sun, Moon, and stars is concerned, if you consider the point seriously, you will find that this is the way of it. And as the heaven is that which contains and cloaks all things, where everything has its place, it is not at once apparent why motion is attributed to that which is contained rather than to the container, to that which is located rather than that which locates it. . . . If this assumption is made there follows another and no lesser problem about the position of the Earth, although almost everyone admits and believes the Earth to be the center of the universe. For if one argues that the Earth does not occupy the center or middle of the universe, not claiming that its distance is great enough to be comparable with the sphere of the fixed stars, but that it is appreciable and significant compared with the orbits of the Sun and other stars,[1] and believing that on this account their motion seems to be variable, as if they were regular with respect to [i.e., revolved around] some center other than the center of the Earth, he would perhaps be able to put forward a not unreasonable account of the apparently variable motion. For the fact that the wandering stars are observed to be sometimes nearer to the Earth and sometimes further away from it necessarily shows that the center of the Earth is not the center of their orbits. It is also undecided whether the Earth veers toward them and away from them or they towards and away from the Earth. It would also not be surprising if in addition to this daily revolution another motion should be supposed for the Earth. Indeed that the

---

[1]**not claiming . . . other stars:** Copernicus is arguing here that the diameter of the earth's orbit is insignificant compared to the distance of the earth from the "fixed stars," which he, like his contemporaries, believed to be embedded in an invisible crystalline sphere, but is comparable to that of the "wandering stars," i.e., the visible planets.

Earth revolves, wanders with several motions, and is one of the stars [i.e., planets] is said to have been the opinion of Philolaus the Pythagorean,[2] no mean mathematician. . . .

Refutation of the Arguments Quoted, and Their Insufficiency[3]

From this and similar arguments, then, they say that the Earth is at rest in the middle of the universe, and that such is undoubtedly the state of affairs. Yet if anyone should hold the opinion that the Earth revolves, he will surely assert that its motion is natural, not violent. What is natural produces contrary effects to what is violent. For objects to which force or impulse is applied must necessarily be destroyed and cannot long subsist; but objects which exist naturally are in their proper state, and continue in their perfect form. There is therefore no need for Ptolemy to fear the scattering of the Earth and of all terrestrial objects in a revolution brought about through the workings of nature, which is far different from artifice, or what can be achieved by human abilities. Further, why is not the same question raised even more strongly about the universe, the motion of which must be much swifter in proportion as the heaven is greater than the Earth? Or has heaven become so immense, because it is drawn outwards from the middle by a motion of ineffable strength [i.e., centrifugal force], that it would collapse if it were not at rest? Certainly if this reasoning were to be accepted, the magnitude of the heaven will rise to infinity. For in proportion it is thrown higher by the impulse of the motion, so the motion will be swifter, on account of the continual increase in the circumference which it must traverse in the space of twenty-four hours; and on the other hand as the motion increased, so would the immensity of the heaven. So the velocity would increase the magnitude, and the magnitude the velocity, to infinity. But according to that axiom in physics, that what is infinite cannot be traversed, nor moved by any means, the heaven will necessarily be at rest. But they say that outside the heaven there is no body, no place, no empty space, in fact nothing whatsoever, and therefore there is nothing to which the heaven can go out. In that case it is remarkable indeed if something can be restrained by nothing. But if the heaven is infinite, and finite only in its hollow interior, perhaps it will be more clearly proved that there is nothing outside the heaven, since every single thing will be within, whatever amount of space it occupies, but the heaven will remain immovable. For the strongest argument by which they try to establish that the universe is finite, is its motion. Therefore let us leave the question whether the universe is finite or infinite for the natural philosophers[4] to argue. What we

---

[2] **Philolaus the Pythagorean**: Greek mathematician and philosopher (ca. 470–385 B.C.E.).

[3] **the arguments quoted . . . insufficiency**: Arguments by ancient authorities, maintaining that "the Earth was at rest in the middle of the universe as if it was the center."

[4] **natural philosophers**: Scientists.

do know for certain is that the Earth is limited by its poles and bounded by a globular surface. . . .

Surely Aristotle's division of simple motion into three types, away from the middle, towards the middle, and round the middle, will be regarded merely as an intellectual division; just as we distinguish between a line, a point, and a surface, although one cannot exist without the other, and none of them without a body. A further point is that immobility is considered a more noble and divine state than that of change and instability, which is for that reason more appropriate to the Earth than to the universe. I also add that it would seem rather absurd to ascribe motion to that which contains and locates, and not rather to that which is contained and located, that is the Earth. Lastly, since it is evident that the wandering stars are sometimes nearer, sometimes further from the Earth, this will also be an example of motion of a single body which is both round the middle, by which they mean the center, away from the middle, and towards it. Motion round the midpoint must therefore be accepted more generally, and as satisfactory, provided that each motion is motion about its own midpoint. You will see then that from all these arguments the mobility of the Earth is more probable than its immobility, especially in the daily revolution, as that is particularly fitting for the Earth.

READING QUESTIONS

1. What justification does Copernicus offer for his opening premise that the universe is spherical? What is his justification for the premise that the earth, too, is spherical?

2. Why does Copernicus accuse Ptolemy of logical inconsistency?

3. On what grounds does Copernicus argue that the heavens (or universe) are of finite extent? Does his logic on this score convince you? Why or why not?

4. Why does Copernicus argue that the earth, like the other planets, is in motion? Why did scientists before him accept the idea that the earth was stationary?

16-2 | A Defense of Science

FRANCIS BACON, *On Superstition and the Virtue of Science* (1620)

Trained as a lawyer, Sir Francis Bacon (1561–1626) served in the court of the English king James I (r. 1603–1625) and conducted numerous experiments designed to explain the natural world. Bacon's most important contribution was to the scientific method itself. He was a

From Francis Bacon, "Aphorisms Concerning the Interpretation of Nature and the Kingdom of Man," in *The Works of Francis Bacon: Popular Edition, Based upon the Complete Edition of Spedding, Ellis, and Heath*, vol. 1 (New York: Hurd and Houghton, 1877), pp. 70–71, 124–126.

proponent of inductive reasoning, the arrival at general principles though the collection and analysis of empirical evidence. He contrasted his method with deductive reasoning, the use of general principles to interpret particular events and phenomena. In this excerpt from his writing, Bacon lays out his general method and seeks to defend it against critics who saw in his work a threat to religion.

There is no soundness in our notions, whether logical or physical. Substance, quality, action, passion, essence itself are not sound notions; much less are heavy, light, dense, rare, moist, dry, generation, corruption, attraction, repulsion, element, matter, form, and the like; but all are fantastical and ill-defined. . . .

The discoveries which have hitherto been made in the sciences are such as lie close to vulgar notions, scarcely beneath the surface. In order to penetrate into the inner and further recesses of nature, it is necessary that both notions and axioms [be] derived from things by a more sure and guarded way, and that a method of intellectual operation be introduced altogether better and more certain. . . .

There are and can be only two ways of searching into and discovering truth. The one flies from the senses and particulars to the most general axioms, and from these principles, the truth of which it takes for settled and immovable, proceeds to judgment and the discovery of middle axioms. And this way is now in fashion. The other derives axioms from the senses and particulars, rising by a gradual and unbroken ascent, so that it arrives at the most general axioms last of all. This is the true way, but as yet untried. . . .

It is not to be forgotten that in every age natural philosophy has had a troublesome adversary and hard to deal with — namely, superstition and the blind and immoderate zeal of religion. For we see among the Greeks that those who first proposed to man's uninitiated ears the natural causes for thunder and for storms were thereupon found guilty of impiety. Nor was much more forbearance shown by some of the ancient fathers of the Christian Church to those who, on most convincing grounds (such as no one in his senses would now think of contradicting), maintained that the earth was round and, of consequence, asserted the existence of the antipodes.[1]

Moreover, as things now are, to discourse of nature is made harder and more perilous by the summaries and systems of the schoolmen; who, having reduced theology into regular order as well as they were able, and fashioned it into the shape of an art, ended in incorporating the contentious and thorny philosophy of Aristotle, more than was fit, with the body of religion. . . .

Lastly . . . some are weakly afraid lest a deeper search into nature should transgress the permitted limits of sobermindedness; wrongfully wresting and

---

[1]**maintained that the earth was round . . . antipodes:** Bacon refers to an ancient debate relating to the shape of the earth; if the earth was round, some Greek theorists argued, then there would be lands (or ocean) on the side of the world directly opposite the one they inhabited. The debate was largely resolved by the fifteenth-century voyages of European explorers, culminating in the 1492 discovery of the New World, when the theorists were proven correct.

transferring what is said in Holy Writ [the Christian Bible] against those who pry into sacred mysteries to the hidden things of nature, which are barred by no prohibition. Others, with more subtlety, surmise and reflect that if secondary causes are unknown everything can be more readily referred to the divine hand and rod,—a point in which they think religion greatly concerned; which is, in fact, nothing else but to seek to gratify God with a lie. Others fear from past example that movements and changes in philosophy will end in assaults on religion; and others again appear apprehensive that in the investigation of nature something may be found to subvert, or at least shake, the authority of religion, especially with the unlearned. But these two last fears seem to me to savor utterly of carnal wisdom; as if men in the recesses and secret thoughts of their hearts doubted and distrusted the strength of religion, and the empire of faith over the senses, and therefore feared that the investigation of truth in nature might be dangerous to them. But if the matter be truly considered, natural philosophy is, after the word of God, at once the surest medicine against superstition and the most approved nourishment for faith; and therefore she is rightly given to religion as her most faithful handmaid, since the one displays the will of God, the other his power.

READING QUESTIONS

1. In Bacon's view, what was, and had always been, the most important adversary of the natural philosopher?

2. Why, according to Bacon, did some observers see natural philosophy as a threat to religion? How did Bacon counter this criticism?

3. What do Bacon's assertions about natural philosophy suggest about the larger relationship between science and faith in the seventeenth century?

16-3 | A Defense of a Sun-Centered Universe

GALILEO GALILEI, *Letter to the Grand Duchess Christina of Tuscany* (1615)

The heliocentric (sun-centered) universe that Nicolaus Copernicus described was defended several decades after his death by Italian astronomer Galileo Galilei. Galileo also made groundbreaking discoveries in mathematics, engineering, and physics and is considered an important contributor to the scientific method. He is probably most famous, however, for the conflict that he had with the Catholic Church over his defense of Copernican heliocentrism. Ultimately, church authorities forced him to publicly recant his defense of heliocentric theory, but the church eventually removed the ban on books concerning the theory centuries later. Galileo refutes the critiques of his ideas in the following letter to the Grand Duchess of Florence, who had recently become interested in the controversy between Copernican theory and the traditional geocentric theory mandated by the Catholic Church.

From Galileo Galilei, trans. Stillman Drake, "Letter to the Grand Duchess Christina," in *Discoveries and Opinions of Galileo* (Garden City, Doubleday, 1957), 175–179, 181–183, 209–211.

As Your Most Serene Highness knows very well, a few years ago I discovered in the heavens many particulars which had been invisible until our time. Because of their novelty, and because of some consequences deriving from them which contradict certain physical propositions commonly accepted in philosophical schools, they roused against me no small number of such professors, as if I had placed these things in heaven with my hands in order to confound nature and the sciences. These people seemed to forget that a multitude of truths contribute to inquiry and to the growth and strength of disciplines rather than to their diminution or destruction, and at the same time they showed greater affection for their own opinions than for the true ones; thus they proceeded to deny and to try to nullify these novelties, about which the senses themselves could have rendered them certain, if they had wanted to look at those novelties carefully. To this end they produced various matters, and they published some writings full of useless discussions and sprinkled with quotations taken from the Holy Scripture, taken from passages which they do not properly understand and which they inappropriately adduce. This was a very serious error, and they might not have fallen into it had they paid attention to Saint Augustine's very useful advice concerning how to proceed with care in reaching definite decisions about things which are obscure and difficult to understand by means of reason alone. For, speaking also about a particular physical conclusion pertaining to heavenly bodies, he writes this: "Now then, always practicing a pious and serious moderation, we ought not to believe anything lightly about an obscure subject, lest we reject (out of love for our error) something which later may be truly shown not to be in any way contrary to the holy books of either the Old or New Testament."
. . .

These people are aware that in my astronomical and philosophical studies, on the question of the constitution of the world's parts, I hold that the sun is located at the center of the revolutions of the heavenly orbs and does not change place, and that the earth rotates on itself and moves around it. Moreover, they hear how I confirm this view not only by refuting Ptolemy's and Aristotle's arguments, but also by producing many for the other side, especially some pertaining to physical effects whose causes perhaps cannot be determined in any other way, and other astronomical ones dependent on many features of the new celestial discoveries; these discoveries clearly confute the Ptolemaic system, and they agree admirably with this other position and confirm it. Now, these people are perhaps confounded by the known truth of the other propositions different from the ordinary which I hold, and so they may lack confidence to defend themselves as long as they remain in the philosophical field. Therefore, since they persist in their original self-appointed task of beating down me and my findings by every imaginable means, they have decided to try to shield the fallacies of their arguments with the cloak of simulated religiousness and with the authority of the Holy Scriptures, unintelligently using the latter for the confutation of arguments they neither understand nor have heard.
. . .

They alleviate their task as much as they can by making it look, at least among common people, as if this opinion were new and especially mine, pretending not to know that Nicolaus Copernicus was its author or rather its reformer and confirmer. Now, Copernicus was not only a Catholic, but also a clergyman and a canon, and he was so highly regarded that he was called to Rome from the remotest parts of Germany when under Leo X the Lateran Council was discussing the reform of the ecclesiastical calendar; at that time this reform remained unfinished only because there was still no exact knowledge of the precise length of the year and of the lunar month. Thus he was charged by the Bishop of Fossonbrone, who was then supervising this undertaking, to try by repeated studies and efforts to acquire more understanding and certainty about those celestial motions; and so he undertook this study, and, by truly Herculanean labor and by his admirable mind, he made so much progress in this science and acquired such an exact knowledge of the periods of celestial motions that he earned the title of supreme astronomer; then, in accordance with his doctrine not only was the calendar regularized, but tables of all planetary motions were constructed. . . .

So the reason they advance to condemn the opinion of the earth's mobility and sun's stability is this: since in many places in the Holy Scripture one reads that the sun moves and the earth stands still, and since Scripture can never lie or err, it follows as a necessary consequence that the opinion of those who want to assert the sun to be motionless and the earth moving is erroneous and damnable. . . .

Therefore I think that in disputes about natural phenomena one must begin not with the authority of scriptural passages, but with sense experiences and necessary demonstrations. For the Holy Scripture and nature derive equally from the Godhead, the former as the dictation of the Holy Spirit and the latter as the most obedient executrix of God's orders; moreover, to accommodate the understanding of the common people it is appropriate for Scripture to say many things that are different (in appearance and in regard to the literal meaning of the words) from the absolute truth; on the other hand, nature is inexorable and immutable, never violates the terms of the laws imposed upon her, and does not care whether or not her recondite reasons and ways of operating are disclosed to human understanding; but not every scriptural assertion is bound to obligations as severe as every natural phenomenon; finally, God reveals Himself to us no less excellently in the effects of nature than in the sacred words of Scripture, as Tertullian perhaps meant when he said, "We postulate that God ought first to be known by nature, and afterwards further known by doctrine—by nature through His works, by doctrine through official teaching" . . .

However, I do not think one has to believe that the same God who has given us senses, language, and intellect would want us to set aside the use of these and give us by other means the information we can acquire with them, so that we would deny our senses and reason even in the case of those physical conclusions which are placed before our eyes and intellect by our sense experiences or by necessary demonstrations. This is especially implausible for those sciences discussed in Scripture to a very minor extent and with disconnected statements; such is precisely the case of astronomy, so little of which is contained therein that one does not find there even the names of the planets, except for the sun, the moon, and only once or twice Venus, under the name of Morning Star. Thus, if the sacred authors had had in mind to teach people about the arrangement and motions of the heavenly bodies, and consequently to have us acquire this information from Holy Scripture, then, in my opinion, they would not have discussed so little of the topic—that is to say, almost nothing in comparison with the innumerable admirable conclusions which are contained and demonstrated in this science.

Indeed, it is the opinion of the holiest and most learned Fathers that the writers of Holy Scripture not only did not pretend to teach us about the structure and the motions of the heavens and of the stars, and their shape, size, and distance, but that they deliberately refrained from doing so, even though they knew all these things very well. For example, on reads the following words in Saint Augustine: "It is also customary to ask what one should believe about the shape and arrangement of heaven according to our Scriptures. In fact, many people argue a great deal about these things, which with greater prudence our authors omitted, which are of no use for eternal life to those who study them, and (what is worse) which take up a lot of time that ought to be spent on things pertaining to salvation. For what does it matter to me whether heaven, like a sphere, completely surrounds the earth, which is balanced at the center of the universe, or whether like a discus it covers the earth on one side from above? However, since the issue here is the authority of Scripture, let me repeat a point I have made more than once; that is, there is a danger that someone who does not understand the divine words may find in our books or infer from them something about these topics which seems to contradict received opinions, and then he might not believe at all the other useful things contained in its precepts, stories, and assertions; therefore, briefly, it should be said that our authors did know the truth about the shape of heaven, but that the Spirit of God, which was speaking through them, did not want to teach men these things which are of no use to salvation." . . .

This let these people apply themselves to refuting the arguments of Copernicus and of the others, and let them leave its condemnation as erroneous and heretical to the proper authorities. . .

READING QUESTIONS

1. According to Galileo, why did Catholic theologians reject the notion of a heliocentric universe?

2. How did Galileo define the relationship between science and religion?

3. How does Galileo use the Bible, St. Augustine, and the history of the Catholic Church itself to rebut the argument that his defense of a heliocentric universe is heretical?

4. How does Galileo say that truth can be established in science, on the one hand, and religion on the other?

Monarchical Power and Responsibility

Enlightenment reformers offered critiques of almost all aspects of European society, from education to religion to economics. For the most part, however, *philosophes* were not revolutionaries. In the determined application of rational thought, they saw a tool for the improvement of human life, not a weapon for destroying all that had come before. Thus, most philosophes supported monarchical government, the European norm in the eighteenth century. Certainly, they saw countless ways in which such governments could be made more efficient, less arbitrary, and more productive of the common good. They did not, however, want to do away with kings.

READ AND COMPARE

1. Which reading would be more threatening to monarchs in Europe? Why do you think so?

2. How do the two excerpts reflect the social status of their authors, who do you suppose was the intended audience for each (aristocracy or commoners), and which reading would appeal better to each class?

16-4 | CHARLES DE SECONDAT, BARON DE MONTESQUIEU, *The Spirit of Laws: On the Separation of Governmental Powers* (1748)

The writings of Frenchman Charles de Secondat (1689–1755), better known as Baron de Montesquieu (mahn-tuhs-KYOO), were composed as the spirit of the Enlightenment swept over Europe in the early eighteenth century. Montesquieu's political writings, excerpted here, were concerned with the makeup of the state and the effect of a government on the lives of those it ruled. In this excerpt from *The Spirit of Laws*, Montesquieu argues for the importance of the separation of powers, or the assignment of executive, legislative, and judicial powers to different individuals or political bodies. As you read, consider the implications for political reform. Why, despite Montesquieu's avowed support of European monarchies, might monarchs have seen his work as a threat?

In every government there are three sorts of power: the legislative; the executive in respect to things dependent on the law of nations; and the executive in regard to matters that depend on the civil law.

From Baron de Montesquieu, *The Spirit of Laws*, trans. T. Nugent (New York: Hafner, 1949), pp. 151–152.

By virtue of the first, the prince or magistrate enacts temporary or perpetual laws, and amends or abrogates those that have been already enacted. By the second, he makes peace or war, sends or receives embassies, establishes the public security, and provides against invasions. By the third, he punishes criminals, or determines the disputes that arise between individuals. The latter we shall call the judiciary power, and the other simply the executive power of the state.

The political liberty of the subject is a tranquility of mind arising from the opinion each person has of his safety. In order to have this liberty, it is requisite the government be so constituted as one man need not be afraid of another.

When the legislative and executive powers are united in the same person, or in the same body of magistrates, there can be no liberty; because apprehensions may arise, lest the same monarch or senate should enact tyrannical laws, to execute them in a tyrannical manner.

Again, there is no liberty, if the judiciary power be not separated from the legislative and executive. Were it joined with the legislative, the life and liberty of the subject would be exposed to arbitrary control; for the judge would be then the legislator. Were it joined to the executive power, the judge might behave with violence and oppression.

There would be an end of everything, were the same man or the same body, whether of the nobles or of the people, to exercise those three powers, that of enacting laws, that of executing the public resolutions, and of trying the causes of individuals.

Most kingdoms in Europe enjoy a moderate government because the prince who is invested with the two first powers leaves the third to his subjects. In Turkey, where these three powers are united in the Sultan's person, the subjects groan under the most dreadful oppression.

In the republics of Italy, where these three powers are united, there is less liberty than in our monarchies. Hence their government is obliged to have recourse to as violent methods for its support as even that of the Turks; witness the state inquisitors, and the lion's mouth into which every informer may at all hours throw his written accusations.

What a situation must the poor subject be in, under those republics! The same body of magistrates are possessed, as executors of the laws, of the whole power they have given themselves in quality of legislators. They may plunder the state by their general determinations; and as they have likewise the judiciary power in their hands, every private citizen may be ruined by their particular decisions.

The whole power is here united in one body; and though there is no external pomp that indicates a despotic sway, yet the people feel the effects of it every moment.

Hence it is that many of the princes of Europe, whose aim has been levelled at arbitrary power, have constantly set out with uniting in their own persons, all the branches of magistracy, and all the great offices of state.

READING QUESTIONS

1. How did Montesquieu define liberty? Why did he believe that a separation of powers was crucial to the protection of liberty?

2. In Montesquieu's view, under what circumstances could liberty be obtained under a monarchy? Under what circumstances could a republic produce tyranny?

3. How does Montesquieu's essay reflect his cultural biases?

4. How might opponents of absolute monarchy have used Montesquieu's ideas to support their position?

16-5 | JEAN-JACQUES ROUSSEAU, *The Social Contract: On Popular Sovereignty and the General Will* (1762)

Jean-Jacques Rousseau (1712–1778) was born in Swiss Geneva and came from the common, not the aristocratic, class. He left Geneva at the age of sixteen; after spending years living on charity and the income from odd jobs, he traveled to Paris seeking to make a name for himself. Rousseau's poverty and origins, combined with his prickly personality, made him something of an outsider in Enlightenment social circles. His 1762 work on political theory, *The Social Contract*, was part of an extended argument in the seventeenth and eighteenth centuries over the sources of governmental power and the conditions, if any, under which one form of government could be replaced with another.

Since no man has any natural authority over his fellow men, and since force is not the source of right, conventions are the basis of all lawful authority among men.

Now, as men cannot create any new forces, but only combine and direct those that exist, they have no other means of preserving themselves than to combine those forces . . . and to make them work in concert.

This sum of forces can be produced only by many people working together; but since every man needs his own strength and freedom to preserve himself, how can he contribute them without injuring himself, and without neglecting to take care of himself? This difficulty, applied to my subject, may be explained this way:

"To find an organization which may use the collective power of the community to defend and protect the person and property of every associate, and while working together, each person may nevertheless obey only himself, and remain as free as he was without the organization." Such is the problem that the social contract addresses. . . .

From Jean-Jacques Rousseau, *The Social Contract*, in *Translations and Reprints from the Original Sources of European History* (Philadelphia: University of Pennsylvania Press, 1898), vol. 5, no. 1:14–16. Language modernized by J. Michael Long.

If we set aside things that are not essential in the social contract, we can explain it as follows: "Each of us puts themselves and their power toward the good of the community, and in return everyone is part of that community."

But the political system or sovereign, which only exists because of the contract, can never compromise itself in anything that undermines the contract, such as giving up control of a part of the system, or submitting to the authority of another sovereign. To violate the contract that created it would be to annihilate itself, and what is nothing produces nothing.

Based upon what we just explained, the will of the people is always right and always best for society; but the policies that the people create are not always the best for society. Men always desire their own good, but do not always understand how to achieve it; the people are never corrupted, but they can be deceived, and it is only then that they intend evil things.

The power of the people, then, needs something to concentrate it and put it in action according to the directions of the will of the people, to be able to communicate between the state and the sovereign, to achieve in society what the connection of soul and body achieves in a man. This is, in the State, the purpose of government, which is often confused with the sovereign, who is actually served and advised by the government.

What, then, is the government? It is an intermediate body established between the people and the sovereign so they can communicate, and intended to execute the laws and maintain civil and political liberties.

It is not enough for the assembled people to create the constitution of the state by approving a set of laws; nor is it enough that they establish a permanent government, or that they create a lasting process for electing magistrates. Besides special assemblies that might become necessary due to emergencies, there should also be fixed assemblies that meet periodically that cannot be abolished; so that, on the appointed day, the people are called together by the law, without needing to be formally summoned.

Once the people are lawfully assembled as a sovereign body, the entire jurisdiction of the government ceases, the executive power is suspended, and the most common citizen is as sacred and inviolable as the most powerful magistrate, because the representatives of that assembly do not need anyone else to represent their interests.

These assemblies, which are meant to maintain the social contract, should always begin their business with two proposals, which no one should be able to suppress, and which should pass separately by vote. The first: "Whether the sovereign wants to maintain the present form of government." The second: "Whether the people want to leave the administration to those who now control it."

I assume that I have proved my belief, that there is no fundamental law in the state which cannot be revoked, not even this social compact; for if all the citizens assembled agree to break that compact, no one can doubt that it could be quite legitimately broken.

READING QUESTIONS

1. What might Rousseau mean when he says "force is not the source of right"?

2. According to Rousseau, what is the origin and reason for the legitimacy of a government?

3. How does Rousseau's concept of the "general will" relate to the concept of majority rule in a representative government?

4. How do you think monarchs and traditional elites would critique the idea of replacing a government that did not represent the will of the people?

16-6 | A Philosophe Argues for Religious Toleration

VOLTAIRE, *A Treatise on Toleration* (1763)

François-Marie Arouet (1694–1778), who used the pen name Voltaire, was arguably the greatest of the Enlightenment philosophes. He was an astonishingly prolific author whose output amounted to hundreds of books and pamphlets. In some respects he was unrepresentative of the general currents of Enlightenment thought, being skeptical of both human rationality and human progress. Like virtually all the philosophes, however, he was an unceasing critic of religious dogma and intolerance. The following excerpts from Voltaire's *Treatise on Toleration* (1763) present the essential components of his argument in favor of religious toleration. As you read, consider what core assumptions form the foundation of his position. How did Voltaire's beliefs about the fundamental equality of human beings and the limits of human knowledge shape his views on religion?

Chapter XXI. Universal Toleration

It does not require any great art or studied eloquence, to prove, that Christians should tolerate each other. I shall go further, and say, that we should regard all men as our brethren. What! a Turk my brother? a Chinese my brother? a Jew? a Siamese? my brother? Yes, without doubt; for are we not all children of the same father, and creatures of the same God?

But these people despise us and treat us as idolaters! It may be so; but I shall only tell them, they are to blame. It seems to me, I should stagger the haughty obstinacy of an Iman,[1] or a Talapoin,[2] if I spoke to them in the following manner:

This little globe, which is but a point, rolls in universal space, in the same manner as other globes, and we are lost in the immensity. Man, a being about five feet in height, is assuredly a thing of no great importance in the creation.

From Voltaire, *A Treatise on Toleration; The Ignorant Philosopher; and A Commentary on the Marquis of Becaria's [sic] Treatise on Crimes and Punishments*, trans. David Williams (London: Fielding and Walker, 1779), pp. 118–123.

[1] **Iman:** Imam; a Muslim religious leader.
[2] **Talapoin:** Buddhist priest or monk.

One of those beings, called men, and who are hardly perceptible, says to some of his neighbors in Arabia or in the country of the Cafres:[3] "Attend to what I say, for the God of all these worlds has enlightened me. There are about nine hundred millions of little ants, such as we are, on this earth, but my ant-hill alone is [in] the care of God, all the rest have been hateful to him from [i.e., for] all eternity; we only shall be happy; all others will be eternally wretched."

They would stop me, and ask, who is this madman, who utters such folly? I should be obliged to answer each of them, It is you. I might then take occasion to meliorate their dispositions into something like humanity; but that I should find difficult.

I will now address myself to Christians; and venture to say to a Dominican,[4] who is an inquisitor, "My brother, you know, that every province of Italy has its jargon; that they do not speak at Venice and Bergamo as they do at Florence. The Academy de la Crusca[5] has fixed the general disposition and construction of the language; its dictionary is a rule from which no deviations are allowed; and the grammar of Buonmattei's[6] is an infallible guide, which must be followed. But do you think that the consul, president of the Academy, or in his absence, Buonmattei, could have the conscience, to order the tongues of all the Venetians and Bergamese to be cut out, who should persist in their provincial dialects?"

The inquisitor would answer me: "The cases are very different. The question here is the salvation of your soul; it is for your good, that the court of inquisition ordains, that you should be seized, on the deposition of a single person, though he be infamous, and in the hands of justice; that you have no advocate[7] to plead for you; that the very name of your accuser should be unknown to you; that the inquisitor should promise you mercy, and afterwards condemn you; that he apply five different kinds of torture to you, and that afterwards you should be whipt [i.e., whipped] or sent to the galleys, or burnt [at the stake] as a spectacle in a religious ceremony.[8] Father Ivonet, [and] Doctor[s] Cuchalon, Zarchinus, Campegius, Royas, Telinus, Gomarus, Diabarus, and Gemelinus[9] lay down these things as laws, and this pious practice must not be disputed. I would take the liberty to answer, "My brother, perhaps you are right; I am convinced of the good you wish to do me; but, without all this, is it not possible to be saved?"

It is true that these absurd horrors do not always deform the face of the earth; but they have been very frequent; and we might collect materials to compose a volume on these practices, much larger than the gospels which condemn them. It is not only cruel to persecute in this short life those who do not think as

---

[3]**Cafres:** Kaffirs; South Africa.

[4]**Dominican:** The Dominicans were a Roman Catholic religious order who, as Voltaire suggests, conducted the Inquisition.

[5]**Academy de la Crusca:** Accademia della Crusca; an Italian learned society founded in 1582. Its members were chiefly linguists and philologists. In 1612 it sponsored publication of a dictionary of the Italian language.

[6]**Buonmattei:** Benedetto Buommattei (1581–1647), also rendered as Boummattei and Buonmattei; Florentine lexicographer, author of *Della Lingua Toscana*.

[7]**advocate:** Lawyer.

[8]Here Voltaire inserted a footnote instructing his readers to "See that excellent book, intitled [sic], The Manual of the Inquisition."

[9]**Father Ivonet, . . . Gemelinus:** Roman Catholic theologians.

we do, but it is audacious to pronounce their eternal damnation. It seems to me, that it little becomes the atoms of a moment [i.e., such insignificant, ephemeral creatures], such as we are, thus to anticipate the decrees of the Creator. I am very far from opposing that opinion, "that out of [i.e., outside] the church there is no salvation." I respect it, as well as everything taught by the church: but, in truth, are we acquainted with all the ways of God, and the whole extent of his mercy? Is it not permitted that we should hope in him, as well as fear him? Is it not sufficient that we are faithful to the church? Is it necessary that every individual should usurp the power of the Deity, and decide, before him, the eternal lot of all mankind?

When we wear mourning for a king of Sweden, Denmark, England, or Prussia, do we say that we mourn for a reprobate who will burn eternally in hell? There are in Europe forty millions of inhabitants, who are not [members] of the Church of Rome; shall we say to each of them, "Sir, as you are to be infallibly damned, I would neither eat, deal, or converse with you."

Is it to be supposed, that an ambassador of France, presented to the Grand Seignior,[10] would say to himself, His highness will be burnt to all eternity, because he has submitted to circumcision? If he really thought that the Grand Seignior was a mortal enemy to God, and the object of his vengeance, could he have spoken to him? Should he have been sent to him? With whom could we have dealings in trade? What duty of civil life could we ever fulfill, if we were in fact possessed with the idea, that we were conversing with persons eternally reprobated?

O ye followers of a merciful God! if you have cruel hearts. If, in adoring him, whose whole law consists in these words, "Love God and your neighbor," you have encumbered that pure and holy law with sophisms, and incomprehensible disputes! If you have lighted the fires of discord, sometimes for a new word, sometimes for a letter of the alphabet! If you have annexed eternal torments to the omission of some words, or some ceremonies, which other people cannot be [i.e., are not] acquainted with—I must say, while shedding tears for mankind: "Transport yourselves with me to that day, in which all men will be judged, and when God will render to every one according to his works."

"I see all the dead, of past and present ages, appearing in his presence. Are you very sure that our Creator and Father will say to the wise and virtuous Confucius, to the legislator Solon, to Pythagoras, Zaleucus, Socrates, Plato, the divine Antonini, the good Trajan, to Titus the delight of mankind, to Epictetus,[11] and to many others who have been the models of human nature: Go, monsters!

---

[10]**Grand Seignior:** Grand signeur; the Ottoman sultan.

[11]**Confucius, Solon, . . . Titus, Epictetus:** Confucius (551–479 B.C.E.), Chinese philosopher; Solon (638–558 B.C.E.), Athenian statesman and lawgiver; Pythagoras (ca. 570–495 B.C.E.), Greek philosopher, theologian, and mathematician; Zaleucus (seventh century B.C.E.), Greek lawgiver; Socrates (ca. 469–399 B.C.E.), Greek philosopher; Plato (428–348 B.C.E.), Greek philosopher and mathematician; Antoninus Pius (r. 138–161), Roman emperor, and Marcus Aurelius Antoninus (r. 161–180), Roman emperor and Stoic philosopher; Trajan (r. 98–117), Roman emperor; Titus Pomponius Atticus (ca. 112–ca. 35 B.C.E.), Roman editor and man of letters; Epictetus (55–135), Greek Stoic philosopher.

Let your punishments be as eternal as my being!—and you, my well-beloved, Jean Châtel, Ravaillac, Damiens, Cartouche,[12] &c. who have died according to the forms which are enjoined, sit at my right hand and partake of my dominion, and of my felicity!"

You shrink with horror at these words; and after they have escaped me, I have nothing more to say to you.

Chapter XXII. Prayer to God

I no longer then look up to men; it is to thee, the God of all beings, of all worlds, and of all ages, I address myself—If weak creatures, lost in immensity and imperceptible to the rest of the universe, may dare to ask any thing of thee, who hast given [us] all things, and whose decrees are immutable and eternal! Deign to regard with pity the errors inseparable from our nature; let not these errors prove our calamities! Thou hast not given us hearts to hate, and hands to destroy each other; dispose us to mutual assistance, in supporting the burden of a painful and transitory life! Let the little differences in the garments which cover our frail bodies; in all our imperfect languages, in our ridiculous customs, our imperfect laws, our idle opinions, in our ranks and conditions, so unequal in our eyes, and so equal in thine: let all those little shades which distinguish the atoms called *men*, be no more signals of hatred and persecution! Let those who light tapers [i.e., candles] at noon-day, to glorify thee—bear with those who content themselves with the light of thy sun! Let not those who throw over their garments a white surplice, while they say it is the duty of men to love thee, hate those who say the same thing in a black woolen cloak! Let it be equal, to adore thee in a jargon formed from an ancient, or from a modern language! May those whose vestments are dipped in scarlet, or in purple who domineer over a small parcel of the small heap of the dirt and mud of this world; and those who possess a few round fragments of a certain metal, enjoy without pride, what they call grandeur and riches; and may others regard them without envy: for thou knowest, there is nothing in these things to inspire envy or pride!

May all men remember that they are brethren! May they regard in horror tyranny, the tyranny exercised over the mind, as they do rapine, which carries away by force the fruits of peaceable labor and industry! If the scourges of war be inevitable, let us not hate and destroy each other in the bosom of peace; let us employ the instant of our existence to praise, in a thousand different languages, from Siam to California, thy goodness which hath granted us that instant!

---

[12]**Jean Châtel, Ravaillac, Damiens, Cartouche:** Jean Châtel (1575–1594), tortured and executed for attempting to assassinate Henry IV of France; François Ravaillac (1578–1610), tortured and drawn and quartered for assassinating Henry IV of France; Robert-François Damiens (1715–1757), tortured and drawn and quartered for attempting to assassinate Louis XV of France; Louis Dominique Bourguignon, known as Cartouche (1693–1721), French highwayman tortured to death.

READING QUESTIONS

1. In Voltaire's view, what important differences, if any, exist between individual human beings? Between different human societies? How did Voltaire's answers to these questions shape his view of religion?

2. What does Voltaire's argument in favor of religious toleration tell you about his beliefs about the limits of human understanding?

3. Do you find Voltaire's argument in favor of universal religious toleration persuasive? Why or why not?

▪ COMPARATIVE AND DISCUSSION QUESTIONS ▪

1. Nicolaus Copernicus and Francis Bacon were separated by a lifetime. (Copernicus died almost twenty years before Bacon was born.) What similarities do you note between their modes of thinking? In what ways did they differ?

2. What was different about how Copernicus and Galileo expressed their supposedly "heretical" views about the universe? Why were their approaches different?

3. What differences do you note between Montesquieu's and Rousseau's theories about the nature of government and how it ought to interact with its citizens? Where do they seem to be in agreement?

4. How did the new vision of the universe created by participants in the Scientific Revolution shape Voltaire's view of human beings and their societies?

5. What would Montesquieu and Rousseau think of Domat's divine-right monarchical theory (Document 15-2), and why?

17

The Expansion of Europe
1650–1800

European overseas expansion in the early modern era (ca. 1500–1800) had profound social and economic consequences, both for Europe and for the rest of the world. European expansion accelerated the integration of the world's regional economies, changed the global balance of wealth and power, and led to the movement, both voluntary and forced, of vast numbers of people from one part of the world to another. It also led to the first true world wars, as competition for colonies and profits around the world fueled a prolonged imperial conflict between France and Great Britain. The two rivals fought over North America, the Caribbean sugar islands, control of the Atlantic slave trade, and trade with India. The eventual outcome was the establishment of British rule over most of North America and much of India. The documents included in this chapter explore early modern efforts to describe and understand the dynamic global economy that emerged during this period. As you examine them, think about the ways in which European expansion changed both how Europeans lived and how they saw themselves and their place in the world.

17-1 | The "Potato Revolution"

WILLIAM SALMON, *The Family Dictionary, or Household Companion* (1695) and THOMAS RUGGLES, *Annals of Agriculture and Other Useful Arts* (1792)

One of the transformative crops brought to Old World Europe from the New World of the Americas was potatoes. European farmers increasingly struggled to make ends meet as more and more lands were enclosed and thus unavailable for common pasturage for their livestock, while wheat, and thus bread, became increasingly expensive for them. Potatoes were an easy

From William Salmon, *The Family Dictionary, or Household Companion* (London: H. Rhodes, 1710), p. 265; and Thomas Ruggles, *Annals of Agriculture and Other Useful Arts* 17 (1792): 205, 353.

solution to this problem. Though it took a while for European farmers to grow the crop widely, it became a staple food and played a role in the significant population growth that occurred in the nineteenth century. Unfortunately, they grew very few types of the plant, and when a disease caused by a plant fungus caused massive crop failures in economically depressed areas of Ireland in 1845, it led to a devastating famine.

William Salmon, *The Family Dictionary, or Household Companion*, 1695

The Leaves of Potato are manifestly hot and dry in the beginning of the second degree, as manifestly appear by their taste. But the roots are temperate in respect to heat or cold, dryness and moisture: They Astringe, are moderately Diuretic, Stomatic, Chylisic, Analeptic, and Spermatogenetic. They nourish the whole body, restore in consumptions, and provoke lust. The preparations of the potato are: (1) boiled, baked or roasted roots, (2) the broth, (3) the blood. *The Prepared Roots:* They stop fluxes of the bowels, nourish much, and restore in a pining consumption; being boiled, baked or roasted, they are eaten with good butter, salt, juice of oranges or lemons, and double refined sugar, as common food: they increase seed and provoke lust, causing fruitfulness in both sexes: and stop all sorts of fluxes of the belly. *The Broth of the Roots:* They are first boiled soft in fair water, then taken out and peeled, afterwards put into the same water again, and boiled till the broth becomes as thick, as very thick cream, or thin Hasty Pudding: some mix an equal quantity of milk with it, and so make broth; others after they are peeled, instead of putting them into the waters they were boiled in, boil them only in milk, till they are dissolved as aforesaid, and the broth is made pleasant with sweet butter, a little salt and double refined sugar, and so eaten. It has all the virtues of the roots eaten in substance, nourishes more, and restores not only in an atrophy, or pining consumption, but also in an ulceration of the lungs. *The Blood of the Potato:* It is made as the Blood of Satyrion, Parsnips, Eddo's Comfrey, and other like roots. It may be taken to a spoonful or two, morning, noon, and night, in a glass of choice Canary, Tent, Alicant, old Malaga, or other good Wines. It restores in deep consumption of all kinds, nourishes to admiration, is good against impotency in men and barrenness in women, and has all the other virtues of both the prepared roots and broth.

Thomas Ruggles, *Annals of Agriculture and Other Useful Arts*, 1792

Everybody knows that bread covers at least two-thirds of the expenditure on food. A laborer's wage must be at least sufficient to maintain himself and his family, and must allow for something over. Were the wages not to do so, then the race of such workers would not last beyond the first generation. In Great Britain, therefore, the wages of the laborer must be evidently more than what is precisely necessary to bring up a family, and the price of grain must determine everything in regard to the economics of labor. However, failure to implement this level of wages may, perhaps, be mitigated by the adoption by the poor of the potato, a nutritious and cheap substitute. Nonetheless, the poor will not eat potatoes if they can get anything else, for the daintiness and ignorance of the poor in regard to the wonderments of this root has been the chief obstacle to its adoption.

READING QUESTIONS

1. According to Salmon and Ruggles, what are some good reasons for poor farmers to grow potatoes? Do you think their arguments would convince farmers to do so? Why or why not?

2. What does Ruggles argue about how to solve the dilemma of farm laborers' food costs, and what obstacle does he mention about that solution?

3. What does his assessment about the poor and potatoes reveal about his cultural biases?

17-2 | Defining and Defending Mercantilism

THOMAS MUN, *England's Treasure by Foreign Trade* (1664)

The overseas trade and colonization policies adopted by early modern European countries were shaped, to a considerable degree, by the economic theory known as mercantilism. Mercantilists saw global wealth as finite and measured its movement from one nation to another exclusively in reference to the balance of trade. Since new wealth could not be created, one nation's gain was always another nation's loss. Thus, in the mercantilist view, the goal of government economic policy should be to maximize exports while minimizing imports. This goal had implications that went far beyond trade policy itself. Mercantilist governments attempted to stimulate economic activities at home that would produce goods with ready foreign markets. At the same time, they sought to acquire colonies abroad that would eliminate the need to purchase raw materials from foreign competitors. In the excerpt below, Thomas Mun (1571–1641), an influential English merchant and economic theorist, lays out the basic premise of mercantilism. As you read it, think about the kinds of policies that might follow from Mun's assumptions.

Although a Kingdom may be enriched by gifts received, or by purchase taken from some other Nations, yet these are things uncertain and of small consideration when they happen. The ordinary means therefore to increase our wealth and treasure is by *Foreign Trade*, wherein we must ever observe this rule; to sell more to strangers yearly than we consume of theirs in value. For suppose that when this Kingdom is plentifully served with the Cloth, Lead, Tinn, Iron, Fish and other native commodities, we do yearly export the overplus to foreign Countries to the value of twenty two hundred thousand pounds; by which means we are enabled beyond the Seas to buy and bring in foreign wares for our use and Consumptions, to the value of twenty hundred thousand pounds; By

---

From Thomas Mun, *England's Treasure by Foreign Trade* (Cambridge: Economic History Society, 1664), pp. 5–6.

this order duly kept in our trading, we may rest assured that the Kingdom shall be enriched yearly two hundred thousand pounds, which must be brought to us in so much Treasure; because that part of our stock which is not returned to us in wares must necessarily be brought home in treasure.

For in this case it cometh to pass in the stock of a Kingdom, as in the estate of a private man; who is supposed to have one thousand pounds yearly revenue and two thousand pounds of ready money in his Chest. If such a man through excess shall spend one thousand five hundred pounds *per annum*, all his ready money will be gone in four years; and in the like time his said money will be doubled if he take a Frugal course to spend but five hundred pounds *per annum*; which rule never faileth likewise in the Commonwealth, but in some cases (of no great moment) which I will hereafter declare, when I shall shew by whom and in what manner this balance of the Kingdoms account ought to be drawn up yearly, or so often as it shall please the State to discover how much we gain or lose by trade with foreign Nations. But first I will say something concerning those ways and means which will increase our exportations and diminish our importations of wares; which being done, I will then set down some other arguments both affirmative and negative to strengthen that which is here declared, and thereby to shew that all the other means which are commonly supposed to enrich the Kingdom with Treasure are altogether insufficient and mere fallacies.

READING QUESTIONS

1. According to Mun, what rule must England follow if it is to increase its wealth?

2. What analogy did Mun use to prove his point? Do you find it convincing? Why or why not?

3. What connections can you draw between mercantilism and the trade wars of the early modern period?

17-3 | Critiquing Mercantilism

ADAM SMITH, *The Wealth of Nations* (1776)

Adam Smith (1723–1790) is widely regarded as the father of modern economics. His most famous work, *An Inquiry into the Nature and Causes of the Wealth of Nations* (1776), from which the following excerpts are drawn, was a sustained critique of mercantilism. Smith was not the first economist to advocate free trade, but he was certainly the most famous and persuasive. At the time *The Wealth of Nations* appeared, government policies throughout Europe were still firmly mercantilistic, but over the following decades his arguments gained more adherents, especially in Britain, and his theories formed the basis for classical liberal economics.

From Adam Smith, *An Inquiry into the Nature and Causes of the Wealth of Nations*, vol. 1, ed. James E. Thorold Rodgers (Oxford: Clarendon Press, 1869), pp. 5–7, 9, 12, 14–15, 30–31, 57–59, 62–65, 125, 128, 136.

Book I, Chapter 1. *Of the Division of Labor*

The greatest improvement in the productive powers of labor, and the greater part of the skill, dexterity, and judgment with which it is anywhere directed, or applied, seem to have been the effects of the division of labor. . . .

To take an example, . . . the trade of the pin-maker; a workman not educated to this business, . . . nor acquainted with the use of the machinery employed in it . . . , could scarce, perhaps, with his utmost industry, make one pin in a day, and certainly could not make twenty. But in the way in which this business is now carried on, not only the whole work is a peculiar trade, but it is divided into a number of branches, of which the greater part are likewise peculiar trades. One man draws out the wire, another straights it, a third cuts it, a fourth points it, a fifth grinds it at the top for receiving the head; to make the head requires two or three distinct operations; to put it on is a peculiar business, to whiten the pins is another; it is even a trade by itself to put them into the paper [container in which they are sold]; and the important business of making a pin is, in this manner, divided into about eighteen distinct operations, which, in some manufactories, are all performed by distinct hands, though in others the same man will sometimes perform two or three of them. I have seen a small manufactory of this kind where ten men only were employed, and where some of them consequently performed two or three distinct operations. But though they were very poor, and therefore but indifferently accommodated with the necessary machinery, they could, when they exerted themselves, make among them about twelve pounds of pins in a day. There are in a pound upwards of four thousand pins of a middling size. Those ten persons, therefore, could make among them upwards of forty-eight thousand pins in a day. Each person, therefore, making a tenth part of forty-eight thousand pins, might be considered as making four thousand eight hundred pins in a day. But if they had all wrought separately and independently, and without any of them having been educated to this peculiar business, they certainly could not each of them have made twenty, perhaps not one pin in a day; that is, certainly, not the two hundred and fortieth, perhaps not the four thousand eight hundredth part of what they are at present capable of performing, in consequence of a proper division and combination of their different operations. . . .

The division of labor, so far as it can be introduced, occasions, in every art, a proportionable increase of the productive powers of labor. The separation of different trades and employments from one another seems to have taken place in consequence of this advantage. This separation, too, is generally called furthest in those countries which enjoy the highest degree of industry and improvement; what is the work of one man in a rude state of society being generally that of several in an improved one. . . .

This great increase of the quantity of work which, in consequence of the division of labor, the same number of people are capable of performing, is owing to three different circumstances; first, to the increase of dexterity in every particular workman; secondly, to the saving of the time which is commonly lost in passing from one species of work to another; and lastly, to the invention of a great number of machines which facilitate and abridge labor, and enable one man to do the work of many. . . .

It is the great multiplication of the productions of all the different arts, in consequence of the division of labor, which occasions, in a well-governed society, that universal opulence which extends itself to the lowest ranks of the people. Every workman has a great quantity of his own work to dispose of beyond what he himself has occasion for; and every other workman being exactly in the same situation, he is enabled to exchange a great quantity of his own goods for a great quantity, or, what comes to the same thing, for the price of a great quantity of theirs. He supplies them abundantly with what they have occasion for, and they accommodate him as amply with what he has occasion for, and a general plenty diffuses itself through all the different ranks of the society. . . .

Book I, Chapter 2. *Of the Principle Which Gives Occasion to the Division of Labor*

This division of labor, from which so many advantages are derived, is not originally the effect of any human wisdom, which foresees and intends that universal opulence to which it gives occasion. It is the necessary, though very slow and gradual consequence of a certain propensity in human nature which has in view no such extensive utility; the propensity to truck, barter, and exchange one thing for another. . . .

Man has almost constant occasion for the help of his brethren, and it is in vain for him to expect it from their benevolence only. He will be more likely to prevail if he can interest their self-love in his favor, and show them that it is for their own advantage to do for him what he requires of them. Whoever offers to another a bargain of any kind, proposes to do this. Give me that which I want, and you shall have this which you want, is the meaning of every such offer; and it is in this manner that we obtain from one another the far greater art of those good offices which we stand in need of. It is not from the benevolence of the butcher, the brewer, or the baker that we expect our dinner, but from their regard to their own interest. . . .

Book I, Chapter 5. *Of the Real and Nominal Price of Commodities, or Their Price in Labor, and Their Price in Money*

Every man is rich or poor according to the degree in which he can afford to enjoy the necessaries, conveniences, and amusements of human life. But after the division of labor has once thoroughly taken place, it is but a very small part of these with which a man's own labor can supply him. The far greater part of them he must derive from the labor of other people, and he must be rich or poor according to the quantity of that labor which he can command, or which he can afford to purchase. The value of any commodity, therefore, to the person who possesses it, and who means not to use or consume it himself, but to exchange it for other commodities, is equal to the quantity of labor which it enables him to purchase or command. Labor, therefore, is the real measure of the exchangeable value of all commodities.

The real price of everything, what everything really costs to the man who wants to acquire it, is the toil and trouble of acquiring it. What everything is really worth to the man who has acquired it, and who wants to dispose of it or exchange it for something else, is the toil and trouble which it can save to himself, and which it can impose upon other people. What is bought with money or with goods is purchased by labor as much as what we acquire by the toil of our own body. That money or those goods indeed save us this toil. . . .

Book I, Chapter 7. *Of the Natural and Market Price of Commodities*

There is in every society or neighborhood an ordinary or average rate both of wages and profit in every different employment of labor and stock. This rate is naturally regulated, as I shall show hereafter, partly by the general circumstances of the society, their riches or poverty, their advancing, stationary, or declining condition; and partly by the particular nature of each employment.

There is likewise in every society or neighborhood an ordinary or average rate of rent, which is regulated too, as I shall show hereafter, partly by the general circumstances of the society or neighborhood in which the land is situated, and partly by the natural or improved fertility of the land.

These ordinary or average rates may be called the natural rates of wages, profit, and rent, at the time and place in which they commonly prevail.

When the price of any commodity is neither more nor less than what is sufficient to pay the rent of the land, the wages of the labor, and the profits of the stock employed in raising, preparing, and bringing it to market, according to their natural rates, the commodity is then sold for what may be called its natural price. . . .

Though the price, therefore, which leaves him this profit is not always the lowest at which a dealer may sometimes sell his goods, it is the lowest at which he is likely to sell them for any considerable time; at least where there is perfect liberty, or where he may change his trade as often as he pleases.

The actual price at which any commodity is commonly sold is called its market price. It may either be above, or below, or exactly the same with its natural price. . . .

When the quantity of any commodity which is brought to market falls short of the effectual demand, all those who are willing to pay the whole value of the rent, wages, and profit, which must be paid in order to bring it thither, cannot be supplied with the quantity which they want. Rather than want it altogether, some of them will be willing to give more. . . .

When the quantity brought to market exceeds the effectual demand, it cannot be all sold to those who are willing to pay the whole value of the rent, wages, and profit, which must be paid in order to bring it thither. Some part must be sold to those who are willing to pay less, and the low price which they give for it must reduce the price of the whole. . . .

When the quantity brought to market is just sufficient to supply the effectual demand, and no more, the market price naturally comes to be either exactly, or as nearly as can be judged of, the same with the natural price. The whole quantity upon hand can be disposed of for this price, and cannot be disposed of for more. . . .

Such fluctuations affect both the value and the rate either of wages or of profit, according as the market happens to be either overstocked or understocked with commodities or with labor; with work done, or with work to be done. . . .

When by an increase in the effectual demand, the market price of some particular commodity happens to rise a good deal above the natural price, those who employ their stocks in supplying that market are generally careful to conceal this change. If it was commonly known, their great profit would tempt so many new rivals to employ their stocks in the same way that, the effectual demand being fully supplied, the market price would soon be reduced to the natural price, and perhaps for some time even below it. If the market is at a great distance from the residence of those who supply it, they may sometimes be able to keep the secret for several years together, and may so long enjoy their extraordinary profits without any new rivals. Secrets of this kind, however, it must be acknowledged, can seldom be long kept; and the extraordinary profit can last very little longer than they are kept. . . .

A monopoly granted either to an individual or to a trading company has the same effect as a secret in trade or manufactures. The monopolists, by keeping the market constantly understocked, by never fully supplying the effectual demand, sell their commodities much above the natural price, and raise their emoluments, whether they consist in wages or profit, greatly above their natural rate. . . .

The exclusive privileges of corporations, statutes of apprenticeship, and all those laws which restrain in particular employments the competition to a smaller number than might otherwise go into them, have the same tendency, though in a less degree. They are a sort of enlarged monopolies, and may frequently, for ages together, and in whole classes of employments, keep up the market price of particular commodities above the natural price, and maintain both the wages of the labor and the profits of the stock employed about them somewhat above their natural rate.

Such enhancements of the market price may last as long as the regulations of policy which give occasion to them. . . .

Book I, Chapter 10. *Of Wages and Profit in the Different Employments of Labor and Stock*

First the policy of Europe occasions a very important inequality in the whole of the advantages and disadvantages of the different employments of labor and stock, by restraining the competition in some employments to a smaller number than might otherwise be disposed to enter into them.

The exclusive privileges of corporations, or guilds, are the principal means it makes use of for this purpose. . . .

The property which every man has in his own labor, as it is the original foundation of all other property, so it is the most sacred and inviolable. The patrimony of a poor man lies in the strength and dexterity of his hands; and to hinder him from employing this strength and dexterity in what manner he thinks proper without injury to his neighbor is a plain violation of this most sacred property. It is a manifest encroachment upon the just liberty both of the workman and of those who might be disposed to employ him. . . .

The pretense that corporations are necessary for the better government of the trade is without any foundation. The real and effectual discipline which is exercised over a workman is not that of his corporation, but that of his customers. It is the fear of losing their employment which restrains his frauds and corrects his negligence. An exclusive corporation necessarily weakens the force of this discipline.

READING QUESTIONS

1. On what grounds does Smith extol the division of labor? Can you think of any drawbacks that might result from such a form of labor organization?

2. What, according to Smith, motivates human activity? What are the consequences of this motive?

3. What, according to Smith, gives goods and services their value?

4. Explain what Smith means by "natural" and "market" prices. Why are the two often not the same?

5. What is Smith's attitude toward monopolies, and why?

SOURCES IN CONVERSATION

The Moral Implications of Expansion

By the end of the eighteenth century, Europeans had built considerable overseas empires. Britain, in particular, stood out, controlling vast territories in both Asia and the Americas. As Britain's empire grew, and the British and colonial economies grew ever more entwined, some British observers began to question the morality of unrestrained exploitation of non-Europeans. The emergence of the antislavery movement in the late eighteenth century is, perhaps, the most notable example of this trend. More broadly, many in Britain came to believe that the British Empire could be sustained only if it operated according to "British values."

READ AND COMPARE

1. How do these two documents demonstrate why the British gradually changed their treatment of non-Europeans?

17-4 | OLAUDAH EQUIANO, *A Description of the Middle Passage* (1789)

African American slavery was key to the economic development of not only the southern colonies of British North America but also the sugar industry in the West Indies and Brazil. Indeed, most of the slaves transported to the Americas during the period 1620–1850 went to those destinations (rather than to North America), chiefly because of the appalling mortality rate among slaves engaged in sugar production. As enslaved Africans died, more were imported to replenish the labor force. In the second half of the eighteenth century, organized opposition to slavery began to form in Britain. Olaudah Equiano (1745–1797), a former slave, was an important participant in that opposition. In the passage from his memoirs included here, Equiano describes the "Middle Passage," the horrific transatlantic crossing made by African slaves on their way to the Americas. As you read it, think about who Equiano might have hoped to influence. What groups might have been most susceptible to his appeal?

The closeness of the place, and the heat of the climate, added to the number in the ship, which was so crowded that each had scarcely room to turn himself, almost suffocated us. This produced copious perspirations, so that the air soon became unfit for respiration, from a variety of loathsome smells, and brought on a sickness among the slaves, of which many died, thus falling victims to the improvident avarice, as I may call it, of their purchasers. This wretched situation was again aggravated by the galling of the chains, now become insupportable; and the filth of the necessary tubs, into which the children often fell, and were almost suffocated. The shrieks of the women, and the groans of the dying, rendered the whole a scene of horror almost inconceivable. Happily perhaps for myself I was soon reduced so low here that it was thought necessary to keep me almost always on deck; and from my extreme youth I was not put in fetters. In this situation I expected every hour to share the fate of my companions, some of whom were almost daily brought upon deck at the point of death, which I began to hope would soon put an end to my miseries. Often did I think many of the inhabitants of the deep much more happy than myself. I envied them the freedom they enjoyed, and as often wished I could change my condition for theirs. Every circumstance I met with served only to render my state more painful, and heighten my apprehensions, and my opinion of the cruelty of the whites. One day they had taken a number of fishes; and when they had killed and satisfied themselves with as many as they thought fit, to our astonishment who were on the deck, rather than give any of them to us to eat as we expected, they tossed the remaining fish into the sea again, although we begged and prayed for some as well as we could, but in vain; and some of my countrymen, being pressed by hunger, took an opportunity, when they thought no one saw them, of trying to get a little privately; but they were discovered, and the attempt procured them some very severe floggings. One day, when we had a smooth sea and moderate wind, two of my wearied countrymen who were chained together

---

From Robert J. Allison, ed., *The Interesting Narrative of the Life of Olaudah Equiano Written by Himself* (Boston: Bedford/St. Martin's, 2007), pp. 67–68.

(I was near them at the time), preferring death to such a life of misery, somehow made through the nettings and jumped into the sea: immediately another quite dejected fellow, who, on one account of his illness, was suffered to be out of irons, also followed their example; and I believe many more would very soon have done the same if they had not been prevented by the ship's crew, who were instantly alarmed. Those of us that were the most active were in a moment put down under the deck, and here was such a noise and confusion amongst the people of the ship as I never heard before, to stop her, and get the boat out to go after the slaves. However two of the wretches were drowned, but they got the other, and afterwards flogged him unmercifully for thus attempting to prefer death to slavery. In this manner we continued to undergo more hardships than I can now relate, hardships which are inseparable from this accursed trade. Many a time we were near suffocation from the want of fresh air, which we were often without for whole days together. This, and the stench of the necessary tubs, carried off many.

READING QUESTIONS

1. According to Equiano, what were conditions like aboard a slave ship?

2. How did the crew treat their cargo? What seems to have been their highest priorities with respect to the slaves?

3. What does Equiano's account tell you about the psychological impact of enslavement and transportation overseas?

17-5 | ROBERT, FIRST BARON CLIVE, *Speech in the House of Commons on India* (1772)

Robert Clive (1725–1774) was born into an English minor gentry family. Apprenticed as a "writer" (clerk) in the British East India Company, he arrived in India in 1744, in the midst of the War of the Austrian Succession. The conflict offered opportunities for bold and ambitious men like Clive, and his bravery won him a commission in the company's army. In 1757 he defeated an Indian army at the Battle of Plassey, and in 1765 he received as a gift from the Mughal emperor the province of Bengal, one of the richest and most populous in India. Clive was thus responsible for transforming the East India Company from a trading entity into a governmental one that directly ruled Indian territory. In the following passage from his writings, Clive defends himself against charges of greed and corruption. As you read it, pay particular attention to the way Clive uses the alleged moral failings of the Indians to justify his own actions.

Indostan [India] was always an absolute despotic government. The inhabitants, especially of Bengal, in inferior stations, are servile, mean [poor],

From "Speech Given in the House of Commons, March 30, 1772," in *The Parliamentary History of England from the Earliest Period to the Year 1803*, vol. 17 (London: T. C. Hansard, 1806–1820), pp. 354–357.

submissive, and humble. In superior stations, they are luxurious, effeminate, tyrannical, treacherous, venal, cruel. The country of Bengal is called, by way of distinction, the paradise of the earth. It not only abounds with the necessaries of life to such a degree, as to furnish a great part of India with its superfluity, but it abounds in very curious and valuable manufactures, sufficient not only for its own use, but for the use of the whole globe. The silver of the west and the gold of the east have for many years been pouring into that country, and goods only have been sent out in return. This has added to the luxury and extravagance of Bengal.

From time immemorial it has been the custom of that country, for an inferior never to come into the presence of a superior without a present. It begins at the nabob,[1] and ends at the lowest man that has an inferior. The nabob has told me, that the small presents he received amounted to £300,000 a year; and I can believe him; because I know that I might have received as much during my last government. The Company's servants have ever been accustomed to receive presents. Even before we took part in the country troubles, when our possessions were very confined and limited, the governor and others used to receive presents; and I will take upon me to assert, that there has not been an officer commanding his Majesty's fleet; nor an officer commanding his Majesty's army; not a governor, not a member of council, not any other person, civil or military, in such a station as to have connection with the country government, who has not received presents. With regard to Bengal, there they flow in abundance indeed. Let the House figure to itself a country consisting of 15 millions of inhabitants, a revenue of four millions sterling, and a trade in proportion. By progressive steps the Company have become sovereigns of that empire. Can it be supposed that their servants will refrain from advantages so obviously resulting from their situation? The Company's servants, however, have not been the authors of those acts of violence and oppression, of which it is the fashion to accuse them. Such crimes are committed by the natives of the country acting as their agents and for the most part without their knowledge. . . . Let us for a moment consider the nature of the education of a young man who goes to India. The advantages arising from the Company's service are now very generally known; and the great object of every man is to get his son appointed a writer to Bengal; which is usually at the age of 16. His parents and relations represent to him how certain he is of making a fortune; that my lord such a one, and my lord such a one, acquired so much money in such a time; and Mr. such a one, and Mr. such a one, so much in such a time. Thus are their principles corrupted at their very setting out, and as they generally go a good many together, they inflame one another's expectations to such a degree, in the course of the voyage, that they fix upon a period for their return[2] before their arrival.

Let us now take a view of one of these writers arrived in Bengal, and not worth a groat.[3] As soon as he lands, a banyan,[4] worth perhaps £100,000 desires

---

[1]**nabob**: More properly, nawab; a provincial ruler.

[2]**they fix upon a period for their return**: In other words, the date by which they expect to return to Britain, fortune in hand.

[3]**groat**: Four pence.

[4]**banyan**: Indian merchant or trader.

he may have the honor of serving this young gentleman, at 4s. 6d.[5] per month. The Company has provided chambers for him, but they are not good enough: the banyan finds better. The young man takes a walk about the town, he observes that other writers, arrived only a year before him, live in splendid apartments or have houses of their own, ride upon fine prancing Arabian horses, and in palanqueens[6] and chaises; that they keep seraglios,[7] make entertainments, and treat with champagne and claret. When he returns he tells the banyan what he has observed. The banyan assures him he may soon arrive at the same good fortune; he furnishes him with money; he is then at his mercy. The advantages of the banyan advance with the rank of his master, who in acquiring one fortune generally spends three. But this is not the worst of it: he is in a state of dependence under the banyan, who commits acts of violence and oppression, as his interest prompts him to, under the pretended sanction and authority of the Company's servant. Hence, Sir, arises the clamor against the English gentlemen in India. But look at them in a retired situation, when returned to England, when they are no longer nabobs and sovereigns of the east: see if there be any thing tyrannical in their disposition towards their inferiors: see if they are not good and humane masters: Are they not charitable? Are they not benevolent? Are they not generous? Are they not hospitable? If they are, thus far, not contemptible members of society, and if in all their dealings between man and man, their conduct is strictly honorable: if, in short, there has not yet been one character found amongst them sufficiently flagitious[8] for Mr. Foote[9] to exhibit on the theatre in the Haymarket, may we not conclude, that if they have erred, it has been because they were men, placed in situations subject to little or no control?

READING QUESTIONS

1. What does Clive's description of Indian character suggest about his racial attitudes?

2. How does Clive justify out-and-out bribery and corruption in Indian government and the East India Company's enrichment by that means?

3. How does Clive excuse the behavior of East India Company employees and exonerate them of "flagitious" actions?

---

[5] **4s. 6d.**: Four shillings, six pence; a modest sum.

[6] **palanqueen**: More properly, palanquin: an enclosed litter, seating one, carried by four or six servants.

[7] **seraglio**: Harem.

[8] **flagitious**: Wicked, villainous.

[9] **Mr. Foote**: Playwright and theater impresario Samuel Foote (1721–1777), who in 1772 staged a play at Haymarket Theater titled *The Nabob*, a satire about the East India Company.

■ COMPARATIVE AND DISCUSSION QUESTIONS ■

1. What do all these documents reveal about social and racial hierarchies during this period?

2. How did Smith undermine mercantilist arguments like the one put forward by Mun?

3. How did the activities described by Equiano and Clive contribute to the growth of British wealth and power?

18

Life in the Era of Expansion
1650–1800

For the social historian, the task of understanding how the "ordinary people" of early modern Europe lived — to say nothing of what they thought — is quite challenging. Most of the non-elite in the seventeenth and eighteenth centuries were illiterate and thus left no self-composed evidence of their existence. Historians studying the period have to rely on the limited writings left by common people or try to interpret their lives through the lens of the better-off classes. Nonetheless, careful attention to the available sources is rewarded with glimpses of various aspects of the changing social and cultural world of the eighteenth century. The documents included in this chapter offer an opportunity to explore eighteenth-century attitudes about mortality, religious belief, children and education, and the state of medical knowledge.

18-1 | The Dangers of Eighteenth-Century Life
EDMOND WILLIAMSON, *Births and Deaths in an English Gentry Family* (1709–1720)

Little is known of Edmond Williamson. He lived in Bedfordshire, one of the "Home Counties" surrounding London. The mere fact that he was literate and kept a diary suggests that he was a man of means, as does his mention of the servants present at his wife's childbirths. Despite their brevity, his diary entries reveal that proximity of death was a central fact of life, even in the lives of the relatively affluent. Three of Williamson's seven children died at birth or shortly afterward, and a fourth succumbed to smallpox before the age of three. Williamson's wife died as well, just a month after the birth of her last child. As you read the diary excerpts, think about the light they shed on eighteenth-century family life.

From Edmond Williamson, "An Account of the Birth of My Children by My Second Wife (1709–1720)," in *The Past Speaks*, 2d ed., ed. Walter Arnstein, Part 2 (Lexington, Mass.: D. C. Heath, 1993), pp. 33–34.

1709

March 29. My wife fell into labor and a little after 9 in the morning was delivered of a son. Present: aunt Taylor, cousin White, sister Smith, cousin Clarkson, widow Hern, Mrs. Howe, midwife, Mr[s]. Wallis, nurse, Mrs. Holms, Eleanor Hobbs, servants.

　April 4. He was baptised by Doctor Battle by the name of John. . . .

　[April] 16. The child died about 1 o'clock in the morning.

1711

Sept. 17. My said wife was delivered of a son just before 4 in the morning. Present: Mrs. Thomas Molyneux's lady and maid, Mrs. Mann, midwife, Margaret Williamson, nurse, Susan Nuthall, servant.

　Oct. 4. He was baptised by Mr. Trabeck by the name of Talbot after my grandmother's name. Sir John Talbot and John Pulteny esquire were gossips [godfathers], with my sister Smith godmother. . . .

1713

June 9. About 8 at night my said wife began her labor.

　[June] 10. Half an hour after 1 in the morning was brought to bed of a son. Present: Mrs. Molyneux, Mrs. Bisset, Mrs. Mann, midwife, Nurse Williamson, Susan Nuthall and Betty Ginger, servants.

　[June] 30. Baptised by Mr. Mompesson of Mansfield by the name of Edmond. . . .

1715

March 7. My said wife was brought to bed of a daughter 10 minutes before 6 in the morning. Present: Mrs. Molyneux, Mrs. Mann, midwife, Nurse Williamson, Mary Evans, Mary Cole and Mary Wheeler, servants.

　[March] 29. Was baptised by Dr. Mandivel, chancellor of Lincoln, by the name of Christian.

1716

March 9. My wife was delivered of a daughter at 7 at night. Present: aunt Taylor, Mrs. Molyneux, Mrs. Oliver, Mrs. Mann, midwife, Mary Smith, nurse, Jane Kensey, and Mary Wheeler, servants.

　[March] 31. Was baptised by Mr. Widmore, the reader of St. Margaret's, by the name of Elizanna. . . . Registered in St. Margaret's, Westminster, as all the rest were.

　April 27. Died, was buried in the new chapel yard in the Broadway.

1718

Jan. 21. [Mrs. Williamson:] I was brought to bed of a son about 2 in the morning, Mrs. Mann, midwife, nurse Chatty, dry-nurse, present; Mrs. Taylor, Mrs. White and Mrs. Molyneux, Jane Beadle; servants: Mary Wells, Jane Griffith, Edmond Kinward. He was baptised by Mr. Widmore, reader of St. Margaret's, Westminster, by the name of Francis. . . .

1719

Feb. 21. [Mrs. Williamson:] I was brought to bed of a son between 6 and 7 in the evening, Mrs. Mann, midwife, nurse Chatty, dry-nurse; present: aunt Taylor, Mrs. Molyneux and Jane Beadle; servants: Rebecca Shippy, Betty Hall and Mathew Dowect.

March 7. He was baptised by Mr. Widmore, reader of St. Margaret's, Westminster, by the name of William. . . .

[Undated]. Died and buried at Hadley.

1720

June. My wife brought to bed of a daughter, but the child did not live a minute.

July 21. My wife died and was buried at Isleworth.

Sept. 9. [Francis] died of the smallpox at Nurse Ward's.

READING QUESTIONS

1. What does the Williamsons' account of the births of their children suggest about pregnancy in early-eighteenth-century England? What factors would account for this?

2. What does Williamson's record of the deaths of his children suggest about the incidence of infant mortality in early modern Europe?

3. Apart from labor, births, and deaths, what else did Williamson record, and what does this tell us?

4. In what ways did the ritual of childbirth in early-eighteenth-century England differ from that in modern developed countries? What could account for the differences?

18-2 | Embracing Innovation in Medicine

MARY WORTLEY MONTAGU, *On Smallpox Inoculations* (ca. 1717)

While medical progress in the eighteenth century was slow, there were some notable breakthroughs, as the combined impact of the Scientific Revolution and the Enlightenment led some to challenge medical orthodoxy. Such breakthroughs did not always come from within the medical profession. Mary Wortley Montagu (1689–1762) is a case in point.

From Lady Mary Wortley Montagu, *Letters of the Right Honourable Lady M — y W — y M — e: Written During Her Travels in Europe, Asia and Africa* . . . , vol. 1 (Aix: Anthony Henricy, 1796), pp. 167–169.

The daughter of an English aristocrat and an unusually well-educated woman, Montagu narrowly survived smallpox, an often fatal disease, in 1715. A year later, while accompanying her diplomat husband in Constantinople, Montagu witnessed what was a common practice in that part of the world, inoculation against smallpox. She subsequently had both of her children inoculated, and, upon returning to England, championed the procedure despite strong anti-"Oriental" sentiment. The following letter was written to a close friend; its substance was made public in the 1720s.

A propos of distempers, I am going to tell you a thing, that will make you wish yourself here. The small-pox, so fatal, and so general amongst us, is here entirely harmless, by the invention of engrafting, which is the term they give it. There is a set of old women, who make it their business to perform the operation, every autumn, in the month of September, when the great heat is abated. People send to one another to know if any of their family has a mind to have the small-pox; they make parties for this purpose, and when they are met (commonly fifteen or sixteen together) the old woman comes with a nut-shell full of the matter of the best sort of smallpox, and asks what vein you please to have opened. She imme-diately rips open that you offer to her, with a large needle (which gives you no more pain than a common scratch) and puts into the vein as much matter as can lie upon the head of her needle, and after that, binds up the little wound with a hollow bit of shell, and in this manner opens four or five veins. The Grecians have commonly the superstition of opening one in the middle of the forehead, one in each arm, and one on the breast, to mark the sign of the Cross; but this has a very ill effect, all these wounds leaving little scars, and is not done by those that are not superstitious, who choose to have them in the legs, or that part of the arm that is concealed. The children or young patients play together all the rest of the day, and are in perfect health to the eighth [day]. Then the fever begins to seize them, and they keep their beds two days, very seldom three. They have very rarely above twenty or thirty [pockmarks] in their faces, which never mark [i.e., leave scars] and in eight days time they are as well as before their illness. Where they are wounded [i.e., where pockmarks appear], there remains running sores during the distemper, which I don't doubt is a great relief to it. Every year, thousands undergo this operation, and the French Ambassador says pleasantly, that they take the small-pox here by way of diversion, as they take the waters[1] in other countries. There is no example of any one that has died in it, and you may believe I am well satisfied of the safety of this experiment, since I intend to try it on my dear little son. I am patriot enough to take the pains to bring this useful invention into fashion in England, and I should not fail to write to some of our doctors very particularly about it, if I knew any one of them that I thought had virtue enough to destroy such a considerable branch of their revenue, for the good of mankind. But that distemper is too beneficial to them, not to expose to

---

[1]**take the waters**: Upper-class men and women across Europe routinely visited spas with mineral waters or hot springs, like Bath in England, to "take the waters." Such trips combined medicinal and recreational motives.

all their resentment, the hardy weight that should undertake to put an end to it. Perhaps if I live to return, I may, however, have courage to war with them. Upon this occasion, admire the heroism in the heart of

    Your friend, etc. etc.

READING QUESTIONS

1. According to Montagu, who administered smallpox inoculations in Constantinople? What does this suggest about Turkish popular medicine in the eighteenth century?

2. What might explain Montagu's skepticism about the willingness of English doctors to adopt the practice of inoculation?

3. What does Montagu's letter suggest about upper-class women's education and empowerment in early modern English society? Do you think she was representative of all women? Of all upper-class women? Why or why not?

4. What are some of the likely reasons English doctors dismissed the smallpox inoculation that was so successful abroad?

18-3 | Shaping Young Minds and Bodies

JOHN LOCKE, *Some Thoughts Concerning Education* (1693)

John Locke's (1632–1704) intellectual curiosity and influence ranged wide, from political theory to the nature of human consciousness, from economics to, in this piece, education. Originally composed as a series of letters to a friend who had sought Locke's advice concerning his son's education, "Some Thoughts" constitutes a companion piece to his "Essay Concerning Human Understanding" (1690), in which he argued that the mind at birth was a "blank slate" upon which ideas were imprinted and that all knowledge was derived from sensory experience and reasoning. As you read the excerpt, ask yourself why education was so important to Locke and, indeed, to so many of the participants in the Enlightenment. What connections can you make between Locke's philosophical positions and his ideas about education?

The well educating of their children is so much the duty and concern of parents, and the welfare and prosperity of the nation so much depends on it, that I would have every one lay it seriously to heart; and after having well examined and distinguished what fancy, custom, or reason advises in the case, set his helping hand to promote everywhere that way of training up youth, with regard to their several conditions, which is the easiest, shortest, and likeliest to produce virtuous, useful, and able men in their distinct callings; tho' that most to be taken care

From *English Philosophers of the Seventeenth and Eighteenth Centuries* (New York: P. F. Collier & Son, 1910), pp. 6–7, 9, 11, 28–29, 33–36, 39, 53–54, 111, 123, 136, 179, 184–185.

of is the gentleman's calling. For if those of that rank are by their education once set right, they will quickly bring all the rest into order. . . .

A sound mind in a sound body, is a short, but full description of a happy state in this world. He that has these two, has little more to wish for; and he that wants either of them, will be but little the better for anything else. Men's happiness or misery is most part of their own making. He, whose mind directs not wisely, will never take the right way; and he, whose body is crazy and feeble, will never be able to advance in it. I confess, there are some men's constitutions of body and mind so vigorous, and well framed by nature, that they need not much assistance from others; but by the strength of their natural genius, they are from their cradles carried towards what is excellent; and by the privilege of their happy constitutions, are able to do wonders. But examples of this kind are but few; and I think I may say, that of all the men we meet with, nine parts of ten are what they are, good or evil, useful or not, by their education. 'Tis that which makes the great difference in mankind. The little, or almost insensible impressions on our tender infancies, have very important and lasting consequences: and there 'tis, as in the fountains of some rivers, where a gentle application of the hand turns the flexible waters in channels, that make them take quite contrary courses; and by this direction given them at first in the source, they receive different tendencies, and arrive at last at very remote and distant places. . . .

I have said he here [as opposed to "she" or "they"], because the principal aim of my discourse is, how a young gentleman should be brought up from his infancy, which in all things will not so perfectly suit the education of daughters; though where the difference of sex requires different treatment, 'twill be no hard matter to distinguish. . . .

[Locke provides extensive advice on healthy eating and drinking habits for children.]

As the strength of the body lies chiefly in being able to endure hardships, so also does that of the mind. And the great principle and foundation of all virtue and worth is placed in this: that a man is able to deny himself his own desires, cross his own inclinations, and purely follow what reason directs as best, tho' the appetite lean the other way.

The great mistake I have observed in people's breeding their children, has been, that this has not been taken care enough of in its due season: that the mind has not been made obedient to discipline, and pliant to reason, when at first it was most tender, most easy to be bowed. Parents being wisely ordained by nature to love their children, are very apt, if reason watch not that natural affection very warily, are apt, I say, to let it run into fondness. They love their little ones and it is their duty; but they often, with them, cherish their faults too. . . .

It seems plain to me, that the principle of all virtue and excellency lies in a power of denying ourselves the satisfaction of our own desires, where reason does not authorize them. This power is to be got and improved by custom, made easy and familiar by an early practice. If therefore I might be heard, I would advise, that, contrary to the ordinary way, children should be used to submit their desires, and go without their longings, even from their very cradles.

The first thing they should learn to know, should be, that they were not to have anything because it pleased them, but because it was thought fit for them. If things suitable to their wants were supplied to them, so that they were never suffered to have what they once cried for, they would learn to be content without it, would never, with bawling and peevishness, contend for mastery, nor be half so uneasy to themselves and others as they are, because from the first beginning they are not thus handled. If they were never suffered to obtain their desire by the impatience they expressed for it, they would no more cry for another thing, than they do for the moon. . . .

Those therefore that intend ever to govern their children, should begin it while they are very little, and look that they perfectly comply with the will of their parents. Would you have your son obedient to you when past a child; be sure then to establish the authority of a father as soon as he is capable of submission, and can understand in whose power he is. If you would have him stand in awe of you, imprint it in his infancy; and as he approaches more to a man, admit him nearer to your familiarity; so shall you have him your obedient subject (as is fit) while he is a child, and your affectionate friend when he is a man. For methinks they mightily misplace the treatment due to their children, who are indulgent and familiar when they are little, but severe to them, and keep them at a distance, when they are grown up: for liberty and indulgence can do no good to children; their want of judgment makes them stand in need of restraint and discipline; and on the contrary, imperiousness and severity is but an ill way of treating men, who have reason of their own to guide them; unless you have a mind to make your children, when grown up, weary of you, and secretly to say within themselves, When will you die, father? . . .

This being laid down in general, as the course that ought to be taken, 'tis fit we now come to consider the parts of the discipline to be used, a little more particularly. I have spoken so much of carrying a strict hand over children, that perhaps I shall be suspected of not considering enough, what is due to their tender age and constitutions. But that opinion will vanish, when you have heard me a little farther: for I am very apt to think, that great severity of punishment does but very little good, nay, great harm in education; and I believe it will be found that . . . those children who have been most chastised, seldom make the best men. All that I have hitherto contended for, is, that whatsoever rigor is necessary, it is more to be used, the younger children are; and having by a due application wrought its effect, it is to be relaxed, and changed into a milder sort of government. . . .

Beating them, and all other sorts of slavish and corporal punishments, are not the discipline fit to be used in the education of those we would have wise, good, and ingenuous men; and therefore very rarely to be applied, and that only in great occasions, and cases of extremity. On the other side, to flatter children by rewards of things that are pleasant to them, is as carefully to be avoided. He that will give to his son apples or sugar-plumbs, or what else of this kind he is most delighted with, to make him learn his book, does but authorize his love of pleasure, and cocker up that dangerous propensity, which he ought by all means to subdue and stifle in him. . . .

[Locke warns against the bad influence of servants upon children.]

Having named company, I am almost ready to throw away my pen, and trouble you no farther on this subject: for since that does more than all precepts, rules, and instructions, methinks 'tis almost wholly in vain to make a long discourse of other things, and to talk of that almost to no purpose. For you will be ready to say, what shall I do with my son? If I keep him always at home, he will be in danger to be my young master; and if I send him abroad, how is it possible to keep him from the contagion of rudeness and vice, which is everywhere so in fashion? In my house he will perhaps be more innocent, but more ignorant too of the world; wanting there change of company, and being used constantly to the same faces, he will, when he comes abroad, be a sheepish or conceited creature.

I confess both sides have their inconveniences. Being abroad, 'tis true, will make him bolder, and better able to bustle and shift among boys of his own age; and the emulation of school-fellows often puts life and industry into young lads. But still you can find a school, wherein it is possible for the master to look after the manners of his scholars, and can show as great effects of his care of forming their minds to virtue, and their carriage to good breeding, as of forming their tongues to the learned languages. . . .

Virtue is harder to be got than a knowledge of the world; and if lost in a young man, is seldom recovered. Sheepishness and ignorance of the world, the faults imputed to a private education, are neither the necessary consequences of being bred at home, nor if they were, are they incurable evils. Vice is the more stubborn, as well as the more dangerous evil of the two; and therefore in the first place to be fenced against. If that sheepish softness which often enervates those who are bred like fondlings [fools] at home, be carefully to be avoided, it is principally so for virtue's sake; for fear lest such a yielding temper should be too susceptible of vicious impressions, and expose the novice too easily to be corrupted. A young man before he leaves the shelter of his father's house, and the guard of a tutor, should be fortified with resolution, and made acquainted with men, to secure his virtues, lest he should be led into some ruinous course, or fatal precipice, before he is sufficiently acquainted with the dangers of conversation, and has steadiness enough not to yield to every temptation. Were it not for this, a young man's bashfulness and ignorance in the world, would not so much need an early care. Conversation would cure it in a great measure; or if that will not do it early enough, it is only a stronger reason for a good tutor at home. For if pains be to be taken to give him a manly air and assurance betimes, it is chiefly as a fence to his virtue when he goes into the world under his own conduct. . . .

[Locke urges parents to choose tutors for their children discriminately, as children learn by example.]

Curiosity in children . . . ought to be encouraged in them, not only as a good sign, but as the great instrument nature has provided to remove that ignorance they were born with; and which, without this busy inquisitiveness, will make them dull and useless creatures. . . .

That which every gentleman . . . desires for his son, besides the estate he leaves him, is contained . . . in these four things, virtue, wisdom, breeding, and learning. . . .

I place virtue as the first and most necessary of those endowments that belong to a man or a gentleman; as absolutely requisite to make him valued and beloved by others, acceptable or tolerable to himself. Without that, I think, he will be happy neither in this nor the other world.

You will wonder, perhaps, that I put learning last, especially if I tell you I think it the least part. This may seem strange in the mouth of a bookish man; and this making usually the chief, if not only bustle and stir about children, this being almost that alone which is thought on, when people talk of education, makes it the greater paradox. When I consider, what ado is made about a little Latin and Greek, how many years are spent in it, and what a noise and business it makes to no purpose, I can hardly forbear thinking that the parents of children still live in fear of the school-master's rod, which they look on as the only instrument of education; as a language or two to be its whole business. How else is it possible that a child should be chained to the oar seven, eight, or ten of the best years of his life, to get a language or two, which, I think, might be had at a great deal cheaper rate of pains and time, and be learned almost in playing? . . .

Reading and writing and learning I allow to be necessary, but yet not the chief business. I imagine you would think him a very foolish fellow, that should not value a virtuous or a wise man infinitely before a great scholar. . . .

To conclude this part . . . , his tutor should remember, that his business is not so much to teach him all that is knowable, as to raise in him a love and esteem of knowledge; and to put him in the right way of knowing and improving himself when he has a mind to it. . . .

Teach him to get a mastery over his inclinations, and submit his appetite to reason. This being obtained, and by constant practice settled into habit, the hardest part of the task is over. To bring a young man to this, I know nothing which so much contributes as the love of praise and commendation, which should therefore be instilled into him by all arts imaginable. Make his mind as sensible of credit and shame as may be; and when you have done that, you have put a principle into him, which will influence his actions when you are not by, to which the fear of a little smart of a rod is not comparable, and which will be the proper stock whereon afterwards to graft the true principles of morality and religion.

READING QUESTIONS

1. Why does Locke advocate beginning a child's education at the earliest possible age?

2. What is Locke's opinion on the education of young women? What in the letter suggests his beliefs on sexual difference and gender roles?

3. What are Locke's views about the need for disciplining children and the nature of the discipline to be used?

4. What are Locke's highest priorities for a childhood education? What sort of person might he have hoped a good education to produce?

SOURCES IN CONVERSATION

The Challenge to Established Religion in the 1700s

By the eighteenth century, established churches in both Catholic and Protestant lands had evolved into extensions of state bureaucracies. Closely tied to the interests of ruling political elites, their purpose was more the preservation of the social and political status quo than it was a true engagement with the spiritual needs of ordinary people. To many Europeans, Christianity promoted by such churches was composed of empty gestures and routines with no real substance. For some Enlightenment thinkers, the ossification of established churches was an indictment of organized religion as a whole, and deism, a rational theology that rejected divine intervention in everyday life, gained popularity in certain circles. Perhaps more important, however, was the challenge to established religion from sincere believers eager for the emergence of a new, more emotionally satisfying form of Christianity. If the eighteenth century was the Age of Enlightenment, it was also an age of popular religious revival, and our understanding of the religious life of the period is incomplete if we do not incorporate both developments.

READ AND COMPARE

1. What similarities do you see in the messages of Wesley and Paine? Where do they differ?

2. Which people in society would find their messages attractive, and who would find them threatening?

3. Which message would be seen as more radical and dangerous to religious and political authorities, and why would it be more of a threat?

18-4 | JOHN WESLEY, *The Ground Rules for Methodism* (1749)

John Wesley (1703–1791), the son of an Anglican clergyman, was himself trained to the ministry. He found little solace in the Anglicanism of his youth, however, and endured years of spiritual yearning until, in 1738, he had a religious awakening. His resulting theological message was quite simple: salvation was possible for all. The appeal of Wesley's message, coupled with his tireless preaching, often to huge crowds outdoors, quickly brought him a large following. These followers became known as "Methodists," after a Bible study group Wesley attended while at Oxford University.

From John Wesley, "A Plain Account of the People Called Methodists," in *The Past Speaks*, 2d ed., ed. Walter Arnstein, Part 2 (Lexington, Mass.: D. C. Heath, 1993), pp. 87–89.

The Nature, Design, and General Rules of the United Societies

1. About ten years ago my brother [Charles Wesley] and I were desired to preach in many parts of London. We had no view therein but, so far as we were able (and we knew God could work by whomsoever it pleased Him) to convince those who would hear, what true Christianity was, and to persuade them to embrace it.

2. The points we chiefly insisted upon were four: First, that orthodoxy or right opinions is, at best, but a very slender part of religion, if it can be allowed to be any part of it at all; that neither does religion consist in negatives, in bare harmlessness of any kind, nor merely in externals in doing good or using the means of grace, in works of piety (so called) or of charity: that it is nothing short of or different from the mind that was in Christ, the image of God stamped upon the heart, inward righteousness attended with the peace of God and joy in the Holy Ghost.

Secondly, that the only way under heaven to this religion is to repent and believe the gospel, of (as the apostle words it) repentance toward God and faith in our Lord Jesus Christ.

Thirdly, that by this faith, he that worketh not, but believeth in Him that justifieth the ungodly, is justified freely by His grace, through the redemption which is in Jesus Christ.

And lastly, that being justified by faith we taste of the heaven to which we are going; we are holy and happy; we tread down sin and fear, and sit in heavenly places with Christ Jesus.

3. Many of those who heard this, began to cry out, that we brought strange things to their ears: that this was doctrine which they never heard before, or, at least, never regarded. They searched the scriptures, whether these things were so, and acknowledged the truth as it is in Jesus. Their hearts also were influenced as well as their understandings, and they determined to follow Jesus Christ and Him crucified.

4. Immediately [those who accepted this new way] were surrounded with difficulties. All the world rose up against them; neighbors, strangers, acquaintances, relations, friends began to cry out amain, "Be not righteous overmuch: why shouldst thou destroy thyself? Let not much religion make thee mad." . . .

Directions Given to the Band Societies

You are supposed to have the faith that "overcometh the world." To you, therefore, it is not grievous:

I. Carefully to abstain from doing evil; in particular:

1. Neither to buy nor sell anything at all on the Lord's day.

2. To taste no spiritous liquor, no dram of any kind, unless prescribed by a physician.

3. To be at a word [i.e., to be honest] both in buying and selling.

4. To pawn nothing, no, not to save life.

5. Not to mention the fault of any behind his back, and to stop those short that do.

6. To wear no needless ornaments, such as rings, earrings, necklaces, lace, ruffles.

7. To use no needless self-indulgence, such as taking snuff or tobacco, unless prescribed by a physician.

II. Zealously to maintain good works; in particular:

1. To give alms of such things as you possess, and that to the uttermost of your power.

2. To reprove all that sin in your sight, and that in love and meekness of wisdom.

3. To be patterns of diligence and frugality, of self-denial, and taking up the cross daily.

III. Constantly to attend on all the ordinances of God; in particular:

1. To be at church and at the Lord's table every week, and at every public meeting of the bands.

2. To attend the ministry of the word every morning unless distance, business or sickness prevent.

3. To use private prayer every day; and family prayer, if you are at the head of a family.

4. To read the scriptures, and meditate therein, at every vacant hour. And

5. To observe, as days of fasting or abstinence, all Fridays in the year.

READING QUESTIONS

1. What, according to Wesley, is the *only* means of obtaining salvation? What is the true nature of religion?

2. What kinds of criticism did Wesley anticipate? What might explain the hostility with which Methodism was sometimes met?

3. Given Wesley's insistence that external behavior has little to do with true religion, what should we make of the detailed directions he laid out for Methodist societies? Why insist on certain behaviors and practices, if they are not part of the essential experience of Christianity?

4. What might explain the appeal of Methodism? How did it differ from other more established forms of Christianity?

18-5 | THOMAS PAINE, *The Age of Reason* (1794)

Thomas Paine (1737–1809) is best known for *Common Sense* (1776), an enormously influential pamphlet in which Paine argued for American independence. *The Age of Reason*, excerpted here, was produced in reaction to another revolution, the French Revolution of 1789.

From Thomas Paine, *The Age of Reason*, ed. Moncure Daniel Conway (New York: G. P. Putnam's Sons, 1924), pp. 21–23.

Paine rejoiced in the revolutionary government's dismantling of the established church, and he was certain that events in France would usher in a new age in European spiritual life, one in which reason, and not revelation, would be the foundation of religious thought and practice. As you read the excerpt, pay particular attention to Paine's views on the relationship between church and state. Why did he see close ties between secular and religious authorities as evil?

It has been my intention, for several years past, to publish my thoughts upon religion; I am well aware of the difficulties that attend the subject, and from that consideration, had reserved it to a more advanced period of life. I intended it to be the last offering I should make to my fellow-citizens of all nations, and that at a time when the purity of the motive that induced me to it could not admit of a question, even by those who might disapprove the work.

The circumstance that has now taken place in France, of the total abolition of the whole national order of priesthood, and of everything appertaining to compulsive systems of religion, and compulsive articles of faith, has not only precipitated my intention, but rendered a work of this kind exceedingly necessary, lest, in the general wreck of superstition, of false systems of government, and false theology, we lose sight of morality, of humanity, and of the theology that is true.

As several of my colleagues, and others of my fellow-citizens of France, have given me the example of making their voluntary and individual profession of faith, I also will make mine; and I do this with all that sincerity and frankness with which the mind of man communicates with itself.

I believe in one God, and no more; and I hope for happiness beyond this life.

I believe the equality of man, and I believe that religious duties consist in doing justice, loving mercy, and endeavouring to make our fellow-creatures happy.

But, lest it should be supposed that I believe many other things in addition to these, I shall, in the progress of this work, declare the things I do not believe, and my reasons for not believing them.

I do not believe in the creed professed by the Jewish church, by the Roman church, by the Greek church, by the Turkish church, by the Protestant church, nor by any church that I know of. My own mind is my own church.

All national institutions of churches, whether Jewish, Christian, or Turkish, appear to me no other than human inventions set up to terrify and enslave mankind, and monopolize power and profit.

I do not mean by this declaration to condemn those who believe otherwise; they have the same right to their belief as I have to mine. But it is necessary to the happiness of man, that he be mentally faithful to himself. Infidelity does not consist in believing, or in disbelieving; it consists in professing to believe what he does not believe.

It is impossible to calculate the moral mischief, if I may so express it, that mental lying has produced in society. When a man has so far corrupted and prostituted the chastity of his mind, as to subscribe his professional belief to things he does not believe, he has prepared himself for the commission of every other crime. He takes up the trade of a priest for the sake of gain, and, in order to qualify himself for that trade, he begins with a perjury. Can we conceive anything more destructive to morality than this?

Soon after I had published the pamphlet Common Sense, in America, I saw the exceeding probability that a revolution in the system of government would be followed by a revolution in the system of religion. The adulterous connection of church and state, wherever it had taken place, whether Jewish, Christian, or Turkish, had so effectually prohibited, by pains and penalties, every discussion upon established creeds, and upon first principles of religion, that until the system of government should be changed, those subjects could not be brought fairly and openly before the world; but that whenever this should be done, a revolution in the system of religion would follow. Human inventions and priest-craft would be detected; and man would return to the pure, unmixed, and unadulterated belief of one God, and no more.

READING QUESTIONS

1. What did Paine believe? What did he *not* believe?

2. How did Paine characterize organized religions? What might explain the intensity of his views?

3. Why did Paine believe that a "revolution in the system of government" would almost certainly produce a "revolution in the system of religion"? What light does this shed on Paine's understanding of the nature of established churches?

■ COMPARATIVE AND DISCUSSION QUESTIONS ■

1. What can be gleaned from Williamson's and Wesley's accounts about the prevalence and nature of religious belief in eighteenth-century England?

2. What do Williamson's and Montagu's accounts suggest about the state and extent of medical knowledge in eighteenth-century Europe?

3. What can be learned from Williamson's, Locke's, and Montagu's accounts about attitudes toward children in the late seventeenth and eighteenth centuries?

4. On which aspects of religious belief and practice might Paine and Wesley agree? On which would they disagree?

Revolutions in Politics

1775–1815

The revolution that erupted in France in 1789, and would, in time, engulf all of Europe in political upheaval and war, was sparked by a financial crisis that had been brewing for more than a century. Over the course of the seventeenth and eighteenth centuries, the cost of warfare rose dramatically, and France was at war for almost all of that time. Under Louis XIV (1638–1715), France launched one war after another in an effort to cement French dominance in Europe. Louis XV (r. 1715–1774) inherited Louis XIV's ambitions and spent much of the eighteenth century unsuccessfully battling Britain for a world empire. By 1789 France's finances had reached the crisis point. With no options left, Louis XVI (r. 1774–1792) gave in to noble pressure to summon the Estates General, the French representative body that had last met in 1614. Louis hoped to use the Estates General as a vehicle for limited financial reform, but events quickly spun out of his control. What had begun as a financial crisis became a far-ranging debate over rights, liberty, and equality, the implications of which would reverberate around the world. While France would return to conservative government, first under Napoleon's dictatorship and then under a restored monarchy, the French Revolution would remain a potent symbol of the possibility of dramatic social and political change for centuries to come.

19-1 | An Englishman Describes the Suffering of the Third Estate

ARTHUR YOUNG, *Travels in France During the Years 1787, 1788, 1789* (1787–1789)

The cost of the wars waged by the French monarchs Louis XIV and Louis XV fell heavily upon the poorest people, who also suffered severe penalties from the French legal system if they

From Arthur Young, *Travels in France During the Years 1787, 1788, 1789*, ed. Betham Edwards (London: George Bell and Sons, 1909), pp. 15–16, 102–104, 313–317, 322–323, 331–332.

were found guilty of breaking any laws. One of the most compelling accounts of conditions in France right before the Revolution began comes from an English agricultural writer, Arthur Young, as he recounts his impressions of France from his tour of the country from 1787 to 1789. In his writing, he reflects both upon conditions immediately before and after the outset of the revolt. He begins by narrating a trip to the royal palace at Versailles, then a visit to Paris, and ends this excerpt by summarizing conditions before and after the Revolution.

The palace of Versailles, one of the objects to which report had given me the greatest expectation, is not in the least striking: I view it without emotion: the impression it makes is nothing. What can compensate the want of unity? From whatever point viewed, it appears an assemblage of buildings; a splendid quarter of a town, but not a fine edifice; an objection from which the garden front is not free, though by far the most beautiful. The great gallery is the finest room I have seen; the other apartments are nothing; but the pictures and statues are well known to be a capital collection. The whole palace, except the chapel, seems to be open to all the world; we pushed through an amazing crowd of all sorts of people to see the procession, many of them not very well dressed, whence it appears, that no questions are asked. But the officers at the door of the apartment in which the King dined, made a distinction, and would not permit all to enter promiscuously. . . .

Again to Versailles. In viewing the king's apartment, which he had not left a quarter of an hour, with those slight traits of disorder that showed he lived in it, it was amusing to see the blackguard figures that were walking uncontrolled about the palace, and even in his bedchamber; men whose rags betrayed them to be in the last stage of poverty, and I was the only person that stared and wondered how the devil they got there. It is impossible not to like this careless indifference and freedom from suspicion. One loves the master of the house, who would not be hurt or offended at seeing his apartment thus occupied if he returned suddenly, for if there was danger of this the intrusion would be prevented. This is certainly a feature of that *good temper* which appears to me so visible everywhere in France. . . .

Ramble through the gardens, and by the grand canal with absolute astonishment at the exaggerations of writers and travelers. There is magnificence in the quarter of the orangery,[1] but no beauty anywhere; there are some statues, good enough to wish them under cover. The extent and breadth of the canal are nothing to the eye, and it is not in such good repair as a farmer's horse pond. The menagerie is well enough, but nothing great. . . .

This great city [Paris] appears to be in many respects the most ineligible and inconvenient for the residence of a person of small fortune of any that I have seen, and vastly inferior to London. The streets are very narrow, and many of them crowded, nine tenths dirty, and all without foot pavements. Walking, which in London is so pleasant and so clean that ladies do it every day, is here a toil and a fatigue to a man, and an impossibility to a well-dressed woman.

---

[1]**orangery**: Greenhouse for growing oranges.

The coaches are numerous, and, what is much worse, there are an infinity of one-horse cabriolets, which are driven by young men of fashion and their imitators, alike fools, with such rapidity as to be real nuisances, and render the streets exceedingly dangerous, without an incessant caution. I saw a poor child run over and probably killed, and have been myself many times blackened with the mud of the kennels. This beggarly practice, of driving a one-horse booby hutch about the streets of a great capital, flows either from poverty or wretched and despicable economy; nor is it possible to speak of it with too much severity. If young noblemen at London were to drive their chaises in streets without footways, as their brethren do at Paris, they would speedily and justly get very well threshed or rolled in the kennel. This circumstance renders Paris an ineligible residence for persons, particularly families that cannot afford to keep a coach; a convenience which is as dear as at London. The fiacres, hackney coaches, are much worse than at that city; and chairs there are none, for they would be driven down in the streets. To this circumstance also it is owing that all persons of small or moderate fortune are forced to dress in black, with black stockings; the dusky hue of this in company is not so disagreeable a circumstance as being too great a distinction; too clear a line drawn in company between a man that has a good fortune and another that has not. With the pride, arrogance, and ill temper of English wealth this could not be borne; but the prevailing good humour of the French eases all such untoward circumstances. Lodgings are not half so good as at London, yet considerably dearer. . . . After the horrid fatigue of the streets, such an elevation is a delectable circumstance. . . .

On the Revolution of France

The gross infamy which attended *lettres de cachet*[2] and the Bastile,[3] during the whole reign of Louis XV made them esteemed in England, by people not well informed, as the most prominent features of the despotism of France. They were certainly carried to an access hardly credible; to the length of being sold, with blanks, to be filled up with names at the pleasure of the purchaser; who was thus able, in the gratification of private revenge, to tear a man from the bosom of his family, and bury him in a dungeon, where he would exist forgotten, and die unknown! . . .

The great mass of the people, by which I mean the lower and middle ranks, could suffer very little from such engines, and as few of them are objects of jealousy, had there been nothing else to complain of, it is not probable that they would ever have been brought to take arms. The abuses attending the levy of taxes are heavy and universal. . . . The rolls of the *taille*,[4] *capitation*,[5] *vingtièmes*,[6] and

---

[2]*lettres de cachet*: Letters that contained orders from the French king that could not be appealed, often used to imprison a person without a trial.

[3]**Bastile**: The Bastille, a fortress in Paris that served as a state prison.

[4]**taille**: Tax levied upon land that peasants had to pay, but not nobility.

[5]**capitation**: Additional tax that was levied first as a wartime supplement to revenue in 1695 but that became a permanent tax in the 1700s.

[6]**vingtièmes**: Income tax of 5 percent payable by all Frenchmen.

other taxes, were distributed among districts, parishes, and individuals, at the pleasure of the intendant, who could exempt, change, add, or diminish, at plea-sure. . . . It must be obvious, that the friends, acquaintances, and dependents of the intendant, and of all his *sub-delegués*, and the friends of these friends . . . might be favoured in taxation at the expence of their miserable neighbours; and that noblemen . . . could find little difficulty in throwing much of the weight of their taxes on others, without a similar support. . . .

The inrolments for the militia, which the *cahiers* call *an injustice without example*, were another dreadful scourge on the peasantry; and, as married men were exempted from it, occasioned in some degree that mischievous population, which brought beings into the world, in order for little else than to be starved. The *corvées*, or police of the roads, were annually the ruin of many hundreds of farmers; more than 300 were reduced to beggary in filling up one vale in Loraine: all these oppressions fell on the *tiers état* only; the nobility and clergy having been equally exempted from *tailles*, militia, and *corvées*. The penal code of finance makes one shudder at the horrors of punishment inadequate to the crime. . . .

1. Smugglers of salt, armed and assembled to the number of five, in Provence, *a fine of* 500 liv. *and nine years gallies;*[7] –in all the rest of the kingdom, *death*.

2. Smugglers armed, assembled, but in number under five, *a fine of* 300 liv. *and three years gallies*. Second offence, *death*. . . .

8. Any persons in employment (I suppose in the salt-works or the revenue), if smug-glers, *death*. And such as assist in the theft of salt in the transport, *hanged*. . . .

The *Capitaineries* were a dreadful scourge on all the occupiers of land. By this term is to be understood the paramountship of certain districts granted by the king to princes of the blood, by which they were put in possession of the prop-erty of all game, even on lands not belonging to them; and what is very singular, on manors granted long before to individuals so that the erecting of a district into a *capitainerie* was an annihilation of all manorial rights to game within it. This was a trifling business in comparison to other circumstances; for in speak-ing of the preservation of the game in these *capitaineries* it must be observed that by game must be understood whole droves of wild boars, and herds of deer not confined by any wall or pale, but wandering at pleasure over the whole country, to the destruction of crops, and to the peopling of the galleys by wretched peas-ants who presumed to kill them in order to save that food which was to support their helpless children.

. . .

It is impossible to justify the excesses of the people on their taking up arms; they were certainly guilty of cruelties; it is idle to deny the facts, for they have been proved too clearly to admit of a doubt. But is it really the people to whom we are to impute the whole? Or to their oppressors who had kept them so long

---

[7]**gallies:** A punishment by which a criminal was sentenced to row ships for long periods of time.

in a state of bondage? . . . [I]t would undoubtedly have done them credit, both as men and christians, if they had possessed their new acquired power with moderation. But let it be remembered, that the populace of no country ever use power with moderation . . . and as every government in the world knows, that violence infallibly attends power in such hands, it is doubly bound in common sense, and for common safety, so to conduct itself, that the people may not find an interest in public confusions . . . and if the government take not warning in time, it is alone answerable for all the burnings and plunderings, and devastation, and blood that follow.

. . .

The public revenue sunk, in one year, 175 millions. . . . But was it a loss to the miserable subjects who formerly paid those taxes; and who paid them by the sweat of their brows, at the expence of the bread out of their children's mouths. . . . Do they feel a loss in having 175 millions in their pockets in 1789, more than they had in 1788? . . . If tythes were to be at one stroke abolished in England, no doubt the clergy would suffer, but would not the agriculture of the kingdom, with every man dependent on it, rise with a vigour never before experienced?

READING QUESTIONS

1. What sorts of abuses does Young describe that contributed to the revolt of the French people against the monarchy, aristocracy, and clergy?

2. Whom does he blame for the Revolution, and why?

3. Does he seem to demonstrate any bias against France as an Englishman? How?

4. Given that he was not an aristocrat, do you think that Young would react the same way if a similar uprising occurred in England? Why or why not?

SOURCES IN CONVERSATION

Imagining a New France

Each phase in the French Revolution was marked by the emergence of a new vision of France's future, of the kind of nation that would embody the French people's essential principles and core qualities. During the first phase, the emphasis of reformers was on equality before the law. Drawing on Enlightenment thought, the members of the National Assembly who drafted the Declaration of the Rights of Man and of the Citizen concentrated on identifying the rights shared by all French citizens and on eliminating legal distinctions that privileged one group within French society over another. During the second revolution, leaders such as Robespierre aimed for a far more radical remaking of France, seeking to change not only France's laws, but its social and cultural values as well. Under the Directory and later under Napoleon, a conservative backlash set in, as French elites sought to reinforce traditional social and economic hierarchies, even as elements of the Revolution were incorporated into the new French state.

READ AND COMPARE

1. In what ways do the principles of the second document violate the stated rights of men in the first document?

2. How do the three documents demonstrate that, even after a revolution that upset the traditional and oppressive monarchical, aristocratic order, the notion of the "general good" of the people could be dangerous? In other words, given this evidence, is a democratically elected state really less prone to abuses of power and suppression of individual liberties?

19-2 | NATIONAL ASSEMBLY OF FRANCE, *Declaration of the Rights of Man and of the Citizen* (1789)

After the fall of the Bastille, rumors that the nobility were plotting to use foreign mercenaries to suppress the Revolution swept through the French countryside. In an effort to quell the "great fear," the National Assembly abolished feudalism and released the Declaration of the Rights of Man and of the Citizen, which laid out the basic principles upon which their government would be founded. While Enlightenment thinkers had used reason to critique social practices and customs but rarely produced actual reforms, the French revolutionaries applied the spirit of reason to practical politics. It is a measure of their success that their ideas about citizens' relationship with their government no longer seem so radical.

The representatives of the French people, organized as a National Assembly, believing that the ignorance, neglect, or contempt of the rights of man are the sole cause of public calamities and of the corruption of governments, have determined to set forth in a solemn declaration the natural, inalienable, and sacred rights of man, in order that this declaration, being constantly before all the members of the social body, shall remind them continually of their rights and duties; in order that the acts of the legislative power, as well as those of the executive power, may be compared at any moment with the objects and purposes of all political institutions and may thus be more respected; and, lastly, in order that the grievances of the citizens, based hereafter upon simple and incontestable principles, shall tend to the maintenance of the constitution and redound to the happiness of all. Therefore the National Assembly recognizes and proclaims, in

From James Harvey Robinson, ed., *Readings in European History*, vol. 2 (Boston: Ginn, 1904), pp. 409–411.

the presence and under the auspices of the Supreme Being, the following rights of man and of the citizen:

ARTICLE 1. Men are born and remain free and equal in rights. Social distinctions may be founded only upon the general good.

2. The aim of all political association is the preservation of the natural and imprescriptible rights of man. These rights are liberty, property, security, and resistance to oppression.

3. The principle of all sovereignty resides essentially in the nation. No body nor individual may exercise any authority which does not proceed directly from the nation.

4. Liberty consists in the freedom to do everything which injures no one else; hence the exercise of the natural rights of each man has no limits except those which assure to the other members of the society the enjoyment of the same rights. These limits can only be determined by law.

5. Law can only prohibit such actions as are hurtful to society. Nothing may be prevented which is not forbidden by law, and no one may be forced to do anything not provided for by law.

6. Law is the expression of the general will. Every citizen has a right to participate personally, or through his representative, in its formation. It must be the same for all, whether it protects or punishes. All citizens, being equal in the eyes of the law, are equally eligible to all dignities and to all public positions and occupations, according to their abilities, and without distinction except that of their virtues and talents.

7. No person shall be accused, arrested, or imprisoned except in the cases and according to the forms prescribed by law. Any one soliciting, transmitting, executing, or causing to be executed, any arbitrary order, shall be punished. But any citizen summoned or arrested in virtue of the law shall submit without delay, as resistance constitutes an offense.

8. The law shall provide for such punishments only as are strictly and obviously necessary, and no one shall suffer punishment except it be legally inflicted in virtue of a law passed and promulgated before the commission of the offense.

9. As all persons are held innocent until they shall have been declared guilty, if arrest shall be deemed indispensable, all harshness not essential to the securing of the prisoner's person shall be severely repressed by law.

10. No one shall be disquieted on account of his opinions, including his religious views, provided their manifestation does not disturb the public order established by law.

11. The free communication of ideas and opinions is one of the most precious of the rights of man. Every citizen may, accordingly, speak, write, and print with freedom, but shall be responsible for such abuses of this freedom as shall be defined by law.

12. The security of the rights of man and of the citizen requires public military forces. These forces are, therefore, established for the good of all and not for the personal advantage of those to whom they shall be intrusted.

13. A common contribution is essential for the maintenance of the public forces and for the cost of administration. This should be equitably distributed among all the citizens in proportion to their means.

14. All the citizens have a right to decide, either personally or by their representatives, as to the necessity of the public contribution; to grant this freely; to know to what uses it is put; and to fix the proportion, the mode of assessment and of collection and the duration of the taxes.

15. Society has the right to require of every public agent an account of his administration.

16. A society in which the observance of the law is not assured, nor the separation of powers defined, has no constitution at all.

17. Since property is an inviolable and sacred right, no one shall be deprived thereof except where public necessity, legally determined, shall clearly demand it, and then only on condition that the owner shall have been previously and equitably indemnified.

READING QUESTIONS

1. Who, according to the authors of this document, make up the "nation"? What is the basis of the government they propose?

2. In what ways is this declaration revolutionary, and in what ways does it continue the status quo?

3. What sort of balance does the declaration attempt to strike between the rights and responsibilities of citizens?

19-3 | *The Law of 22 Prairial* (1794)

The Terror took place against a backdrop of war with Austria and Prussia, as increasingly radicalized French revolutionary leaders struggled to contend with enemies, both foreign and domestic. Seeking national unity, Maximilien Robespierre (1758–1794) and his allies pursued a comprehensive program of republican reforms, which they argued were necessary for the full expression of the general will. Anyone who was perceived as an obstacle to the implementation of that program was, by definition, an enemy of the French people. The Law of 22 Prairial, promulgated shortly before Robespierre's fall, concentrated power in the hands of Robespierre's select committees, at the same time that it removed the last vestiges of legal protection for those accused of political crimes. As you read it, think about how Robespierre and his allies might have justified the new law. Why might they have believed that the Law of 22 Prairial was necessary for the survival of the Revolution?

The revolutionary tribunal is established to punish the enemies of the people.

From *Histoire Socialiste de la Révolution Française* (Paris, Éditions Sociales, 1968). Translated for Marxists.org by Mitchell Abidor.

The enemies of the people are those who seek to destroy public liberty either by force or by ruse.

The enemies of the people are those who provoked the reestablishment of royalty or sought to demean or dissolve the National Convention and the revolutionary and republican government of which it is the center;

Those who betrayed the Republic in the command of forts and armies and any other military function;

Those who sought to prevent the provisioning of Paris or caused famine in the republic;

Those who assisted the projects of the enemies of France, either by favoring the freeing and the impunity granted conspirators and the aristocracy, or by corrupting the elected representatives of the people, or by abusing the principles of the Revolution, or the laws and measures of the government by false and perfidious applications of them;

Those who mislead the people or the representatives of the people in order to lead them to undertake measures contrary to the interest of liberty;

Those who seek to inspire discouragement in order to favor the undertakings of the tyrannies leagued against the Republic;

Those who spread false news in order to divide and trouble the people;

Those who seek to lead public opinion astray and to prevent the education of the people, to deprave morals, and to corrupt the public consciousness.

. . .

The punishment for all crimes falling under the jurisdiction of the revolutionary tribunal is death.

The proof necessary to condemn the enemies of the people is any kind of document, either material or moral, either verbal or written, which would naturally obtain the assent of any fear or reasonable person. The rule governing judgement is the conscience of the jurors enlightened by the love of the Fatherland. Their goal: the triumph of the Republic and the ruin of its enemies. The procedure: the simple methods that good sense indicates to arrive at the knowledge of truth in the forms determined by the law.

If there exist either material or moral proofs independent of testimonial proofs no witnesses shall be heard until this formality appears to be necessary in order to uncover accomplices or for other major considerations of public interest.

The law grants patriotic jurors as defenders of slandered patriots. It grants none to conspirators.

READING QUESTIONS

1. What groups and individuals are defined as "enemies of the people"?

2. What powers did the law give the state to identify and punish such people?

3. How might the law's authors have justified the lack of legal protections for those accused?

4. In your opinion, does the law constitute a betrayal of the Revolution? Why or why not?

19-4 | NAPOLEON BONAPARTE, *The Napoleonic Code* (1804)

Napoleon Bonaparte (1769–1821) first gained fame as a general in France's revolutionary army, but his military achievements proved less lasting than his civil ones. When he took power in 1799, Napoleon ordered a new law code written for France, incorporating many of the National Assembly's 1789 reforms. Finished in 1804, the new civil code was easily read and understood by the average citizen. While it enshrined greater legal equality for men than had prevailed prior to 1789, it was, nonetheless, a socially conservative document. Nowhere is this more apparent than in the code's treatment of women. As had been the case under the monarchy, the new law code was predicated on a vision of politics and society centered on the authority of fathers and husbands. As you read this excerpt from the code, pay particular attention to the way it differentiates between the legal status of men and women.

Preliminary Title: Of the Publication, Effect, and Application of the Laws in General

1. The laws are executory throughout the whole French territory, by virtue of the promulgation thereof made by the First Consul. They shall be executed in every part of the Republic, from the moment at which their promulgation can have been known. The promulgation made by the First Consul shall be taken to be known in the department which shall be the seat of government, one day after the promulgation; and in each of the other departments, after the expiration of the same interval augmented by one day for every ten myriameters[1] (about twenty ancient leagues[2]) between the town in which the promulgation shall have been made, and the chief place of each department.

2. The law ordains for the future only; it has no retrospective operation.

3. The laws of police and public security bind all the inhabitants of the territory. Immovable property, although in the possession of foreigners, is governed by the French law. The laws relating to the condition and privileges of persons govern Frenchmen, although residing in a foreign country. . . .

6. Private agreements must not contravene the laws which concern public order and good morals.

Book I: Of Persons

Title I: Of the Enjoyment and Privation of Civil Rights

1. The exercise of civil rights is independent of the quality of citizen, which is only acquired and preserved conformably to the constitutional law. . . .

8. Every Frenchman shall enjoy civil rights.

From E. A. Arnold, ed. and trans., *A Documentary Survey of Napoleonic France* (Lanham, Md.: University Press of America, 1993), pp. 151–164. Reprinted by permission of Rowman & Littlefield.

[1]**myriameters**: Ten thousand meters, or ten kilometers. One of the Revolution's accomplishments was to replace the many local systems of measurement in France with a unified, easy-to-use metric system.

[2]**leagues**: Roman leagues; about two kilometers. The Roman Empire's systems of measurement survived long after its political structure crumbled.

Chapter VI: Of the Respective Rights and Duties of Married Persons

212. Married persons owe to each other fidelity, succor, assistance.

213. The husband owes protection to his wife, the wife obedience to her husband.

214. The wife is obliged to live with her husband, and to follow him to every place where he may judge it convenient to reside: the husband is obliged to receive her, and to furnish her with every necessity for the wants of life, according to his means and station.

215. The wife cannot plead in her own name, without the authority of her husband, even though she should be a public trader, or non-communicant, or separate in property.

216. The authority of the husband is not necessary when the wife is prosecuted in a criminal manner, or relating to police.

217. A wife, although noncommunicant or separate in property, cannot give, pledge, or acquire by free or chargeable title, without the concurrence of her husband in the act, or his consent in writing.

218. If the husband refuses to authorize his wife to plead in her own name, the judge may give her authority.

219. If the husband refuses to authorize his wife to pass an act, the wife may cause her husband to be cited directly before the court of the first instance, of the circle of their common domicil[e], which may give or refuse its authority, after the husband shall have been heard, or duly summoned before the chamber of council.

220. The wife, if she is a public trader, may, without the authority of her husband, bind herself for that which concerns her trade; and in the said case she binds also her husband, if there be a community between them. She is not reputed a public trader if she merely retails goods in her husband's trade, but only when she carries on a separate business.

221. When the husband is subjected to a condemnation, carrying with it an afflictive or infamous punishment, although it may have been pronounced merely for contumacy,[3] the wife, though of age, cannot, during the continuance of such punishment, plead in her own name or contract, until after authority given by the judge, who may in such case give his authority without hearing or summoning the husband. . . .

226. The wife may make a will without the authority of her husband. . . .

Title VI: Of Divorce

Section II: Of the Provisional Measures to Which the Petition for Cause Determinate May Give Rise

267. The provisional management of the children shall rest with the husband, petitioner, or defendant, in the suit for divorce, unless it be otherwise ordered for the greater advantage of the children, on petition of either the mother, or the family, or the government commissioner. . . .

---

[3]**contumacy**: Refusal to obey legal authority.

271. Every obligation contracted by the husband at the expense of the community, every alienation made by him of immovable property dependent upon it, subsequent to the date of the order mentioned in article 238, shall be declared void, if proof be given, moreover, that it has been made or contracted in fraud of the rights of the wife. . . .

Title IX: Of Paternal Power

375. A father who shall have cause of grievous dissatisfaction at the conduct of a child, shall have the following means of correction.

376. If the child has not commenced his sixteenth year, the father may cause him to be confined for a period which shall not exceed one month; and to this effect the president of the court of the circle shall be bound, on his petition, to deliver an order of arrest.

377. From the age of sixteen years commenced to the majority or emancipation, the father is only empowered to require the confinement of his child during six months at the most; he shall apply to the president of the aforesaid court, who, after having conferred thereon with the commissioner of government, shall deliver an order of arrest or refuse the same, and may in the first case abridge the time of confinement required by the father. . . .

379. The father is always at liberty to abridge the duration of the confinement by him ordered or required. If the child after his liberation fall into new irregularities, his confinement may be ordered anew, according to the manner prescribed in the preceding articles. . . .

Book III: Modes of Acquiring Property

Title I: Of Successions

818. The husband may, without the concurrence of his wife, claim a distribution of objects movable or immovable fallen to her and which come into community; with respect to objects which do not come into community, the husband cannot claim the distribution thereof without the concurrence of his wife; he can only demand a provisional distribution in case he has a right to the enjoyment of her property. The co-heirs of the wife cannot claim final distribution without suing the husband and his wife. . . .

Title II: Donations and Wills

905. A married woman cannot make donation during life without the assistance or the special consent of her husband, or without being thereto authorized by the law, conformably to what is prescribed by articles 217 and 219, under the title "Of Marriage." She shall not need either the consent of her husband, or the authorization of the law, in order to dispose by will. . . .

Chapter IV: Of Donations During Life

Section II: Of the Administration of the Community, and of the Effect of the Acts of Either of the Married Parties Relating to the Conjugal Union

1421. The husband alone administers the property of the community. He may sell it, alienate and pledge it without the concurrence of his wife. . . .

1424. Fines incurred by the husband for a crime not importing civil death, may be sued for out of the property of the community, saving the compensation due to the wife; such as are incurred by the wife cannot be put in execution except out of her bare property in her personal goods, so long as the community continues. . . .

1427. The wife cannot bind herself nor engage the property of the community, even to free her husband from prison, or for the establishment of their children in case of her husband's absence, until she shall have been thereto authorized by the law.

1428. The husband has the management of all the personal property of the wife. He may prosecute alone all possessory actions and those relating to movables, which belong to his wife. He cannot alienate the personal immovables of his wife without her consent. He is responsible for all waste in the personal goods of his wife, occasioned by the neglect of conservatory acts.

READING QUESTIONS

1. What groups in French society would benefit most from these laws?

2. What about these laws seems radical, and what seems rooted in tradition?

3. What legal and economic rights do women enjoy under the code?

4. What similarities are there in the way the code treats women and children? What significance should we attach to these similarities?

19-5 | Challenging the Limits of Equality

MARY WOLLSTONECRAFT, *A Vindication of the Rights of Woman* (1792)

The French Constitution of 1791, drafted by the same National Assembly that passed the Declaration of the Rights of Man, confined full citizenship to a limited number of property-holding men. While many Enlightenment ideals that underlay the Revolution had developed in salons overseen by upper-class women, prevailing thought held that women lacked the intellectual and emotional capacity to participate in politics. The English radical Mary Wollstonecraft disagreed. Her response was *A Vindication of the Rights of Woman*, written to French diplomat Charles Talleyrand, who had recently advocated a very limited and almost exclusively domestic education for women.

My own sex, I hope, will excuse me, if I treat them like rational creatures, instead of flattering their fascinating graces, and viewing them as if they were in a state

From Mary Wollstonecraft, *A Vindication of the Rights of Woman*, ed. Carol H. Poston (New York: W. W. Norton, 1975), pp. 9–10, 27, 31.

of perpetual childhood, unable to stand alone. I earnestly wish to point out in what true dignity and human happiness consists — I wish to persuade women to endeavor to acquire strength, both of mind and body, and to convince them that the soft phrases, susceptibility of heart, delicacy of sentiment, and refinement of taste, are almost synonymous with epithets of weakness, and that those beings who are only the objects of pity will soon become objects of contempt.

Dismissing those soft pretty feminine phrases, which the men condescendingly use to soften our slavish dependence, and despising that weak elegancy of mind, exquisite sensibility, and sweet docility of manners, supposed to be the sexual characteristics of the weaker vessel, I wish to show that elegance is inferior to virtue, that the first object of laudable ambition is to obtain a character as a human being, regardless of the distinction of sex.
. . .

Youth is the season for love in both sexes; but in those days of thoughtless enjoyment provision should be made for the more important years of life, when reflection takes place of sensation. The woman who has only been taught to please will soon find that her charms are oblique sunbeams and that they cannot have much effect on her husband's heart when they are seen every day, when the summer is passed and gone. Will she then have sufficient native energy to look into herself for comfort, and cultivate her dormant faculties? or, is it not more rational to expect that she will try to please other men?

Why must the female mind be tainted by coquettish arts to gratify the sensualist and prevent love from subsiding into friendship, or compassionate tenderness, when there are not qualities on which friendship can be built? Let the honest heart show itself, and reason teach passion to submit to necessity; or, let the dignified pursuit of virtue and knowledge raise the mind above those emotions. . . .

If then women are not a swarm of ephemeron triflers, why should they be kept in ignorance under the specious name of innocence? . . . As to the argument respecting the subjection in which the sex has ever been held, it retorts on man. The many have always been enthralled by the few; and monsters, who scarcely have shown any discernment of human excellence, have tyrannized over thousands of their fellow-creatures. . . . China is not the only country where a living man has been made a God. Men have submitted to superior strength to enjoy with impunity the pleasure of the moment; women have only done the same, and therefore till it is proved that the courtier, who servilely resigns the birthright of a man, is not a moral agent, it cannot be demonstrated that woman is essentially inferior to man because she has always been subjugated.

READING QUESTIONS

1. How might a man and a woman read this document differently? Is it addressed to men or women?

2. In what ways does Wollstonecraft accept that women are inferior? Does this weaken or strengthen her argument?

3. Based on Wollstonecraft's argument, what can you discern about a stereotypical woman of the time? How does she behave? How do men respond to her?

4. What connection might Wollstonecraft have made between education and fitness for the exercise of political rights? How might her vision of female education have differed from that promoted by Talleyrand?

19-6 | The Revolution in the French Colonies

FRANÇOIS DOMINIQUE TOUSSAINT L'OUVERTURE, *A Black Revolutionary Leader in Haiti* (1797)

The impact of the French Revolution and the Napoleonic Wars was not limited to Europe. Societies across the Americas were shaken by events in France. In the United States, support or opposition to the Revolution was a key line of division between emerging political parties. In South America, independence movements flared up in colony after colony. And, in the sugar islands of the Caribbean, oppressed slaves rose in revolt, determined to have their full share in the rights of men. In 1792, after French colonial rulers arrested the leader of a Caribbean slave delegation in Paris, freed slave Toussaint Breda (who later changed his name to "L'Ouverture," as he had "opened" the way to liberty) emerged as the leader of a massive revolt on the French island of Saint-Domingue (known since gaining its independence as Haiti). In the letter included here, L'Ouverture appealed to French leaders to reject calls by the colonial planter class for re-establishment of slavery in the French colonies and to support the cause of liberty.

The impolitic and incendiary discourse of Vaublanc[1] has not affected the blacks nearly so much as their certainty of the projects which the proprietors of San Domingo are planning: insidious declarations should not have any effect in the eyes of wise legislators who have decreed liberty for the nations. But the attempts on that liberty which the colonists propose are all the more to be feared because it is with the veil of patriotism that they cover their detestable plans. We know that they seek to impose some of them on you by illusory and specious promises, in order to see renewed in this colony its former scenes of horror. Already perfidious emissaries have stepped in among us to ferment the destructive leaven prepared by the hands of liberticides [i.e., murderers of liberty]. But they will not succeed. I swear it by all that liberty holds most sacred. My attachment to France, my knowledge of the blacks, make it my duty not to leave you ignorant either of the crimes which they meditate or the oath that we renew, to bury ourselves under the ruins of a country revived by liberty rather than suffer the return of slavery.

It is for you, Citizens Directors, to turn from over our heads the storm which the eternal enemies of our liberty are preparing in the shades of silence. It is for you to enlighten the legislature, it is for you to prevent the enemies of the present

---

From François Dominique Toussaint L'Ouverture, Letter, in *The Black Jacobins*, 2nd Edition, edited by C. L. R. James. Reproduced by permission of Curtis Brown Group Ltd., London on behalf of the Estate of C L R James. Copyright © C L R James, 1938.

[1]**Vaublanc:** The count of Vaublanc was a royalist and proponent of freeing the slaves and giving them citizenship, in opposition to L'Ouverture's more moderate views.

system from spreading themselves on our unfortunate shores to sully it with new crimes. Do not allow our brothers, our friends, to be sacrificed to men who wish to reign over the ruins of the human species. But no, your wisdom will enable you to avoid the dangerous snares which our common enemies hold out for you. . . .

I send you with this letter a declaration which will acquaint you with the unity that exists between the proprietors of San Domingo who are in France, those in the United States, and those who serve under the English banner. You will see there a resolution, unequivocal and carefully constructed, for the restoration of slavery; you will see there that their determination to succeed has led them to envelop themselves in the mantle of liberty in order to strike it more deadly blows. You will see that they are counting heavily on my complacency in lending myself to their perfidious views by my fear for my children. It is not astonishing that these men who sacrifice their country to their interests are unable to conceive how many sacrifices a true love of country can support in a better father than they, since I unhesitatingly base the happiness of my children on that of my country, which they and they alone wish to destroy.

I shall never hesitate between the safety of San Domingo and my personal happiness; but I have nothing to fear. It is to the solicitude of the French Government that I have confided my children. . . . I would tremble with horror if it was into the hands of the colonists that I had sent them as hostages; but even if it were so, let them know that in punishing them for the fidelity of their father, they would only add one degree more to their barbarism, without any hope of ever making me fail in my duty. . . . Blind as they are! They cannot see how this odious conduct on their part can become the signal of new disasters and irreparable misfortunes, and that far from making them regain what in their eyes liberty for all has made them lose, they expose themselves to a total ruin and the colony to its inevitable destruction. Do they think that men who have been able to enjoy the blessing of liberty will calmly see it snatched away? They supported their chains only so long as they did not know any condition of life more happy than that of slavery. But to-day when they have left it, if they had a thousand lives they would sacrifice them all rather than be forced into slavery again. But no, the same hand which has broken our chains will not enslave us anew. France will not revoke her principles, she will not withdraw from us the greatest of her benefits. She will protect us against all our enemies; she will not permit her sublime morality to be perverted, those principles which do her most honor to be destroyed, her most beautiful achievement to be degraded, and her Decree of 16 Pluviose[2] which so honors humanity to be revoked. But if, to re-establish slavery in San Domingo, this was done, then I declare to you it would be to attempt the impossible: we have known how to face dangers to obtain our liberty, we shall know how to brave death to maintain it.

---

[2]**Decree of 16 Pluviose**: In 1793, French revolutionaries reorganized their calendar to remove the Christian elements; the event marking year one moved from the birth of Jesus to the adoption of the French constitution in 1792. The fifth month, roughly corresponding to April, known for its rains, became Pluviose, which loosely translates as "rainy." The specific decree to which L'Ouverture refers abolished slavery in French colonies in April 1794.

This, Citizens Directors, is the morale of the people of San Domingo, those are the principles that they transmit to you by me.

My own you know. It is sufficient to renew, my hand in yours, the oath that I have made, to cease to live before gratitude dies in my heart, before I cease to be faithful to France and to my duty, before the god of liberty is profaned and sullied by the liberticides, before they can snatch from my hands that sword, those arms, which France confided to me for the defense of its rights and those of humanity, for the triumph of liberty and equality.

READING QUESTIONS

1. Who is the intended audience of this document? What is L'Ouverture trying to convince them to do?

2. What reasons might persuade the French to reimpose slavery in Haiti, and what reasons might they have for defending its abolition?

3. In what way is L'Ouverture seeking to find common ground with the French? Why?

■ COMPARATIVE AND DISCUSSION QUESTIONS ■

1. In what ways did the points expressed in Young's travel account find their way into the Declaration of the Rights of Man? Were any points left out of the declaration? If so, why do you suppose they were excluded?

2. Compare and contrast the Declaration of the Rights of Man and of the Citizen, the Law of 22 Prairial, and the Napoleonic Code. What light do they shed on the evolution of French politics between 1789 and 1804?

3. What similarities exist between the arguments of Mary Wollstonecraft and Toussaint L'Ouverture for their groups' inclusion in the new political order? What differences can you discern?

4. Based on the Declaration of the Rights of Man, Mary Wollstonecraft's argument, and Toussaint L'Ouverture's letter, what were the limits of liberty and equality promised by the Revolution?

20

The Revolution in Energy and Industry

ca. 1780–1850

The term *Industrial Revolution* was coined almost 150 years ago to describe the technological, economic, and social transformations that took place first in Great Britain and then elsewhere in Europe and the United States. Between 1780 and 1850, traditional English society, in which the overwhelming majority of the population worked in agriculture, gave way to an industrial society wherein the majority lived in urban settings and worked in the manufacturing or service sectors. These changes gave rise to similarly momentous alterations in patterns of work, social hierarchies, material culture, and the regional and global balance of power. In the short run, working and living conditions for ordinary Europeans worsened. In the long run, industrialization led to a vast expansion in the economy, providing jobs and goods for a rapidly growing population and fueling the West's global pre-eminence in the nineteenth and twentieth centuries. Historians still debate whether "revolution" is an apt description for changes that took place over many decades, but there is little doubt that the consequences of those changes were profound.

20-1 | Predicting a Population Catastrophe

THOMAS MALTHUS, *An Essay on the Principle of Population* (1798)

Thomas Malthus (1766–1834) was an Anglican clergyman by training but was deeply interested in demography, or the study of human population. His 1798 book *An Essay on the Principle of Population* is widely regarded as the foundational text on the subject, and his

---

From Thomas Malthus, *An Essay on the Principle of Population* (London: J. Johnson, 1798), pp. 18–38.

argument—that, unchecked by birth control, human populations increase faster than their food supplies—remains relevant today, as manufacturers, farmers, politicians, and scientists alike debate the earth's ability to sustain its population indefinitely.

I said that population, when unchecked, increased in a geometrical ratio, and subsistence for man in an arithmetical ratio.

Let us examine whether this position be just. I think it will be allowed, that no state has hitherto existed (at least that we have any account of) where the manners were so pure and simple, and the means of subsistence so abundant, that no check whatever has existed to early marriages, among the lower classes, from a fear of not providing well for their families, or among the higher classes, from a fear of lowering their condition in life. Consequently in no state that we have yet known has the power of population been left to exert itself with perfect freedom.

Whether the law of marriage be instituted or not, the dictate of nature and virtue seems to be an early attachment to one woman. Supposing a liberty of changing in the case of an unfortunate choice, this liberty would not affect population till it arose to a height greatly vicious; and we are now supposing the existence of a society where vice is scarcely known. In a state therefore of great equality and virtue, where pure and simple manners prevailed, and where the means of subsistence were so abundant that no part of the society could have any fears about providing amply for a family, the power of population being left to exert itself unchecked, the increase of the human species would evidently be much greater than any increase that has been hitherto known.

In the United States of America, where the means of subsistence have been more ample, the manners of the people more pure, and consequently the checks to early marriages fewer, than in any of the modern states of Europe, the population has been found to double itself in twenty-five years. This ratio of increase, though short of the utmost power of population, yet as the result of actual experience, we will take as our rule, and say, that population, when unchecked, goes on doubling itself every twenty-five years or increases in a geometrical ratio.

Let us now take any spot of earth, this Island for instance, and see in what ratio the subsistence it affords can be supposed to increase. We will begin with it under its present state of cultivation. If I allow that by the best possible policy, by breaking up more land and by great encouragements to agriculture, the produce of this Island may be doubled in the first twenty-five years, I think it will be allowing as much as any person can well demand.

In the next twenty-five years, it is impossible to suppose that the produce could be quadrupled. It would be contrary to all our knowledge of the qualities of land. The very utmost that we can conceive, is, that the increase in the second twenty-five years might equal the present produce. Let us then take this for our rule, though certainly far beyond the truth, and allow that, by great exertion, the whole produce of the Island might be increased every twenty-five years, by a quantity of subsistence equal to what it at present produces. The most enthusiastic speculator cannot suppose a greater increase than this. In a few centuries it would make every acre of land in the Island like a garden.

Yet this ratio of increase is evidently arithmetical. It may be fairly said, therefore, that the means of subsistence increase in an arithmetical ratio.

Let us now bring the effects of these two ratios together. The population of the Island is computed to be about seven millions, and we will suppose the present produce equal to the support of such a number. In the first twenty-five years the population would be fourteen millions, and the food being also doubled, the means of subsistence would be equal to this increase. In the next twenty-five years the population would be twenty-eight millions, and the means of subsistence only equal to the support of twenty-one millions. In the next period, the population would be fifty-six millions, and the means of subsistence just sufficient for half that number. And at the conclusion of the first century the population would be one hundred and twelve millions and the means of subsistence only equal to the support of thirty-five millions, which would leave a population of seventy-seven millions totally unprovided for.

A great emigration necessarily implies unhappiness of some kind or other in the country that is deserted. For few persons will leave their families, connections, friends, and native land, to seek a settlement in untried foreign climes, without some strong subsisting causes of uneasiness where they are, or the hope of some great advantages in the place to which they are going. But to make the argument more general and less interrupted by the partial views of emigration, let us take the whole earth, instead of one spot, and suppose that the restraints to population were universally removed. If the subsistence for man that the earth affords was to be increased every twenty-five years by a quantity equal to what the whole world at present produces, this would allow the power of production in the earth to be absolutely unlimited, and its ratio of increase much greater than we can conceive that any possible exertions of mankind could make it.

Taking the population of the world at any number, a thousand millions, for instance, the human species would increase in the ratio of — 1, 2, 4, 8, 16, 32, 64, 128, 256, 512, etc. and subsistence as — 1, 2, 3, 4, 5, 6, 7, 8, 9, 10, etc. In two centuries and a quarter, the population would be to the means of subsistence as 512 to 10: in three centuries as 4096 to 13, and in two thousand years the difference would be almost incalculable, though the produce in that time would have increased to an immense extent.

No limits whatever are placed to the productions of the earth; they may increase for ever and be greater than any assignable quantity. Yet still the power of population being a power of a superior order, the increase of the human species can only be kept commensurate to the increase of the means of subsistence by the constant operation of the strong law of necessity acting as a check upon the greater power. The effects of this check remain now to be considered.

Among plants and animals the view of the subject is simple. They are all impelled by a powerful instinct to the increase of their species, and this instinct is interrupted by no reasoning or doubts about providing for their offspring. Wherever therefore there is liberty, the power of increase is exerted, and the superabundant effects are repressed afterwards by want of room and nourishment, which is common to animals and plants, and among animals by becoming the prey of others.

The effects of this check on man are more complicated. Impelled to the increase of his species by an equally powerful instinct, reason interrupts his career and asks him whether he may not bring beings into the world for whom he cannot provide the means of subsistence. In a state of equality, this would be the simple question. In the present state of society, other considerations occur. Will he not lower his rank in life? Will he not subject himself to greater difficulties than he at present feels? Will he not be obliged to labor harder? And if he has a large family, will his utmost exertions enable him to support them? May he not see his offspring in rags and misery, and clamoring for bread that he cannot give them? And may he not be reduced to the grating necessity of forfeiting his independence, and of being obliged to the sparing hand of charity for support?

These considerations are calculated to prevent, and certainly do prevent, a very great number in all civilized nations from pursuing the dictate of nature in an early attachment to one woman. And this restraint almost necessarily, though not absolutely so, produces vice. Yet in all societies, even those that are most vicious, the tendency to a virtuous attachment is so strong that there is a constant effort towards an increase of population. This constant effort as constantly tends to subject the lower classes of the society to distress and to prevent any great permanent amelioration of their condition.

The way in which these effects are produced seems to be this. We will suppose the means of subsistence in any country just equal to the easy support of its inhabitants. The constant effort towards population, which is found to act even in the most vicious societies, increases the number of people before the means of subsistence are increased. The food therefore which before supported seven millions must now be divided among seven millions and a half or eight millions. The poor consequently must live much worse, and many of them be reduced to severe distress. The number of laborers also being above the proportion of the work in the market, the price of labor must tend toward a decrease, while the price of provisions would at the same time tend to rise. The laborer therefore must work harder to earn the same as he did before. During this season of distress, the discouragements to marriage, and the difficulty of rearing a family are so great that population is at a stand. In the mean time the cheapness of labor, the plenty of laborers, and the necessity of an increased industry amongst them, encourage cultivators to employ more labor upon their land, to turn up fresh soil, and to manure and improve more completely what is already in tillage, till ultimately the means of subsistence become in the same proportion to the population as at the period from which we set out. The situation of the laborer being then again tolerably comfortable, the restraints to population are in some degree loosened, and the same retrograde and progressive movements with respect to happiness are repeated. . . .

Many reasons occur why this oscillation has been less obvious, and less decidedly confirmed by experience, than might naturally be expected. One principal reason is that the histories of mankind that we possess are histories only of the higher classes. We have but few accounts that can be depended upon of the manners and customs of that part of mankind where these retrograde and progressive movements chiefly take place. A satisfactory history of this kind, on one people, and of one period, would require the constant and minute attention of an observing mind during a long life. Some of the objects of inquiry would be, in what proportion to the number of adults was the number of marriages, to what extent vicious customs prevailed in consequence of the restraints upon matrimony, what was the comparative mortality among the children of the most distressed part of the community and those who lived rather more at their ease, what were the variations in the real price of labor, and what were the observable differences in the state of the lower classes of society with respect to ease and happiness, at different times during a certain period.

Such a history would tend greatly to elucidate the manner in which the constant check upon population acts and would probably prove the existence of the retrograde and progressive movements that have been mentioned, though the times of their vibrations must necessarily be rendered irregular from the operation of many interrupting causes, such as the introduction or failure of certain manufactures, a greater or less prevalent spirit of agricultural enterprise, years of plenty, or years of scarcity, wars and pestilence, poor laws, the invention of processes for shortening labor without the proportional extension of the market for the commodity, and, particularly, the difference between the nominal and real price of labor, a circumstance which has perhaps more than any other contributed to conceal this oscillation from common view. . . .

But the want of freedom in the market of labor, which occurs more or less in all communities, either from parish laws, or the more general cause of the facility of combination among the rich, and its difficulty among the poor, operates to prevent the price of labor from rising at the natural period, and keeps it down some time longer; perhaps till a year of scarcity, when the clamor is too loud and the necessity too apparent to be resisted. The true cause of the advance in the price of labor is thus concealed, and the rich affect to grant it as an act of compassion and favor to the poor, in consideration of a year of scarcity, and, when plenty returns, indulge themselves in the most unreasonable of all complaints, that the price does not again fall, when a little rejection would show them that it must have risen long before but from an unjust conspiracy of their own. But though the rich by unfair combinations contribute frequently to prolong a season of distress among the poor, yet no possible form of society could prevent the almost constant action of misery upon a great part of mankind, if in a state of inequality, and upon all, if all were equal.

The theory on which the truth of this position depends appears to me so extremely clear that I feel at a loss to conjecture what part of it can be denied. That population cannot increase without the means of subsistence is a proposition so evident that it needs no illustration. That population does invariably increase where there are the means of subsistence, the history of every people that have ever existed will abundantly prove. And that the superior power of population cannot be checked without producing misery or vice, the ample portion of these too bitter ingredients in the cup of human life and the continuance of the physical causes that seem to have produced them bear too convincing a testimony.

READING QUESTIONS

1. How, according to Malthus, do wages and the availability of work influence population growth?

2. What do Malthus's arguments, especially those on the means of limiting human population growth voluntarily, suggest about views on gender relations? What does he mean in arguing that the considerations that lead men not to marry at an early age "almost necessarily, though not absolutely so, [produce] vice"?

3. Why did Malthus's predictions fail to come true in Europe and the United States? What factors did he fail to take into account?

SOURCES IN CONVERSATION

Life as an Industrial Worker at Midcentury

By the mid-nineteenth century, industrialization had taken a firm hold in Britain, the northern United States, and much of northern Europe. Britain was still the most industrialized nation on earth, but Germany and the United States were rapidly gaining ground. As workers and their families poured into industrial centers in search of work, conditions in industrial cities grew grim. Unplanned and unregulated growth combined with industrial pollution to produce crowded and unhealthy working-class neighborhoods. For individuals who were new to factory work, almost as challenging as the industrial urban environment was the adjustment to industrial labor itself. Men, women, and children who were accustomed to the informality and relative slow pace of the rural economy and the artisanal shop found themselves subjected to rigid industrial discipline. In time, urban conditions would improve and industrial workers would fight for, and win, greater control of their working lives. In the 1830s and 1840s, however, such gains were far in the future.

READ AND COMPARE

1. What do these three documents reveal about social-class relationships in the mid-nineteenth century in Europe? How did middle-class people and wealthy factory owners feel about workers, and how do you suppose the workers felt about their "social betters"?

2. How are the two social environments (the "old town" of Manchester versus the factory in Berlin) different, and what accounts for the difference between them?

20-2 | FRIEDRICH ENGELS, *The Condition of the Working Class in England in 1844* (1844)

Friedrich Engels (1820–1895) is best known today as Karl Marx's collaborator and coauthor of *The Communist Manifesto* (1848). He was also a social scientist in his own right, and *The Condition of the Working Class in England in 1844* was a pioneering sociological study. His account of conditions in Manchester's working-class neighborhoods was based on extensive firsthand experience acquired while overseeing his family's cotton textile interests in the city.

Manchester lies at the foot of the southern slope of a range of hills, which stretch hither from Oldham . . . and contains about four hundred thousand inhabitants, rather more than less. The town itself is peculiarly built, so that a person may live in it for years, and go in and out daily without coming into contact with a working-people's quarter or even with workers, that is, so long as he confines himself to his business or to pleasure walks. This arises chiefly from the fact, that by unconscious tacit agreement, as well as with outspoken conscious determination, the working-people's quarters are sharply separated from the sections of the city reserved for the middle-class. . . .

I may mention just here that the mills almost all adjoin the rivers or the different canals that ramify throughout the city, before I proceed at once to describe the laboring quarters. First of all, there is the old town of Manchester, which lies between the northern boundary of the commercial district and the Irk. Here the streets, even the better ones, are narrow and winding, as Todd Street, Long Millgate, Withy Grove, and Shude Hill, the houses dirty, old, and tumble-down, and the construction of the side streets utterly horrible. Going from the Old Church to Long Millgate, the stroller has at once a row of old-fashioned houses at the right, of which not one has kept its original level; these are remnants of the old pre-manufacturing Manchester, whose former inhabitants have removed with their descendants into better built districts, and have left the houses, which were not good enough for them, to a population strongly mixed with Irish blood. Here one is in an almost undisguised working-men's quarter, for even the shops and beer houses hardly take the trouble to exhibit a trifling degree of cleanliness. But all this is nothing in comparison with the courts and lanes which lie behind, to which access can be gained only through covered passages, in which no two human beings can pass at the same time. Of the irregular cramming together of dwellings in ways which defy all rational plan, of the tangle in which they are crowded literally one upon the other, it is impossible to convey an idea. And it is not the buildings surviving from the old times of Manchester which are to blame for this; the confusion has only recently reached its height when every scrap of space left by the old

From Friedrich Engels, *The Condition of the Working-Class in England in 1844* (London: Swan Sonnenschein & Co., 1892), pp. 45, 48–53.

way of building has been filled up and patched over until not a foot of land is left to be further occupied.

The south bank of the Irk is here very steep and between fifteen and thirty feet high. On this declivitous hillside there are planted three rows of houses, of which the lowest rise directly out of the river, while the front walls of the highest stand on the crest of the hill in Long Millgate. Among them are mills on the river, in short, the method of construction is as crowded and disorderly here as in the lower part of Long Millgate. Right and left a multitude of covered passages lead from the main street into numerous courts, and he who turns in thither gets into a filth and disgusting grime, the equal of which is not to be found—especially in the courts which lead down to the Irk, and which contain unqualifiedly the most horrible dwellings which I have yet beheld. In one of these courts there stands directly at the entrance, at the end of the covered passage, a privy without a door, so dirty that the inhabitants can pass into and out of the court only by passing through foul pools of stagnant urine and excrement. This is the first court on the Irk above Ducie Bridge—in case any one should care to look into it. Below it on the river there are several tanneries which fill the whole neighborhood with the stench of animal putrefaction [i.e., rotting carcasses]. Below Ducie Bridge the only entrance to most of the houses is by means of narrow, dirty stairs and over heaps of refuse and filth. The first court below Ducie Bridge, known as Allen's Court, was in such a state at the time of the cholera[1] that the sanitary police ordered it evacuated, swept, and disinfected with chloride of lime. Dr. Kay[2] gives a terrible description of the state of this court at that time. Since then, it seems to have been partially torn away and rebuilt; at least looking down from Ducie Bridge, the passer-by sees several ruined walls and heaps of debris with some newer houses. The view from this bridge, mercifully concealed from mortals of small stature by a parapet as high as a man, is characteristic for the whole district. At the bottom flows, or rather stagnates, the Irk, a narrow, coal-black, foul-smelling stream, full of debris and refuse, which it deposits on the shallower right bank.

In dry weather, a long string of the most disgusting, blackish-green, slime pools are left standing on this bank, from the depths of which bubbles of miasmatic gas constantly arise and give forth a stench unendurable even on the bridge forty or fifty feet above the surface of the stream. But besides this, the stream itself is checked every few paces by high weirs, behind which slime and refuse accumulate and rot in thick masses. Above the bridge are tanneries, bone mills, and gasworks, from which all drains and refuse find their way into the Irk, which receives further the contents of all the neighboring sewers and privies. It may be easily imagined, therefore, what sort of residue the stream deposits. Below the bridge you look upon the piles of debris, the refuse, filth, and offal from the courts on the steep left bank; here each house is packed close

---

[1]**at the time of the cholera**: Cholera, a disease caused by the contamination of water supplies with human excrement, first appeared in Britain in 1831.

[2]**Dr. Kay**: Dr. James Kay, later Sir James Kay-Shuttlesworth (1804–1877), author of *The Moral and Physical Condition of the Working-Class Employed in the Cotton Manufacture in Manchester* (1832).

behind its neighbor and a piece of each is visible, all black, smoky, crumbling, ancient, with broken panes and window frames. The background is furnished by old barrack-like factory buildings. On the lower right bank stands a long row of houses and mills; the second house being a ruin without a roof, piled with debris; the third stands so low that the lowest floor is uninhabitable, and therefore without windows or doors. Here the background embraces the pauper burial-ground, the station of the Liverpool and Leeds railway, and, in the rear of this, the Workhouse, the "Poor-Law Bastille"[3] of Manchester, which, like a citadel, looks threateningly down from behind its high walls and parapets on the hilltop, upon the working-people's quarter below.

Above Ducie Bridge, the left bank grows more flat and the right bank steeper, but the condition of the dwellings on both banks grows worse rather than better. He who turns to the left here from the main street, Long Millgate, is lost; he wanders from one court to another, turns countless corners, passes nothing but narrow, filthy nooks and alleys, until after a few minutes he has lost all clue, and knows not whither to turn. Everywhere half or wholly ruined buildings, some of them actually uninhabited, which means a great deal here; rarely a wooden or stone floor to be seen in the houses, almost uniformly broken, ill-fitting windows and doors, and a state of filth! Everywhere heaps of debris, refuse, and offal; standing pools for gutters, and a stench which alone would make it impossible for a human being in any degree civilized to live in such a district. The newly-built extension of the Leeds railway, which crosses the Irk here, has swept away some of these courts and lanes, laying others completely open to view. Immediately under the railway bridge there stands a court, the filth and horrors of which surpass all the others by far, just because it was hitherto so shut off, so secluded that the way to it could not be found without a good deal of trouble. I should never have discovered it myself, without the breaks made by the railway, though I thought I knew this whole region thoroughly. Passing along a rough bank, among stakes and washing-lines, one penetrates into this chaos of small one-storied, one-roomed huts, in most of which there is no artificial floor; kitchen, living and sleeping-room all in one. In such a hole, scarcely five feet long by six broad, I found two beds — and such bedsteads and beds! — which, with a staircase and chimney-place, exactly filled the room. In several others I found absolutely nothing, while the door stood open, and the inhabitants leaned against it. Everywhere before the doors refuse and offal; that any sort of pavement lay underneath could not be seen but only felt, here and there, with the feet. This whole collection of cattle-sheds for human beings was surrounded on two sides by houses and a factory, and on the third by the river, and besides the narrow stair up the bank, a narrow doorway alone led out into another almost equally ill-built, ill-kept labyrinth of dwellings. . . .

---

[3] **Poor-Law Bastille:** The Poor Law legislation passed in 1834 mandated that all able-bodied recipients of public charity forfeit any property they possessed and live and labor in workhouses.

If we leave the Irk and penetrate once more on the opposite side from Long Millgate into the midst of the working-men's dwellings, we shall come into a somewhat newer quarter, which stretches from St. Michael's Church to Withy Grove and Shude Hill. Here there is somewhat better order. In place of the chaos of buildings, we find at least long straight lanes and alleys or courts, built according to a plan and usually square. But if, in the former case, every house was built according to caprice, here each lane and court is so built, without reference to the situation of the adjoining ones. . . .

Here, as in most of the working-men's quarters of Manchester, the pork-raisers rent the courts and build pig-pens in them. In almost every court one or even several such pens may be found, into which the inhabitants of the court throw all refuse and offal, whence the swine grow fat; and the atmosphere, confined on all four sides, is utterly corrupted by putrefying animal and vegetable substances. . . .

Such is the Old Town of Manchester, and on re-reading my description, I am forced to admit that instead of being exaggerated, it is far from black enough to convey a true impression of the filth, ruin, and uninhabitableness, the defiance of all considerations of cleanliness, ventilation, and health which characterize the construction of this single district, containing at least twenty to thirty thousand inhabitants. And such a district exists in the heart of the second city of England, the first manufacturing city of the world. If any one wishes to see in how little space a human being can move, how little air—and *such* air!—he can breathe, how little of civilization he may share and yet live, it is only necessary to travel hither. True, this is the *Old* Town, and the people of Manchester emphasize the fact whenever any one mentions to them the frightful condition of this Hell upon Earth; but what does that prove? Everything which here arouses horror and indignation is of recent origin, belongs to the *industrial epoch.*

READING QUESTIONS

1. How was it possible, as Engels claimed, that middle-class residents of Manchester's suburbs could pass through the working-class districts closer to the city center on their way to and from work, "without coming into contact with a working-people's quarter or even with workers"? What does this claim suggest about economic segregation in the city?

2. "Of the irregular cramming together of dwellings in ways which defy all rational plan, of the tangle in which they are crowded literally one upon the other, it is impossible to convey an idea," Engels remarked of one district. Why might Manchester have developed in this way?

3. What might his remark about the Long Millgate district containing a "population strongly mixed with Irish blood" suggest about Engels's racial attitudes?

20-3 | *Factory Rules in Berlin* (1844)

The rigid rules and regulations of the factory floor offered a stark contrast to the chaos and squalor of working-class neighborhoods in industrial cities. Determined to maximize efficiency, and with it profits, factory owners imposed strict rules on their workers. This 1844 set of rules for a Berlin factory provides an example of industrial discipline. As you read the rules, ask yourself why factory owners might have thought them to be necessary. What light do they shed on the power of owners over workers in mid-nineteenth-century Europe?

In every large works, and in the co-ordination of any large number of workmen, good order and harmony must be looked upon as the fundamentals of success, and therefore the following rules shall be strictly observed.

Every man employed in the concern named below shall receive a copy of these rules, so that no one can plead ignorance. Its acceptance shall be deemed to mean consent to submit to its regulations.

(1) The normal working day begins at all seasons at 6 a.m. precisely and ends, after the usual break of half an hour for breakfast, an hour for dinner and half an hour for tea, at 7 p.m., and it shall be strictly observed.

Five minutes before the beginning of the stated hours of work until their actual commencement, a bell shall ring and indicate that every worker employed in the concern has to proceed to his place of work, in order to start as soon as the bell stops.

The doorkeeper shall lock the door punctually at 6 a.m., 8.30 a.m., 1 p.m. and 4.30 p.m.

Workers arriving 2 minutes late shall lose half an hour's wages; whoever is more than 2 minutes late may not start work until after the next break, or at least shall lose his wages until then. Any disputes about the correct time shall be settled by the clock mounted above the gatekeeper's lodge.

These rules are valid both for time- and for piece-workers, and in cases of breaches of these rules, workmen shall be fined in proportion to their earnings. The deductions from the wage shall be entered in the wage-book of the gate-keeper whose duty they are; they shall be unconditionally accepted as it will not be possible to enter into any discussions about them.

(2) When the bell is rung to denote the end of the working day, every work-man, both on piece- and on day-wage, shall leave his workshop and the yard, but is not allowed to make preparations for his departure before the bell rings. Every breach of this rule shall lead to a fine of five silver groschen to the sick fund. Only those who have obtained special permission by the overseer may stay on in the workshop in order to work. —If a workman has worked beyond the closing bell, he must give his name to the gatekeeper on leaving, on pain of losing his payment for the overtime.

From S. Pollard and C. Holmes, ed., *Documents of European Economic History*, vol. 1 (London: Edward Arnold Ltd., 1968), pp. 534–536.

(3) No workman, whether employed by time or piece, may leave before the end of the working day, without having first received permission from the overseer and having given his name to the gatekeeper. Omission of these two actions shall lead to a fine of ten silver groschen payable to the sick fund.

(4) Repeated irregular arrival at work shall lead to dismissal. This shall also apply to those who are found idling by an official or overseer, and refuse to obey their order to resume work.

(5) Entry to the firm's property by any but the designated gateway, and exit by any prohibited route, e.g. by climbing fences or walls, or by crossing the Spree, shall be punished by a fine of fifteen silver groschen to the sick fund for the first offences, and dismissal for the second.

(6) No worker may leave his place of work otherwise than for reasons connected with his work.

(7) All conversation with fellow-workers is prohibited; if any worker requires information about his work, he must turn to the overseer, or to the particular fellow-worker designated for the purpose.

(8) Smoking in the workshops or in the yard is prohibited during working hours; anyone caught smoking shall be fined five silver groschen for the sick fund for every such offence.

(9) Every worker is responsible for cleaning up his space in the workshop, and if in doubt, he is to turn to his overseer. — All tools must always be kept in good condition, and must be cleaned after use. This applies particularly to the turner, regarding his lathe.

(10) Natural functions must be performed at the appropriate places, and whoever is found soiling walls, fences, squares, etc., and similarly, whoever is found washing his face and hands in the workshop and not in the places assigned for the purpose, shall be fined five silver groschen for the sick fund.

(11) On completion of his piece of work, every workman must hand it over at once to his foreman or superior, in order to receive a fresh piece of work. Pattern makers must on no account hand over their patterns to the foundry without express order of their supervisors. No workman may take over work from his fellow-workman without instruction to that effect by the foreman.

(12) It goes without saying that all overseers and officials of the firm shall be obeyed without question, and shall be treated with due deference. Disobedience will be punished by dismissal.

(13) Immediate dismissal shall also be the fate of anyone found drunk in any of the workshops.

(14) Untrue allegations against superiors or officials of the concern shall lead to stern reprimand, and may lead to dismissal. The same punishment shall be meted out to those who knowingly allow errors to slip through when supervising or stocktaking.

(15) Every workman is obliged to report to his superiors any acts of dishonesty or embezzlement on the part of his fellow workmen. If he omits to do so, and it is shown after subsequent discovery of a misdemeanour that he knew about it at the time, he shall be liable to be taken to court as an accessory after

the fact and the wage due to him shall be retained as punishment. Conversely, anyone denouncing a theft in such a way as to allow conviction of the thief shall receive a reward of two Thaler, and, if necessary, his name shall be kept confidential. — Further, the gatekeeper and the watchman, as well as every official, are entitled to search the baskets, parcels, aprons etc. of the women and children who are taking the dinners into the works, on their departure, as well as search any worker suspected of stealing any article whatever. . . .

(18) Advances shall be granted only to the older workers, and even to them only in exceptional circumstances. As long as he is working by the piece, the workman is entitled merely to his fixed weekly wage as subsistence pay; the extra earnings shall be paid out only on completion of the whole piece contract. If a workman leaves before his piece contract is completed, either of his own free will, or on being dismissed as punishment, or because of illness, the partly completed work shall be valued by the general manager with the help of two overseers, and he will be paid accordingly. There is no appeal against the decision of these experts.

(19) A free copy of these rules is handed to every workman, but whoever loses it and requires a new one, or cannot produce it on leaving, shall be fined 2½ silver groschen, payable to the sick fund.

Moabit, August, 1844.

READING QUESTIONS

1. How did the author of the rules explain their necessity? How might the workers' view of the rules have differed from that of the factory owner?

2. What aspects of worker behavior seem to be of most concern to the factory owner?

3. What do the rules suggest about differences between industrial and rural notions of time?

20-4 | NED LUDD, *Yorkshire Textile Workers Threaten a Factory Owner* (ca. 1811–1812)

In the early nineteenth century, the new mechanization of textile manufacturing endangered the livelihoods of the handworkers engaged in manual textile production. During the years 1811–1816, many English hosiery weavers found themselves replaced by stocking frames,

From G. D. H. Cole and A. W. Filson, eds., *British Working Class Documents: Selected Documents 1789–1875* (London: Macmillan, 1951), pp. 113–115.

new machines that could knit stockings. Croppers, whose task was to finish woven cloth by cropping (shearing) it, were threatened by the introduction of the shearing frame, a machine that could replace the work of several men cutting by hand. The workers retaliated by smashing the "detestable" machines that had claimed their jobs. They adopted the name *Luddites* after a likely apocryphal Edward "Ned" Ludd, lauded as the first to destroy a shearing frame. Hostile missives, like that which follows, were often sent to the owners of stocking or shearing frames and made frequent reference to "King Ludd," a protector of the downtrodden.

Sir,

Information has just been given in, that you are a holder [owner] of those detestable Shearing Frames, and I was desired by my men to write to you, and give you fair warning to pull them down, and for that purpose I desire that you will understand I am now writing to you, you will take notice that if they are not taken down by the end of next week, I shall detach one of my lieutenants with at least 300 men to destroy them, and further more take notice that if you give us the trouble of coming thus far, we will increase your misfortunes by burning your buildings down to ashes. . . . We hope for assistance from the French Emperor[1] in shaking off the Yoke of the Rottenest, wickedest, and most Tyrannical Government that ever existed. . . . We will never lay down our arms till the House of Commons passes an act to put down all the machinery hurtfull [*sic*] to the Commonality and repeal that[2] to the Frame Breakers. . . .

Signed by the General of the Army of Redressers,
Ned Ludd, Clerk

READING QUESTIONS

1. Why do you think the Luddites resorted to threats and violence rather than peacefully seeking redress through the political process?

2. Why, in a threat to an individual factory owner, do you think the anonymous author of this letter denounced Britain's government as "the Rottenest, wickedest, and most Tyrannical . . . that ever existed"?

3. Why might the Luddites have expected the French emperor Napoleon to be their savior?

---

[1]**assistance from the French Emperor:** Great Britain was engaged in a lengthy war against the French emperor, Napoleon Bonaparte.

[2]**repeal that:** In response to the wave of machine breaking, Parliament made such crimes capital offenses.

20-5 | Creating an Industrial Utopia
ROBERT OWEN, *A New View of Society* (1813)

Robert Owen (1771–1858) first gained prominence as a successful textile manufacturer who treated his employees generously and beneficently. He later became a tireless promoter of educational reform and was an early "utopian" socialist and trade-union advocate, providing the inspiration for the founding of the Grand National Consolidated Trades Union in 1834. None of Owen's schemes for socialist communities succeeded, nor did the early trade unions, but his theories about educating children were very influential during his own lifetime and remain current today.

According to the last returns under the Population Act, the poor and working classes of Great Britain and Ireland have been found to exceed twelve millions of persons, or nearly three-fourths of the population of the British Islands.

The characters of these persons are now permitted to be very generally formed without proper guidance or direction, and, in many cases, under circumstances which *must* train them to the extreme of vice and misery; and of course render them the worst and most dangerous subjects in the empire; while the far greater part of the remainder of the community are educated upon the most mistaken principles of human nature, such, indeed, as cannot fail to produce a general conduct throughout society, totally unworthy of the character of rational beings.

The first thus unhappily situated are the poor and the uneducated profligate among the working classes, who are now trained to commit crimes, which they are afterwards *punished* for committing.

The second is the remaining mass of the population, who are now *instructed* to *believe*, or at least to acknowledge, that certain principles are *unerringly true*, and to *act* as though they were *grossly false*; thus filling the world with *folly* and *inconsistency*, and making society, throughout all its ramifications, a scene of insincerity.

This state of matters has continued for a long period, its evils have been and are continually increasing, until they now cry aloud for efficient corrective measures, or general disorder must ensue. . . .

Did these circumstances not exist to an extent almost incredible, could it be necessary *now* to contend for a principle regarding Man, which scarcely requires more than to be fairly stated to make it self-evident? This principle is, "THAT ANY CHARACTER, FROM THE BEST TO THE WORST, FROM THE MOST IGNORANT TO THE MOST ENLIGHTENED, MAY BE GIVEN TO ANY COMMUNITY, EVEN TO THE WORLD AT LARGE, BY APPLYING CERTAIN MEANS WHICH ARE TO A GREAT EXTENT AT THE COMMAND AND UNDER THE CONTROL, OR EASILY MADE SO, OF THOSE WHO POSSESS THE GOVERNMENT OF NATIONS."

From Robert Owen, *A New View of Society, or Essays on the Principle of the Formation of Human Character and the Application of the Principle to Practice* (London: Richard Taylor and Co., 1813), pp. 5–6, 9, 26–28, 35–36, 38–41, 49–51.

The principle as now stated is a broad one, and, if it should be found to be true, cannot fail to give a new character to legislative proceedings, and *such* a character as will be most favorable to the well-being of society. . . .

Children are without exception passive agents, or wonderfully contrived compounds, which by due preparation and accurate attention, founded on a correct knowledge of the subject, may be formed collectively into any Human character. And although these original compounds like all the other works of the Great Directing Power of the Universe, possess endless varieties, yet they all partake of that plastic nature or quality, which, by perseverance under judicious management, may be ultimately molded into the very image of rational wishes and desires.

And in the next place, these principles cannot fail soon to create those feelings, which without force, or the production of any counteracting motive, will irresistibly lead those who possess them to make due allowance for the difference of sentiments and manners not only among their friends and countrymen, but also among the inhabitants of every region on the earth, even including their enemies. For, with this insight into the formation of character, where is there any conceivable foundation for private displeasure or public enmity? Say, if it be within the sphere of possibility that children can be trained to acquire *that* knowledge and *these* feelings? The child of eight years growth, who from infancy has been rationally trained in these principles, will readily discover and trace from whence the opinions and habits of his associates have arisen, and why they possess them. And at the same age he will have acquired reasons sufficiently powerful to exhibit to him in strong colors the irrationality of being angry with an individual for possessing qualities which, as an unavoidable passive agent during the formation of those qualities, he had not the means of preventing. Such must be the impressions which these principles will make on the mind of every such child; and in lieu of generating anger or displeasure, they will produce commiseration and pity for those individuals, who possess either habits or sentiments which appear to him to be destructive of their own comfort, pleasure, or happiness, and will promote in him a desire to remove those causes of distress, that his own feelings of commiseration and pity may be also removed. And the pleasure which he cannot avoid experiencing by this mode of conduct, will likewise stimulate him to the most active endeavors to withdraw all those circumstances which surround any part of mankind with causes of misery, and to replace them with others which have a tendency to increase their happiness. He must then also strongly entertain the desire to "do good to *all* men," and even to "love his enemies."

In the year 1784 the late Mr. Dale[1] of Glasgow founded a spinning and weaving manufactory near the falls of the Clyde, in the county of Lanark in Scotland; and about that period cotton mills were first introduced into the northern part of the kingdom.

---

[1]**the late Mr. Dale**: Robert Owen's father-in-law.

It was the power which could be obtained from the falls of water which induced Mr. Dale to erect his mills in this situation, for in other respects it was not well chosen: the country around was uncultivated; the inhabitants were poor, and few in number; and the roads in the neighborhood were so bad, that the falls of Clyde now so celebrated were then unknown to strangers.

It was therefore necessary to collect a new population to supply the infant establishment with laborers. This however was no light task; for all the regularly trained Scotch peasantry disdained the idea of working from early till late, day after day, within cotton mills. Two modes only to obtain these laborers occurred: the one, to procure children from the various public charities in the country; and the other, to induce families to settle around the works.

To accommodate the first, a large house was erected, which ultimately contained about five hundred children, who were procured chiefly from workhouses and charities in Edinburgh.

These children were to be fed, clothed, and educated; and these duties Mr. Dale performed with the benevolence which he was known to possess. . . .

The benevolent proprietor spared no expense which could give comfort to the poor children which it contained. The rooms provided for them were spacious, always clean, and well ventilated; the food was of the best quality, and most abundant; the clothes were neat and useful; a surgeon was kept in constant pay to direct how to prevent as well as cure disease; and the best instructors which the country afforded were appointed to teach such branches of education as were deemed likely to be useful to children in their situation; and kind, well disposed persons were appointed to superintend all their proceedings. Nothing, in short, at first sight seemed wanting to render it a most complete charity.

But to defray the expense of these well devised arrangements, and support the establishment generally, it was absolutely necessary that the children should be employed within the mills from six o'clock in the morning to seven in the evening summer and winter; and after these hours their education commenced. The directors of the public charities from mistaken economy, would not consent to send the children under their care to cotton mills, unless the children were received by the proprietors at the ages of six, seven, and eight. And Mr. Dale was under the necessity of accepting them at those ages, or stopping the manufactory which he had commenced.

It is not to be supposed that children so young could remain, with the interval of meals only, from six in the morning until seven in the evening, in constant employment on their feet within cotton mills, and afterwards acquire much proficiency in education. And so it proved; for the greater part of them became dwarfs in body and mind, and many of them deformed. Their labor through the day, and their education at night, became so irksome, that numbers of them continually ran away, and almost all looked forward with impatience and anxiety to the expiration of their apprenticeship of seven, eight, and nine years, which generally expired when they were from thirteen to fifteen years old. At this period of life, unaccustomed to provide for themselves, and unacquainted with the world, they usually went to Edinburgh or Glasgow, where boys and girls were soon assailed by the innumerable temptations which all large towns present; and many of them fell sacrifices to those temptations.

Thus were Mr. Dale's arrangements and kind solicitude for the comfort and happiness of these children rendered in their ultimate effect almost nugatory. They were sent to be employed, and without their labor he could not support them; but, while under his care, he did all that any individual circumstanced as he was could do for his fellow-creatures.

The error proceeded from the children being sent from the workhouses at an age far too young for employment; they ought to have been detained four years longer, and educated; and then all the evils which followed would have been prevented.

And if such be a true picture not overcharged of parish apprentices to our manufacturing system under the best and most humane regulations, in what colors must it be exhibited under the worst? . . .

[Once Owen himself was put in charge of the factory,] the system of receiving apprentices from public charities was abolished; permanent settlers with large families were encouraged, and comfortable houses were built for their accommodation.

The practice of employing children in the mills, of six, seven, and eight years of age, was discontinued, and their parents advised to allow them to acquire health and education until they were ten years old. (It may be remarked, that even this age is too early to keep them at constant employment in manufactories, from six in the morning to seven in the evening. Far better would it be for the children, their parents, and for society, that the first should not commence employment until they attain the age of twelve, when their education might be finished, and their bodies would be more competent to undergo the fatigue and exertions required of them. When parents can be trained to afford this additional time to their children without inconvenience, they will, of course, adopt the practice now recommended.)

The children were taught reading, writing, and arithmetic, during five years, that is, from five to ten, in the village school, without expense to their parents; and all the modern improvements in education have been adopted, or are in process of adoption: some facilities in teaching arithmetic have been also introduced, which were peculiar to this school, and found very advantageous. They may therefore be taught and well trained before they engage in any regular employment. Another important consideration is, that all their instruction is rendered a pleasure and delight to them; they are much more anxious for the hour of school time to arrive, than end: they therefore make a rapid progress; and it may be safely asserted, that if they shall not be trained to form such characters as may be the most wished and desired, not one particle of the fault will proceed from the children; but the cause will rest in the want of a true knowledge of human nature, in those who have the management of them and their parents.

READING QUESTIONS

1. Why was Owen opposed to child labor?

2. What did Owen believe regarding human nature and behavior, especially as they pertain to the poor, criminal, or undereducated?

3. According to Owen, what purposes did education serve for the children of the working class?

20-6 | Child Labor in an Industrial Age
The Child of the Factory (1842)

Child labor was neither a novelty nor a product of the Industrial Revolution; children in traditional agricultural societies were (and are) put to work as soon as they were capable of contributing to the family economy. Yet the circumstances associated with industrialization, in particular the factory system of labor organization, focused public attention on the phenomenon as never before—first in Britain and then, as the illustration suggests, in continental Europe. The consequence, again beginning in Britain, was a humanitarian outcry leading to legislation limiting and eventually prohibiting child labor in factories. This illustration accompanied an article written about children in the cotton textile industry in France.

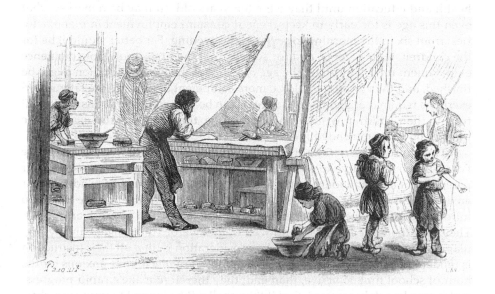

The Child of the Factory, c. 1842 (engraving) (b/w photo)/French School, (19th century)/INDIVISION CHARMET/Bibliotheque des Arts Decoratifs, Paris, France/Bridgeman Images.

READING QUESTIONS

1. On what grounds might contemporaries, including many members of the working class, have defended child labor?

2. Are all of the children depicted in the illustration actually working? If not, then why might they be in the factory?

■ COMPARATIVE AND DISCUSSION QUESTIONS ■

1. What similarities do you see between Malthus's arguments and those of Adam Smith (Document 17-3) regarding the "wages of labor"? What differences?

2. How might Malthus have reacted to the conditions in Manchester described by Engels, and why might he have reacted that way?

3. What do you think Malthus would say about Owen's views on human nature? Why? What do you think John Locke (Document 15-6) would say about them, and why?

4. What do you think Owen thought of the Luddites? Why?

5. What might Owen have thought about the Berlin factory rules? What kinds of rules would you expect him to devise for his own workers?

21

Ideologies and Upheavals
1815–1850

The rapid social changes brought about by the Industrial Revolution combined with the political and intellectual legacy of the French Revolution to give rise to a number of competing ideologies, each offering a different response to the social and economic challenges of the early nineteenth century. Conservatives were committed to protecting the social status quo, prerevolutionary political norms, and what they saw as traditional values. Liberals, by contrast, sought an end to government controls over the economy and called for the establishment of representative political institutions grounded in written constitutions. Communists offered yet another solution—the seizure of the means and ownership of production by the working class—while Chartists sought the enfranchisement of all adult males. While all these ideologies competed with one another, the population of England rose dramatically in the nineteenth century. At the same time, the population of Ireland shrank from about 8 million to scarcely 6 million during the 1840s as people fled the devastating conditions of the potato famine.

21-1 | Touting the Values of Industrial Technology
ANDREW URE, *The Philosophy of the Manufacturers* (1835)

Part of the impetus behind the ideological struggles of the nineteenth century was the rapid growth of industrialization and the mechanization of factories. While the new technologies and practices increased manufacturing output, they also meant changes in working conditions and wages for workers. In this document, Scottish physician Andrew Ure extols the virtues of the new technologies, speaking for the emerging, wealthy upper middle class of factory owners.

From Andrew Ure, *The Philosophy of Manufactures*, ed. P. L. Simmonds (London: H. G. Bohn, 1861), pp. 5–8, 14–15, 20–21, 23, 29–31.

This island is pre-eminent among civilized nations for the prodigious development of its factory wealth, and has been therefore long viewed with a jealous admiration by foreign powers. This very pre-eminence, however, has been contemplated in a very different light by many influential members of our own community, and has been even denounced by them as the certain origin of innumerable evils to the people, and of revolutionary convulsions to the state. If the affairs of the kingdom be wisely administered, I believe such allegations and fears will prove to be groundless, and to proceed more from the envy of one ancient and powerful order of the commonwealth, towards another suddenly grown into political importance, than from the nature of things. . . .

The blessings which physio-mechanical science has bestowed on society, and the means it has still in store for ameliorating the lot of mankind, have been too little dwelt upon; while, on the other hand, it has been accused of lending itself to the rich capitalists as an instrument for harassing the poor, and of exacting from the operative an accelerated rate of work. It has been said, for example, that the steam-engine now drives the power-looms with such velocity as to urge on their attendant weavers at the same rapid pace; but that the hand-weaver, not being subjected to this restless agent, can throw his shuttle[1] and move his treddles[2] at his convenience. There is, however, this difference in the two cases, that in the factory, every member of the loom is so adjusted, that the driving force leaves the attendant nearly nothing at all to do, certainly no muscular fatigue to sustain, while it procures for him good, unfailing wages, besides a healthy workshop *gratis*: whereas the non-factory weaver, having everything to execute by muscular exertion, finds the labour irksome, makes in consequence innumerable short pauses, separately of little account, but great when added together; earns therefore proportionally low wages, while he loses his health by poor diet and the dampness of his hovel. . . .

The constant aim and effect of scientific improvement in manufactures are philanthropic, as they tend to relieve the workmen either from niceties of adjustment which exhaust his mind and fatigue his eyes, or from painful repetition of efforts which distort or wear out his frame. At every step of each manufacturing process described in this volume the humanity of science will be manifest. . . .

In its precise acceptation, the Factory system is of recent origin, and may claim England for its birthplace. The mills for throwing silk, or making organzine,[3] which were mounted centuries ago in several of the Italian states, and furtively transferred to this country by Sir Thomas Lombe in 1718, contained indeed certain elements of a factory, and probably suggested some hints of those grander and more complex combinations of self-acting machines, which were first embodied half a century later in our cotton manufacture by Richard Arkwright, assisted by gentlemen of Derby, well acquainted with its celebrated silk establishment. But the spinning of an entangled flock of fibres into a smooth thread, which constitutes the main operation with cotton, is in silk superfluous;

---

[1]**shuttle**: A hand tool used to weave thread on a loom.
[2]**treddles**: Treadles: foot pedals used to drive the motion of a machine.
[3]**organzine**: A type of silk thread.

being already performed by the unerring instinct of a worm, which leaves to human art the simple task of doubling and twisting its regular filaments. The apparatus requisite for this purpose is more elementary, and calls for few of those gradations of machinery which are needed in the carding, drawing, roving, and spinning processes of a cotton-mill.

When the first water-frames for spinning cotton were erected at Cromford, in the romantic valley of the Derwent, about sixty years ago, mankind were little aware of the mighty revolution which the new system of labour was destined by Providence to achieve, not only in the structure of British society, but in the fortunes of the world at large. Arkwright alone had the sagacity to discern, and the boldness to predict in glowing language, how vastly productive human industry would become, when no longer proportioned in its results to muscular effort, which is by its nature fitful and capricious, but when made to consist in the task of guiding the work of mechanical fingers and arms, regularly impelled with great velocity by some indefatigable physical power. What his judgment so clearly led him to perceive, his energy of will enabled him to realize with such rapidity and success, as would have done honour to the most influential individuals, but were truly wonderful in that obscure and indigent artisan. . . .

The principle of the factory system then is, to substitute mechanical science for hand skill, and the partition of a process into its essential constituents, for the division or graduation of labour among artisans. On the handicraft plan, labour more or less skilled was usually the most expensive element of production. . . . but on the automatic plan, skilled labour gets progressively superseded, and will, eventually, be replaced by mere overlookers of machines.

By the infirmity of human nature it happens, that the more skilful the workman, the more self-willed and intractable he is apt to become, and, of course, the less fit a component of a mechanical system, in which, by occasional irregularities, he may do great damage to the whole. The grand object therefore of the modern manufacturer is, through the union of capital and science, to reduce the task of his work-people to the exercise of vigilance and dexterity, — faculties, when concentred to one process, speedily brought to perfection in the young. In the infancy of mechanical engineering, a machine-factory displayed the division of labour in manifold gradations — the file, the drill, the lathe, having each its different workmen in the order of skill: but the dextrous hands of the filer and driller are now superseded by the planing, the key groove cutting, and the drilling-machines; and those of the iron and brass turners, by the self-acting slide-lathe. . . .

It is, in fact, the constant aim and tendency of every improvement in machinery to supersede human labour altogether, or to diminish its cost, by substituting the industry of women and children for that of men; or that of ordinary labourers for trained artisans. In most of the water-twist, or throstle cotton-mills, the spinning is entirely managed by females of sixteen years and upwards. The effect of substituting the self-acting mule for the common mule, is to discharge the greater part of the men spinners, and to retain adolescents and children. The proprietor of a factory near Stockport states, in evidence to the commissioners, that, by such substitution, he would save 50*l.* a week in wages in consequence of dispensing with nearly forty male spinners, at about 25s. of wages each. . . .

Steam-engines furnish the means not only of their support but of their multiplication. They create a vast demand for fuel; and, while they lend their powerful arms to drain the pits and to raise the coals, they call into employment multitudes of miners, engineers, shipbuilders, and sailors, and cause the construction of canals and railways. Thus therefore, in enabling these rich fields of industry to be cultivated to the utmost, they leave thousands of fine arable fields free for the production of food to man, which must have been otherwise allotted to the food of horses. Steam-engines moreover, by the cheapness and steadiness of their action, fabricate cheap goods, and procure in their exchange a liberal supply of the necessaries and comforts of life produced in foreign lands.

Improvements in the machinery have a three-fold bearing: —

lst. They make it possible to fabricate some articles which, but for them, could not be fabricated at all.

2nd. They enable an operative to turn out a greater quantity of work than he could before, — time, labour, and quality of work remaining constant.

3rd. They effect a substitution of labour comparatively unskilled, for that which is more skilled.

READING QUESTIONS

1. How does Ure respond to critiques that the factory system leads to poor working conditions?

2. According to Ure, how is a mechanical system superior to a skilled artisan?

3. What are the various economic benefits that the mechanization of labor makes possible, according to Ure?

4. What elements of his arguments display the significant differences in cultural norms about work that have developed between the nineteenth century and today?

SOURCES IN CONVERSATION

Conservatism, Liberalism, and Socialism

The differences between conservatism, liberalism, and socialism were not ones of emphasis or degree. They were, instead, rooted in fundamental disagreements about human nature, the relationship between society and the individual, and the possibility and desirability of social, economic, and political change. Conservatives, liberals, and socialists had different views of Europe's past and different visions of Europe's future. In significant ways, the political upheavals of the nineteenth century were battles over these competing outlooks. As you read these excerpts from the writings of Metternich, Mill, Marx, and Engels, concentrate on identifying the core assumptions that inform each author's work. How did each author's assumptions shape the solutions he proposed to the challenges facing nineteenth-century Europe?

READ AND COMPARE

1. What do Metternich on the one hand, and Marx and Engels on the other, identify as the chief problems inherent in European society at that time? What do they prescribe as the solution?

2. How would Mill feel about potential outcomes of the revolution that is advocated by Marx and Engels? Would he support it or fear it? Why do you think so?

21-2 | KLEMENS VON METTERNICH, *Political Confession of Faith* (1820)

Prince Klemens von Metternich (1773–1859) was Austria's foreign secretary from 1809 until driven into exile during the revolution of 1848. As the key figure at the Congress of Vienna, he was widely credited as principal architect of the peace settlement that ended the Napoleonic Wars and ushered in the "long peace" of the nineteenth century. As a member of the landed aristocracy and a staunch upholder of the established social hierarchy, Metternich was a fervent foe of liberalism and nationalism, both of which he regarded as dangerous revolutionary doctrines.

The Source of the Evil

Man's nature is immutable. The first needs of society are and remain the same, and the differences which they seem to offer find their explanation in the diversity of influences, acting on the different races by natural causes, such as the diversity of climate, barrenness or richness of soil, insular or continental position, &c. &c. These local differences no doubt produce effects which extend far beyond purely physical necessities; they create and determine particular needs in a more elevated sphere; finally, they determine the laws, and exercise an influence even on religions.

It is, on the other hand, with institutions as with everything else. Vague in their origin, they pass through periods of development and perfection, to arrive

From Klemens von Metternich, *Memoirs of Prince Metternich, 1815–1829*, vol. 3, ed. Richard von Metternich (New York: Charles Scribner and Sons, 1881), pp. 456–458, 461–463, 469–471, 473–476.

in time at their decadence; and, conforming to the laws of man's nature, they have, like him, their infancy, their youth, their age of strength and reason, and their age of decay.

Two elements alone remain in all their strength, and never cease to exercise their indestructible influence with equal power. These are the precepts of morality, religious as well as social, and the necessities created by locality. From the time that men attempt to swerve from these bases, to become rebels against these sovereign arbiters of their destinies, society suffers from a *malaise* which sooner or later will lead to a state of convulsion. The history of every country, in relating the consequences of such errors, contains many pages stained with blood, but we dare to say, without fear of contradiction, one seeks in vain for an epoch when an evil of this nature has extended its ravages over such a vast area as it has done at the present time. . . .

The progress of the human mind has been extremely rapid in the course of the last three centuries. This progress having been accelerated more rapidly than the growth of wisdom (the only counterpoise to passions and to error); a revolution prepared by the false systems, the fatal errors into which many of the most illustrious sovereigns of the last half of the eighteenth century fell, has at last broken out in a country advanced in knowledge [i.e., France], and enervated by pleasure, in a country inhabited by a people whom one can only regard as frivolous, from the facility with which they comprehend and the difficulty they experience in judging calmly. . . .

France had the misfortune to produce the greatest number of these men. It is in her midst that religion and all that she holds sacred, that morality and authority, and all connected with them, have been attacked with a steady and systematic animosity, and it is there that the weapon of ridicule has been used with the most ease and success.

Drag through the mud the name of God and the powers instituted by His divine decrees, and the revolution will be prepared! Speak of a social contract, and the revolution is accomplished! The revolution was already completed in the palaces of Kings, in the drawing-rooms and boudoirs of certain cities, while among the great mass of the people it was still only in a state of preparation. . . .

The scenes of horror which accompanied the first phases of the French Revolution prevented the rapid propagation of its subversive principles beyond the frontiers of France, and the wars of conquest which succeeded them gave to the public mind a direction little favorable to revolutionary principles. Thus the Jacobin propaganda failed entirely to realize criminal hopes.

Nevertheless the revolutionary seed had penetrated into every country and spread more or less. It was greatly developed under the *régime* of the military despotism of Bonaparte. His conquests displaced a number of laws, institutions, and customs; broke through bonds sacred among all nations, strong enough to resist time itself; which is more than can be said of certain benefits conferred by these innovators. From these perturbations it followed that the revolutionary spirit could in Germany, Italy, and later on in Spain, easily hide itself under the veil of patriotism. . . .

We are convinced that society can no longer be saved without strong and vigorous resolutions on the part of the Governments still free in their opinions and actions.

We are also convinced that this may yet be, if the Governments face the truth, if they free themselves from all illusion, if they join their ranks and take their stand on a line of correct, unambiguous, and frankly announced principles.

By this course the monarchs will fulfill the duties imposed upon them by Him who, by entrusting them with power, has charged them to watch over the maintenance of justice, and the rights of all, to avoid the paths of error, and tread firmly in the way of truth. Placed beyond the passions which agitate society, it is in days of trial chiefly that they are called upon to despoil realities of their false appearances, and to show themselves as they are, fathers invested with the authority belonging by right to the heads of families, to prove that, in days of mourning, they know how to be just, wise, and therefore strong, and that they will not abandon the people whom they ought to govern to be the sport of factions, to error and its consequences, which must involve the loss of society. The moment in which we are putting our thoughts on paper is one of these critical moments. The crisis is great; it will be decisive according to the part we take or do not take. . . .

Union between the monarchs is the basis of the policy which must now be followed to save society from total ruin. . . .

The first principle to be followed by the monarchs, united as they are by the coincidence of their desires and opinions, should be that of maintaining the stability of political institutions against the disorganized excitement which has taken possession of men's minds — the immutability of principles against the madness of their interpretation; and respect for laws actually in force against a desire for their destruction. . . .

Let [the governments] in these troublous times be more than usually cautious in attempting real ameliorations, not imperatively claimed by the needs of the moment, to the end that good itself may not turn against them — which is the case whenever a Government measure seems to be inspired by fear.

Let them not confound concessions made to parties with the good they ought to do for their people, in modifying, according to their recognized needs, such branches of the administration as require it.

Let them give minute attention to the financial state of their kingdoms, so that their people may enjoy, by the reduction of public burdens, the real, not imaginary, benefits of a state of peace.

Let them be just, but strong; beneficent, but strict.

Let them maintain religious principles in all their purity, and not allow the faith to be attacked and morality interpreted according to the *social contract* or the visions of foolish sectarians.

Let them suppress Secret Societies, that gangrene of society.

In short, let the great monarchs strengthen their union, and prove to the world that if it exists, it is beneficent, and ensures the political peace of Europe: that it is powerful only for the maintenance of tranquility at a time when so many attacks are directed against it; that the principles which they profess are paternal and protective, menacing only the disturbers of public tranquility. . . .

To every great State determined to survive the storm there still remain many chances of salvation, and a strong union between the States on the principles we have announced will overcome the storm itself.

READING QUESTIONS

1. According to Metternich, what aspects of human society are changeable? Which are not?

2. From Metternich's point of view, why was the French Revolution a great evil? What steps did he suggest must be taken to prevent a similar revolutionary outbreak in the future?

3. What is Metternich's attitude toward organized religion? What connection does he make between religion, morality, and the stability of society and the state?

4. Why does Metternich place such emphasis on monarchical power?

21-3 | JOHN STUART MILL, *On Liberty* (1859)

The English philosopher John Stuart Mill (1806–1873) was, perhaps, the most important liberal theorist of the nineteenth century. His numerous works explored the relationship between the individual, society, and the state in an effort to identify and define the rights and interests of each. For Mill, the freedom of the individual was paramount, and any state that placed unjust or unwarranted limitations on individual liberty was, by definition, tyrannical. Thus, in Mill's work we see a clear connection between liberty and the term *liberalism*. In this excerpt from *On Liberty*, Mill identifies the central principles that guided his political philosophy.

The object of this Essay is to assert one very simple principle, as entitled to govern absolutely the dealings of society with the individual in the way of compulsion and control, whether the means used be physical force in the form of legal penalties, or the moral coercion of public opinion. That principle is, that the sole end for which mankind are warranted, individually or collectively, in interfering with the liberty of action of any of their number, is self-protection. That the only purpose for which power can be rightfully exercised over any member of a civilized community, against his will, is to prevent harm to others. His own good, either physical or moral, is not a sufficient warrant. He cannot rightfully be compelled to do or forbear because it will be better for him to do so, because it will make him happier, because, in the opinions of others, to do so would be wise, or even right. These are good reasons for remonstrating with him, or reasoning with him, or persuading him, or entreating him, but not for compelling him, or visiting him with any evil in case he do otherwise. To justify that, the conduct from which it is desired to deter him, must be calculated to produce evil to some one else. The only part of the conduct of any one, for which he is amenable to society, is that which concerns others. In the part which merely concerns

From John Stuart Mill, *On Liberty* (London: John W. Parker and Son, West Strand, 1859), pp. 21–22, 26–27.

himself, his independence is, of right, absolute. Over himself, over his own body and mind, the individual is sovereign. . . .

This, then, is the appropriate region of human liberty. It comprises, first, the inward domain of consciousness; demanding liberty of conscience, in the most comprehensive sense; liberty of thought and feeling; absolute freedom of opinion and sentiment on all subjects, practical or speculative, scientific, moral, or theological. The liberty of expressing and publishing opinions may seem to fall under a different principle, since it belongs to that part of the conduct of an individual which concerns other people; but, being almost of as much importance as the liberty of thought itself, and resting in great part on the same reasons, is practically inseparable from it. Secondly, the principle requires liberty of tastes and pursuits; of framing the plan of our life to suit our own character; of doing as we like, subject to such consequences as may follow: without impediment from our fellow-creatures, so long as what we do does not harm them, even though they should think our conduct foolish, perverse, or wrong. Thirdly, from this liberty of each individual, follows the liberty, within the same limits, of combination among individuals; freedom to unite, for any purpose not involving harm to others: the persons combining being supposed to be of full age, and not forced or deceived.

No society in which these liberties are not, on the whole, respected, is free, whatever may be its form of government; and none is completely free in which they do not exist absolute and unqualified. The only freedom which deserves the name, is that of pursuing our own good in our own way, so long as we do not attempt to deprive others of theirs, or impede their efforts to obtain it. Each is the proper guardian of his own health, whether bodily, or mental and spiritual. Mankind are greater gainers by suffering each other to live as seems good to themselves, than by compelling each to live as seems good to the rest.

READING QUESTIONS

1. According to Mill, what single principle should govern the dealings of society with the individual?

2. What individual rights did Mill identify? Why did he think they were so important?

3. What role did individual conscience play in Mill's philosophy? What does this suggest about his attitude toward state-sponsored religion?

21-4 | KARL MARX AND FRIEDRICH ENGELS, *The Communist Manifesto* (1848)

Karl Marx (1818–1883) and Friedrich Engels (1820–1895) are credited as the founders of communism. In formulating their theories, Marx and Engels drew on the work of

From Karl Marx and Friedrich Engels, *Selected Works*, vol. 1 (Moscow: Progress Publishers, 1969), pp. 2–12, 32, www.marxists.org/archive/marx/works/download/manifest.pdf.

earlier economists, particularly Adam Smith and David Ricardo, and on Thomas Malthus's demographic theories, as well as their familiarity with living and working conditions in England's industrial centers. Their *Communist Manifesto*, first published in London as a pamphlet (written in German), opens with the proclamation that "the history of all hitherto existing society is the history of class struggles." The authors predicted the eventual triumph of the working class (proletariat) over the middle class (bourgeoisie) and the establishment of a classless society in which wealth would be equally distributed.

[Preamble]

A specter is haunting Europe—the specter of communism. All the powers of old Europe have entered into a holy alliance to exorcise this specter: Pope and Tsar, Metternich and Guizot,[1] French Radicals and German police-spies.

Where is the party in opposition that has not been decried as communistic by its opponents in power? Where is the opposition that has not hurled back the branding reproach of communism, against the more advanced opposition parties, as well as against its reactionary adversaries?

Two things result from this fact:

I. Communism is already acknowledged by all European powers to be itself a power.

II. It is high time that Communists should openly, in the face of the whole world, publish their views, their aims, their tendencies, and meet this nursery tale of the Specter of Communism with a manifesto of the party itself.

To this end, Communists of various nationalities have assembled in London and sketched the following manifesto, to be published in the English, French, German, Italian, Flemish, and Danish languages.

Chapter 1: Bourgeois and Proletarians

The history of all hitherto existing society is the history of class struggles.

Freeman and slave, patrician and plebeian, lord and serf, guild-master and journeyman, in a word, oppressor and oppressed, stood in constant opposition to one another, carried on an uninterrupted, now hidden, now open fight, a fight that each time ended, either in a revolutionary reconstitution of society at large, or in the common ruin of the contending classes.

In the earlier epochs of history, we find almost everywhere a complicated arrangement of society into various orders, a manifold gradation of social rank. In ancient Rome we have patricians, knights, plebeians, slaves; in the Middle Ages, feudal lords, vassals, guild-masters, journeymen, apprentices, serfs; in almost all of these classes, again, subordinate gradations.

---

[1]**Guizot:** François Pierre Guillaume Guizot (1787–1874), French politician and prime minister (1847–1848).

The modern bourgeois society that has sprouted from the ruins of feudal society has not done away with class antagonisms. It has but established new classes, new conditions of oppression, new forms of struggle in place of the old ones.

Our epoch, the epoch of the bourgeoisie, possesses, however, this distinct feature: it has simplified class antagonisms. Society as a whole is more and more splitting up into two great hostile camps, into two great classes directly facing each other—Bourgeoisie and Proletariat.

From the serfs of the Middle Ages sprang the chartered burghers of the earliest towns. From these burgesses the first elements of the bourgeoisie were developed.

The discovery of America, the rounding of the Cape, opened up fresh ground for the rising bourgeoisie. . . .

The feudal system of industry, in which industrial production was monopolized by closed guilds, now no longer sufficed for the growing wants of the new markets. The manufacturing system took its place. The guild-masters were pushed on one side by the manufacturing middle class; division of labor between the different corporate guilds vanished in the face of division of labor in each single workshop.

Meantime the markets kept ever growing, the demand ever rising. Even manufacturer no longer sufficed. Thereupon, steam and machinery revolutionized industrial production. The place of manufacture was taken by the giant, Modern Industry; the place of the industrial middle class by industrial millionaires, the leaders of the whole industrial armies. . . . The modern bourgeoisie is itself the product of a long course of development, of a series of revolutions in the modes of production and of exchange.

Each step in the development of the bourgeoisie was accompanied by a corresponding political advance of that class. An oppressed class under the sway of the feudal nobility, an armed and self-governing association in the medieval commune: here independent urban republic (as in Italy and Germany); there taxable "third estate" of the monarchy (as in France); afterwards, in the period of manufacturing proper, serving either the semi-feudal or the absolute monarchy as a counterpoise against the nobility, and, in fact, cornerstone of the great monarchies in general, the bourgeoisie has at last, since the establishment of Modern Industry and of the world market, conquered for itself, in the modern representative State, exclusive political sway. The executive of the modern state is but a committee for managing the common affairs of the whole bourgeoisie.

The bourgeoisie, historically, has played a most revolutionary part.

The bourgeoisie, wherever it has got the upper hand, has put an end to all feudal, patriarchal, idyllic relations . . . [and] has substituted naked, shameless, direct, brutal exploitation.

The bourgeoisie has stripped of its halo every occupation hitherto honored and looked up to with reverent awe. It has converted the physician, the lawyer, the priest, the poet, the man of science, into its paid wage laborers.

The bourgeoisie has torn away from the family its sentimental veil, and has reduced the family relation to a mere money relation. . . .

The bourgeoisie cannot exist without constantly revolutionizing the instruments of production, and thereby the relations of production, and with them the whole relations of society. Conservation of the old modes of production in unaltered form, was, on the contrary, the first condition of existence for all earlier industrial classes. Constant revolutionizing of production, uninterrupted disturbance of all social conditions, everlasting uncertainty and agitation distinguish the bourgeois epoch from all earlier ones. . . .

The need of a constantly expanding market for its products chases the bourgeoisie over the entire surface of the globe. It must nestle everywhere, settle everywhere, establish connections everywhere.

The bourgeoisie has through its exploitation of the world market given a cosmopolitan character to production and consumption in every country. To the great chagrin of Reactionists, it has drawn from under the feet of industry the national ground on which it stood. All old-established national industries have been destroyed or are daily being destroyed. They are dislodged by new industries, whose introduction becomes a life and death question for all civilized nations, by industries that no longer work up indigenous raw material, but raw material drawn from the remotest zones; industries whose products are consumed, not only at home, but in every quarter of the globe. . . .

The bourgeoisie, by the rapid improvement of all instruments of production, by the immensely facilitated means of communication, draws all, even the most barbarian, nations into civilization. The cheap prices of commodities are the heavy artillery with which it batters down all Chinese walls, with which it forces the barbarians' intensely obstinate hatred of foreigners to capitulate. It compels all nations, on pain of extinction, to adopt the bourgeois mode of production; it compels them to introduce what it calls civilization into their midst, i.e., to become bourgeois themselves. In one word, it creates a world after its own image.

The bourgeoisie has subjected the country to the rule of the towns. It has created enormous cities, has greatly increased the urban population as compared with the rural, and has thus rescued a considerable part of the population from the idiocy of rural life. Just as it has made the country dependent on the towns, so it has made barbarian and semi-barbarian countries dependent on the civilized ones, nations of peasants on nations of bourgeois, the East on the West.

The bourgeoisie keeps more and more doing away with the scattered state of the population, of the means of production, and of property. . . .

We see then: the means of production and of exchange, on whose foundation the bourgeoisie built itself up, were generated in feudal society. At a certain stage in the development of these means of production and of exchange, the conditions under which feudal society produced and exchanged, the feudal organization of agriculture and manufacturing industry, in one word, the feudal relations of property became no longer compatible with the already developed productive forces; they became so many fetters. They had to be burst asunder; they were burst asunder.

Into their place stepped free competition, accompanied by a social and political constitution adapted in it, and the economic and political sway of the bourgeois class.

A similar movement is going on before our own eyes. . . . It is enough to mention the commercial crises that by their periodical return put the existence of the entire bourgeois society on its trial, each time more threateningly. In these crises, a great part not only of the existing products, but also of the previously created productive forces, are periodically destroyed. In these crises, there breaks out an epidemic that, in all earlier epochs, would have seemed an absurdity — the epidemic of over-production. Society suddenly finds itself put back into a state of momentary barbarism; it appears as if a famine, a universal war of devastation, had cut off the supply of every means of subsistence; industry and commerce seem to be destroyed; and why? Because there is too much civilization, too much means of subsistence, too much industry, too much commerce. The productive forces at the disposal of society no longer tend to further the development of the conditions of bourgeois property; on the contrary, they have become too powerful for these conditions, by which they are fettered, and so soon as they overcome these fetters, they bring disorder into the whole of bourgeois society, endanger the existence of bourgeois property. The conditions of bourgeois society are too narrow to comprise the wealth created by them. And how does the bourgeoisie get over these crises? On the one hand by enforced destruction of a mass of productive forces; on the other, by the conquest of new markets, and by the more thorough exploitation of the old ones. That is to say, by paving the way for more extensive and more destructive crises, and by diminishing the means whereby crises are prevented.

The weapons with which the bourgeoisie felled feudalism to the ground are now turned against the bourgeoisie itself.

But not only has the bourgeoisie forged the weapons that bring death to itself; it has also called into existence the men who are to wield those weapons — the modern working class — the proletarians.

In proportion as the bourgeoisie, i.e., capital, is developed, in the same proportion is the proletariat, the modern working class, developed — a class of laborers, who live only so long as they find work, and who find work only so long as their labor increases capital. These laborers, who must sell themselves piecemeal, are a commodity, like every other article of commerce, and are consequently exposed to all the vicissitudes of competition, to all the fluctuations of the market.

Owing to the extensive use of machinery, and to the division of labor, the work of the proletarians has lost all individual character, and, consequently, all charm for the workman. He becomes an appendage of the machine, and it is only the most simple, most monotonous, and most easily acquired knack, that is required of him. Hence, the cost of production of a workman is restricted, almost entirely, to the means of subsistence that he requires for maintenance, and for the propagation of his race. But the price of a commodity, and therefore also of labor, is equal to its cost of production. In proportion, therefore, as the repulsiveness of the work increases, the wage decreases. Nay more, in proportion as the use of machinery and division of labor increases, in the same proportion the burden of toil also increases, whether by prolongation of the working hours, by the increase of the work exacted in a given time or by increased speed of machinery, etc.

Modern Industry has converted the little workshop of the patriarchal master into the great factory of the industrial capitalist. Masses of laborers, crowded into the factory, are organized like soldiers. As privates of the industrial army they are placed under the command of a perfect hierarchy of officers and sergeants. Not only are they slaves of the bourgeois class, and of the bourgeois State; they are daily and hourly enslaved by the machine, by the overlooker, and, above all, by the individual bourgeois manufacturer himself. The more openly this despotism proclaims gain to be its end and aim, the more petty, the more hateful and the more embittering it is.

The less the skill and exertion of strength implied in manual labor, in other words, the more modern industry becomes developed, the more is the labor of men superseded by that of women. Differences of age and sex have no longer any distinctive social validity for the working class. All are instruments of labor, more or less expensive to use, according to their age and sex.

No sooner is the exploitation of the laborer by the manufacturer, so far, at an end, that he receives his wages in cash, than he is set upon by the other portions of the bourgeoisie, the landlord, the shopkeeper, the pawnbroker, etc.

The lower strata of the middle class — the small tradespeople, shopkeepers, and retired tradesmen generally, the handicraftsmen and peasants — all these sink gradually into the proletariat, partly because their diminutive capital does not suffice for the scale on which Modern Industry is carried on, and is swamped in the competition with the large capitalists, partly because their specialized skill is rendered worthless by new methods of production. Thus the proletariat is recruited from all classes of the population.

The proletariat goes through various stages of development. With its birth begins its struggle with the bourgeoisie. At first the contest is carried on by individual laborers, then by the workpeople of a factory, then by the operative of one trade, in one locality, against the individual bourgeois who directly exploits them. They direct their attacks not against the bourgeois conditions of production, but against the instruments of production themselves; they destroy imported wares that compete with their labor, they smash to pieces machinery, they set factories ablaze, they seek to restore by force the vanished status of the workman of the Middle Ages.

At this stage, the laborers still form an incoherent mass scattered over the whole country, and broken up by their mutual competition. If anywhere they unite to form more compact bodies, this is not yet the consequence of their own active union, but of the union of the bourgeoisie, which class, in order to attain its own political ends, is compelled to set the whole proletariat in motion, and is moreover yet, for a time, able to do so. At this stage, therefore, the proletarians do not fight their enemies, but the enemies of their enemies, the remnants of absolute monarchy, the landowners, the non-industrial bourgeois, the petty bourgeois. Thus, the whole historical movement is concentrated in the hands of the bourgeoisie; every victory so obtained is a victory for the bourgeoisie.

But with the development of industry, the proletariat not only increases in number; it becomes concentrated in greater masses, its strength grows, and it feels that strength more. The various interests and conditions of life within the ranks of the proletariat are more and more equalized, in proportion as machinery obliterates all distinctions of labor, and nearly everywhere reduces wages to the same low level. The growing competition among the bourgeois, and the resulting commercial crises, make the wages of the workers ever more fluctuating. The increasing improvement of machinery, ever more rapidly developing, makes their livelihood more and more precarious; the collisions between individual workmen and individual bourgeois take more and more the character of collisions between two classes. Thereupon, the workers begin to form combinations (Trades Unions) against the bourgeois; they club together in order to keep up the rate of wages; they found permanent associations in order to make provision beforehand for these occasional revolts. Here and there, the contest breaks out into riots.

Now and then the workers are victorious, but only for a time. The real fruit of their battles lies, not in the immediate result, but in the ever expanding union of the workers. This union is helped on by the improved means of communication that are created by modern industry, and that place the workers of different localities in contact with one another. It was just this contact that was needed to centralize the numerous local struggles, all of the same character, into one national struggle between classes. But every class struggle is a political struggle. And that union, to attain which the burghers of the Middle Ages, with their miserable highways, required centuries, the modern proletarian, thanks to railways, achieve in a few years.

This organization of the proletarians into a class, and, consequently into a political party, is continually being upset again by the competition between the workers themselves. But it ever rises up again, stronger, firmer, mightier. It compels legislative recognition of particular interests of the workers, by taking advantage of the divisions among the bourgeoisie itself. Thus, the ten-hours' bill in England was carried.

Altogether collisions between the classes of the old society further, in many ways, the course of development of the proletariat. The bourgeoisie finds itself involved in a constant battle. At first with the aristocracy; later on, with those portions of the bourgeoisie itself, whose interests have become antagonistic to the progress of industry; at all time with the bourgeoisie of foreign countries. In all these battles, it sees itself compelled to appeal to the proletariat, to ask for help, and thus, to drag it into the political arena. The bourgeoisie itself, therefore, supplies the proletariat with its own elements of political and general education, in other words, it furnishes the proletariat with weapons for fighting the bourgeoisie. . . .

Of all the classes that stand face to face with the bourgeoisie today, the proletariat alone is a really revolutionary class. The other classes decay and finally disappear in the face of Modern Industry; the proletariat is its special and essential product.

The lower middle class, the small manufacturer, the shopkeeper, the artisan, the peasant, all these fight against the bourgeoisie, to save from extinction their existence as fractions of the middle class. They are therefore not revolutionary, but conservative. Nay more, they are reactionary, for they try to roll back the wheel of history. If by chance, they are revolutionary, they are only so in view of their impending transfer into the proletariat; they thus defend not their present, but their future interests, they desert their own standpoint to place themselves at that of the proletariat.

The "dangerous class" [*lumpenproletariat*], the social scum, that passively rotting mass thrown off by the lowest layers of the old society, may, here and there, be swept into the movement by a proletarian revolution; its conditions of life, however, prepare it far more for the part of a bribed tool of reactionary intrigue.

In the condition of the proletariat, those of old society at large are already virtually swamped. . . .

All the preceding classes that got the upper hand sought to fortify their already acquired status by subjecting society at large to their conditions of appropriation. The proletarians cannot become masters of the productive forces of society, except by abolishing their own previous mode of appropriation, and thereby also every other previous mode of appropriation. They have nothing of their own to secure and to fortify; their mission is to destroy all previous securities for, and insurances of, individual property.

All previous historical movements were movements of minorities, or in the interest of minorities. The proletarian movement is the self-conscious, independent movement of the immense majority, in the interest of the immense majority. The proletariat, the lowest stratum of our present society, cannot stir, cannot raise itself up, without the whole superincumbent strata of official society being sprung into the air. Though not in substance, yet in form, the struggle of the proletariat with the bourgeoisie is at first a national struggle. The proletariat of each country must, of course, first of all settle matters with its own bourgeoisie.

In depicting the most general phases of the development of the proletariat, we traced the more or less veiled civil war, raging within existing society, up to the point where that war breaks out into open revolution, and where the violent overthrow of the bourgeoisie lays the foundation for the sway of the proletariat.

Hitherto, every form of society has been based, as we have already seen, on the antagonism of oppressing and oppressed classes. But in order to oppress a class, certain conditions must be assured to it under which it can, at least, continue its slavish existence. . . . The essential conditions for the existence and for the sway of the bourgeois class is the formation and augmentation of capital; the condition for capital is wage-labor. Wage-labor rests exclusively on competition between the laborers. The advance of industry, whose involuntary promoter is the bourgeoisie, replaces the isolation of the laborers, due to competition, by the revolutionary combination, due to association. The development of Modern Industry, therefore, cuts from under its feet the very foundation on which the bourgeoisie produces and appropriates products. What the bourgeoisie therefore produces, above all, are its own grave-diggers. Its fall and the victory of the proletariat are equally inevitable. . . .

Chapter 4: Position of the Communists in Relation to the Various Existing Opposition Parties

The Communists disdain to conceal their views and aims. They openly declare that their ends can be attained only by the forcible overthrow of all existing social conditions. Let the ruling classes tremble at a Communistic revolution. The proletarians have nothing to lose but their chains. They have a world to win.

WORKERS OF ALL COUNTRIES, UNITE!

READING QUESTIONS

1. How do Marx and Engels describe the power relationship between the bourgeoisie and the proletariat? How is it changing?

2. In Marx and Engels's view, what is the fundamental source of historical change?

3. Why, according to Marx and Engels, is a working-class revolution against the capitalist middle class inevitable? What do they suggest workers do to hasten the arrival of the revolution?

21-5 | Following Mademoiselle Liberté
EUGÈNE DELACROIX, *Liberty Leading the People* (1830)

Marianne, a female figure representing liberty and reason, became a central element in French political iconography during the French Revolution. From that point forward, French artists have used Marianne to connect the political events of their day to France's revolutionary legacy, drawing on this powerful symbol of the promise of the Revolution to give meaning to their own struggles. The work of French artist Eugène Delacroix (1798–1863) provides an example of this phenomenon. In 1830, with France once again convulsed by revolutionary upheaval, Delacroix placed Marianne in the thick of the Parisian street fighting, leading a crowd of revolutionaries forward over their fallen comrades, pointing the way toward the realization of France's national destiny.

Gianni Dagli Orti/Shutterstock.

READING QUESTIONS

1. What social classes are represented in the painting? What do they suggest about the political alliances that shaped the revolution of 1830?

2. How might we interpret the fact that liberty is portrayed as a young woman? How might we react to the fact that her dress is torn to reveal her breasts?

3. What does Delacroix's painting suggest about the place of the French Revolution in French national identity in the early nineteenth century?

21-6 | Workers Demand the Vote

The People's Charter (1838)

In 1832 a major reform of Britain's Parliament took place. Although working-class agitation was a significant factor in pressuring the government to act, the newly created uniform borough (town) voting franchise excluded almost the entire working class from the electorate. One response to this outcome was Chartism, an explicitly working-class political movement

London Working Men's Association, "Six Points of the People's Charter," www.chartists.net/The-six-points.htm, accessed March 11, 2013.

based on "The People's Charter," a list of demands embodied in a petition to Parliament. The charter was drawn up by six members of Parliament—Daniel O'Connell, John Arthur Roebuck, John Temple Leader, Charles Hindley, Thomas Perronet Thompson, and William Sharman Crawford—and six working-class radicals—Henry Hetherington, John Cleave, James Watson, Richard Moore, William Lovett, and Henry Vincent. Although overwhelmingly rejected when it was presented to Parliament in 1839, 1842, and 1848, five of the charter's six demands (annual parliamentary elections being the exception) became law by 1918.

1. **A vote** for every man twenty-one years of age, of sound mind, and not undergoing punishment for crime.

2. **The ballot**[1]—To protect the elector in the exercise of his vote.

3. **No property qualification** for Members of Parliament[2]—thus enabling the constituencies to return the man of their choice, be he rich or poor.

4. **Payment of members**, thus enabling an honest tradesman, working man, or other person, to serve a constituency, when taken from his business to attend to the interests of the Country.

5. **Equal constituencies** securing the same amount of representation for the same number of electors, instead of allowing small constituencies to swamp the votes of large ones.

6. **Annual Parliaments**, thus presenting the most effectual check to bribery and intimidation, since though a constituency might be bought once in seven years (even with the ballot), no purse could buy a constituency (under a system of universal suffrage) in each ensuing twelve-month; and since members, when elected for a year only, would not be able to defy and betray their constituents as now.

READING QUESTIONS

1. Given that roughly 80 percent of Great Britain's population was working class, what would have been the political consequences of the first point of the Charter's enactment?

2. The Charter calls for an end to property qualifications for members of Parliament and also for payment of members of Parliament. What do these two demands suggest about the nature of parliamentary representation in early- and mid-nineteenth-century Britain? Who was running the country?

---

[1]**The ballot**: Secret ballot. At the time voting took place viva voce, out loud and in public, which many argued led to intimidation of voters.

[2]**No property qualification . . . Parliament**: At the time candidates for Parliament had to possess at least £300 in property. Since a skilled working man might earn £75 a year, the property qualification amounted to four years' wages.

21-7 | The Misery of the Potato Famine

WILLIAM STEUART TRENCH, *Realities of Irish Life* (1847)

As an Irish land agent, William Steuart Trench (1808–1872) was a firsthand witness to the ravages of the potato famine. A fungus, the potato blight, attacked the crop repeatedly during the years 1845–1848. The British government's limited efforts to provide help for the Irish were wholly inadequate. The Irish poor, whose diets consisted of little other than potatoes, were the victims of a Malthusian demographic disaster; between 1841 and 1851 Ireland's population fell between 20 and 25 percent. Estimates of the death toll range from around 750,000 to double that figure. Hundreds of thousands of the more fortunate Irish emigrated.

I did not see a child playing in the streets or on the roads; no children are to be seen outside the doors but a few sick and dying children. . . . In the districts which are now being depopulated by starvation, coffins are only used for the more wealthy. The majority were taken to the grave without any coffin, and buried in their rags: in some instances even the rags are taken from the corpse to cover some still living body. . . .

I then proceeded to Cappagh, which is a coast-guard station, in the midst of a starving population, which had been collected round mines which are not now worked. . . . On the evening before, I had heard of a boy living on the road to Cappagh, who had seen a dog tearing the head, and neck, and ribs of a man. I wished to learn the truth of this from the boy himself. He told me that the fact was so, and that his little brother had on another occasion seen another dog tearing the head of a man. The younger boy remarked that he had seen the remains of the head the day before in an adjoining field. I asked him to lead me to the spot, which he did, and I there found a part of the human head and under-jaw, gnawed, but marked with blood. I placed it under ground. . . .

On arriving at Cappagh, in the first house I saw a dead child lying in a corner of the house, and two children, pale as death, with their heads hanging down upon their breasts sitting by a small fire. The father had died on the road coming home from work. One of the children, a lad seventeen years of age, had been found, in the absence of his mother, who was looking for food, lying dead, with his legs held out of the fire by the little child which I then saw lying dead. Two other children had also died. The mother and the two children still alive had lived on one dish of barley for the last four days. On entering another house the doctor said, "Look there, Sir, you can't tell whether they are boys or girls." Taking up a skeleton child, he said, "Here is the way it is with them all; their legs swing and rock like the legs of a doll, they have the smell of mice."

From William Steuart Trench, *Realities of Irish Life* (London: Longmans, Green, 1868), pp. 394–398.

READING QUESTIONS

1. Why do you think the British government failed to take effectual action to alleviate the famine?

2. The blight, which affected potato harvests throughout northern Europe, did not produce a similar catastrophe in Britain. Why might Britain have been spared?

▪ COMPARATIVE AND DISCUSSION QUESTIONS ▪

1. Compare and contrast the vision of human nature articulated by Metternich, Mill, and Marx and Engels. How did the authors' ideas about the individual shape their views of society and social change?

2. What would Marx and Engels make of Ure's defense of the mechanization of industry, and how would they use it to support their arguments?

3. Why do you think Marx and Engels specifically named Metternich as one of communism's foes in the preamble to the *Communist Manifesto*? Was their emphasis warranted? What would Metternich think of his detractors, and why?

4. How do you think Marx and Engels regarded the Chartist movement, and why?

5. How might Metternich have responded to Delacroix's *Liberty Leading the People*? What alternative description of the legacy of the French Revolution might he have offered?

Life in the Emerging Urban Society
1840–1914

In the second half of the nineteenth century, Germany, France, and the United States followed Britain's lead and became industrialized nations. All witnessed the growth of the middle and working classes — and experienced the deplorable sanitary conditions that accompanied rapid urbanization. By the 1860s, however, significant advances in public health and medical science had increased the life expectancy of the urban poor. Politically, the expansion of the electorate in Britain, Germany, and France meant that, by 1884, the working class was the largest voting bloc in all three nations, although throughout Europe, women of all classes still lacked the vote. In the intellectual realm, literary Realists challenged the Romanticism of the first half of the century, basing their work on observation instead of emotion and rejecting pastoral scenes for gritty depictions of urban working-class life, while the theory of evolution and its outgrowth, Social Darwinism, seemed to directly defy the religious revival cultivated during the Romantic movement. The following documents reflect the facts that Britain set the mold for urbanization and industrialization — modernity — and that British thinkers were at the forefront of public health, scientific, and pseudoscientific trends.

22-1 | Sanitation and Public Health

SIR EDWIN CHADWICK, *Inquiry into the Sanitary Conditions of the Poor* (1842)

Sir Edwin Chadwick (1800–1880), a disciple of the radical philosopher Jeremy Bentham, spent his life in pursuit of social and sanitary reform. Bentham, Chadwick, and other radicals known as utilitarians shared many views with nineteenth-century liberals. Both liberals and utilitarians believed in human rationality and the concept of human progress, and both believed that poverty was chiefly the consequence of individual moral failings. The two groups parted ways sharply, however, over the role of government. Nineteenth-century liberals argued that government intervention was an impediment to social and economic progress. Utilitarians, in contrast, believed that the only measure of a policy's worth was its utility—that is, the degree to which it improved society as a whole. If, in particular situations, such as public health, government intervention could be shown to have a positive effect, the utilitarians had no ideological objection to such intervention.

After as careful an examination of the evidence collected as I have been enabled to make, I beg leave to recapitulate the chief conclusions which that evidence appears to me to establish.

First, as to the extent and operation of the evils which are the subject of this inquiry: —

That the various forms of epidemic, endemic, and other disease[1] caused, or aggravated, or propagated chiefly amongst the laboring classes by atmospheric impurities produced by decomposing animal and vegetable substances, by damp and filth, and close and overcrowded dwellings prevail amongst the population in every part of the kingdom, whether dwelling in separate houses, in rural villages, in small towns, in the larger towns—as they have been found to prevail in the lowest districts of the metropolis.

That such disease, wherever its attacks are frequent, is always found in connection with the physical circumstances above specified, and that where those circumstances are removed by drainage, proper cleansing, better ventilation, and other means of diminishing atmospheric impurity, the frequency and intensity of such disease is abated; and where the removal of the noxious agencies appears to be complete, such disease almost entirely disappears.

From Edwin Chadwick, *Report . . . from the Poor Law Commissioners on an Inquiry into the Sanitary Conditions of the Labouring Population of Great Britain* (London: W. Clowes and Sons, 1842), pp. 369–372.

[1]**epidemic, endemic, and other disease**: The laboring classes were plagued by cholera, typhus, typhoid fever, tuberculosis (known then as "consumption"), and numerous respiratory ailments primarily caused by air pollution and occupational hazards such as cotton dust ("Brown Lung").

The high prosperity in respect to employment and wages, and various and abundant food, have afforded to the laboring classes no exemptions from attacks of epidemic disease, which have been as frequent and as fatal in periods of commercial and manufacturing prosperity as in any others.

That the formation of all habits of cleanliness is obstructed by defective supplies of water.

That the annual loss of life from filth and bad ventilation are greater than the loss from death or wounds in any wars in which the country has been engaged in modern times.

That of the 43,000 cases of widowhood, and 112,000 cases of destitute orphanage relieved from the poor's rates in England and Wales alone, it appears that the greatest proportion of deaths of the heads of families occurred from the above specified and other removable causes; that their ages were under 45 years; that is to say, 13 years below the natural probabilities of life as shown by the experience of the whole population of Sweden. . . .

That, measuring the loss of working ability amongst large classes by the instances of gain, even from incomplete arrangements for the removal of noxious influences from places of work or from abodes, that this loss cannot be less than eight or ten years.

That the ravages of epidemics and other diseases do not diminish but tend to increase the pressure of population.

That in the districts where the mortality is greatest the births are not only sufficient to replace the numbers removed by death, but to add to the population.

That the younger population, bred up under noxious physical agencies, is inferior in physical organization and general health to a population preserved from the presence of such agencies.

That the population so exposed is less susceptible of moral influences, and the effects of education are more transient than with a healthy population.

That these adverse circumstances tend to produce an adult population short-lived, improvident, reckless, and intemperate, and with habitual avidity for sensual gratifications.

That these habits lead to the abandonment of all the conveniences and decencies of life, and especially lead to the overcrowding of their homes, which is destructive to the morality as well as the health of large classes of both sexes.

That defective town cleansing fosters habits of the most abject degradation and tends to the demoralization of large numbers of human beings, who subsist by means of what they find amidst the noxious filth accumulated in neglected streets and bye-places.

That the expenses of local public works are in general unequally and unfairly assessed, oppressively and uneconomically collected, by separate collections, wastefully expended in separate and inefficient operations by unskilled and practically irresponsible officers.

That the existing law for the protection of the public health and the constitutional machinery for reclaiming its execution, such as the Courts Leet,[2] have fallen into desuetude, and are in the state indicated by the prevalence of the evils they were intended to prevent.

Secondly. As to the means by which the present sanitary condition of the laboring classes may be improved: —

The primary and most important measures, and at the same time the most practicable, and within the recognized province of public administration, are drainage, the removal of all refuse of habitations, streets, and roads, and the improvement of the supplies of water.

That the chief obstacles to the immediate removal of decomposing refuse of towns and habitations have been the expense and annoyance of the hand labor and cartage requisite for the purpose.

That this expense may be reduced to one-twentieth or to one-thirtieth, or rendered inconsiderable, by the use of water and self-acting means of removal by improved and cheaper sewers and drains. . . .

That appropriate scientific arrangements for public drainage would afford important facilities for private land-drainage, which is important for the health as well as sustenance of the laboring classes.

That the expense of public drainage, of supplies of water laid on in houses, and of means of improved cleansing would be a pecuniary [monetary] gain, by diminishing the existing charges attendant on sickness and premature mortality.

That for the protection of the laboring classes and of the ratepayers against inefficiency and waste in all new structural arrangements for the protection of the public health, and to ensure public confidence that the expenditure will be beneficial, securities should be taken that all new local public works are devised and conducted by responsible officers qualified by the possession of the science and skill of civil engineers. . . .

That for the prevention of the disease occasioned by defective ventilation and other causes of impurity in places of work and other places where large numbers are assembled, and for the general promotion of the means necessary to prevent disease, that it would be good economy to appoint a district medical officer independent of private practice, and with the securities of special qualifications and responsibilities to initiate sanitary measures and reclaim the execution of the law.

That by the combinations of all these arrangements, it is probable that the full ensurable period of life indicated by the Swedish tables; that is, an increase of 13 years at least, may be extended to the whole of the laboring classes.

That the attainment of these and the other collateral advantages of reducing existing charges and expenditure are within the power of the legislature, and are

---

[2]**Courts Leet**: Law courts dating back to medieval times, when the administration of justice was overseen by individual noblemen. Many early industrial towns, Manchester among them, lacked comprehensive municipal governments until the 1830s and afterward, and thus such antiquated institutions like Courts Leet confronted situations that their creators had never envisioned and for which they were, as Chadwick suggests, wholly inadequate.

dependent mainly on the securities taken for the application of practical science, skill, and economy in the direction of local public works.

And that the removal of noxious physical circumstances, and the promotion of civic, household, and personal cleanliness, are necessary to the improvement of the moral condition of the population; for that sound morality and refinement in manners and health are not long found coexistent with filthy habits amongst any class of the community.

READING QUESTIONS

1. What, according to Chadwick, was the chief source of disease? Why does he say this?

2. What sorts of solutions does he offer to improve public health? What role did he believe government should play?

3. According to Chadwick, what is the relationship between sanitation and morality? Do you agree with his assessment? Why or why not?

22-2 | Life in London's East End

JACK LONDON, *The People of the Abyss* (1902)

Although known chiefly for works of fiction like *The Call of the Wild*, American author (and socialist) Jack London (1876–1916) also published nonfiction works. *The People of the Abyss* was based on his firsthand experience of living in the slums of London's East End for several months, where he pretended to be a stranded American sailor in order to observe the realities of working-class life. London's project reflects the larger trend toward Realism in nineteenth- and early-twentieth-century art and literature. In both Europe and the United States, artists, writers, and reformers sought to document social reality as a first step toward advancing the cause of social justice.

Chapter XLX: The Ghetto

The City of Dreadful Monotony the East End is often called, especially by well-fed, optimistic sightseers, who look over the surface of things and are merely shocked by the intolerable sameness and meanness of it all. If the East End is worthy of no worse title than The City of Dreadful Monotony, and if working people are unworthy of variety and beauty and surprise, it would not be such a bad place in which to live. But the East End does merit a worse title. It should be called The City of Degradation.

While it is not a city of slums, as some people imagine, it may well be said to be one gigantic slum. From the standpoint of simple decency and clean

From Jack London, *The People of the Abyss* (New York: Macmillan, 1903), pp. 210–218, 276–277, 314–317.

manhood and womanhood, any mean street, of all its mean streets, is a slum. Where sights and sounds abound which neither you nor I would care to have our children see and hear is a place where no man's children should live, and see and hear. Where you and I would not care to have our wives pass their lives is a place where no other man's wife should have to pass her life. For here, in the East End, the obscenities and brute vulgarities of life are rampant. There is no privacy. The bad corrupts the good, and all fester together. Innocent childhood is sweet and beautiful; but in East London innocence is a fleeting thing, and you must catch them before they crawl out of the cradle, or you will find the very babes as unholily wise as you.

The application of the Golden Rule determines that East London is an unfit place in which to live. Where you would not have your own babe live, and develop, and gather to itself knowledge of life and the things of life, is not a fit place for the babes of other men to live. . . . Political economy and the survival of the fittest can go hang if they say otherwise. What is not good enough for you is not good enough for other men, and there's no more to be said. . . .

The mean streets merely look mean from the outside, but inside the walls are to be found squalor, misery, and tragedy. While the following tragedy may be revolting to read, it must not be forgotten that the existence of it is far more revolting. In Devonshire Place, Lisson Grove, a short while back died an old woman of seventy-five years of age. At the inquest the coroner's officer stated that "all he found in the room was a lot of old rags covered with vermin. He had got himself smothered with the vermin. The room was in a shocking condition, and he had never seen anything like it. Everything was absolutely covered with vermin."

The doctor said: "He found deceased lying across the fender on her back. She had one garment and her stockings on. The body was quite alive with vermin, and all the clothes in the room were absolutely gray with insects. Deceased was very badly nourished and was very emaciated. She had extensive sores on her legs, and her stockings were adherent to those sores. The sores were the result of vermin."

A man present at the inquest wrote: "I had the evil fortune to see the body of the unfortunate woman as it lay in the mortuary; and even now the memory of that grewsome [sic] sight makes me shudder. There she lay in the mortuary shell, so starved and emaciated that she was a mere bundle of skin and bones. Her hair, which was matted with filth, was simply a nest of vermin. Over her bony chest leaped and rolled hundreds, thousands, myriads of vermin."

If it is not good for your mother and my mother so to die, then it is not good for this woman, whosoever's mother she might be, so to die. . . .

In such conditions, the outlook for children is hopeless. They die like flies, and those that survive, survive because they possess excessive vitality and a capacity of adaptation to the degradation with which they are surrounded. They have no home life. In the dens and lairs in which they live they are exposed to all that is obscene and indecent. And as their minds are made rotten, so are their bodies made rotten by bad sanitation, overcrowding, and underfeeding. When a father and mother live with three or four children in a room where the children take turn about in sitting up to drive the rats away from the sleepers, when those children never have enough to eat and are preyed upon and made miserable and weak by swarming vermin, the sort of men and women the survivors will make can readily be imagined. . . .

Five men can produce bread for a thousand. One man can produce cotton cloth for 250 people, woolens for 300, and boots and shoes for 1000. Yet it has been shown throughout the pages of this book that English folk by the millions do not receive enough food, clothes, and boots. Then arises the third and inexorable question: *If Civilization has increased the producing power of the average man, why has it not bettered the lot of the average man?*

There can be one answer only — MISMANAGEMENT. Civilization has made possible all manner of creature comforts and heart's delights. In these the average Englishman does not participate. If he shall be forever unable to participate, then Civilization falls. There is no reason for the continued existence of an artifice so avowed a failure. But it is impossible that men should have reared this tremendous artifice in vain. It stuns the intellect. To acknowledge so crushing a defeat is to give the death-blow to striving and progress.

One other alternative, and one other only, presents itself. *Civilization must be compelled to better the lot of the average man.* This accepted, it becomes at once a question of business management. Things profitable must be continued; things unprofitable must be eliminated. Either the Empire is a profit to England or it is a loss. If it is a loss, it must be done away with. If it is a profit, it must be managed so that the average man comes in for a share of the profit.

If the struggle for commercial supremacy is profitable, continue it. If it is not, if it hurts the worker and makes his lot worse than the lot of a savage, then fling foreign markets and industrial empire overboard. For it is a patent fact that if 40,000,000 people, aided by Civilization, possess a greater individual producing power than the Inuit,[1] then those 40,000,000 people should enjoy more creature comforts and heart's delights than the Inuits enjoy. . . .

In short, society must be reorganized, and a capable management put at the head. That the present management is incapable, there can be no discussion. . . . Blood empire is greater than political empire, and the English of the New World and the Antipodes are strong and vigorous as ever. But the political empire under which they are nominally assembled is perishing. The political machine known as the British Empire is running down. In the hands of its management it is losing momentum every day.

It is inevitable that this management, which has grossly and criminally mismanaged, shall be swept away. Not only has it been wasteful and inefficient, but it has misappropriated the funds. Every worn-out, pasty-faced pauper, every blind man, every prison babe, every man, woman, and child whose belly is gnawing with hunger pangs, is hungry because the funds have been misappropriated by the management.

Nor can one member of this managing class plead not guilty before the judgment bar of Man. "The living in their houses, and in their graves the dead,"

---

[1]**Inuit:** Aboriginal peoples of the arctic regions of Russia, North America, and Greenland.

are challenged by every babe that dies of innutrition, by every girl that flees the sweater's den to the nightly promenade of Piccadilly,[2] by every worked-out toiler that plunges into the canal. The food this managing class eats, the wine it drinks, the shows it makes, and the fine clothes it wears, are challenged by eight million mouths which have never had enough to fill them, and by twice eight million bodies which have never been sufficiently clothed and housed.

There can be no mistake. Civilization has increased man's producing power an hundred fold, and through mismanagement the men of Civilization live worse than the beasts, and have less to eat and wear and protect them from the elements than the savage Inuit in a frigid climate who lives to-day as he lived in the stone age ten thousand years ago.

READING QUESTIONS

1. To what causes does Jack London attribute the widespread poverty and misery among metropolitan London's poor?

2. Whom might he have hoped to influence with his work? What strategies did he employ in his effort to persuade his readers to take action?

3. What connections did London make between conditions in the East End and the condition of the British Empire? What were the political implications of the connections he made?

SOURCES IN CONVERSATION

Separate Spheres

The nineteenth-century societal ideal of separate spheres for men and women was predicated on the assumption that men and women had very different natures. Men were seen as both physically and mentally suited to the rough-and-tumble world of economic competition. It was men, therefore, that would provide the income that made the middle-class lifestyle possible, doing battle on behalf of their families in the office and the marketplace. Women, in contrast, were soft and yielding. Providers of comfort and care by nature, their job was to create a home that was a refuge for their husbands from the rigors of the outside world. It was the wife's role to remind her husband through her behavior, appearance, and the home she made of the values that made the struggle for advancement worthwhile. Thus, in theory, men and women formed a partnership, with each making a contribution to their joint achievement of the middle-class ideal.

---

[2]**that flees the sweater's den . . . Piccadilly:** That leaves work in a sweatshop to engage in prostitution.

READ AND COMPARE

1. These three documents all reflect a middle- to upper-class perspective of women's roles in British society. How do you suppose lower-class women in Britain would respond to these documents, and why do you think so?

2. How do you think Pankhurst would respond to the advice presented in the first two documents? How would Beeton respond to Pankhurst's ideas?

22-3 | ISABELLA BEETON, *Mrs. Beeton's Book of Household Management* (1861)

Isabella Beeton (1836–1865) was a British journalist whose earliest articles appeared in the *English Woman's Domestic Magazine*, one of the first magazines targeted specifically at middle-class women. *Mrs. Beeton's Book of Household Management*, first published in 1861, contained more than 2,700 entries of recipes and practical instructions, from how to keep moths from attacking clothes to how to care for horses. A bestseller that was continually reprinted, it was almost certainly the most widely consulted book on the subject in the decades following its appearance. The excerpts included here focus on the responsibilities of servants. For middle-class and elite women, management of servants was one of the most important tasks. Such women were not expected to cook and clean, but they were responsible for making sure that their households were the well-ordered havens of cleanliness and tranquility demanded by promoters of the late-nineteenth-century cult of domesticity.

Masters and Mistresses. — It has been said that good masters and mistresses make good servants, and this to a great extent is true. There are certainly some men and women in the wide field of servitude whom it would be impossible to train into good servants, but the conduct of both master and mistress is seldom without its effect upon these dependents. They are not mere machines, and no one has a right to consider them in that light. The sensible master and the kind mistress know, that if servants depend on them for their means of living, in their turn they are dependent on their servants for very many of the comforts of life; and that, with a proper amount of care in choosing servants, and treating them like reasonable beings, and making slight excuses for the shortcomings of human nature, they will, save in some exceptional case, be tolerably well served, and, in most instances, surround themselves with attached domestics. . . .

The Lady's-Maid. — The qualifications a lady's maid should possess are a thorough knowledge of hair dressing, dressmaking and repairing and restoring clothes. She should be able to pack well, and her taste, being often called into requisition in matters of dress, should be good. It is also essential that she be well spoken, quiet in manner and quick; that she should be clean and honest goes

From Isabella Beeton, *Mrs. Beeton's Book of Household Management* (London: Ward, Lock and Co., 1888), pp. 1454, 1471, 1473, 1478–1479, 1481–1482.

without saying. A lady's maid having so much more intercourse with her mistress than any other servant should not only possess, but learn, discretion from day to day. To know when to speak and when to be silent, and to be willing to bear with patience any little caprices of taste and temper with which she may have to contend.

Her first duty in the morning, after having performed her own toilet, is to prepare the bath and everything for dressing for her mistress, taking her an early cup of tea if she requires one. She then examines the clothes put off by her mistress the evening before, either to put them away, or to see that they are all in order to put on again. During the winter and in wet weather, the dresses should be carefully examined, and the mud removed. Dresses of tweed, and other woolen materials may be laid out on a table and brushed all over; but in general, even in woolen fabrics, the lightness of the tissues renders brushing unsuitable to dresses, and it is better to remove the dust from the folds by beating them lightly with a handkerchief or thin cloth. Silk dresses should never be brushed, but rubbed with a piece of merino, or other soft material, of a similar color, kept for the purpose. Summer dresses . . . simply require shaking; but if the muslin be tumbled, it must be ironed afterwards. If the dresses require slight repair, it should be done at once: "a stitch in time saves nine." . . .

A waiting-maid who wishes to make herself useful will study the fashion-books with attention, so as to be able to aid her mistress's judgment in dressing, according to the prevailing fashion, with such modifications as her style and figure require. She will also, if she has her mistress's interest at heart, employ her spare time in repairing and making up dresses which have served one purpose, to serve another also; or turning many things, unfitted for her mistress, to use for the younger branches of the family. The lady's-maid may thus render herself invaluable to her mistress, and increase her own happiness in so doing. The exigencies of fashion and luxury are such, that all ladies, except those of the very highest rank, will consider themselves fortunate in having about them a thoughtful person, capable of diverting their finery to a useful purpose. . . .

Duties of the Housemaid. — "Cleanliness is next to godliness," saith the proverb, and "order" is in the next degree; the housemaid, then, may be said to be the handmaiden to two of the most prominent virtues. Her duties are very numerous, and many of the comforts of the family depend on their performance; but they are simple and easy to a person naturally clean and orderly, and desirous of giving satisfaction. . . .

The first duty of the housemaid in winter is to open the shutters of all the lower rooms in the house, and take up the hearthrugs of those rooms which she is going to "do" before breakfast. In some families, where there is only a cook and housemaid kept, and where the drawing-rooms are large, the cook has the care of the dining-room, and the housemaid that of the breakfast-room, library, and drawing-rooms. After the shutters are all opened, she sweeps the breakfast-room, sweeping the dust towards the fire-place, of course previously removing the fender. She should then lay a cloth (generally made of coarse wrappering) over the carpet in front of the stove, and on this should place her housemaid's box, containing black-lead brushes, leathers, emery-paper, cloth, black lead, and all utensils necessary for cleaning a grate, with the cinder-pail on the other side. She now sweeps up the ashes, and deposits them in her cinder-pail, which is a japanned tin pail, with a wire-sifter inside, and a closely-fitting top. In this pail the cinders are sifted, and reserved for use in the kitchen or under the copper, the ashes only being thrown away. The cinders disposed of, she proceeds to black-lead the grate, producing the black lead, the soft brush for laying it on, her blacking and polishing brushes, from the box which contains her tools. This housemaid's box should be kept well stocked. Having blackened, brushed, and polished every part, and made all clean and bright, she now proceeds to lay the fire. . . .

Bright grates require unceasing attention to keep them in perfect order. A day should never pass without the housemaid rubbing with a dry leather the polished parts of a grate, as also the fender and fire-irons. A careful and attentive housemaid should have no occasion ever to use emery-paper for any part but the bars, which, of course, become blackened by the fire. (Some mistresses, to save labor, have a double set of bars, one set bright for the summer, and another black set to use when fires are in requisition.) . . .

The several fires lighted, the housemaid proceeds with her dusting, and polishing the several pieces of furniture in the breakfast-parlor, leaving no corner unvisited. Before sweeping the carpet, it is a good practice to sprinkle it all over with tea-leaves, which not only lay all dust, but give a slightly fragrant smell to the room. It is now in order for the reception of the family; and where there is neither footman nor parlor-maid, she now proceeds to the dressing-room, and lights her mistress's fire, if she is in the habit of having one to dress by. Her mistress is called, hot water placed in the dressing-room for her use, her clothes—as far as they are under the house-maid's charge—put before the fire to air, hanging a fire-guard on the bars where there is one, while she proceeds to prepare the breakfast. . . .

READING QUESTIONS

1. What do Beeton's instructions about the management and duties of household servants tell us about how life in modern urban societies has altered over the past century and a half?

2. What does Beeton infer are some of the most typical problems that exist between masters and servants?

3. What does this excerpt tell us about class divisions and about Beeton's attitudes toward the "lower orders," from which servants came?

4. What do the daily chores described here reveal about nineteenth-century attitudes toward work and the use of time?

5. Britain's aristocracy had been managing servants for centuries at the time this guide was published. To whom do you think Beeton was imparting her instructions, regardless of the grandeur of the households she describes?

22-4 | *Dressing the Respectable Woman* (ca. 1890)

The clothes worn by late-nineteenth-century middle-class and elite women concerned with respectability were form-fitting, multilayered, cumbersome, and uncomfortable. In order to achieve what was seen as the ideal female silhouette, women began by putting on a set of rigid undergarments, including whale-bone corsets, an operation that required the assistance of a servant. Once dressed, the fashionable woman remained dependent on her servants, since her attire restricted her movement and made physical labor all but impossible.

Reception dress, bodice and skirt (silk, velvet, lace & damask)/Cregmile, Kate R. (1891–1923)/CINCINNATI ART MUSEUM/Cincinnati Art Museum, Ohio, USA/Bridgeman Images.

READING QUESTIONS

1. What details about the dress catch your attention? Why?

2. Do you think it likely that nineteenth-century women had waists as narrow as this dress suggests? What would have been required for a typical woman to fit into this dress?

3. What does the dress tell you about late-nineteenth-century ideas about the "perfect" female body?

4. What connections can you make between this dress and nineteenth-century ideas about the social and economic roles of elite and middle-class women?

22-5 | EMMELINE PANKHURST, *My Own Story* (1914)

The political struggle over whether women should vote in Britain was particularly intense, and the women who fought so bitterly to win suffrage would not be vindicated until 1928, when the Representation of the People Act gave all women over the age of twenty-one the right to vote. Emmeline Pankhurst played a pivotal role in the conflict, and the Women's Social and Political Union that she founded was criticized for using very militant tactics, including vandalism, arson, and assault, for which members were often jailed. In jail, the union's members engaged in hunger and thirst strikes to politically pressure authorities. The following excerpt is Emmeline's recounting of a speech she made to a judge in 1913 before being sentenced to three years of prison labor.

I spoke once more to the Judge.

"The jury have found me guilty, with a strong recommendation to mercy, and I do not see, since motive is not taken into account in human laws, that they could do otherwise after your summing up. But since motive is not taken into account in human laws, and since I, whose motives are not ordinary motives, am about to be sentenced by you to the punishment which is accorded to people whose motives are selfish motives, I have only this to say: If it was impossible for a different verdict to be found; if it is your duty to sentence me, as it will be presently, then I want to say to you, as a private citizen, and to the jury as private citizens, that I, standing here, found guilty by the laws of my country, I say to you it is your duty, as private citizens, to do what you can to put an end to this intolerable state of affairs. I put that duty upon you. And I want to say, *whatever the sentence you pass upon me, I shall do what is humanly possible to terminate that sentence at the earliest possible moment. I have no sense of guilt. I feel I have done my duty. I look upon myself as a prisoner of war. I am under no moral obligation to conform to, or in any way accept, the sentence imposed upon me.* I shall take the desperate remedy that other women have taken. It is obvious to you that the struggle will be an unequal one, but I shall make it—I shall make it as long as I have an ounce of strength left in me, or any life left in me.

From Emmeline Pankhurst, *My Own Story* (London: Eveleigh Nash, 1914), pp. 297–299.

"I shall fight, I shall fight, I shall fight, from the moment I enter prison to struggle against overwhelming odds; I shall resist the doctors if they attempt to feed me. I was sentenced last May in this court to nine months' imprisonment. I remained in prison six weeks. There are people who have laughed at the ordeal of hunger-striking and forcible feeding. All I can say is, and the doctors can bear me out, that I was released because, had I remained there much longer, I should have been a dead woman.

"I know what it is because I have gone through it. My own daughter has only just left it. There are women there still facing that ordeal, facing it twice a day. Think of it, my lord, twice a day this fight is gone through. Twice a day a weak woman resisting overwhelming force, fights and fights as long as she has strength left; fights against women and even against men, resisting with her tongue, with her teeth, this ordeal. Last night in the House of Commons some alternative was discussed, or rather, some additional punishment. Is it not a strange thing, my lord, that laws which have sufficed to restrain men through-out the history of this country do not suffice now to restrain women — decent women, honourable women?

"Well, my lord, I do want you to realise it. I am not whining about my pun-ishment, I invited it. I deliberately broke the law, not hysterically or emotionally, but of set serious purpose, because I honestly feel it is the only way. Now, I put the responsibility of what is to follow upon you, my lord, as a private citizen, and upon the gentlemen of the jury, as private citizens, and upon all the men in this court — what are you, with your political powers, going to do to end this intolerable situation?

"*To the women I have represented, to the women who, in response to my incitement, have faced these terrible consequences, have broken laws, to them, I want to say I am not going to fail them, but to face it as they face it, to go through with it, and I know that they will go on with the fight whether I live or whether I die.*

"*This movement will go on and on until we have the rights of citizens in this coun-try, as women have in our Colonies, as they will have throughout the civilised world before this woman's war is ended.*

"That is all I have to say."

READING QUESTIONS

1. What social norms for British women in the early twentieth century did Pankhurst and other suffragettes violate?

2. How did the actions of these militant women refute the assumptions about the nature of women that informed British society at that time?

3. Pankhurst and other especially militant British suffragettes were criticized by more moderate suffragettes for their tactics. Were their tactics really necessary to effect change? Why or why not?

22-6 | A New Creation Story
CHARLES DARWIN, *The Descent of Man* (1871)

Charles Darwin (1809–1882) was the most prominent scientist in nineteenth-century Britain. His major works, *On the Origin of Species by Means of Natural Selection* (1859) and *The Descent of Man* (1871), put forward the theory of natural selection and argued that humans were closely related to the great apes, respectively. They are the foundational texts for modern evolutionary science, although they were immensely controversial on publication and are still objects of heated contention.

The main conclusion here arrived at, and now held by many naturalists who are well competent to form a sound judgment, is that man is descended from some less highly organized form. . . . He who is not content to look, like a savage, at the phenomena of nature as disconnected, cannot any longer believe that man is the work of a separate act of creation. He will be forced to admit that the close resemblance of the embryo of man to that, for instance, of a dog—the construction of his skull, limbs, and whole frame on the same plan with that of other mammals, independently of the uses to which the parts may be put—the occasional re-appearance of various structures, for instance of several muscles, which man does not normally possess, but which are common to the Quadrumana[1]—and a crowd of analogous facts—all point in the plainest manner to the conclusion that man is the co-descendant with other mammals of a common progenitor.

We have seen that man incessantly presents individual differences in all parts of his body and in his mental faculties. These differences or variations seem to be induced by the same general causes, and to obey the same laws as with the lower animals. In both cases similar laws of inheritance prevail. Man tends to increase at a greater rate than his means of subsistence; consequently he is occasionally subjected to a severe struggle for existence, and natural selection will have effected whatever lies within its scope. A succession of strongly-marked variations of a similar nature is by no means requisite; slight fluctuating differences in the individual suffice for the work of natural selection; not that we have any reason to suppose that in the same species, all parts of the organization tend to vary to the same degree. . . .

By considering the embryological structure of man,—the homologies which he presents with the lower animals,—the rudiments which he retains,—and the reversions to which he is liable, we can partly recall in imagination the former condition of our early progenitors; and can approximately place them in their proper place in the zoological series. We thus learn that man is descended from a hairy, tailed quadruped, probably arboreal in its habits, and an inhabitant

---

From Charles Darwin, *The Descent of Man and Selection in Relation to Sex* (New York: Appleton and Co., 1883), pp. 620–621, 623–624, 626–629, 633–634.

[1]**Quadrumana**: Term once used to describe primates with opposable digits (thumbs) on all four feet.

of the Old World. This creature, if its whole structure had been examined by a naturalist, would have been classed amongst the Quadrumana, as surely as the still more ancient progenitor of the Old and New World monkeys. The Quadrumana and all the higher mammals are probably derived from an ancient marsupial animal, and this through a long line of diversified forms, from some amphibian-like creature, and this again from some fish-like animal. In the dim obscurity of the past we can see that the early progenitor of all the Vertebrata must have been an aquatic animal, provided with branchiæ,[2] with the two sexes united in the same individual, and with the most important organs of the body (such as the brain and heart) imperfectly or not at all developed. This animal seems to have been more like the larvæ of the existing marine Ascidians[3] than any other known form.

The high standard of our intellectual powers and moral disposition is the greatest difficulty which presents itself, after we have been driven to this conclusion on the origin of man. But every one who admits the principle of evolution, must see that the mental powers of the higher animals, which are the same in kind with those of man, though so different in degree, are capable of advancement. . . .

The moral nature of man has reached its present standard, partly through the advancement of his reasoning powers and consequently of a just public opinion, but especially from his sympathies having been rendered more tender and widely diffused through the effects of habit, example, instruction, and reflection. It is not improbable that after long practice virtuous tendencies may be inherited. With the more civilized races, the conviction of the existence of an all-seeing Deity has had a potent influence on the advance of morality. Ultimately man does not accept the praise or blame of his fellows as his sole guide though few escape this influence, but his habitual convictions, controlled by reason, afford him the safest rule. His conscience then becomes the supreme judge and monitor. Nevertheless the first foundation or origin of the moral sense lies in the social instincts, including sympathy; and these instincts no doubt were primarily gained, as in the case of the lower animals, through natural selection.

The belief in God has often been advanced as not only the greatest but the most complete of all the distinctions between man and the lower animals. It is however impossible, as we have seen, to maintain that this belief is innate or instinctive in man. On the other hand a belief in all-pervading spiritual agencies seems to be universal, and apparently follows from a considerable advance in man's reason, and from a still greater advance in his faculties of imagination, curiosity, and wonder. I am aware that the assumed instinctive belief in God has been used by many persons as an argument for His existence. But this is a rash argument, as we should thus be compelled to believe in the existence of many cruel and malignant spirits, only a little more powerful than man; for the belief in them is far more general than in a beneficent Deity. The idea of a universal and beneficent Creator does not seem to arise in the mind of man, until he has been elevated by long-continued culture. . . .

---

[2]**branchiæ**: Gills.
[3]**Ascidians**: Genus of mollusks.

I am aware that the conclusions arrived at in this work will be denounced by some as highly irreligious; but he who denounces them is bound to show why it is more irreligious to explain the origin of man as a distinct species by descent from some lower form, through the laws of variation and natural selection, than to explain the birth of the individual through the laws of ordinary reproduction. The birth both of the species and of the individual are equally parts of that grand sequence of events, which our minds refuse to accept as the result of blind chance. The understanding revolts at such a conclusion, whether or not we are able to believe that every slight variation of structure, — the union of each pair in marriage, — the dissemination of each seed, — and other such events, have all been ordained for some special purpose.

Sexual selection has been treated at great length in this work, for, as I have attempted to show, it has played an important part in the history of the organic world. I am aware that much remains doubtful, but I have endeavored to give a fair view of the whole case. In the lower divisions of the animal kingdom, sexual selection seems to have done nothing. . . . When, however, we come to the Arthropoda and Vertebrata,[4] even to the lowest classes in these two great Sub-Kingdoms, sexual selection has effected much. . . .

Sexual selection depends on the success of certain individuals over others of the same sex, in relation to the propagation of the species; while natural selection depends on the success of both sexes, at all ages, in relation to the general conditions of life. The sexual struggle is of two kinds; in the one it is between the individuals of the same sex, generally the males, in order to drive away or kill their rivals, the females remaining passive; while in the other, the struggle is likewise between the individuals of the same sex, in order to excite or charm those of the opposite sex, generally the females, which no longer remain passive, but select the more agreeable partners. . . .

The main conclusion arrived at in this work, namely that man is descended from some lowly organized form, will, I regret to think, be highly distasteful to many. But there can hardly be a doubt that we are descended from barbarians. The astonishment which I felt on first seeing a party of Fuegians[5] on a wild and broken shore will never be forgotten by me, for the reflection at once rushed into my mind—such were our ancestors. These men were absolutely naked and bedaubed with paint, their long hair was tangled, their mouths frothed with excitement, and their expression was wild, startled, and distrustful. They possessed hardly any arts, and like wild animals lived on what they could catch; they had no government, and were merciless to every one not of their own small tribe. He who has seen a savage in his native land will not feel much shame, if forced to acknowledge that the blood of some more humble creature flows in his veins. For my own part I would as soon be descended from that heroic little monkey, who braved his dreaded enemy in order to save the life of his keeper,

---

[4]**Arthropoda and Vertebrata:** Insects and vertebrates (animals with spinal columns), respectively.

[5]**Fuegians:** Inhabitants of Tierra del Fuego, at the tip of South America; Patagonians.

or from that old baboon, who descending from the mountains, carried away in triumph his young comrade from a crowd of astonished dogs—as from a savage who delights to torture his enemies, offers up bloody sacrifices, practices infanticide without remorse, treats his wives like slaves, knows no decency, and is haunted by the grossest superstitions.

Man may be excused for feeling some pride at having risen, though not through his own exertions, to the very summit of the organic scale; and the fact of his having thus risen, instead of having been aboriginally placed there, may give him hope for a still higher destiny in the distant future. But we are not here concerned with hopes or fears, only with the truth as far as our reason permits us to discover it; and I have given the evidence to the best of my ability. We must, however, acknowledge, as it seems to me, that man with all his noble qualities, with sympathy which feels for the most debased, with benevolence which extends not only to other men but to the humblest living creature, with his god-like intellect which has penetrated into the movements and constitution of the solar system—with all these exalted powers—Man still bears in his bodily frame the indelible stamp of his lowly origin.

READING QUESTIONS

1. On what grounds does Darwin base his argument that "man is descended from some less highly organized form"? Are they compelling? Why or why not?

2. Why does Darwin maintain that the "assumed instinctive belief in God [that] has been used by many persons as an argument for His existence," is "a rash argument"?

3. What assumptions about human civilization and progress are hinted at in this work?

22-7 | Weeding Out the Weak

HERBERT SPENCER, *Social Statics: Survival of the Fittest Applied to Humankind* (1851)

Like Darwin, Herbert Spencer (1820–1903) was an English intellectual, although his work concerned philosophy and social theory rather than science. Spencer was one of the earliest champions of what would later be called Social Darwinism—the use of the concept of evolution to justify social inequality and to "demonstrate" the racial superiority of people of northern European ancestry. The following excerpt comes from his first major work, *Social Statics* (1851), which attracted relatively little attention on publication but which contains many of the ideas that would make Spencer one of the most well-known and influential British intellectuals during the 1870s and 1880s.

From Herbert Spencer, "Social Statics," in *Liberalism: Its Meaning and History*, ed. J. Salwyn Schapiro (New York: Van Nostrand Reinhold, 1958), pp. 136–137.

In common with its other assumptions of secondary offices, the assumption by a government of the office of Reliever-general to the poor, is necessarily forbidden by the principle that a government cannot rightly do anything more than protect. In demanding from a citizen contributions for the mitigation of distress — contributions not needed for the due administration of men's rights — the state is, as we have seen, reversing its function, and diminishing that liberty to exercise the faculties which it was instituted to maintain. Possibly . . . some will assert that by satisfying the wants of the pauper, a government is in reality extending his liberty to exercise his faculties. . . . But this statement of the case implies a confounding of two widely different things. To enforce the fundamental law — to take care that every man has freedom to do all that he wills, provided he infringes not the equal freedom of any other man — this is the special purpose for which the civil power exists. Now insuring to each the right to pursue within the specified limits the objects of his desires without let or hindrance, is quite a separate thing from insuring him satisfaction. . . .

Pervading all nature we may see at work a stern discipline, which is a little cruel that it may be very kind. That state of universal warfare maintained throughout the lower creation, to the great perplexity of many worthy people, is at bottom the most merciful provision which the circumstances admit of. . . . The poverty of the incapable, the distresses that come upon the imprudent, the starvation of the idle, and those shoulderings aside of the weak by the strong, which leave so many "in shallows and in miseries," are the decrees of a large, farseeing benevolence. It seems hard that an unskillfulness which with all its efforts he cannot overcome, should entail hunger upon the artisan. It seems hard that a laborer incapacitated by sickness from competing with his stronger fellows, should have to bear the resulting privations. It seems hard that widows and orphans should be left to struggle for life or death. Nevertheless, when regarded not separately, but in connection with the interests of universal humanity, these harsh fatalities are seen to be full of the highest beneficence — the same beneficence which brings to early graves the children of diseased parents, and singles out the low-spirited, the intemperate, and the debilitated as the victims of an epidemic.

READING QUESTIONS

1. What, according to Spencer, is the "fundamental law"? Do you agree with it? Why or why not? Where else have you seen this "fundamental law"?

2. On what grounds could Spencer argue that the death of "the children of diseased parents" was in the "interests of universal humanity" and "full of the highest beneficence" for mankind?

3. What might explain the appeal of Spencer's ideas? In what ways did he provide "scientific" support for prevailing social, cultural, and racial assumptions?

■ COMPARATIVE AND DISCUSSION QUESTIONS ■

1. In what ways does Beeton's *Book of Household Management* reflect the new nineteenth-century awareness of sanitation's relationship to health, made explicit in Chadwick's report?

2. Contrast Beeton's depiction of a middle-class home with London's description of the housing of the working-class poor. What does this contrast suggest about the distribution of wealth in industrial Britain?

3. How might Spencer respond to the condition of the British poor as described by Chadwick and London? What might Chadwick and London say to Spencer?

4. What would Robert Owen (Document 20-5) propose as a solution to the problems described by London and Chadwick?

5. How would Locke (Document 18-3) and Metternich (Document 21-2) respond to Darwin's contention that "the moral nature of man has reached its present standard, partly through the advancement of his reasoning powers and consequently of a just public opinion, but especially from his sympathies having been rendered more tender and widely diffused through the effects of habit, example, instruction, and reflection"?

6. Compare and contrast Darwin's and Spencer's views on civilization and human survival. How might Darwin have responded to the pseudo-Darwinian arguments put forward by late-nineteenth and early-twentieth-century proponents of white racial supremacy?

7. What do you think Darwin and Spencer would say in response to Pankhurst's assertions about the moral imperative of women's suffrage? Why do you think so?

23

The Age of Nationalism
1850–1914

Before 1848, nationalism was a revolutionary ideology, often concerned with rebelling against autocratic forms of government or against external rule. Romantics saw in the shared history and culture of particular peoples an argument for the overthrow of imperial domination. Liberals linked nationalism to economic progress and the protection of individual liberty, convinced that both could be achieved only if the will of the people was expressed through representative government. In the second half of the nineteenth century, however, conservative leaders such as Germany's Otto von Bismarck harnessed the power of nationalism to garner support for conservative, even reactionary, governments and policies. While nationalism served as a catalyst for political unification in Italy and Germany, just as often it led to division and conflict. The United States fought a bloody and bitter civil war between 1861 and 1865 over the power of the federal government to stop the expansion of slavery. France went from the Second Republic to the Second Empire, and then faced the secession of Paris from France in 1871. Conflicting nationalisms undermined the strength and stability of the Austro-Hungarian Empire. Toward the end of the century, the adoption of nationalism as the basis for personal identity led to horrifying violence against perceived outsiders, particularly Europe's Jewish population. The Dreyfus affair in France (1894–1906) spurred a Jewish nationalist movement—Zionism—as some members of Europe's Jewish community became convinced that lasting peace and security for Jews could be achieved only through the foundation of a Jewish nation-state.

23-1 | Romantic Nationalism in Italy
A Good Offer (1860)

The movement for Italian unification and independence culminated in 1870, but it was a long and protracted process, and it required brilliant political, diplomatic, and military maneuvers by Count Cavour, the prime minister of Sardinia-Piedmont, and the capable support of patriot fighter Giuseppe Garibaldi. After supporting progressive causes earlier in his reign, Pope Pius IX opposed unification from 1848 to 1870 and liberal reforms in Italy until 1878. In September 1860, when Count Cavour's army vanquished a papal army, the pope's resistance to unification and liberalism was dealt a serious blow. This cartoon from the English publication *Punch* depicts Garibaldi offering the pope the cap of liberty, symbolic of liberal reforms in a united Italy, to replace his heavy papal crown, calling it "a good offer."

PUNCH, OR THE LONDON CHARIVARI.—SEPTEMBER 29, 1860.

A GOOD OFFER.

GARIBALDI. "TAKE TO THIS CAP, PAPA PIUS. YOU WILL FIND IT MORE COMFORTABLE THAN YOUR OWN."

The Cartoon Collector/Print Collector/Hulton Archive/Getty Images.

READING QUESTIONS

1. Why would the pope, as leader of the Catholic Church, oppose liberal reforms and a united Italy?

2. What do the postures and body language of the two figures suggest about the power dynamics in Italy at that time?

3. What would be the consequences for the papacy if the pope didn't accept this "good offer"?

SOURCES IN CONVERSATION

Nationalism and the Conservative Order

In the early nineteenth century, nationalism was strongly associated with revolution, with a desire to overthrow the existing political order. Thus, in the decades following the defeat of Napoleon, conservatives were generally united in their hatred of nationalism. Over time, however, many conservatives came to see nationalism as a powerful weapon for defeating their ideological rivals and reinforcing the political and social status quo. By co-opting the nationalist program of their ideological rivals, conservatives could claim to represent the interests of "the people," even as they maintained the power of traditional elites. The documents included below represent two very different perspectives on this development.

READ AND COMPARE

1. What is similar in the arguments and aims of Mazzini and Bismarck? What seems to be different, and how is it different?

2. Whom do you suppose each author is trying to reach with his message, and how are the authors trying to convince their audience?

23-2 | GIUSEPPE MAZZINI, *On Nationality* (1852)

After the Congress of Vienna in 1815, Italy was organized into separate states, but various formulas were imagined for unifying Italy. Giuseppe Mazzini's vision was the most liberal and democratic; he believed that a republic should be created to rule all of Italy, hearkening back to the republican governments of the medieval city-states, and even the ancient Roman

From Giuseppe Mazzini, "Europe: Its Condition and Prospects," in *Essays: Selected from the Writings, Literary, Political and Religious of Joseph Mazzini*, ed. William Clark (London: Walter Scott, 1880), pp. 266–267, 277–278, 291–292.

Republic. In this republic, all men would be able to vote, and all people would unite behind their common interests as Italians. His hopes were dashed numerous times, however, by his numerous arrests and periods of exile, as well as by French and Austrian interventions in Italy. After 1856, the struggle for independence fell to King Victor Emmanuel II of Sardinia-Piedmont. In this 1852 essay, Mazzini talks about the reorganization of Europe through a combination of nationalism and liberalism.

Europe . . . no longer believes in the sanctity of royal races; she may still accept them here and there as a guarantee of stability, as a defence against the encroachments of some other dangerous element; but she no longer believes in the *principle*, in any special virtue residing in them, in a divine right consecrating and protecting them. Whenever they rule despotically, she conspires against them; wherever liberty exists under their sway, in however small a degree, she supports them under a brevet of impotence. . . .

Europe no longer believes in the Papacy; she no longer believes that it possesses the right, mission, or capacity of spiritual education or guidance; she no longer believes in the immediate revelation, in the direction transmission of the designs and laws of Providence, by virtue of election, to any individual whatsoever; five years ago she was seized with enthusiasm for a Pope who seemed disposed to bless the progress of the human race, and to constitute himself the representative of the most advanced ideas of his age; she despised him as soon as he retraced his steps and recommenced the brutal career of his predecessors.

. . .

There are in Europe two great questions; or, rather, the question of the transformation of authority, that is to say, of the Revolution, has assumed two forms; the question which all have agreed to call social, and the question of nationalities. The first is more exclusively agitated in France, the second in the heart of the other peoples of Europe. . . . The question there is now, above all, to establish better relations between labour and capital, between production and consumption, between the workman and the employer.

It is probable that the European initiative, that which will give a new impulse to intelligence and to events, will spring from the question of nationalities. The social question may, in effect, although with difficulty, be partly resolved by a single people; it is an internal question for each, and the French Republicans of 1848 so understood it, when, determinately abandoning the European initiative, they placed Lamartine's[1] manifesto by the side of their aspirations towards the organisation of labour. The question of nationality can only be resolved by destroying the treaties of 1815, and changing the map of Europe and its public Law. The question of *Nationalities*, rightly understood, is the Alliance of the Peoples; the balance of powers based upon new foundations; the organisation of the work that Europe has to accomplish.

. . .

---

[1]**Lamartine:** A French poet and politician who helped found the Second Republic.

It was not for a material interest that the people of Vienna fought in 1848; in weakening the empire they could only lose power. It was not for an increase of wealth that the people of Lombardy fought in the same year; the Austrian Government had endeavoured in the year preceding to excite the peasants against the landed proprietors, as they had done in Gallicia; but everywhere they had failed. They struggled, they still struggle, as do Poland, Germany, and Hungary, for country and liberty; for a word inscribed upon a banner, proclaiming to the world that they also live, think, love, and labour for the benefit of all. They speak the same language, they bear about them the impress of consanguinity, they kneel beside the same tombs, they glory in the same tradition; and they demand to associate freely, without obstacles, without foreign domination, in order to elaborate and express their idea; to contribute their stone also to the great pyramid of history. It is something moral which they are seeking; and this moral something is in fact, even politically speaking, the most important question in the present state of things. It is the organisation of the European task. It is no longer the savage, hostile, quarrelsome nationality of two hundred years ago which is invoked by these peoples. The nationality . . . founded upon the following principle: — *Whichever people, by its superiority of strength, and by its geographical position, can do us an injury, is our natural enemy; whichever cannot do us an injury, but can by the amount of its force and by its position injure our enemy, is our natural ally,* — is the princely nationality of aristocracies or royal races. The nationality of the peoples has not these dangers; it can only be founded by a common effort and a common movement; sympathy and alliance will be its result. In principle, as in the ideas formerly laid down by the men influencing every national party, nationality ought only to be to humanity that which the division of labour is in a workshop — the recognised symbol of association; the assertion of the individuality of a human group called by its geographical position, its traditions, and its language, to fulfil a special function in the European work of civilisation.

The map of Europe has to be remade. This is the key to the present movement; herein lies the initiative. Before acting, the instrument for action must be organised; before building, the ground must be one's own. The social idea cannot be realised under any form whatsoever before this reorganisation of Europe is effected; before the peoples are free to interrogate themselves; to express their vocation, and to assure its accomplishment by an alliance capable of substituting itself for the absolutist league which now reigns supreme.

READING QUESTIONS

1. What is Mazzini's argument about how Europeans feel about traditional institutions? What does he offer as evidence of his assertions?

2. How does Mazzini contrast the European nationalist movements of the nineteenth century with earlier forms of nationalism?

3. Do you see any potential problems with his idealized combination of nationalism and liberalism? Considering the French Revolution of 1789 and the revolutions of 1848, what could possibly go wrong?

23-3 | OTTO VON BISMARCK, *Speech Before the Reichstag: On the Law for Workers' Compensation* (1884)

Otto von Bismarck, the chancellor of Germany from 1871 to 1890, combined two ideas that were considered opposites in the first half of the century: nationalism and conservatism. The nineteenth-century liberal focus on individualism stripped the upper classes of their obligation to the lower, creating an opportunity for conservatives like Bismarck. By offering support to the working classes, Bismarck undermined the claim made by liberals that their policies expressed the will of the people. At the same time, he made the revolutionary platforms put forward by socialists and communists less appealing to working people. One of the places this struggle played out was in the protections afforded to workers, which liberals saw as interfering with the property rights of factory owners. Below, Bismarck lays out his vision of the proper relationship between the state and its citizens. As you read this excerpt, ask yourself what obligations Bismarck believed the state had to the people. What obligations did the people owe the state in return?

Deputy von Vollmar has expressed his astonishment that . . . we are making new and different proposals. Gentlemen, that is not our fault. Yesterday Deputy Bamberger[1] compared the business of government with that of a cobbler who measures shoes, which he thereupon examines as to whether they are suitable for him or not and accordingly accepts or rejects them. I am by no means dissatisfied with this humble comparison, by which you place the united governments in the perspective of a shoemaker taking measurements for Herr Bamberger. The profession of government in the sense of Frederick the Great is to serve the people, and may it be also as a cobbler; the opposite is to dominate the people. We want to serve the people. But I make the demand on Herr Bamberger that he act as my co-shoemaker in order to make sure that no member of the public goes barefoot, and to create a suitable shoe for the people in this crucial area.

Deputy von Vollmar[2] then proceeded to the connection that he imputes between our proposal and the Socialist Law.[3] It is not correct, as he conceives it, that we made the proposal in order to win more support for the Socialist Law. There is, indeed, a connection between the two, but it is quite different. At the time of the submission of the Socialist Law the government, and particularly His Majesty the Emperor and, if I am not in error, also the majority of the Reichstag, underwrote certain promissory notes for the future and gave assurances that as a corollary to this Socialist Law a serious effort for the betterment of the fate

[1]**Deputy Bamberger**: Ludwig Bamberger (1823–1899) was an economist and founder of the German Liberal Party, one of Bismarck's sometimes reluctant allies.

[2]**Deputy von Vollmar**: Georg Heinrich von Vollmar (1850–1922) was a Socialist politician and thus one of Bismarck's opponents in this debate.

[3]**the Socialist Law**: Passed in 1878, it made illegal the meetings and publications of the German Social Democratic Party, though members could (and did) still run for office.

of the workers should go hand in hand. In my opinion that is the complement to the Socialist Law; if you have persistently decided not to improve the situation of the workers, then I understand that you reject the Socialist Law. For it is an injustice on the one hand to hinder the self-defense of a large class of our fellow citizens and on the other hand not to offer them aid for the redress of that which causes the dissatisfaction. That the Social Democratic leaders wish no advantage for this law, that I understand; dissatisfied workers are just what they need. Their mission is to lead, to rule, and the necessary prerequisite for that is numerous dissatisfied classes. They must naturally oppose any attempt of the government, however well intentioned it may be, to remedy this situation, if they do not wish to lose control over the masses they mislead. Therefore, I place no value on the objections that come from the leaders of the Social Democrats; I would place a very high value on the objections that come from the workers in general. Our workers, thank God, are not all Social Democrats and are not to such a degree unresponsive to the efforts of the confederated governments to help them, perhaps also not to the difficulties that these efforts meet in the parliamentary arena. . . . I in no way support an absolutist government. . . .

[The real question] is whether the state — by state I always mean the empire — whether the state has the right to abandon to chance the performance of a responsibility of the state, namely, to protect the worker from accidents and need when he is injured or becomes old, so that private companies form that charge premiums from the workers and the employers at whatever rates the market will bear. . . . As soon as the state concerns itself with these matters at all, however — and I believe that it is the state's duty to concern itself — it must strive for the least expensive form and must take no advantage from it, and above all not lose sight of the benefit for the poor and the needy. Otherwise one could indeed relinquish the fulfillment of certain state duties, such as among other things the care of the poor, in the widest sense of the word, as well as schools and national defense to private stock companies. . . . In the same way one can continue to believe that the whole of the state's responsibility must in the end be left to the voluntary formation of private stock companies. The whole problem is rooted in the question: does the state have the responsibility to care for its helpless fellow citizens, or does it not? I maintain that it does have this duty, and to be sure, not simply the Christian state, as I once permitted myself to allude to with the words "practical Christianity," but rather every state by its very nature. It would be madness for a corporate body or a collectivity to take charge of those objectives that the individual can accomplish; those goals that the community can fulfill with justice and profit should be relinquished to the community. There are objectives that only the state in its totality can fulfill. . . . Among the last mentioned objectives [of the state] belong national defense [and] the general system of transportation. . . . To these belong also the help of persons in distress and the prevention of such justified complaints as in fact provide excellent material for exploitation by the Social Democrats. That is the responsibility of the state from which the state will not be able to withdraw in the long run.

If one argues against my position that this is socialism, then I do not fear that at all. The question is, where do the justifiable limits of state socialism lie?

Without such a boundary we could not manage our affairs. Each law for poor relief is socialism. . . .

There scarcely exists nowadays a word with which more abuse is committed than the word *free*. . . . According to my experience, everyone understands by *freedom* only the freedom for oneself and not for others, as well as the responsibility of others to refrain absolutely from any limitation of one's own freedom. In short, by *freedom* they actually mean *domination*; by *freedom of speech* they understand the domination of the speaker; by *freedom of the press* the predominant and preponderant influence of editorial offices and of newspapers. Indeed gentlemen, and I am not speaking here in confessional terms, in all confessions, by *freedom of the church* the domination of the priests is very frequently understood. . . . I have no desire to speak of human weakness, but rather of the human custom which establishes the importance of the individual person, the dominance of individual persons and their influence over the general public, precisely on the pretext that freedom demands it. That is indeed more strikingly realized in our own history than in any other. In the centuries of the decay of the German Empire, German freedom was always sharply accentuated. What did this mean? The freedom of the princes from the emperor, and the power of the nobles over the serfs! They wanted for their part to be free; that means, *to be free* was for them and also for others identical with the concept *to dominate*. They did not feel themselves to be free unless they dominated. Therefore, whenever I read the word *free* before another adjective, I become very suspicious. . . . Deputy Bamberger expressed subsequently his regret concerning the "socialist fad." It is, however, a harsh expression when one characterizes as a "socialist fad" the careful decision of the allied governments in Germany, weighed for three years, which they again, for the third time, propose to you in the hope finally to obtain your approval. Perhaps the whole institution of the state is a socialist fad. If everyone could live on his own, perhaps everyone would be much more free, but also much less protected and guarded. If the Deputy calls the proposal a socialist whim, I reply simply that it is untrue, and my assertion is as justified as his. He uses further the expression that the old age and disability care "were chimerical plans." . . . There is nothing about our proposal that is chimerical. Our proposals are completely genuine; they are the result of an existing need. . . . The fulfillment of a state responsibility is never a chimera, and as such I recognize it as a legislative responsibility. It is in fact not a pleasant occupation to devote these public cobbler services to a customer like Deputy Bamberger, who treats us with scorn and ingratitude in the face of real exertions, and who characterizes as a "fad" and a "chimera" the proposal that was worked out in order to make it acceptable to you. I would like to suggest in general that we might be somewhat milder in the expressions with which we mutually characterize our efforts.

READING QUESTIONS

1. What is Bismarck's conception of "freedom," and what role does he see for it in the German Empire over which he presides?

2. What, according to Bismarck, makes his proposals different from those of the socialists he opposes?

3. What areas did Bismarck think were fit for private for-profit activity? What areas did he reserve for the state? Why?

23-4 | A Revolution in Paris

JOHN LEIGHTON, *Paris Under the Commune* (1871)

The triumph of the centralized nation-state was not predestined, and there were periodic outbursts of resistance to the centralization of political power and identity it represented. One such uprising came in Paris in the spring of 1871, sparked by the defeat of France in the Franco-Prussian War and the election of a large majority of conservatives and monarchists to the National Assembly. Convinced that the forces of conservatism were responsible for France's military humiliation and that the incoming National Assembly would betray the principles of the French Revolution, the people of Paris rose in revolt and declared their independence from the national government. For a few months, the Paris Commune promoted a decentralized, bottom-up approach to government, before it was brutally suppressed by the armed forces of the newly formed Third Republic in attacks that left twenty thousand Parisians dead. Here an Englishman, John Leighton, gives his (often hostile) impressions of the Commune. In this excerpt from his description of life under the Commune, Leighton focuses on a decree that annulled the payment of rents for the last quarter of 1871.

"Citizens," says the *Official Journal* this morning, "your Commune is constituted." Then follows decree upon decree. White posters are being stuck up everywhere. Why are they at the Hôtel de Ville, if not to publish decrees? The conscription is abolished. We shall see no more poor young fellows marching through the town with their numbers in their caps, and fired with that noble patriotism which is imbibed in the cabarets at so much a glass. We shall have no more soldiers, but to make up for that we shall all be National Guards. As to the landlords, their vexation is extreme; even the tenants do not seem so satisfied as they ought to be. Not to have to pay any rent is very delightful, certainly, but they scarcely dare believe in such good fortune. Thus when Orpheus, trying to rescue Eurydice from "the infernal regions," interrupts with "his harmonious strains" the tortures of eternal punishment, Prometheus did not doubtless show as much delight as he ought to have done, on discovering that the beak of the vulture was no longer gnawing at his vitals, "scarcely daring to believe in such good fortune." Orpheus is the Commune; Eurydice, Liberty; "the infernal regions," the Government of the 4th September; "the harmonious strains,"

From John Leighton, *Paris Under the Commune, or, The Seventy-three Days of the Second Siege* (London: Bradbury, Evans, and Co., 1871), pp. 79–82.

the decrees of the Commune; Prometheus, the tenant; and the vulture, the landlord![1]

In plain terms, however—forgive me for joking on such a subject—the decree which annuls the payment of the rents for the quarters ending October 1870, January 1871, and April 1871, does not appear to me at all extravagant, and really I do not see what there is to object to in the following lines which accompany it:—

> In consideration of the expenses of the war having been chiefly sustained by the industrial, commercial, and working portion of the population, it is but just that the proprietors of houses and land should also bear their part of the burthen. . . .

Let us talk it over together, Mr. Landlord. You have a house and I live in it. It is true that the chimneys smoke, and that you most energetically refuse to have them repaired. However, the house is yours, and you possess most decidedly the right of making a profit by it. Understand, once for all, that I never contest your right. As for me, I depend upon my wit, I do not possess much, but I have a tool—it may be either a pen, or a pencil, or a hammer—which enables me, in the ordinary course of things, to live and to pay with more or less regularity my quarter's rent. If I had not possessed this tool, you would have taken good care not to let me inhabit your house or any part or portion thereof, because you would have considered me in no position to pay you your rent. Now, during the war my tool has unquestionably rendered me but poor service. It has remained ignobly idle in the inkstand, in the folio, or on the bench. Not only have I been unable to use it, but I have also in some sort lost the knack of handling it; I must have some time to get myself into working order again. While I was working but little, and eating less, what were you doing? Oh! I do not mean to say that you were as flourishing as in the triumphant days of the Empire, but still I have not heard of any considerable number of landlords being found begging at the corners of the streets, and I do not fancy you made yourselves conspicuous by your assiduous attendance at the Municipal Cantines. I have even heard that you or many of your brother-landlords took pretty good care not to be in Paris during the Prussian siege, and that you contented yourselves with forming the most ardent wishes, for the final triumph of French arms, from beneath the wide-spreading oaks of your châteaux in Touraine and Beauce, or from the safe haven of a Normandy fishing village; while we, accompanied it is true by your most fervent prayers, took our turn at mounting guard, on the fortifications during the bitter cold nights, or knee-deep in the mud of the trenches. However, I do not blame those who sought safety in flight; each person is free to do

---

[1]**Orpheus . . . the landlord**: In Greek mythology, Orpheus, who charmed the king and queen of the underworld with the music from his lyre, was allowed to bring his dead wife Eurydice back to earth as long as he did not look behind him. When he turned around too soon, Eurydice had to return to the underworld forever. Prometheus stole fire from the god Zeus and gave it to humans; as punishment, Zeus chained him to a rock, where every day a vulture came to eat his liver, and every day it grew back, so that he had to endure the torment over again.

as he pleases; what I object to is your coming back and saying, "During seven or eight months you have done no work, you have been obliged to pawn your furniture to buy bread for your wife and children; I pity you from the bottom of my heart — be so kind as to hand me over my three quarters' rent." No, a thousand times no; such a demand is absurd, wicked, ridiculous; and I declare that if there is no possible compromise between the strict execution of the law and his decree of the Commune, I prefer, without the least hesitation, to abide by the latter; I prefer to see a little poverty replace for a time the long course of prosperity that has been enjoyed by this very small class of individuals, than to see the last articles of furniture of five hundred thousand suffering wretches, put up to auction and knocked down for one-twentieth part of their value. There must, however, be some way of conciliating the interests of both landlords and tenants. Would it be sufficient to accord delays to the latter, and force the former to wait a certain time for their money? I think not; if I were allowed three years to pay off my three quarters' rent, I should still be embarrassed. The tool of the artisan is not like the peasant's plot of ground, which is more productive after having lain fallow. During the last few sad months, when I had no work to do, I was obliged to draw upon the future, a future heavily mortgaged; when I shall perhaps scarcely be able to meet the expenses of each day, will there be any possibility of acquitting the debts of the past? You may sell my furniture if the law gives you the right to do so, but I shall not pay!

The only possible solution, believe me, is that in favor of the tenants, only it ought not to be applied in so wholesale a fashion. Inquiries should be instituted, and to those tenants from whom the war has taken away all possibility of payment an unconditional receipt should be delivered: to those who have suffered less, a proportionate reduction should be allowed; but those whom the invasion has not ruined or seriously impoverished — and the number is large, among provision merchants, café keepers, and private residents — let those pay directly. In this way the landlords will lose less than one may imagine, because it will be the lowest rents that will be forfeited. The decree of the Commune is based on a right principle, but too generally applied.

The new Government — for it is a Government — does not confine itself to decrees. It has to install itself in its new quarters and make arrangements.

In a few hours it has organized more than ten committees — the executive, the financial, the public-service, the educational, the military, the legal, and the committee of public safety. No end of committees and committeemen: it is to be hoped that the business will be promptly dispatched!

READING QUESTIONS

1. Who, based on Leighton's discussion, makes up the nation? How does it affect your reading of this passage to know that Leighton spent much of his book mocking and denouncing the Paris Commune?

2. What is Leighton's complaint regarding this specific decree of the Commune? Does he seem reasonable? What groups in French society might have agreed with him? What groups might have disagreed with him?

23-5 | An Indictment of France's Military Elite
ÉMILE ZOLA, *"J'Accuse" the French Army* (1898)

In 1898 and 1899 the case of Alfred Dreyfus, a Jewish captain in the French army who was falsely accused and convicted of treason on the basis of falsified evidence, split France apart. On one side was the army, joined by anti-Semites and most of the Catholic establishment. On the other side stood civil libertarians and most of the more radical republicans. The support offered to Dreyfus by prominent republicans and intellectuals, including novelist Émile Zola, proved critical to securing the reopening of his case and his eventual exoneration. In this excerpt from Zola's famous letter entitled "J'Accuse," Zola accused the French military high command of conspiracy to subvert justice, an action that opened Zola up to a retaliatory prosecution for libel.

Dreyfus knows several languages: a crime. No compromising papers were found in his possession: a crime. He sometimes visited his native country:[1] a crime. He is industrious and likes to find out about everything: a crime. He is calm: a crime. He is worried: a crime. . . .

I accuse Lieutenant-Colonel du Paty de Clam[2] of having been the diabolical, but I would fain believe the unwitting, artisan of the miscarriage of justice, and thereafter of having defended his unhallowed work for three years by the most clumsy and culpable machinations.

I accuse General Mercier[3] of having become, at all events through weakness, an accomplice in one of the greatest iniquities of the age.

I accuse General Billot[4] of having had in his hands sure proofs of the innocence of Dreyfus and of having hushed them up, of having incurred the guilt of crimes against humanity and justice, for political ends and to save the face of the General Staff.

I accuse General de Boisdeffre and General Gonse[5] of having been participators in the same crime, actuated, the one no doubt by clerical partisanship, the

---

From Émile Zola, "J'Accuse," in Armand Charpentier, *The Dreyfus Case*, trans. Lewis May (London: Geoffrey Bles, 1935), pp. 142–144.

[1]**his native country**: Dreyfus was from Alsace (Alsatia in German), a French province at the time of his birth, but taken by Germany in 1871. For Dreyfus to visit his childhood home, he had to cross the new national border.

[2]**Lieutenant-Colonel du Paty de Clam**: Armand Mercier Paty de Clam was the French counterintelligence officer who conducted the first accusation against Dreyfus and who remained convinced of Dreyfus's guilt long after the actual author of the document that began the case was revealed.

[3]**General Mercier**: Mercier was the war minister who originated the case against Dreyfus and continued it to avoid political embarrassment after making public pronouncements of his certainty of Dreyfus's guilt.

[4]**General Billot**: Jean-Baptiste Billot was a French general and war minister during the later stages of the Dreyfus affair, 1896–1898.

[5]**General de Boisdeffre and General Gonse**: Boisdeffre was the chief of staff of the French army—its highest-ranking soldier—at the time of the initial accusation, and according to Zola, a strong supporter of the Catholic clergy in France. General Gonse was the general to whom the counterintelligence division (called for secrecy purposes the Statistical Section) reported.

other, it may be, by that esprit de corps which would make the Army and the War Office the sacred Ark of the Covenant.

I accuse General de Pellieux and Major Ravary[6] of conducting a disgraceful inquiry, by which I mean an inquiry characterized by the most monstrous partiality, of which we have, in the report of the latter of these two men, an imperishable monument of stupid audacity.

I accuse the three handwriting experts, MM. Belhomme, Varinard, and Couard, of drawing up misleading and lying reports, unless, indeed, a medical examination should reveal them to be suffering from some pathological abnormality of sight and judgment.

I accuse the War Office of conducting an abominable campaign in the Press, and particularly in the newspapers *l'Eclair* and *l'Echo de Paris*, in order to mislead public opinion and to conceal their own misdeeds.

I accuse the first Court-Martial of acting contrary to law by condemning an accused man on the strength of a secret document; and I accuse the second Court-Martial of having, in obedience to orders, concealed that illegality, and of committing in its turn the crime of knowingly acquitting a guilty man.

In bringing these charges, I am not unaware that I render myself liable to prosecution under Clauses 30 and 31 of the Act of the 29th of July, which deals with defamation of character in the public Press. But I do so of my own free will and with my eyes open.

As for those whom I accuse, I do not know them, I have never seen them. I entertain for them neither hatred nor ill-will. They are so far as I am concerned mere entities, spirits of social maleficence, and the action to which I have here committed myself is but a revolutionary means of hastening the explosion of Truth and Justice.

I have but one passion, and that is for light, and I plead in the name of that humanity which has so greatly suffered and has a right to happiness. My fiery protest is but the outcry of my soul. Let them drag me, then, into a Court of Justice and let the matter be thrashed out in broad daylight. I am ready.

READING QUESTIONS

1. What risks did Zola take by publishing this letter? What might explain his willingness to take those risks?

2. Based on this document, what was the relationship between the needs of the accused and the needs of the state in nineteenth-century France? How did Zola oppose this conception of justice?

3. Although the actions of the court that convicted Dreyfus were popular, were they compatible with the idea of government by the consent of the governed, which the French Third Republic claimed to embody?

---

[6]**General de Pellieux and Major Ravary**: Pellieux was the general who investigated the accusations against Esterhazy — the man later proved to have committed the crime of which Dreyfus was accused — and found him innocent. Ravary oversaw the handwriting analysts and reported on their findings, which turned out to be inaccurate.

■ COMPARATIVE AND DISCUSSION QUESTIONS ■

1. How might Mazzini interpret the image of the "Good Offer" to Pope Pius IX?

2. What connections can you make between nationalism and the resurgence of conservatism in the second half of the nineteenth century? What light do the documents by Mazzini, Leighton, and Bismarck shed on this question?

3. What picture of French politics in the decades following the defeat of France in the Franco-Prussian War is painted in the documents by Leighton and Zola? What connections can you make between the suppression of the Paris Commune and the Dreyfus affair?

24

The West and the World
1815–1914

Industrialization played a central role in nineteenth-century European imperialism. At the same time that industrialization created skyrocketing demand in Europe for raw materials and new markets, it provided Europeans with the wealth and technology that made global domination possible. While Europeans often cast imperialism in economic terms, they also justified expansion and colonization in other ways. Some believed that Europeans had a responsibility to spread their "superior" Western culture and religion to less fortunate regions of the world. Others, drawing on distorted interpretations of Darwin's theory of evolution, claimed a biological right of conquest, arguing that human progress depended on the subjugation of the weak by the strong. The results of European imperialism were mixed. The fortunes made from the extraction of raw materials and the exploitation of colonial labor were offset by limited success in establishing new markets and the costs associated with conquest and colonial rule. Moreover, the penetration of European culture into colonized societies was often shallow, and European missionaries and educators were dismayed to discover that many non-Europeans were quite content with their own culture and religion. Finally, while industrial innovation catapulted Europe into a position of global dominance, native resistance never fully faded, and an undercurrent of fear persisted among the uninvited occupiers.

Economic Imperialism and Military Expansion

While cultural and religious considerations played a prominent role in creating public support for imperialism, the decisions of policymakers were most often driven by economic and military concerns. From the point of view of governments and commercial interests, competition for overseas colonies was an extension of the internal competition between European nations for dominance. Economic and military considerations often went hand in hand, and, in the end, the control of colonial empires depended on military force. The effective deployment of such force required the acquisition of new naval ports and military outposts. Thus, the need to defend colonial possessions justified further imperial expansion, which, in turn, required ever larger, more advanced armies and navies.

READ AND COMPARE

1. What is similar in the arguments of Lin Zexu and the Earl of Cromer when they speak of their home countries?

2. How do the documents demonstrate or critique the ideology of nationalism from the English, Egyptian, and Chinese perspectives?

24-1 | COMMISSIONER LIN ZEXU, *Letter to Queen Victoria* (1839)

China, the most populous country on earth in the nineteenth century, was an irresistible target for Europeans interested in finding new markets for their products. Unfortunately for such would-be traders, the Chinese showed little interest in aiding Western economic expansion. The Chinese imperial government's reluctance to allow Western access, combined with poverty and general disinterest in Western goods, restricted trade until the British discovered they had a product that would sell in China—opium. Lin Zexu, the imperial commissioner for the southern province of Guangdong, attempted to suppress the opium trade and published this open letter to the British queen in 1839. The British were, evidently, unimpressed with Lin Zexu's appeal. That same year, the British started the first Opium War (1839–1842) to ensure their continued right to sell opium in China.

We have heard that in your own country opium is prohibited with the utmost strictness and severity: this is a strong proof that you know full well how hurtful it is to mankind. Since then you do not permit it to injure your own country,

From William H. McNeil and Mitsuko Iriye, eds., *Readings in World History*, vol. 9: *Modern Asia and Africa* (New York: Oxford University Press, 1971), pp. 111–118.

you ought not to have the injurious drug transferred to another country, and above all others, how much less to the Inner Land! Of the products which China exports to your foreign countries, there is not one which is not beneficial to mankind in some shape or other. There are those which serve for food, those which are useful, and those which are calculated for re-sale; but all are beneficial. Has China (we should like to ask) ever yet sent forth a noxious article from its soil? Not to speak of our tea and rhubarb, things which your foreign countries could not exist a single day without, if we of the Central Land were to grudge you what is beneficial, and not to compassionate your wants, then wherewithal could you foreigners manage to exist? And further, as regards your woolens, camlets [goat or camel hair cloth], and longells [cloth of a specific weave], were it not that you get supplied with our native raw silk, you could not get these manufactured! If China were to grudge you those things which yield a profit, how could you foreigners scheme after any profit at all? Our other articles of food, such as sugar, ginger, cinnamon, &c., and our other articles for use, such as silk piece-goods, chinaware, &c., are all so many necessaries of life to you; how can we reckon up their number! On the other hand, the things that come from your foreign countries are only calculated to make presents of, or serve for mere amusement. It is quite the same to us if we have them, or if we have them not. If then these are of no material consequence to us of the Inner Land, what difficulty would there be in prohibiting and shutting our market against them? It is only that our heavenly dynasty most freely permits you to take off her tea, silk, and other commodities, and convey them for consumption everywhere, without the slightest stint or grudge, for no other reason, but that where a profit exists, we wish that it be diffused abroad for the benefit of all the earth!

Your honorable nation takes away the products of our Central Land, and not only do you thereby obtain food and support for yourselves, but moreover, by re-selling these products to other countries you reap a threefold profit. Now if you would only not sell opium, this threefold profit would be secured to you: how can you possibly consent to forgo it for a drug that is hurtful to men, and an unbridled craving after gain that seems to know no bounds! Let us suppose that foreigners came from another country, and brought opium into England, and seduced the people of your country to smoke it, would not you, the sovereign of the said country, look upon such a procedure with anger, and in your just indignation endeavor to get rid of it? . . .

We have heard that in London the metropolis where you dwell, as also in Scotland, Ireland, and other such places, no opium whatever is produced. It is only in sundry parts of your colonial kingdom of Hindostan,[1] such as Bengal, Madras, Bombay, Patna, Malwa, Benares, Malacca, and other places where the very hills are covered with the opium plant, where tanks are made for the preparing of the drug; month by month, and year by year, the volume of the poison increases, its unclean stench ascends upwards, until heaven itself grows angry,

---

[1]**Hindostan:** British India, particularly the northwestern section, in today's India and Pakistan.

and the very gods thereat get indignant! You, the queen of the said honorable nation, ought immediately to have the plant in those parts plucked up by the very root! Cause the land there to be hoed up afresh, sow in its stead the five grains, and if any man dare again to plant in these grounds a single poppy, visit his crime with the most severe punishment. . . .

Suppose the subject of another country were to come to England to trade, he would certainly be required to comply with the laws of England, then how much more does this apply to us of the celestial empire! Now it is a fixed statute of this empire, that any native Chinese who sells opium is punishable with death, and even he who merely smokes it, must not less die.

READING QUESTIONS

1. What tone did Lin assume in his letter to the English queen? In what ways did he appeal to Victoria's sense of fairness and morality?

2. How did Lin characterize the commercial relationship between China and Britain? What light does this shed on Chinese resistance to British imports?

3. How might a British imperialist have justified the export of opium into China in defiance of the wishes of the Chinese government?

4. What does the fact that the British government was willing to go to war over opium exports tell you about the motives behind British imperialism?

24-2 | EVELYN BARING, EARL OF CROMER, *Why Britain Acquired Egypt in 1882* (1908)

Egypt, after being ruled by foreign powers for many centuries, was transformed by another foreign-born Ottoman-backed governor known as Muhammad Ali beginning in 1805. Muhammad Ali modernized the military, improved the government bureaucracy, built transportation infrastructure, and expanded agricultural production, though as a result Egyptian peasants became impoverished tenant farmers forced to produce cash-crop exports. Europeans flocked to the modernized country, and Muhammad Ali's policies were continued by his grandson Ismail. Ismail contracted with a French company to complete the Suez Canal in 1869, and he also improved irrigation for agriculture, but his programs were very expensive and required hefty loans from European creditors. By 1876 Egypt had fallen behind in loan payments, and Egyptian and French commissioners were sent in to force the government to prioritize paying the debts. Ismail was removed from power, and a revolt broke out in 1882; the British government then intervened and occupied Egypt. In this document, the Earl of Cromer justifies that occupation, using the assumptions of European imperialism to back his arguments.

Egypt may now almost be said to form part of Europe. It is on the high road to the far East. It can never cease to be an object of interest to all the Powers of Europe, and especially to England. A numerous and intelligent body

---

From Evelyn Baring, Earl of Cromer, *Modern Egypt* (New York: Macmillan, 1916), pp. 326–330.

of Europeans and of non-Egyptian Orientals have made Egypt their home. European capital to a large extent has been sunk in the country. The rights and privileges of Europeans are jealously guarded, and, moreover, give rise to complicated questions, which it requires no small amount of ingenuity and technical knowledge to solve. Exotic institutions have sprung up and have taken root in the country. The Capitulations[1] impair those rights of internal sovereignty which are enjoyed by the rulers or legislatures of most States. The population is heterogeneous and cosmopolitan to a degree almost unknown elsewhere. Although the prevailing faith is that of Islam, in no country in the world is a greater variety of religious creeds to be found among important sections of the community.

In addition to these peculiarities, which are of a normal character, it has to be borne in mind that in 1882 the army was in a state of mutiny; the Treasury was bankrupt; every branch of the administration had been dislocated; the ancient and arbitrary method, under which the country had for centuries been governed, had received a severe blow, whilst, at the same time, no more orderly and law-abiding form of government had been inaugurated to take its place.

Is it probable that a Government composed of the rude elements described above, and led by men of such poor ability as Arabi[2] and his co-adjutors, would have been able to control a complicated machine of this nature? Were the Sheikhs of the El-Azhar Mosque likely to succeed where Tewfik Pasha and his Ministers, who were men of comparative education and enlightenment, acting under the guidance and inspiration of a first-class European Power, only met with a modified success after years of patient labour? There can be but one answer to these questions. Sentimental politicians may consider that the quasi-national character of Arabi's movement gives it a claim to their sympathies, but others who are not carried away by sentiment may reasonably maintain that the fact of its having been a quasi-national movement was one of the reasons which foredoomed it to failure; for, in order to justify its national character, it had to run counter, not only to the European, but also to the foreign Eastern elements of Egyptian government and society. Neither is it in the nature of things that any similar movement should, under the present conditions of Egyptian society, meet with any better success. The full and immediate execution of a policy of "Egypt for the Egyptians," as it was conceived by the Arabists in 1882, was, and still is impossible.

History, indeed, records some very radical changes in the forms of government to which a State has been subjected without its interests being absolutely and permanently shipwrecked. But it may be doubted whether any instance can be quoted of a sudden transfer of power in any civilised or semi-civilised community to a class so ignorant as the pure Egyptians, such as they were in the year 1882. These latter have, for centuries past, been a subject race. Persians,

---

[1]**Capitulations**: Treaties between the Ottoman Empire and European countries that gave Europeans economic and legal benefits in the empire.

[2]**Arabi**: Egyptian colonel who led the revolts against the government that British forces defeated in 1882.

Greeks, Romans, Arabs from Arabia and Baghdad, Circassians, and finally, Ottoman Turks, have successively ruled over Egypt, but we have to go back to the doubtful and obscure precedents of Pharaonic times to find an epoch when, possibly, Egypt was ruled by Egyptians. Neither, for the present, do they appear to possess the qualities which would render it desirable, either in their own interests, or in those of the civilized world in general, to raise them at a bound to the category of autonomous rulers with full rights of internal sovereignty.

If, however, a foreign occupation was inevitable, or nearly inevitable, it remains to be considered whether a British occupation was preferable to any other. From the purely Egyptian point of view, the answer to this question cannot be doubtful. The intervention of any European Power was preferable to that of Turkey. The intervention of one European Power was preferable to international intervention. The special aptitude shown by Englishmen in the government of Oriental races pointed to England as the most effective and beneficent instrument for the gradual introduction of European civilization into Egypt. An Anglo-French or an Anglo-Italian occupation, from both of which we narrowly and also accidentally escaped, would have been detrimental to Egyptian interests and would ultimately have caused friction, if not serious dissension, between England on the one side and France or Italy on the other.

The only thing to be said in favour of Turkish intervention is that it would have relieved England from the responsibility of intervening. It has been shown in the course of this narrative that, in the early stages of the proceedings, the policy of the two Western Powers, which was guided by the anti-Turkish sentiments prevalent in France, was not of a nature to invite or encourage Turkish cooperation. At a later period, the shortsightedness of the Sultan was such as to cause the Porte[3] to commit political suicide in so far as decisive Turkish action was concerned. Perhaps it was well that it did so, for it is highly probable that armed Turkish intervention in Egypt, accompanied as it might well have been, by misgovernment, paltry intrigue, corruption, and administrative and financial confusion, would only have been the prelude to further, and possibly more serious international complications.

By a process of exhausting all other expedients, we arrive at the conclusion that armed British intervention was, under the special circumstances of the case, the only possible solution of the difficulties which existed in 1882. Probably also it was the best solution. The arguments against British intervention, indeed, were sufficiently obvious. It was easy to foresee that, with a British garrison in Egypt, it would be difficult that the relations of England either with France or Turkey should be cordial. With France especially, there would be a danger that our relations might become seriously strained. Moreover, we lost the advantages of insular position. The occupation of Egypt necessarily dragged England to a certain extent within the arena of Continental politics. In the event of war, the presence of a British garrison in Egypt would possibly be

---

[3]**Porte:** The central government of the Ottoman Empire.

a source of weakness rather than of strength. Our position in Egypt placed us in a disadvantageous diplomatic position, for any Power, with whom we had a difference of opinion about some non-Egyptian question, was at one time able to retaliate by opposing our Egyptian policy. The complicated rights and privileges possessed by the various Powers of Europe in Egypt facilitated action of this nature.

There can be no doubt of the force of these arguments. The answer to them is that it was impossible for Great Britain to allow the troops of any other European Power to occupy Egypt. When it became apparent that some foreign occupation was necessary, that the Sultan would not act save under conditions which were impossible of acceptance, and that neither French nor Italian cooperation could be secured, the British Government acted with promptitude and vigour. A great nation cannot throw off the responsibilities which its past history and its position in the world have imposed upon it. English history affords other examples of the Government and people of England drifting by accident into doing what was not only right but was also most in accordance with British interests.

READING QUESTIONS

1. How does Cromer characterize the capabilities of Egyptians to rule themselves, and how does he support his argument about them?

2. Why does he argue that Britain was the best country to restore order to Egypt?

3. What were the potential consequences for Britain when it decided to occupy Egypt?

4. How might Colonel Arabi, or another Egyptian nationalist, refute Cromer's arguments justifying the occupation?

24-3 | British Conquests in Africa
The Rhodes Colossus (1892)

There were no limits to the British fortune hunter Cecil Rhodes's (1853–1902) ambitions or to the steps he was willing to take to achieve his ends. Rhodes saw in the British imperialist expansion in Africa an opportunity both to amass a fabulous personal fortune and to add to Britain's global power and prestige. A committed Social Darwinist, Rhodes had no moral qualms about the conquest and economic exploitation of native peoples. In his view, human progress was achieved through racial competition, a competition Rhodes was certain would end in British domination of the globe. In this 1892 cartoon first published in the British magazine *Punch*, Rhodes is depicted as the embodiment of Britain's African empire.

THE RHODES COLOSSUS

STRIDING FROM CAPE TOWN TO CAIRO.

The Art Archive/Shutterstock.

READING QUESTIONS

1. How might the majority of British readers have responded to this cartoon? What is your personal reaction to the cartoon?

2. What does the cartoon suggest about British ambitions in Africa? What obstacles stood in the way of the achievement of those ambitions?

24-4 | A White Explorer in Black Africa

HENRY MORTON STANLEY, *Autobiography* (1909)

In 1871, while working as a journalist for the *New York Herald*, Sir Henry Morton Stanley (1841–1904) led an expedition to locate Dr. David Livingstone, a popular explorer and missionary who had gone missing in Central Africa. Upon reading about Stanley's exploration of the Congo basin, Leopold II, king of the Belgians, became interested in acquiring an empire in Africa and hired Stanley to carry out a series of expeditions on his behalf. In time, Leopold would establish a personal empire in the Congo that was notorious, even among Europeans, for its unspeakably brutal exploitation of the native population. Stanley's autobiography, however, paints a very different picture of the interactions between whites and blacks in Central Africa. As you read this excerpt, pay particular attention to Stanley's assumptions about white racial superiority. How did racial thinking shape his understanding of his experiences in the Congo?

Ngalyema, chief of Stanley Pool district, had demanded and received four thousand five hundred dollars' worth of cotton, silk, and velvet goods for granting me the privilege of establishing a station in a wilderness of a place at the commencement of up-river navigation. Owing to this, I had advanced with my wagons to within ten miles of the Pool. I had toiled at this work the best part of two years, and whenever I cast a retrospective glance at what the task had cost me, I felt that it was no joke, and such that no money would bribe me to do over again. Such a long time had elapsed since Ngalyema had received his supplies, that he affected to forget that he had received any; and, as I still continued to advance towards him after the warnings of his messengers, he collected a band of doughty warriors, painted their bodies with diagonal stripes of ochre, soot, chalk, and yellow, and issued fiercely to meet me.

Meantime, the true owners of the soil had enlightened me respecting Ngalyema's antecedents. He was only an enterprising native trader in ivory and slaves, who had fled from the north bank; but, though he had obtained so much money from me by pretences, I was not so indignant at this as at the audacity with which he chose to forget the transaction, and the impudent demand for another supply which underlay this. Ngalyema, having failed to draw any promise by sending messengers, thought he could extort it by

From Henry Morton Stanley, *Autobiography*, ed. Dorothy Stanley (New York: Houghton Mifflin, 1909), pp. 339–344, 384–385.

appearing with a warlike company. Meantime, duly warned, I had prepared a surprise for him.

I had hung a great Chinese Gong conspicuously near the principal tent. Ngalyema's curiosity would be roused. All my men were hidden, some in the steamboat on top of the wagon, and in its shadow was a cool place where the warriors would gladly rest after a ten-mile march; other of my men lay still as death under tarpaulins, under bundles of grass, and in the bush round about the camp. By the time the drum-taps and horns announced Ngalyema's arrival, the camp seemed abandoned except by myself and a few small boys. I was indolently seated in a chair, reading a book, and appeared too lazy to notice anyone; but suddenly looking up and seeing my "brother Ngalyema" and his warriors scowlingly regarding me, I sprang up, and seized his hands, and affectionately bade him welcome, in the name of sacred fraternity, and offered him my own chair.

He was strangely cold, and apparently disgruntled, and said: —

"Has not my brother forgotten his road? What does he mean by coming to this country?"

"Nay, it is Ngalyema who has forgotten the blood-bond which exists between us. It is Ngalyema who has forgotten the mountains of goods which I paid him. What words are these of my brother?"

"Be warned, Rock-Breaker. Go back before it is too late. My elders and people all cry out against allowing the white man to come into our country. Therefore, go back before it be too late. Go back, I say, the way you came."

Speech and counter-speech followed. Ngalyema had exhausted his arguments; but it was not easy to break faith and be uncivil, without plausible excuse. His eyes were reaching round seeking to discover an excuse to fight, when they rested on the round, burnished face of the Chinese gong.

"What is that?" he said.

"Ah, that—that is a fetish."

"A fetish! A fetish for what?"

"It is a war-fetish, Ngalyema. The slightest sound of that would fill this empty camp with hundreds of angry warriors; they would drop from above, they would spring up from the ground, from the forest about, from everywhere."

"Sho! Tell that story to the old women, and not to a chief like Ngalyema. My boy tells me it is a kind of a bell. Strike it and let me hear it."

"Oh, Ngalyema, my brother, the consequences would be too dreadful! Do not think of such a thing!"

"Strike it, I say."

"Well, to oblige my dear brother Ngalyema, I will."

And I struck hard and fast, and the clangorous roll rang out like thunder in the stillness. Only for a few seconds, however, for a tempest of human voices was heard bursting into frightful discords, and from above, right upon the heads of the astonished warriors, leaped yelling men; and from the tents, the huts, the forest round about, they came by sixes, dozens, and scores, yelling like madmen, and seemingly animated with uncontrollable rage. The painted warriors became panic-stricken; they flung their guns and powder-kegs away, forgot their chief, and all thoughts of loyalty, and fled on the instant, fear lifting their heels high in the air; or, tugging at their eyeballs and kneading the senses confusedly, they saw, heard, and suspected nothing, save that the limbo of fetishes had broken loose!

But Ngalyema and his son did not fly. They caught the tails of my coat, and we began to dance from side to side, a loving triplet, myself being the foremost, to ward off the blow savagely aimed at my "brothers," and cheerfully crying out, "Hold fast to me, my brothers. I will defend you to the last drop of my blood. Come one, come all," etc.

Presently the order was given, "Fall in!" and quickly the leaping forms became rigid, and the men stood in two long lines in beautiful order, with eyes front, as though "at attention." Then Ngalyema relaxed his hold of my coat-tails, and crept from behind, breathing more freely; and, lifting his hand to his mouth, exclaimed, in genuine surprise "Eh, Mamma! Where did all these people come from?"

"Ah, Ngalyema, did I not tell you that thing was a powerful fetish? Let me strike it again, and show you what else it can do."

"No! No! No!" he shrieked. "I have seen enough!"

The day ended peacefully. I was invited to hasten on to Stanley Pool. The natives engaged themselves by the score to assist me in hauling the wagons. My progress was thenceforward steady and uninterrupted, and in due time the wagons and goods-columns arrived at their destination. . . .

Some of you may, perhaps, wonder at the quiet inoffensiveness of the natives, who, on a former expedition, had worried my soul by their ferocity and wanton attacks, night and day; but a very simple explanation of it may be found in Livingstone's Last Journals, dated 28th October, 1870. He says: "Muini Mukata, who has travelled further than most Arabs, said to me, 'If a man goes with a good-natured, civil tongue, he may pass through the worst people in Africa unharmed.' This is true, but time also is required; one must not run through a country, but give the people time to become acquainted with you, and let their worst fears subside."

Now on the expedition across Africa I had no time to give, either to myself or to them. The river bore my heavy canoes downward; my goods would never have endured the dawdling requirement by the system of teaching every tribe I met who I was. To save myself and my men from certain starvation, I had to rush on and on, right through. But on this expedition, the very necessity of making roads to haul my enormous six-ton wagons gave time for my reputation to travel ahead of me. My name, purpose, and liberal rewards for native help, naturally exaggerated, prepared a welcome for me, and transformed my enemies of the old time into workmen, friendly allies, strong porters, and firm friends. I was greatly forbearing also; but, when a fight was inevitable, through open violence, it was sharp and decisive. Consequently, the natives rapidly learned that though everything was to be gained by friendship with me, wars brought nothing but ruin. . . .

The dark faces light up with friendly gleams, and a budding of good will may perhaps date from this trivial scene. To such an impressionable being as an African native, the self-involved European, with his frigid, imperious manner, pallid white face, and dead, lustreless eyes, is a sealed book.

We had sown seeds of good-will at every place we had touched, and each tribe would spread diffusively the report of the value and beauty of our labors. Pure benevolence contains within itself grateful virtues. Over natural people nothing has greater charm or such expansible power; its influence grows without effort; its subtlety exercises itself on all who come within hearing of it. Coming in such innocent guise, it offends not; there is naught in it to provoke resentment. Provided patience and good temper guides the chief of Stanley Falls station, by the period of the return of the steamers, the influence of the seedling just planted there will have been extended from tribe to tribe far inland, and amid the persecuted fugitives from the slave-traders. . . .

When a young white officer quits England for the first time, to lead blacks, he has got to learn to unlearn a great deal. . . . We must have white men in Africa; but the raw white is a great nuisance there during the first year. In the second year, he begins to mend; during the third year, if his nature permits it, he has developed into a superior man, whose intelligence may be of transcendent utility for directing masses of inferior men.

My officers were possessed with the notion that my manner was "hard," because I had not many compliments for them. That is the kind of pap which we may offer women and boys. Besides, I thought they were superior natures, and required none of that encouragement, which the more childish blacks almost daily received.

READING QUESTIONS

1. In what ways did Stanley seek to present himself as a "great" explorer? What factors did he see as decisive in his success?

2. What attitudes did Stanley display toward the natives he encountered? In his view, how did the blacks benefit from his "friendship"?

3. How did Stanley seem to view the Europeans with whom he worked? What does the final paragraph reveal about nineteenth-century attitudes toward masculinity?

4. In what ways does the excerpt hint at the violence that would characterize Belgian rule in the years to come?

24-5 | An Anti-Imperialist Pamphlet
MARK TWAIN, *King Leopold's Soliloquy* (1905)

Belgium led the way in colonizing sub-Saharan Africa under the flag of the Congo Free State, an organization that claimed to bring the benefits of European civilization to Africa. In fact, it produced massive profits for Leopold II at tremendous human cost to the Congo natives. Despite tight Belgian control over travel to the Congo, reports filtered out of forced labor and horrific punishments for workers who failed to meet rubber production quotas. In 1905 Mark Twain published an anti-imperialist pamphlet written from Leopold's perspective, interspersed with images like the ones included here.

It is all the same old thing—tedious repetitions and duplications of shop-worn episodes; mutilations, murders, massacres, and so on, and so on, till one gets drowsy over it. Mr. Morel[1] intrudes at this point, and contributes a comment which he could just as well have kept to himself—and throws in some italics, of course; these people can never get along without italics:

"It is one heartrending story of human misery from beginning to end, and *it is all recent.*"

Meaning 1904 and 1905. I do not see how a person can act so. This Morel is a king's subject, and reverence for monarchy should have restrained him from reflecting upon me with that exposure. This Morel is a reformer; a Congo reformer. That sizes *him* up. He publishes a sheet in Liverpool called *The West African Mail*, which is supported by the voluntary contributions of the sap-headed and the soft-hearted; and every week it steams and reeks and festers with up-to-date "Congo atrocities" of the sort detailed in this pile of pamphlets here. I will suppress it. I suppressed a Congo atrocity book there, after it was actually in print; it should not be difficult for me to suppress a newspaper.

[Studies some photographs of mutilated negroes—throws them down. Sighs.]

The kodak has been a sore calamity to us. The most powerful enemy that has confronted us, indeed. In the early years we had no trouble in getting the press to "expose" the tales of the mutilations as slanders, lies, inventions of busy-body American missionaries and exasperated foreigners who found the "open door" of the Berlin-Congo charter closed against them when they innocently went out there to trade; and by the press's help we got the Christian nations everywhere to turn an irritated and unbelieving ear to those tales and say hard things about the tellers of them. Yes, all things went harmoniously and pleasantly in those good days, and I was looked up to as the benefactor of a down-trodden and friendless people. Then all of a sudden came the crash! That is to say, the incorruptible *kodak*—and all the harmony went to hell! The only witness I have encountered in my long experience that I couldn't bribe.

---

[1]**Mr. Morel**: E. D. Morel (1873–1924); British author and socialist politician who wrote important exposés of Leopold's brutality in the Congo.

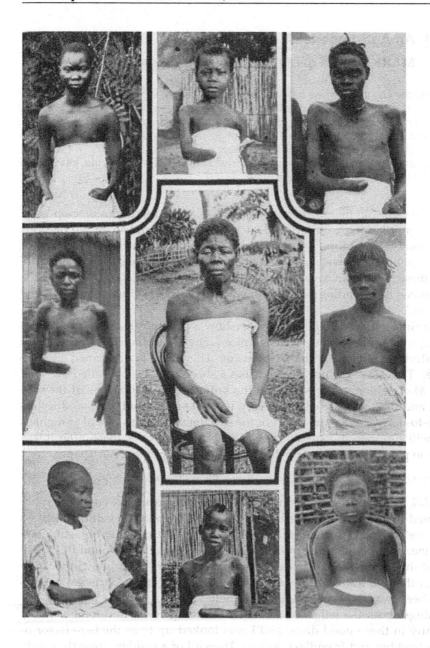

Every Yankee missionary and every interrupted trader sent home and got one; and now — oh, well, the pictures get sneaked around everywhere, in spite of all we can do to ferret them out and suppress them. Ten thousand pulpits and ten thousand presses are saying the good word for me all the time and placidly and convincingly denying the mutilations. Then that trivial little kodak, that a child can carry in its pocket, gets up, uttering never a word, and knocks them dumb!

READING QUESTIONS

1. What does this pamphlet suggest about the role of public opinion in nineteenth- and early-twentieth-century imperialism?

2. In Twain's opinion, how did the invention of the handheld camera change the debate over imperialism? What similarities do you see between the dynamic Twain described and the role of new information technology in shaping current global political debates?

24-6 | Questioning the Economics of Imperialism

J. A. HOBSON, *Imperialism* (1902)

Not all Europeans were imperialists, although anti-imperialists were typically in the minority. One of the underlying assumptions of empire was that colonies would trade exclusively with their mother countries, a theory at odds with Adam Smith's eighteenth-century vision of free trade. In 1902, John Atkinson Hobson, an English economist, published a critique of the prevailing link between colonies, economies, and national security, questioning the benefits of imperialism for the colonizing countries. His work influenced the communist leader Lenin's later critique of imperialism.

Although the new Imperialism has been bad business for the nation, it has been good business for certain classes and certain trades within the nation. The vast expenditure on armaments, the costly wars, the grave risks and embarrassments of foreign policy, the stoppage of political and social reforms within Great Britain, though fraught with great injury to the nation, have served well the present business interests of certain industries and professions.

It is idle to meddle with politics unless we clearly recognize this central fact and understand what these sectional interests are which are the enemies of national safety and the commonwealth. We must put aside the merely sentimental diagnosis which explains wars or other national blunders by outbursts of patriotic animosity or errors of statecraft. Doubtless at every outbreak of war not only the man in the street but the man at the helm is often duped by the cunning with which aggressive motives and greedy purposes dress themselves in defensive clothing. There is, it may be safely asserted, no war within memory, however nakedly aggressive it may seem to the dispassionate historian, which has not been presented to the people who were called upon to fight as a necessary defensive policy, in which the honor, perhaps the very existence, of the State was involved. . . .

What is the direct economic outcome of Imperialism? A great expenditure of public money upon ships, guns, military and naval equipment and stores, growing and productive of enormous profits when a war, or an alarm of war, occurs; new public loans and important fluctuations in the home and foreign Bourses [essentially a stock market]; more posts for soldiers and sailors and in the diplomatic and consular services; improvement of foreign investments by

From Louis L. Snyder, ed., *The Imperialism Reader: Documents and Readings on Modern Expansionism* (Princeton, N.J.: Van Nostrand, 1962), pp. 322–323.

the substitution of the British flag for a foreign flag; acquisition of markets for certain classes of exports, and some protection and assistance for trades representing British houses in these manufactures; employment for engineers, missionaries, speculative miners, ranchers, and other emigrants.

Certain definite business and professional interests feeding upon imperialistic expenditure, or upon the results of that expenditure, are thus set up in opposition to the common good, and, instinctively feeling their way to one another, are found united in strong sympathy to support every new imperialist exploit. . . .

With them stand the great manufacturers for export trade, who gain a living by supplying the real or artificial wants of the new countries we annex or open up. . . . The proportion which such trade bears to the total industry of Great Britain is very small, but some of it is extremely influential and able to make a definite impression upon politics, through chambers of commerce, Parliamentary representatives, and semi-political, semi-commercial bodies like the Imperial South African Association or the China League.

The shipping trade has a very definite interest which makes for Imperialism. This is well illustrated by the policy of State subsidies now claimed by shipping firms as a retainer, and in order to encourage British shipping for purposes of imperial safety and defense.

The services are, of course, imperialist by conviction and by professional interest, and every increase of the army and navy enhances their numerical strength and the political power they exert. . . .

What is true of Great Britain is true likewise of France, Germany, the United States, and of all countries in which modern capitalism has placed large surplus savings in the hands of a plutocracy or of a thrifty middle class. A well-recognized distinction is drawn between creditor and debtor countries. Great Britain has been for some time by far the largest creditor country, and the policy by which the investing classes use the instrument of the State for private business purposes is most richly illustrated in the recent history of her wars and annexations.[1] But France, Germany, and the United States are advancing fast along the same path. . . .

Investors who have put their money in foreign lands, upon terms which take full account of risks connected with the political conditions of the country, desire to use the resources of their Government to minimize these risks, and so to enhance the capital value and the interest of their private investments. The investing and speculative classes in general also desire that Great Britain should take other foreign areas under her flag in order to secure new areas for profitable investment and speculation.

---

[1]**recent history of . . . wars and annexations**: One such example was the British government's decision to buy the khedive of Egypt's stock shares in the Suez Canal Company in 1875, about 40 percent of the company. This led to British control of the canal, and of Egypt when the khedive was unable to pay his debts. The most recent example would have been the expansion of the British Cape Colony into the Boers' (European farmers of Dutch descent) Transvaal territories, resulting in the 1899–1902 South African War. British companies gained access to gold and diamond mining as a result of the war.

READING QUESTIONS

1. Based on this selection, what groups does Hobson see benefiting from imperialism? In what ways are the interests of these groups the same as or different from the interests of the nation as a whole?

2. What negative outcomes does Hobson believe result from imperial competition?

3. What is Hobson's attitude toward war, particularly regarding the relationship between the government and the citizens of the nation in wartime?

▪ COMPARATIVE AND DISCUSSION QUESTIONS ▪

1. Based on the documents included in this chapter, how would you characterize the motives behind the New Imperialism? Who primarily benefited from it, who tended to bear the costs of it, and how do these documents reflect these conclusions?

2. Compare the documents produced by the Westerners Stanley, Twain, and Hobson. Where do they seem to differ, and what similarities can you see? What differences in perspective might account for their different ideas on colonization?

3. Based on their documents, would Commissioner Lin agree with Hobson's views on the dangers of imperial trade?

4. Compare and contrast the Twain pamphlet and the Cecil Rhodes cartoon. How did each try to shape public opinion about imperialism? How might Rhodes have responded to accusations similar to those leveled by Twain against Leopold II?

5. How might Hobson and the Earl of Cromer agree about the outcomes of imperialism, and how might they disagree? Based upon his social status, why do you suppose the Earl of Cromer defends the occupation of Egypt?

25

War and Revolution

1914–1919

The outbreak of World War I was greeted with widespread European enthusiasm. For decades, Europe's Great Powers had been divided into alliance blocs in anticipation of a conflict. The currents of extreme nationalism, competition for overseas colonies, and Social Darwinism that characterized the prewar era convinced many that war was not only inevitable, but desirable — a brief, decisive test of "survival of the fittest." In reality, the conflict was a long, brutal contest in which the combatants had to mobilize all of their resources — people, raw materials, transportation infrastructure, and factories — in a "total war" that made little distinction between soldiers and civilians. In the trenches on the western front, the war stagnated into a contest of attrition. In the east, the collapse of the Russian Empire paved the way for the eventual Soviet state, but it did not lead to a German victory. In the end, the human and economic costs of the war dwarfed all previous conflicts. Despite these costs, and despite the efforts of U.S. president Woodrow Wilson to use the subsequent peace negotiations to forge a new, more peaceful international order, the world emerged from global war in 1919 as divided and unstable as ever. Within two decades, a new round of conflict in Europe would spark a second world war, this one even more destructive than the first.

SOURCES IN CONVERSATION

World War I in the Trenches and in the Air

Trench warfare epitomized the anonymity of warfare in the industrial era. Each side rained down countless artillery shells on the enemy lines, bringing death to men the gunners would never see. Machine guns were not aimed at individuals, but at crowds of men. The victims of poison gas were selected by chance, as shifting winds pushed gas clouds in one direction or another. In order to counter the hideous, impersonal, and seemingly hopeless reality of trench warfare and maintain support for the war effort, political leaders used propaganda to present the conflict as a morally directed struggle between good and evil forces.

READ AND COMPARE

1. How does the image in Document 25-3 differ from the account and picture in Documents 25-1 and 25-2?

2. Why was it important to present the realities of the war so differently in propagandistic posters?

25-1 | HENRI BARBUSSE, *The Story of a Squad* (1916)

Although it would be impossible to sufficiently convey the horrifying experiences of soldiers on the front lines in World War I, some authors attempted to do so. The fighting on the western front ground down by late 1914 to a series of largely stationary fortification trenches that wound roughly four hundred miles through Belgium and France, with barbed wire and mines between the fortifications. New weapons such as grenades, machine guns, poison gas, improved long-range artillery, planes, and tanks all made the fighting incredibly deadly, with casualties measured in hundreds of thousands of men. Meanwhile, in between the largely futile and almost suicidal offensive charges, soldiers suffered from boredom, rampant disease, hunger, and lack of sleep. This fictional account is one of the earliest, first published in 1916 by Frenchman Henri Barbusse. Although it is a novel, it is based on Barbusse's experiences with his "squad." The first section describes the general atmosphere of the trenches, and the second narrates part of an offensive charge.

The great pale sky is alive with thunderclaps. Each detonation reveals together a shaft of red falling fire in what is left of the night, and a column of smoke in what has dawned of the day. Up there—so high and so far that they are heard unseen—a flight of dreadful birds goes circling up with strong and palpitating cries to look down upon the earth.

. . .

From Henri Barbusse, *Under Fire: The Story of a Squad*, trans. Fitzwater Wray (London: J. M. Dent & Sons, 1917), pp. 5–6, 243–246, 248–250.

Now you can make out a network of long ditches where the lave of the night still lingers. It is the trench. It is carpeted at bottom with a layer of slime that liberates the foot at each step with a sticky sound; and by each dug-out it smells of the night's excretions. The holes themselves, as you stoop to peer in, are foul of breath.

Crack! Crack! Boom!—rifle fire and cannonade. Above us and all around, it crackles and rolls, in long gusts or separate explosions. The flaming and melancholy storm never, never ends. For more than fifteen months, for five hundred days in this part of the world where we are, the rifles and the big guns have gone on from morning to night and from night to morning. We are buried deep in an everlasting battlefield; but like the ticking of the clocks at home in the days gone by—in the now almost legendary Past—you only hear the noise when you listen.
. . .

A man arrives running, and speaks to Bertrand, and then Bertrand turns to us—"Up you go," he says, "it's our turn."

All move at once. We put our feet on the steps made by the sappers, raise ourselves, elbow to elbow, beyond the shelter of the trench, and climb on to the parapet.

Bertrand is out there on the sloping ground. He covers us with a quick glance, and when we are all there he says, "Allons, forward!" . . .

We descend over the rough and slippery ground with involuntary gestures, helping ourselves sometimes with the rifle. . . . No, there is no firing against us. The wide exodus of the battalion out of the ground seems to have passed unnoticed! This truce is full of an increasing menace, increasing. The pale light confuses us.
. . .

Bertrand shouts at us to reserve our bombs and wait till the last moment.

But the sound of his voice is carried away. Abruptly, across all the width of the opposite slope, lurid flames burst forth that strike the air with terrible detonations. In line from left to right fires emerge from the sky and explosions from the ground. It is a frightful curtain which divides us from the world, which divides us from the past and from the future. We stop, fixed to the ground, stupefied by the sudden host that thunders from every side; then a simultaneous effort uplifts our mass again and throws it swiftly forward. We stumble and impede each other in the great waves of smoke. With harsh crashes and whirlwinds of pulverized earth, towards the profundity into which we hurl ourselves pell-mell, we see craters opened here and there, side by side, and merging in each other. Then one knows no longer where the discharges fall. Volleys are let loose so monstrously resounding that one feels himself annihilated by the mere sound of the downpoured thunder of these great constellations of destruction that form in the sky. One sees and one feels the fragments passing close to one's head with their hiss of red-hot iron plunged in water. The blast of one explosion so burns my hands that I let my rifle fall. I pick it up again, reeling, and set off in the tawny-gleaming tempest with lowered head, lashed by spirits of dust and soot in a crushing downpour like volcanic lava. The stridor of the bursting shells hurts your ears, beats you on the neck, goes through your temples, and you cannot endure it without a cry. The gusts of death drive us on, lift us up, rock us to and fro. We leap, and do not know whither we go. Our eyes are blinking and weeping and obscured. The view before us is blocked by a flashing avalanche that fills space.

It is the barrage fire. We have to go through that whirlwind of fire and those fearful showers that vertically fall. We are passing through. We are through it, by chance. Here and there I have seen forms that spun round and were lifted up and laid down, illumined by a brief reflection from over yonder. I have glimpsed strange faces that uttered some sort of cry—you could see them without hearing them in the roar of annihilation. A brasier full of red and black masses huge and furious fell about me, excavating the ground, tearing it from under my feet, throwing me aside like a bouncing toy. I remember that I strode over a smouldering corpse, quite black, with a tissue of rosy blood shriveling on him; and I remember, too, that the skirts of the greatcoat flying next to me had caught fire, and left a trail of smoke behind. On our right, all along Trench 97, our glances were drawn and dazzled by a rank of frightful flames, closely crowded against each other like men.

Forward!

Now we are nearly running. I see some who fall solidly flat, face forward, and others who founder meekly, as though they would sit down on the ground. We step aside to avoid the prostrate dead, quiet and rigid, or else offensive, and also—more perilous snares!—the wounded that hook on to you, struggling.

The International Trench! We are there. The wire entanglements have been torn up into long roots and creepers, thrown afar and coiled up, swept away and piled in great drifts by the guns. Between these big bushes of rain-damped steel the ground is open and free.

The trench is not defended. The Germans have abandoned it, or else a first wave has already passed over it. Its interior bristles with rifles placed against the bank. In the bottom are scattered corpses. From the jumbled litter of the long trench, hands emerge that protrude from grey sleeves with red facings, and booted legs. In places the embankment is destroyed and its woodwork splintered—all the flank of the trench collapsed and fallen into an indescribable mixture. In other places, round pits are yawning. And of all that moment I have best retained the vision of a whimsical trench covered with many-coloured rags and tatters. For the makings of the sandbags the Germans had used cotton and woolen stuffs of motley design pillaged from some house-furnisher's shop; and all this hotch-potch of coloured remnants, mangled and frayed, floats and flaps and dances in our faces.

. . .

We can indeed make out the little round grey caps which rise and then drop on the ground level, fifty yards away, beyond a belt of dark earth, furrowed and humped. Encouraged, they spring forward, they who now form the group where I am. So near the goal, so far unscathed, shall we not reach it? Yes, we will reach it! We make great strides and no longer hear anything. Each man plunges straight ahead, fascinated by the terrible trench, bent rigidly forward, almost incapable of turning his head to right or to left. I have a notion that many of us missed their footing and fell to the ground. I jump sideways to miss the suddenly erect bayonet of a toppling rifle. Quite close to me, Farfadet jostles me with his face bleeding, throws himself on Volpatte who is beside me and clings to him. Volpatte doubles up without slackening his rush and drags him along some paces, then shakes him off without looking at him and without knowing who he is, and shouts at him in a breaking voice almost choked with exertion: "Let me go, let me go, *nom de Dieu!* They'll pick you up directly — don't worry."

The other man sinks to the ground, and his face, plastered with a scarlet mask and void of all expression, turns in every direction; while Volpatte, already in the distance, automatically repeats between his teeth, "Don't worry," with a steady forward gaze on the line.

. . .

Behind us voices urge us — "Forward, boys, forward, nom de Dieu!"

"All the regiment is behind us!" they cry. We do not turn round to see, but the assurance electrifies our rush once more.

No more caps are visible behind the embankment of the trench we are nearing. Some German dead are crumbling in front of it, in pinnacled heaps or extended lines. We are there. The parapet takes definite and sinister shape and detail; the loopholes — we are prodigiously, incredibly close!

Something falls in front of us. It is a bomb. With a kick Corporal Bertrand returns it so well that it rises and bursts just over the trench.

With that fortunate deed the squad reaches the trench.

Pepin has hurled himself flat on the ground and is involved with a corpse. He reaches the edge and plunges in — the first to enter. Fouillade, with great gestures and shouts, jumps into the pit almost at the same moment that Pepin rolls down it. Indistinctly I see — in the time of the lightning's flash — a whole row of black demons stooping and squatting for the descent, on the ridge of the embankment, on the edge of the dark ambush.

A terrible volley bursts point-blank in our faces, flinging in front of us a sudden row of flames the whole length of the earthen verge. After the stunning shock we shake ourselves and burst into devilish laughter — the discharge has passed too high. And at once, with shouts and roars of salvation, we slide and roll and fall alive into the belly of the trench!

READING QUESTIONS

1. What does this account reveal about the impact of trench warfare upon the perceptions and behavior of soldiers and their evolving responses to combat?

2. How would most Europeans have responded if they understood the realities of trench warfare as the war dragged on?

3. In light of the horrendous casualties and costs of the war, what would governments need to do to ensure public support for the war?

25-2 | *Klaxon Horn Used to Warn of Gas Attacks* (1917)

In this 1917 photograph, a French soldier wearing a gas mask mans a Klaxon horn used to warn his fellow soldiers of an impending gas attack. As you examine the photograph, focus on the details that reveal aspects of industrial warfare. What does this photograph tell you about the differences between World War I and earlier conflicts?

A Klaxon horn used to give warning against German gas-attacks in a French trench, illustration from "The Illustrated War News," 24th January 1917 (sepia photo)/French Photographer (20th century)/STAPLETON COLLECTION/Private Collection/Bridgeman Images.

READING QUESTIONS

1. What light does the photograph shed on the role of new military technology in World War I?

2. How does the photograph reflect the anonymity of modern warfare?

3. What does the photograph suggest to you about the experience of ordinary soldiers in World War I?

25-3 | *Is* _YOUR_ *Home Worth Fighting For?* (1915)

This war recruiting poster from 1915 was meant to encourage Irish men to enlist as soldiers, despite the perils that they would face if they were assigned to combat duties.

IS **YOUR** HOME
WORTH FIGHTING FOR?

IT WILL BE TOO LATE TO FIGHT
WHEN THE ENEMY IS AT YOUR DOOR
SO JOIN TO-DAY

Universal History Archive/UIG/Shutterstock.

READING QUESTIONS

1. How would this image motivate young men and families to support the war, despite the realities reflected in Documents 25-1 and 25-2?

2. If a soldier were motivated to enlist by this poster, and he were sent to the trenches, how would his experience of trench warfare differ from the way the war is represented in this propagandistic image?

25-4 | Women and the War

HELENA SWANWICK, *The War in Its Effect upon Women* (1916)

The years immediately preceding World War I had witnessed a massive and sometimes violent campaign for women's suffrage in Britain. Helena Swanwick, a German-born academic and journalist, was one of the prominent participants in that campaign, editing the suffragist newspaper *Common Cause* from 1909 to 1914. When war broke out, Swanwick split with much of the suffragist leadership that supported Britain's participation. Throughout the conflict, she advocated a negotiated peace and the establishment of an international organization to maintain it, unlike Emmeline Pankhurst, the suffragette highlighted in Document 22-5, who urged women to abandon their struggle to vote to fight the "German Peril." As a feminist and a socialist, Swanwick regarded the war as an opportunity for women to improve their social, economic, and political status.

How has the war affected women? How will it affect them? Women, as half the human race, are compelled to take their share of evil and good with men, the other half. The destruction of property, the increase of taxation, the rise of prices, the devastation of beautiful things in nature and art—these are felt by men as well as by women. Some losses doubtless appeal to one or the other sex with peculiar poignancy, but it would be difficult to say whose sufferings are the greater, though there can be no doubt at all that men get an exhilaration out of war which is denied to most women. When they see pictures of soldiers encamped in the ruins of what was once a home, amidst the dead bodies of gentle milch [*sic*] cows, most women would be thinking too insistently of the babies who must die for need of milk to entertain the exhilaration which no doubt may be felt at "the good work of our guns." When they read of miles upon miles of kindly earth made barren, the hearts of men may be wrung to think of wasted toil, but to women the thought suggests a simile full of an even deeper pathos; they will think of the millions of young lives destroyed, each one having cost the travail and care of a mother, and of the millions of young bodies made barren by the premature death

---

From Helena Swanwick, "The War in Its Effect upon Women," in *World War I and European Society*, ed. Marilyn Shevin-Coetzee and Frans Coetzee (Lexington, Mass.: D. C. Heath, 1995), pp. 160–164, 166.

of those who should have been their mates. The millions of widowed maidens in the coming generation will have to turn their thoughts away from one particular joy and fulfillment of life. While men in war give what is, at the present stage of the world's development, the peculiar service of men, let them not forget that in rendering that very service they are depriving a corresponding number of women of the opportunity of rendering what must, at all stages of the world's develop-ment, be the peculiar service of women. After the war, men will go on doing what has been regarded as men's work; women, deprived of their own, will also have to do much of what has been regarded as men's work. These things are going to affect women profoundly, and one hopes that the reconstruction of society is going to be met by the whole people—men and women—with a sympathetic under-standing of each other's circumstances. When what are known as men's questions are discussed, it is generally assumed that the settlement of them depends upon men only; when what are known as women's questions are discussed, there is never any suggestion that they can be settled by women independently of men. Of course they cannot. But, then, neither can "men's questions" be rightly settled so. In fact, life would be far more truly envisaged if we dropped the silly phrases "men's and women's questions"; for, indeed, there are no such matters, and all human questions affect all humanity.

Now, for the right consideration of human questions, it is necessary for humans to understand each other. This catastrophic war will do one good thing if it opens our eyes to real live women as they are, as we know them in worka-day life, but as the politician and the journalist seem not to have known them. When war broke out, a Labour newspaper, in the midst of the news of men's activities, found space to say that women would feel the pinch, because their supply of attar of roses would be curtailed. It struck some women like a blow in the face. When a great naval engagement took place, the front page of a pro-gressive daily was taken up with portraits of the officers and men who had won distinction, and the back page with portraits of simpering mannequins in extrav-agantly fashionable hats; not frank advertisement, mind you, but exploitation of women under the guise of news supposed to be peculiarly interesting to the feeble-minded creatures.

When a snapshot was published of the first women ticket collectors in England, the legend underneath the picture ran "Super-women"! It took the life and death of Edith Cavell[1] to open the eyes of the Prime Minister to the fact that there were thousands of women giving life and service to their country. "A year ago we did not know it," he said, in the House of Commons. Is that indeed so? Surely in our private capacities as ordinary citizens, we knew not only of the women whose portraits are in the picture papers (mostly pretty ladies of the music hall or of society), but also of the toiling millions upon whose cour-age and ability and endurance and goodness of heart the great human family rests. Only the politicians did not know, because their thoughts were too much engrossed with faction fights to think humanly; only the journalists would not

---

[1]**Edith Cavell:** British nurse working in Belgium, who was executed by the Germans for providing aid to Belgian insurgents.

write of them, because there was more money in writing the columns which are demanded by the advertisers of feminine luxuries. Anyone who has conducted a woman's paper knows the steady commercial pressure for that sort of "copy." . . .

The Need for Production

It is often forgotten that for full prosperity a country needs to be producing as much wealth as possible, consistently with the health, freedom, and happiness of its people. To arrive at this desired result, it is quite clear that as many people as possible should be employed productively, and it is one of the unhappy results of our economic anarchy that employers have found it profitable to have a large reserve class of unemployed and that wage-earners have been driven to try and diminish their own numbers and to restrict their own output. To keep women out of the "labor market" (by artificial restrictions, such as the refusal to work with them, or the refusal to allow them to be trained, or the refusal to adapt conditions to their health requirements) is in truth antisocial. But it is easy to see how such antisocial restrictions have been forced upon the workers, and it is futile to blame them. A way must be found out of industrial war before we can hope that industry will be carried on thriftily. Men and women must take counsel together and let the experience of the war teach them how to solve economic problems by co-operation rather than conflict. Women have been increasingly conscious of the satisfaction to be got from economic independence, of the sweetness of earned bread, of the dreary depression of subjection. They have felt the bitterness of being "kept out"; they are feeling the exhilaration of being "brought in." They are ripe for instruction and organization in working for the good of the whole. . . .

Readjustment of Employment

Most people were astonished in 1914 at the rapidity with which industry and social conditions adapted themselves to the state of war, and there are those who argue that, because the fears of very widespread and continued misery at the outbreak of the war were not justified, we need not have any anxiety about any widespread and continued misery at the establishment of peace. Certainly depression or panic are worse than useless, and a serene and cheerful heart will help to carry the nation beyond difficulties. But comfortable people must beware of seeming to bear the sorrows of others with cheerfulness, and a lack of preparation for easily foreseen contingencies will not be forgiven by those who suffer from carelessness or procrastination. We know quite well what some, at least, of our problems are going to be, and the fool's paradise would lead straight to revolution.

It would be wise to remember that the dislocation of industry at the outbreak of the war was easily met; first, because the people thrown out by the cessation of one sort of work were easily absorbed by the increase of another sort; second, because there was ample capital and credit in hand; third, because the State was prepared to shoulder many risks and to guarantee stability; fourth, because there was an untapped reservoir of women's labor to take the place of men's. The problems after the war will be different, greater, and more lasting. . . . Because it will obviously be impossible for all to find work quickly (not to speak of the right kind of work), there is almost certain to be an outcry for the restriction of work in various directions, and one of the first cries (if we may judge from the past) will be to women: "Back to the Home!" This cry will be raised whether the women have a home or not. . . . We must understand the unimpeachable right of the man who has lost his work and risked his life for his country, to find decent employment, decent wages and conditions, on his return to civil life. We must also understand the enlargement and enhancement of life which women feel when they are able to live by their own productive work, and we must realize that to deprive women of the right to live by their work is to send them back to a moral imprisonment (to say nothing of physical and intellectual starvation), of which they have become now for the first time fully conscious. And we must realize the exceeding danger that conscienceless employers may regard women's labor as preferable, owing to its cheapness and its docility, and that women, if unsympathetically treated by their male relatives and fellow workers, may be tempted to continue to be cheap and docile in the hands of those who have no desire except that of exploiting them and the community. The kind of man who likes "to keep women in their place" may find he has made slaves who will be used by his enemies against him. Men need have no fear of free women; it is the slaves and the parasites who are a deadly danger.

The demand for equal wage for equal work has been hotly pressed by men since the war began, and it is all to the good so far as it goes. But most men are still far from realizing the solidarity of their interests with those of women in all departments of life, and are still too placidly accepting the fact that women are sweated over work which is not the same as that of men. They don't realize yet that starved womanhood means starved manhood, and they don't enough appreciate the rousing and infectious character of a generous attitude on the part of men, who, in fighting the women's battles unselfishly and from a love of right, would stimulate the women to corresponding generosity. There are no comrades more staunch and loyal than women, where men have engaged their truth and courage. But men must treat them as comrades; they must no longer think only of how they can "eliminate female labor"; they must take the women into their trade unions and other organizations, and they must understand that the complexities of a woman's life are not of her invention or choosing, but are due to her function as mother of men. The sexual side of a woman's life gravely affects the economic side, and we can never afford to overlook this. As mothers and home-makers women are doing work of the highest national importance and economic value, but this value is one which returns to the nation as a whole and only in small and very uncertain part to the women themselves. . . . Unless men are prepared to socialize the responsibilities of parenthood, one does not see how women's labor is ever to be organized for the welfare of the whole, nor does one see how women are to perform their priceless functions of motherhood as well as possible if they are to be penalized for them in the future as they have been in the past. . . .

Enfranchisement and Emancipation

The course and conduct of the war, throwing upon women greater and greater responsibilities, bringing home to them how intimately their own lives and all they hold dear and sacred are affected by the government of the country, will tend greatly to strengthen and enlarge their claim for a share in the government. The growth of what was known as "militancy," in the last few years of the British suffrage movement, was the disastrous result of the long denial of justice, the acrid fruit of government which had become coercion, because it was no longer by consent.[2] Now that, for two years past, the women of Great Britain have made common cause with their men in this time of stress, the heat of the internal conflict has died down, and one hears on all sides that prominent anti-suffragists have become ardent suffragists, while others have declared their resolve at any rate never again to *oppose* the enfranchisement of women. The battle of argument was won long ago, but we are not, as a people, much given to theory; custom has a very strong hold over us. The shock of war has loosened that hold, and now almost every one who used to oppose, when asked whether women should be given votes, would reply: "Why not? They have earned them!" I cannot admit that representation is a thing that people should be called upon to "earn," nor that, if essential contribution to the nation is to count as "earning," the women have not earned the vote for just as long as the men. . . .

What the war has put in a fresh light, so that even the dullest can see, is that if the State may claim women's lives and those of their sons and husbands and lovers, if it may absorb all private and individual life, as at present, then indeed the condition of those who have no voice in the State is a condition of slavery, and Englishmen don't feel quite happy at the thought that their women are still slaves, while their Government is saying they are waging a war of liberation. Many women had long ago become acutely aware of their ignominious position, but the jolt of the war has made many more aware of it.

READING QUESTIONS

1. Having studied Swanwick's essay, how would you answer the two questions she poses at its beginning: "How has the war affected women? How will it affect them?"

2. Swanwick noted that the war brought about a major increase in the number of women in the workforce. What did she foresee happening to those women when the war ended?

3. What connections can you make between the developments Swanwick described and the achievement of women's suffrage in countries across Europe in the decade following the war?

---

[2]**"militancy," in the last few years . . . consent:** During the years preceding the war's outbreak, "militant" suffragists, led by Emmeline Pankhurst, had conducted a campaign of domestic terrorism to publicize their cause.

25-5 | Preparing for the Coming Revolution

VLADIMIR I. LENIN, *What Is to Be Done?* (1902)

Marx's vision of revolutionary change was developed with the industrialized countries of northern Europe in mind. It was the industrial working class that would create the revolution. Through workers' groups, trade unions, and political parties, the proletariat would organize themselves into an irresistible force that would crush the bourgeoisie. The expansion of male suffrage in Britain, France, Germany, and Italy facilitated this process by bringing working-class people into the electorate. Russian socialist revolutionaries were, therefore, faced with two key problems. First, Russia remained staunchly autocratic, and the formation of political opposition groups was illegal. Second, Russian industry was still in its infancy, and, thus, there was no sizable industrial working class to serve as the bulwark of the revolution. With these problems in mind, the Russian revolutionary Vladimir Lenin (1870–1924) outlined a revised socialist strategy in his pamphlet "What Is to Be Done?"

The history of all countries shows that the working class, exclusively by its own effort, is able to develop only trade union consciousness, *i.e.,* it may itself realize the necessity for combining in unions, for fighting against the employers and for striving to compel the government to pass necessary labor legislation, etc. The theory of socialism, however, grew out of the philosophic, historical, and economic theories that were elaborated by the educated representatives of the propertied classes, the intellectuals. According to their social status, the founders of modern scientific socialism, Marx and Engels, themselves belonged to the bourgeois intelligentsia. Similarly, in Russia, the theoretical doctrine of Social Democracy[1] arose quite independently of the spontaneous growth of the labor movement; it arose as a natural and inevitable outcome of the development of ideas among the revolutionary socialist intelligentsia. At the time of which we are speaking, *i.e.,* the middle of the nineties [1890s], this doctrine not only represented the completely formulated program of the Emancipation of Labor group,[2] but had already won the adherence of the majority of the revolutionary youth in Russia. . . .

It is only natural that a Social Democrat, who conceives the political struggle as being identical with the "economic struggle against the employers and the government," should conceive of an "organization of revolutionaries" as being more or less identical with an "organization of workers." And this, in fact, is what actually happens; so that when we talk about organization, we literally talk in different tongues. I recall a conversation I once had with a fairly consistent Economist, with whom I had not been previously acquainted. We were discussing the pamphlet *Who Will Make the Political Revolution?* and we were very

From *Collected Works of Vladimir Ilyich Lenin,* vol. 5 (Moscow: Foreign Languages Publishing House, 1961). Marxists Internet Archive. Web. February 23, 2010.

[1]**Social Democracy:** Lenin is referring to revolutionary communism, rather than moderate, democratic socialist parties.

[2]**Emancipation of Labor group:** First Russian Marxist political organization, founded in 1883.

soon agreed that the principal defect in that brochure was that it ignored the question of organization. We were beginning to think that we were in complete agreement with each other—but as the conversation proceeded, it became clear that we were talking of different things. My interlocutor accused the author of the brochure just mentioned of ignoring strike funds, mutual aid societies, etc.; whereas I had in mind an organization of revolutionaries as an essential factor in "making" the political revolution. After that became clear, I hardly remember a single question of importance upon which I was in agreement with that Economist!

What was the source of our disagreement? The fact that on questions of organization and politics the Economists are forever lapsing from Social Democracy into trade unionism. The political struggle carried on by the Social Democrats is far more extensive and complex than the economic struggle the workers carry on against the employers and the government. Similarly (and indeed for that reason), the organization of a revolutionary Social Democratic Party must inevitably *differ* from the organizations of the workers designed for the latter struggle. A workers' organization must in the first place be a trade organization; secondly, it must be as wide as possible; and thirdly, it must be as public as conditions will allow (here, and further on, of course, I have only autocratic Russia in mind). On the other hand, the organizations of revolutionaries must consist first and foremost of people whose profession is that of a revolutionary (that is why I speak of organizations of *revolutionaries*, meaning revolutionary Social Democrats). In view of this common feature of the members of such an organization, *all distinctions as between workers and intellectuals*, and certainly distinctions of trade and profession, must be obliterated. Such an organization must of necessity be not too extensive and as secret as possible. . . .

I assert:

1. that no movement can be durable without a stable organization of leaders to maintain continuity;
2. that the more widely the masses are spontaneously drawn into the struggle and form the basis of the movement and participate in it, the more necessary is it to have such an organization, and the more stable must it be (for it is much easier for demagogues to sidetrack the more backward sections of the masses);
3. that the organization must consist chiefly of persons engaged in revolutionary activities as a profession;
4. that in a country with an autocratic government, the more we *restrict* the membership of this organization to persons who are engaged in revolutionary activities as a profession and who have been professionally trained in the art of combating the political police, the more difficult will it be to catch the organization, and the *wider* will be the circle of men and women of the working class or of other classes of society able to join the movement and perform active work in it. . . .

The active and widespread participation of the masses will not suffer; on the contrary, it will benefit by the fact that a "dozen" experienced revolutionaries, no less professionally trained than the police, will centralize all the secret side of the work—prepare leaflets, work out approximate plans and appoint bodies of leaders for each urban district, for each factory district and to each educational institution, etc. (I know that exception will be taken to my "undemocratic" views, but I shall reply to this altogether unintelligent objection later on.) The centralization of the more secret functions in an organization of revolutionaries will not diminish, but rather increase the extent and the quality of the activity of a large number of other organizations intended for wide membership and which, therefore, can be as loose and as public as possible, for example, trade unions, workers' circles for self-education and the reading of illegal literature, and socialist and also democratic circles for *all other sections of the population*, etc., etc. We must have *as large a number as possible* of such organizations having the widest possible variety of functions, but it is absurd and dangerous to *confuse those with organizations of revolutionaries*, to erase the line of demarcation between them, to dim still more the masses' already incredibly hazy appreciation of the fact that in order to "serve" the mass movement we must have people who will devote themselves exclusively to Social Democratic activities, and that such people must *train* themselves patiently and steadfastly to be professional revolutionaries.

Aye, this appreciation has become incredibly dim. The most grievous sin we have committed in regard to organization is that *by our primitiveness we have lowered the prestige of revolutionaries in Russia*. A man who is weak and vacillating on theoretical questions, who has a narrow outlook, who makes excuses for his own slackness on the ground that the masses are awakening spontaneously; who resembles a trade union secretary more than a people's tribune, who is unable to conceive of a broad and bold plan, who is incapable of inspiring even his opponents with respect for himself, and who is inexperienced and clumsy in his own professional art—the art of combating the political police—such a man is not a revolutionary but a wretched amateur!

Let no active worker take offense at these frank remarks, for as far as insufficient training is concerned, I apply them first and foremost to myself. I used to work in a circle that set itself great and all-embracing tasks; and every member of that circle suffered to the point of torture from the realization that we were proving ourselves to be amateurs at a moment in history when we might have been able to say, paraphrasing a well-known epigram: "Give us an organization of revolutionaries, and we shall overturn the whole of Russia!"

READING QUESTIONS

1. Judging by his remarks, what sort of attitude did Lenin have toward the working class?

2. Why, if Lenin advocated establishing *"as large a number as possible"* of traditional trade unions and similar organizations, did he also maintain that there was urgent need for a secret organization of "professional revolutionaries"?

3. What connections can you make between the positions Lenin outlined in this pamphlet and the future development of Communist government under the Bolsheviks?

25-6 | Making the World Safe for Democracy

WOODROW WILSON, *The Fourteen Points* (1918)

When war broke out in 1914, the overwhelming majority of Americans were opposed to U.S. involvement, seeing the war as an "Old World" conflict that had little to do with America's national interests. President Woodrow Wilson (1856–1924) matched his policies to public opinion, running for re-election in 1916 on the slogan "He kept us out of war." As the war dragged on, however, it became increasingly difficult for the United States to remain neutral, and by the spring of 1917 Wilson was ready to ask Congress for a declaration of war against Germany. In his message to Congress, Wilson justified his request by linking the war to essential American political values. Those values were further elaborated in his "Fourteen Points," Wilson's plan for a postwar international order that would keep the peace and pave the way for the spread of democracy around the world.

1. Open covenants of peace, openly arrived at. Diplomacy shall proceed always frankly and in the public view.
2. Absolute freedom of navigation upon the seas, outside territorial waters.
3. The removal, so far as possible, of all economic barriers and the establishment of an equality of trade conditions.
4. Adequate guarantees given and taken that national armaments will be reduced.
5. A free, open-minded, and absolutely impartial adjustment of all colonial claims. In determining all such questions of sovereignty the interests of the populations concerned must have equal weight with the equitable claims of the Government whose title is to be determined.
6. The evacuation of all Russian territory.
7. Belgium must be evacuated and restored. Without this healing act the whole structure and validity of international law is forever impaired.
8. All French territory should be freed and the invaded portions restored; and the wrong done to France by Prussia in 1871 in the matter of Alsace-Lorraine[1] should be righted.
9. A readjustment of the frontiers of Italy should be effected along clearly recognizable lines of nationality.
10. The peoples of Austria-Hungary, whose place among the nations we wish to see safeguarded and assured, should be accorded the freest opportunity of autonomous development.
11. Rumania, Serbia, and Montenegro should be evacuated; occupied territories restored; Serbia accorded free and secure access to the sea; and international guarantees of the political and economic independence and territorial integrity of the several Balkan states should be entered into.

Woodrow Wilson, "The Fourteen Points," in *The Great Events of the Great War*, vol. 6, ed. Charles F. Horne (New York: National Alumni, 1920), pp. 3–6.

[1]**the wrong done to . . . Alsace-Lorraine:** The German states, headed by Prussia, defeated France in the Franco-German War (1870–1871) and annexed all of Alsace and about two-thirds of Lorraine, both of them French provinces prior to the war.

12. Nationalities which are now under Turkish rule should be assured an unmolested opportunity of autonomous development, and the Dardanelles should be permanently opened as a free passage to the ships and commerce of all nations.

13. An independent Polish state should be erected which should be assured a free and secure access to the sea.

14. A general association of nations must be formed, for the purpose of affording mutual guarantees of political independence and territorial integrity to great and small states alike.

READING QUESTIONS

1. How did Wilson want to treat Germany?

2. On what underlying principles did Wilson base points six through thirteen?

3. What do you think prompted Wilson's demand for "absolute freedom of the seas"?

4. In your opinion, was Wilson's plan practical and realistic? Why or why not?

25-7 | The Bitter Taste of Defeat

A Defeated Germany Contemplates the Peace Treaty (1919)

Unlike the Congress of Vienna (1814–1815), in which defeated France participated, the Treaty of Versailles was written without German input. Indeed, the German government was only presented with the completed treaty and told that it faced the choice of signing it or having the Allied armies resume their advance. By June 1919, the German army had been entirely demobilized. Moreover, the Allied naval blockade, which contributed to approximately 750,000 civilian deaths by starvation and disease during its duration, remained in place until Germany signed the treaty on June 28, 1919. The following document captures the reaction of Germany's most important legislative body, the National Assembly of the Germany Republic, to the treaty.

Bauer,[1] [Social Democratic Party, acting chancellor]: Ladies and gentlemen!

The Reich president has entrusted me with the formation of a new cabinet, to replace the Scheidemann[2] government which has resigned. . . . The resignation of the cabinet resulted from its inability to reach an undivided position

---

From "Deutsche Parlamentsdebatten," in *The Making of Modern Germany*, ed. and trans. Benjamin Sax and Dieter Kuntz (Lexington, Mass.: D. C. Heath, 1992), pp. 45–47.

[1]**Bauer**: Gustav Adolf Bauer (1870–1944); German chancellor, August 1919–March 1920.

[2]**Scheidemann**: German journalist and politician Philipp Scheidemann (1865–1939), who led a short-lived government from February to June of 1919.

regarding the peace treaty that has been presented to us. . . . For each of us who were members of the former government it was a bitterly difficult matter to take a position between feelings of indignation and cold rage. And not less difficult was the decision to join this new government whose first and most pressing task it is to conclude this unjust peace. . . . We are here because of our sense of responsibility, aware that it is our damnable duty to try to salvage what can be salvaged. . . .

No matter how each one of us feels about the question of acceptance or rejection, we are all united about one thing: in strong criticism of this peace treaty (*"Very true!"*) to which we are being forced to affix our signatures! When this draft was first presented to us, it was greeted with a unanimous protest of indignation and rejection from our people. We defied disappointment and hoped for the indignation of the entire world. . . .

Rejection did not mean averting the treaty. (*"Very true!" from the Social Democrats.*) A no vote would only have meant a short delay of the yes vote. (*"Very true!"*) Our ability to resist has been broken; we do not have the capability to avert [signing]. . . . In the name of the national government, ladies and gentlemen, I ask you in view of the circumstances and pending ratification by the National Assembly,[3] to sign the peace treaty laid before you! . . .

The government of the German Republic pledges to fulfill the imposed conditions of the peace. The government, however, wishes during this solemn occasion to express its views quite clearly. . . . The imposed conditions exceed the limits of Germany's ability to comply. . . .

Moreover, we emphatically declare that we cannot accept Article 231 of the peace treaty, which demands that Germany accept responsibility for singly initiating the war. (*Applause.*)

Gröber,[4] *delegate of the Center Party:* Honored Assembly! The Center Party delegation of the National Assembly wishes to acknowledge the government's declaration. We accept this program and will support this government and accept [cabinet] participation. . . . We say we are prepared to accept the responsibility of fulfilling its terms as far as is humanly possible, but we do not recognize a responsibility for carrying out conditions that are impossible or intolerable. However, although these are oppressive and hardly fulfillable conditions and will have a detrimental effect on the German people, we must also take other facts into account.

First, the peace will shortly bring hundreds of thousands of prisoners back to German families. . . . Second, the peace will end starvation. . . . Third, only the peace will give us the possibility of economically rebuilding Germany. . . . Fourth, the peace also allows us to maintain our German unity. . . .

---

[3]**pending ratification . . . Assembly**: It was a vote by individual delegates, and, as the Socialists were in a majority, the treaty was accepted even though, as Bauer states, they hated it too. The vote was 237 to 138 for conditional acceptance.

[4]**Gröber**: Conrad Gröber (1872–1948); Catholic archbishop and politician.

Schiffer,[5] *delegate of the DDP* [German Democratic Party]: Contrary to the first two speakers, I wish to declare to this esteemed assembly, that the great majority of my political friends have decided to withhold their approval of the peace treaty laid before us. . . .

Count von Posadowsky,[6] *delegate of the DNVP* [German National People's Party]: Our Fatherland finds itself in the most difficult hour of its history. The enemy stands before our gates, and in the country there are disconcerting signs of internal breakup. . . . We in our party are aware of the ramifications for our people which a rejection of the peace treaty will entail. (*"Very true!" from the right.*) The resultant harm, however, will only be temporary, but if we accept this treaty we will abandon countless generations of our people to misery. . . . For us, acceptance of the treaty is impossible for many reasons. . . . In addition to making Germany defenseless, there is also the matter of theft of our territory. . . .

Haase,[7] *delegate of the USPD* [Independent Social Democratic Party]: We know that the peace treaty will bring incredible burdens for our people. . . . Nonetheless, we have no choice but to accept the treaty. Not only will rejection increase the harm, it will moreover mean sure ruin. (*Agreement from the Independent Social Democrats.*) Our people are in this desperate situation only because of the wicked warmongers and war extenders. . . .

Kahl,[8] *delegate of the DVP* [German People's Party]: Gentlemen! The German People's Party unanimously rejects this peace. . . . We reject it because to accept it would mean the destruction of the German state. . . . We reject because we cannot justify the separation of precious segments of German earth, such as the eastern provinces, from the Motherland. . . . Yes, if only we had swords in our hands! (*Laughter from the Social Democrats.*) Then we would easily find a response! (*"Very true" from the right.*)

READING QUESTIONS

1. Why were all of the speakers unhappy with the Treaty of Versailles?

2. On what grounds did Bauer, Gröber, and Haase advocate accepting the treaty?

3. On what grounds did Schiffer, Posadowsky, and Kahl advocate its rejection?

4. In your opinion, does this document help support the charge, later leveled by right-wing Germans, that by accepting the treaty the left had "stabbed Germany in the back"? Why or why not?

---

[5]**Schiffer**: Eugen Schiffer (1860–1954); German politician.
[6]**Count von Posadowsky**: Arthur Adolf Graf von Posadowsky-Wehner (1845–1932); German politician.
[7]**Haase**: Hugo Haase (1863–1919); German jurist, politician, and pacifist.
[8]**Kahl**: Wilhelm Kahl (1849–1932); German academic and politician.

■ COMPARATIVE AND DISCUSSION QUESTIONS ■

1. Compare and contrast the photograph of a French soldier wearing a gas mask and the recruiting poster from 1915. How might images like the former have made images like the latter necessary?

2. Compare and contrast Swanwick's views regarding women's place in the workforce during World War I with those of Emmeline Pankhurst (Document 22-5) regarding prewar industrial society. What had changed? How? Why did Swanwick argue for a diplomatic solution, while Pankhurst supported defeating Germany militarily?

3. What do Swanwick's and Lenin's differing views about the route to social and economic progress (women's emancipation in Swanwick's case, workers' emancipation in Lenin's) suggest about the political environments in which each lived?

4. How might Woodrow Wilson have responded to the German debate over the peace treaty? With what aspects of the German position might he have sympathized?

26

The Age of Anxiety
1880–1940

The Enlightenment faith in the power of reason and the inevitability of human progress increasingly came under attack in the late nineteenth century. Scientific advances, technological innovation, and increased productive capacity had not led to dramatic social progress. In the view of critics of Enlightenment rationalism like Friedrich Nietzsche and Sigmund Freud, the fact that the march of civilization had not, apparently, civilized human beings pointed toward the need for new models of human behavior, models that gave more weight to instincts, emotions, and irrationality. While the beginnings of twentieth-century cultural and intellectual trends can be found in the late nineteenth century, the true turning point was World War I. The unprecedented death and destruction of the Great War shook Europeans' confidence in rationality and progress to the core. For many, after the events of 1914–1919, the world would never be the same. This feeling of fundamental disruption was heightened by the continuing tensions between the combatants over the terms of the peace. It was against this backdrop of uncertainty and disorientation that the world was plunged into depression in the 1930s. When the Great Depression (1929–1939) hit the United States, the subsequent worldwide financial crisis forced many Europeans to reconsider their most basic beliefs about economic, political, and social relationships.

26-1 | Discovering the Self
SIGMUND FREUD, *The Interpretation of Dreams* (1900)

Sigmund Freud (1856–1939), a Viennese psychoanalyst, stunned the European intellectual world when he published *The Interpretation of Dreams* in 1900, in which he argued that human behavior was largely irrational, driven by instincts and memories that were buried deep within the unconscious mind. Thus, Freud offered a direct challenge to the intellectual and moral certainties of the previous century. In this excerpt from *The Interpretation of Dreams*, Freud explains the value of his study of dreams, describing them as vital evidence for uncovering the true relationship between the conscious and unconscious mind.

The unconscious is the true psychical reality; *in its innermost nature it is as much unknown to us as the reality of the external world, and it is as incompletely presented by the data of consciousness as is the external world by the communications of our sense organs.*

Now that the old antithesis between conscious life and dream-life has been reduced to its proper proportions by the establishment of unconscious psychical reality, a number of dream-problems with which earlier writers were deeply concerned have lost their significance. Thus some of the activities whose successful performance in dreams excited astonishment are no longer to be attributed to dreams but to unconscious thinking, which is active during the day no less than at night. If, as Scherner[1] has said, dreams appear to engage in making symbolic representations of the body, we now know that those representations are the product of certain unconscious fantasies (deriving, probably, from sexual impulses) which find expression not only in dreams but also in hysterical phobias and other symptoms. If a dream carries on the activities of the day and completes them and even brings valuable fresh ideas to light, all we need do is strip it of the dream disguise, which is the product of dream-work and the mark of assistance rendered by obscure forces from the depths of the mind . . . the intellectual achievement is due to the same mental forces which produce every similar result during the daytime. We are probably inclined greatly to overestimate the conscious character of intellectual and artistic production as well. Accounts given us by some of the most highly productive men, such as Goethe[2] and Helmholtz,[3] show rather that what is essential and new in their creations came to them without premeditation and as an almost ready-made whole. There is nothing strange if in other cases, where a concentration of every intellectual faculty was needed, conscious activity also contributed its share. But it is the much-abused privilege of conscious activity, wherever it plays a part, to conceal every other activity from our eyes.

It would scarcely repay the trouble if we were to treat the historical significance of dreams as a separate topic. A dream may have impelled some chieftain to embark upon a bold enterprise the success of which has changed history. But this only raises a fresh problem so long as a dream is regarded as an alien

---

[1]**Scherner**: Karl Albert Scherner; psychologist who published an 1861 work on dream theory, *The Life of Dreams*.
[2]**Goethe**: Johann Wolfgang von Goethe (1749–1832); German author of the classical and Romantic schools, most famous for his dramatic retelling of Faust's deal with the Devil.
[3]**Helmholtz**: Hermann Ludwig Ferdinand von Helmholtz (1821–1894); German doctor who wrote extensively on perception and theory of science.

power in contrast to the other more familiar forces of the mind; no such problem remains if a dream is recognized as a *form of expression* of impulses which are under the pressure of resistance during the day but which have been able to find reinforcement during the night from deep-lying sources of excitation. The respect paid to dreams in antiquity is, however, based upon correct psychological insight and is the homage paid to the uncontrolled and indestructible forces in the human mind, to the "demonic" power which produces the dream-wish and which we find at work in our unconscious. . . .

What role is now left, in our representation of things, to the phenomenon of consciousness, once so all-powerful and over-shadowing all else? None other than that of a sense-organ for the perception of psychic qualities. . . .

The whole multiplicity of the problems of consciousness can only be grasped by an analysis of the thought processes in hysteria. These give one the impression that the transition from a preconscious to a conscious cathexis[4] is marked by a censorship similar to that between the *Ucs.* [unconscious] and the *Pcs.* [preconscious]. This censorship, too, only comes into force above a certain quantitative limit, so that thought-structures of low intensity escape it. Examples of every possible variety of how a thought can be withheld from consciousness or can force its way into consciousness under certain limitations are to be found included within the framework of psychoneurotic phenomena; and they all point to the intimate and reciprocal relations between censorship and consciousness. I will bring these psychological reflections to an end with a report. . . .

I was called in to a consultation last year to examine an intelligent and unembarrassed-looking girl. She was most surprisingly dressed. For though as a rule a woman's clothes are carefully considered down to the last detail, she was wearing one of her stockings hanging down and two of the buttons on her blouse were undone. She complained of having pains in her leg and, without being asked, exposed her calf. But what she principally complained of was, to use her own words, that she had a feeling in her body as though there was something "stuck into it" which was "moving backwards and forwards" and was "shaking" her through and through: sometimes it made her whole body feel "stiff." My medical colleague, who was present at the examination, looked at me; he found no difficulty in understanding the meaning of her complaint. But what struck both of us as extraordinary was the fact that it meant nothing to the patient's mother—though she must often have found herself in the situation which her child was describing. The girl herself had no notion of the bearing of her remarks; for if she had, she would never have given voice to them. In this case it had been possible to hoodwink the censorship into allowing a fantasy which would normally have been kept in the preconscious to emerge into consciousness under the innocent disguise of making a complaint. . . .

---

[4]**cathexis:** For Freud, this term represented the libido's energy, the driving force in most human behavior.

Thus I would look for the *theoretical* value of the study of dreams in the contributions it makes to psychological knowledge and in the preliminary light it throws on the problems of psychoneuroses. Who can guess the importance of the results which might be obtained from a thorough understanding of the structure and functions of the mental apparatus, since even the present state of our knowledge allows us to exert a favorable therapeutic influence on the curable forms of psychoneurosis? But what of the *practical* value of this study — I hear the question raised — as a means towards an understanding of the mind, towards a revelation of the hidden characteristics of individual men? Have not the unconscious impulses brought out by dreams the importance of real forces in mental life? Is the ethical significance of suppressed wishes to be made light of — wishes which, just as they lead to dreams, may some day lead to other things?

I do not feel justified in answering these questions. I have not considered this side of the problem of dreams further. I think, however, that the Roman emperor was in the wrong when he had one of his subjects executed because he had dreamt of murdering the emperor. He should have begun by trying to find out what the dream meant; most probably its meaning was not what it appeared to be. And even if a dream with another content had had this act of *lèse majesté*[5] as its meaning, would it not be right to bear in mind Plato's dictum that the virtuous man is content to *dream* what a wicked man really *does*? I think it is best, therefore, to acquit dreams. Whether we are to attribute *reality* to unconscious wishes, I cannot say. It must be denied, of course, to any transitional or intermediate thoughts. If we look at unconscious wishes reduced to their most fundamental and truest shape, we shall have to conclude, no doubt, that *psychical* reality is a particular form of existence not to be confused with *material* reality. Thus there seems to be no justification for people's reluctance in accepting responsibility for the immorality of their dreams. When the mode of functioning of the mental apparatus is rightly appreciated and the relation between the conscious and the unconscious understood, the greater part of what is ethically objectionable in our dream and fantasy lives will be found to disappear. In the words of Hanns Sachs:[6] "If we look in our consciousness at something that has been told us by a dream about a contemporary (real) situation, we ought not to be surprised to find that the monster which we saw under the magnifying glass of analysis turns out to be a tiny infusorian."[7]

Actions and consciously expressed opinions are as a rule enough for practical purposes in judging men's characters. Actions deserve to be considered first and foremost; for many impulses which force their way through to consciousness are even then brought to nothing by the real forces of mental life before they can mature into deeds. In fact, some impulses often meet with no psychical

---

[5]*lèse majesté*: Insulting the monarch; an act of treason.
[6]**Hanns Sachs**: Viennese psychologist (1881–1947) and student of Freud who later wrote an admiring biography of his teacher.
[7]**infusorian**: Single-celled organism.

obstacles to their progress, for the very reason that the unconscious is certain that they will be stopped at some other stage. It is in any case instructive to get to know the much trampled soil from which our virtues proudly spring. Very rarely does the complexity of a human character, driven hither and thither by dynamic forces, submit to a choice between simple alternatives, as our antiquated morality would have us believe.

And the value of dreams for giving us knowledge of the future? There is of course no question of that. It would be truer to say instead that they give us knowledge of the past. For dreams are derived from the past in every sense. Nevertheless the ancient belief that dreams foretell the future is not wholly devoid of truth. By picturing our wishes as fulfilled, dreams are after all leading us into the future. But this future, which the dreamer pictures as the present, has been molded by his indestructible wish into a perfect likeness of the past.

READING QUESTIONS

1. According to Freud, what forms the basis of human behavior? What does he present as evidence of this pathway to expression?

2. What role did Freud assign the conscious mind in directing and controlling human behavior?

3. How might someone who believed in the absolute responsibility of individuals for their actions, particularly their moral actions, respond to Freud's theories?

26-2 | The Great Depression in America

Unemployed Men Arrive at the Capitol in Washington, D.C. (1932)

The American stock market crash in 1929 caused a rapid series of cascading consequences that resulted in the international financial crisis known as the Great Depression. By 1932, the Great Depression was causing mass unemployment in America, with millions of men out of work, and the administration of President Herbert Hoover had done little to remedy the situation. As a result, Franklin Delano Roosevelt was overwhelmingly elected to succeed Hoover as president, but he would not take office and begin his reform measures until the following year, 1933. In this image, unemployed men are pictured, having traveled to Washington, D.C., in 1932 to seek work or federal aid to reduce their economic misery.

Bettmann/Getty Images.

READING QUESTIONS

1. What would have been the political impact of the publication of pictures like this one, and why do you suppose it was published in 1932 specifically?

2. Why do you suppose the men were willing to pose for the picture, given their economic woes?

3. How does this image visually mirror the relationship between suffering Americans and the federal government before FDR began his administration? How does it represent a departure from previous cultural norms of Americans concerning the role of the federal government?

26-3 | An Analysis of the Versailles Treaty

JOHN MAYNARD KEYNES, *The Economic Consequences of the Peace* (1920)

Of all the observers at Versailles, British economist John Maynard Keynes was one of the most prescient. Upset that negotiators had given insufficient thought to the economic consequences of the treaty, Keynes warned Europe's leaders that their actions would lead to economic disaster, a prediction that seemed to come true in 1923, with the German economic collapse, and again in 1929 with the U.S. stock market crash and ensuing Great Depression. As you read Keynes's criticism of the treaty, pay particular attention to the connections he makes between economic policy and political stability.

The Treaty includes no provisions for the economic rehabilitation of Europe,—nothing to make the defeated Central Empires[1] into good neighbors, nothing to stabilize the new States of Europe,[2] nothing to reclaim Russia; nor does it promote in any way a compact of economic solidarity amongst the Allies themselves; no agreement was reached at Paris for restoring the disordered finances of France and Italy, or to adjust the systems of the Old World and the New.

The Council of Four[3] paid no attention to these issues, being preoccupied with others, — Clemenceau to crush the economic life of his enemy, Lloyd George to do a deal and bring home something which would pass muster for a week, the President to do nothing that was not just and right. It is an extraordinary fact that the fundamental economic problems of a Europe starving and disintegrating before their eyes, was the one question in which it was impossible to arouse the interest of the Four. Reparation was their main excursion into the economic field, and they settled it as a problem of theology, of politics, of electoral chicane, from every point of view except that of the economic future of the States whose destiny they were handling. . . .

For the immediate future events are taking charge, and the near destiny of Europe is no longer in the hands of any man. The events of the coming year will not be shaped by the deliberate acts of statesmen, but by the hidden currents, flowing continually beneath the surface of political history, of which no

---

From John Maynard Keynes, *The Economic Consequences of the Peace* (New York: Harcourt, Brace and Howe, 1920), pp. 226–227, 296–297.

[1]**Central Empires**: Germany, Austria-Hungary, and the Ottoman Empire—the losing alliance in the Great War.

[2]**new States of Europe**: The Treaty of Versailles dismembered the Austro-Hungarian and German Empires, in the process creating newly independent states, including Czechoslovakia, Hungary, Yugoslavia, Lithuania, Latvia, and Estonia.

[3]**Council of Four**: The leaders of the Allied nations at Versailles: Woodrow Wilson of the United States, Georges Clemenceau of France, David Lloyd George of Great Britain, and Vittorio Orlando of Italy.

one can predict the outcome. In one way only can we influence these hidden currents, — by setting in motion those forces of instruction and imagination which change opinion. The assertion of truth, the unveiling of illusion, the dissipation of hate, the enlargement and instruction of men's hearts and minds, must be the means.

In this autumn of 1919, in which I write, we are at the dead season of our fortunes. The reaction from the exertions, the fears, and the sufferings of the past five years is at its height. Our power of feeling or caring beyond the immediate questions of our own material well-being is temporarily eclipsed. The greatest events outside our own direct experience and the most dreadful anticipations cannot move us.

We have been moved already beyond endurance, and need rest. Never in the lifetime of men now living has the universal element in the soul of man burnt so dimly.

READING QUESTIONS

1. What motivations does Keynes believe shaped the treaty that emerged from the Versailles negotiations? Whose motivations were they? What does he think should have influenced the treaty instead?

2. In what ways does Keynes think Europeans have lost control of their lives? What, if any, ideas does he seem to offer to help them recover that control?

3. What about Keynes's document suggests that reason is not the driving force in international relations?

4. As Keynes portrays them, how have the citizens of the warring countries responded to the peace?

26-4 | Postwar Economic Crisis in Germany
Hyperinflation in Germany (1923)

The French occupation of the Ruhr in 1923 set off a chain of events that had cataclysmic consequences for the German economy. In response to the occupation, the German government ordered the people of the Ruhr to stop working. As the cost of supporting the striking workers and their employers mounted, the government began printing money to meet its obligations. The result was runaway inflation that obliterated the value of the German mark. This German cartoon from 1923 dramatized the impact of inflation on German families. In it, a mother holds up her starving child above a rising sea of bank notes, crying out for bread as she struggles to keep herself from being drowned in the accumulating piles of worthless money.

Papiergeld! Papiergeld!

„Brot! Brot!"

Photo12/UIG/Getty Images.

READING QUESTIONS

1. What does the cartoon suggest about the consequences of hyperinflation for ordinary Germans? What might explain the artist's choice to use the metaphor of drowning to illustrate those consequences?

2. How might the experience of hyperinflation have challenged the values and expectations of middle-class Germans?

3. What connections can you make between hyperinflation and political developments in Germany in the 1920s and 1930s?

SOURCES IN CONVERSATION

The Great Depression
in Great Britain and Germany

As the Great Depression took hold and unemployment and economic insecurity grew, European governments struggled to respond to the crisis. Although the impact of the depression was uneven, with some countries experiencing a longer and deeper downturn than others, all European governments found their legitimacy challenged by their inability, or unwillingness, to ameliorate the suffering of millions of their citizens. The sources included below explore the economic and political impact of the depression in Great Britain and Germany.

READ AND COMPARE

1. How do these two documents reflect the comparative conditions in England and Germany after World War I? How do the public responses to those conditions in each document differ, and why do you suppose the people responded as they did in each situation?

2. Why were the conditions in Germany so much worse than in Britain after the war?

26-5 | OSCAR DE LACY AND LILY WEBB, *Hunger March Speeches* (1932)

Mirroring classical economic theory, throughout the 1930s Great Britain matched declines in government revenue with cuts in spending, and it did little to intervene in the economy on behalf of the unemployed. Unemployment benefits were made available based upon need in August 1931, but Parliament imposed a Means Test wherein people seeking benefits would have to prove their economic need for aid, including an intrusive government inspection of their finances. Though the economy recovered in subsequent years, the recovery was uneven, as new industries grew in the south, while in the industrial north long-term decline only deepened. Long-term unemployed people in the north were hardest hit by the Means Test, and they resented it bitterly. In 1932, the National Unemployed Worker's Movement organized thousands of people to march in protest of the situation. In response, seventy thousand police officers were sent in to violently disperse the marchers and tens of thousands of onlookers once they reached Hyde Park in London on October 27. A police sergeant present at the event recorded and transcribed the two following documents, which are recollected accounts of speeches by two of the march leaders.

From Oscar de Lacy and Lily Webb, notes taken by Sergeant A. Davies, HO 144/18186, UK National Archives website, http://www.nationalarchives.gov.uk/education/resources/thirties-britain/hunger-march-speeches/.

Oscar de Lacy, leader of the Brighton hunger marchers said:

"As a leader and deputy organizer of the Southern contingent, it was my duty to see that the hunger marchers in 1932 marched against the national government of starvation, war and degradation, and paved the way for the smashing of the means test. When our marchers heard that the "Daily Mail" had referred to them as dupes of Communist party, they were very indignant, and some of them said if they could only get hold of the "Daily Mail" reporter they would stuff him full of his own dirty rotten reports. Comrades, we did not come here for fun. We came for business and we are not going back until the dirty means test as every unemployed man knows it, is taken away from the statute book. I must say this, comrades, that coming through from Brighton to London, right to Hyde park, the rank and file of the police force have acted as toffs.[1] I must be honest. We have no fight with the man in blue. Comrades I want to say this, that the national government and Lord Trenchard must take warning and understand that before they can depend on the marchers being batoned down, they will have to reckon with the seething discontent inside their own ranks. I suppose that is sedition, but it is common knowledge that through the cuts in their pay the police are seething with discontent, and they have a right to be discontented. We have no quarrel with them."

Comrade Lily Webb said:

"Comrades and fellow workers, as one of the leaders of the women hunger marchers who have marched from Burnley to London, I went first of all to convey the greetings of the women marchers to the London workers. I also want to thank you on behalf of the women marchers for the magnificent reception that you have accorded to us women marchers, not only on entering London yesterday but at this great demonstration this afternoon. I have never had the honour of speaking in London before to-day, and I can say, comrades, I have never seen a sight like this in the working class movement, outside Russia. I am proud to be able to speak at this meeting. We are fighting to abolish the rotten means test. The workers all over the country are fighting against it as they never fought against anything before, and we will continue to fight it until it is smashed. The way we have been received in London has made us more determined than ever. The reception by the Islington workers exceeded all our expectations. Whilst our immediate task is to fight the means test, we shall have to follow the example of the workers of Soviet Russia, to be able to abolish unemployment. Before we can overthrow unemployment we shall have to overthrow capitalism."

READING QUESTIONS

1. What do these speeches suggest about the threat that the depression posed to social order, and particularly to political authorities and social elites, in Britain?

---

[1]**toffs:** A mid-nineteenth-century slang word used to refer to upper-class people or those of aristocratic descent.

2. How does de Lacy attempt to drive a wedge between ordinary people and elites
    with his speech? Whom is he trying to assert alliance with that would aid the
    cause of the unemployed?

3. According to Webb, what needs to happen to solve the economic problems of
    the British people?

4. Which of these two speeches would probably be considered more threatening to
    British political leaders and social elites, and why?

26-6 | HEINRICH HAUSER, *With the Unemployed in Germany* (1933)

The Great Depression struck Germany with greater force than any other country, with
unemployment soaring to nearly 40 percent. Still suffering from the hardships created by
wartime destruction, reparations payments, and hyperinflation, the German people were
faced with the second economic catastrophe in less than a decade. These excerpts from the
writings of German journalist Heinrich Hauser capture something of the suffering and despair
of Germany's unemployed.

An almost unbroken chain of homeless men extends the whole length of the
great Hamburg-Berlin highway.

There are so many of them moving in both directions, impelled by the wind
or making their way against it, that they could shout a message from Hamburg
to Berlin by word of mouth.

It is the same scene for the entire two hundred miles, and the same scene
repeats itself. . . . All the highways in Germany over which I traveled this year
presented the same aspect. . . .

Most of the hikers paid no attention to me. They walked separately or in
small groups, with their eyes on the ground. And they had the queer, stum-
bling gait of barefooted people, for their shoes were slung over their shoulders.
Some of them were guild members — carpenters with embroidered wallets, knee
breeches, and broad felt hats; milkmen with striped red shirts, and bricklayers
with tall black hats, — but they were in a minority. Far more numerous were
those whom one could assign to no special profession or craft — unskilled young
people, for the most part, who had been unable to find a place for themselves in
any city or town in Germany, and who had never had a job and never expected
to have one. There was something else that had never been seen before — whole
families that had piled all their goods into baby carriages and wheelbarrows that
they were pushing along as they plodded forward in dumb despair. It was a
whole nation on the march.

I saw them — and this was the strongest impression that the year 1932 left
with me — I saw them, gathered into groups of fifty or a hundred men, attacking

From Heinrich Hauser, "With Germany's Unemployed," *The Living Age* 344 (March 1933):
27–38.

fields of potatoes. I saw them digging up the potatoes and throwing them into sacks while the farmer who owned the field watched them in despair and the local policeman looked on gloomily from the distance. I saw them staggering toward the lights of the city as night fell, with their sacks on their backs. What did it remind me of? Of the War, of the worst periods of starvation in 1917 and 1918, but even then people paid for the potatoes. . . .

I saw that the individual can know what is happening only by personal experience. I know what it is to be a tramp. I know what cold and hunger are. I know what it is to spend the night outdoors or behind the thin walls of a shack through which the wind whistles. I have slept in holes such as hunters hide in, in hayricks, under bridges, against the warm walls of boiler houses, under cattle shelters in pastures, on a heap of fir-tree boughs in the forest. But there are two things that I have only recently experienced—begging and spending the night in a municipal lodging house.

I entered the huge Berlin municipal lodging house in a northern quarter of the city. . . .

There was an entrance arched by a brick vaulting, and a watchman sat in a little wooden sentry box. His white coat made him look like a doctor. We stood waiting in the corridor. Heavy steam rose from the men's clothes. Some of them sat down on the floor, pulled off their shoes, and unwound the rags that were bound around their feet. More people were constantly pouring in the door, and we stood closely packed together. Then another door opened. The crowd pushed forward, and people began forcing their way almost eagerly through this door, for it was warm in there. Without knowing it I had already caught the rhythm of the municipal lodging house. It means waiting, waiting, standing around, and then suddenly jumping up. . . .

We now stand in a long hall, down the length of which runs a bar dividing the hall into a narrow and a wide space. All the light is on the narrow side. There under yellow lamps that hang from the ceiling on long wires sit men in white smocks. We arrange ourselves in long lines, each leading up to one of these men, and the mill begins to grind. . . .

As the line passes in single file the official does not look up at each new person to appear. He only looks at the paper that is handed to him. These papers are for the most part invalid cards or unemployment certificates. The very fact that the official does not look up robs the homeless applicant of self-respect, although he may look too beaten down to feel any. . . .

Now it is my turn and the questions and answers flow as smoothly as if I were an old hand. But finally I am asked, "Have you ever been here before?"

"No."

"No?" The question reverberates through the whole room. The clerk refuses to believe me and looks through his card catalogue. But no, my name is not there. The clerk thinks this strange, for he cannot have made a mistake, and the terrible thing that one notices in all these clerks is that they expect you to lie. They do not believe what you say. They do not regard you as a human being but as an infection, something foul that one keeps at a distance. He goes on. "How did you come here from Hamburg?"

"By truck."

"Where have you spent the last three nights?"

I lie coolly.

"Have you begged?"

I feel a warm blush spreading over my face. It is welling up from the bourgeois world that I have come from. "No."

A coarse peal of laughter rises from the line, and a loud, piercing voice grips me as if someone had seized me by the throat: "Never mind. The day will come, comrade, when there's nothing else to do." And the line breaks into laughter again, the bitterest laughter I have ever heard, the laughter of damnation and despair. . . .

Again the crowd pushes back in the kind of rhythm that is so typical of a lodging house, and we are all herded into the undressing room. . . . I cling to the man who spoke to me. He is a Saxon with a friendly manner and he has noticed that I am a stranger here. A certain sensitiveness, an almost perverse, spiritual alertness makes me like him very much.

Out of a big iron chest each of us takes a coat hanger that would serve admirably to hit somebody over the head with. As we undress the room becomes filled with the heavy breath of poverty. We are so close together that we brush against each other every time we move. Anyone who has been a soldier, anyone who has been to a public bath is perfectly accustomed to the look of naked bodies. But I have never seen anything quite so repulsive as all these hundreds of withered human frames. For in the homeless army the majority are men who have already been defeated in the struggle of life, the crippled, old, and sick. There is no repulsive disease of which traces are not to be seen here. There is no form of mutilation or degeneracy that is not represented, and the naked bodies of the old men are in a disgusting state of decline. . . .

It is superfluous to describe what follows. Towels are handed out . . . then nightgowns—long, sacklike affairs made of plain unbleached cotton but freshly washed. Then slippers. . . .

Distribution of spoons, distribution of enameled-ware bowls with the words "Property of the City of Berlin" written on their sides. Then the meal itself. A big kettle is carried in. Men with yellow smocks have brought it and men with yellow smocks ladle out the food. These men, too, are homeless and they have been expressly picked by the establishment and given free food and lodging and a little pocket money in exchange for their work about the house.

Where have I seen this kind of food distribution before? In a prison that I once helped to guard in the winter of 1919 during the German civil war. There was the same hunger then, the same trembling, anxious expectation of rations. Now the men are standing in a long row, dressed in their plain nightshirts that reach to the ground, and the noise of their shuffling feet is like the noise of big wild animals walking up and down the stone floor of their cages before feeding time. . . .

My next recollection is sitting at table in another room on a crowded bench that is like a seat in a fourth-class railway carriage. Hundreds of hungry mouths make an enormous noise eating their food. The men sit bent over their food like animals who feel that someone is going to take it away from them. They hold their bowl with their left arm part way around it, so that nobody can take it away, and they also protect it with their other elbow and with their head and mouth, while they move the spoon as fast as they can between their mouth and the bowl. . . .

We shuffle into the sleeping room, where each bed has a number painted in big letters on the wall over it. You must find the number that you have around your neck, and there is your bed, your home for one night. It stands in a row with fifty others and across the room there are fifty more in a row. . . .

Only a few people, very few, move around at all. The others lie awake and still, staring at their blankets, wrapped up in themselves but not sleeping. Only an almost soldierly sense of comradeship, an inner self-control engendered by the presence of so many people, prevents the despair that is written on all these faces from expressing itself. The few who are moving about do so with the tormenting consciousness of men who merely want to kill time. They do not believe in what they are doing.

Going to sleep means passing into the unconscious, eliminating the intelligence. And one can read deeply into a man's life by watching the way he goes to sleep. For we have not always slept in municipal lodgings. There are men among us who still move as if they were in a bourgeois bedchamber. . . .

The air is poisoned with the breath of men who have stuffed too much food into empty stomachs. There is also a sickening smell of lysol. It seems completely terrible to me. . . . Animals die, plants wither, but men always go on living.

READING QUESTIONS

1. To what other period in Germany's history did Hauser compare the depression? How might that have influenced his perception of the current situation?

2. In this account, what was the attitude of the people with power toward those without it, and how did that affect the job and relief seekers?

3. According to Hauser, what impact did the depression have on perceptions of social and economic class?

26-7 | *German Communist Party Poster* (1932)

Economic turmoil in Germany increased the appeal of radical political parties, as Germans from across the social spectrum grew convinced that mainstream parties were incapable of solving the country's problems. Seeking to take advantage of this favorable economic climate, Nazis and Communists alike promised to address the fundamental needs of the German people. The slogan on this 1932 Communist Party election poster captures the desperate mood of the early 1930s: "If you want work, freedom, and food, vote red!" The document in the background is a worker's unemployment card.

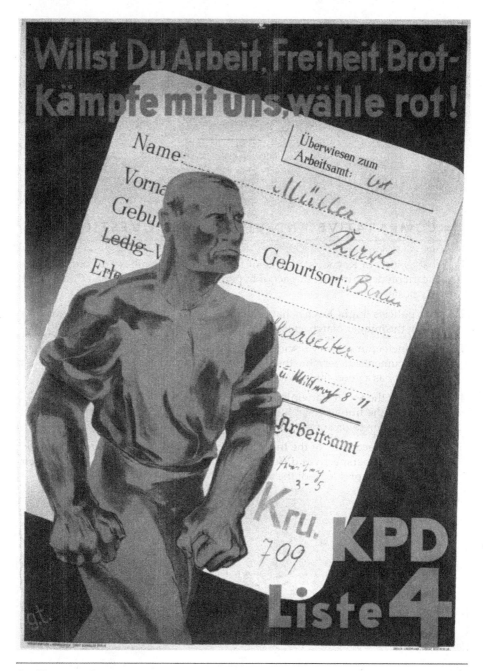

Cci/Shutterstock.

READING QUESTIONS

1. What does the poster's slogan suggest about the focus of political debate in early 1930s Germany?

2. At what groups in German society might this poster have been aimed? What clues does the poster provide about its intended target audience?

■ COMPARATIVE AND DISCUSSION QUESTIONS ■

1. What aspects of Keynes's critique of the Treaty of Versailles are confirmed by the cartoon depicting the impact of hyperinflation and the German Communist Party poster?

2. What policies might Keynes have suggested in response to the problems outlined in the hunger march speeches?

3. If the nineteenth century's science was defined by certainty, in what ways do these documents undermine that certainty? Do any of these authors see this loss of certainty as a good thing? Why or why not?

4. How might the Social Darwinists, particularly Herbert Spencer (Document 22-7), respond to the hunger march speeches or Hauser's narrative? In what ways might the depression support or undercut Spencer's ideology?

5. Compare the accounts of the hunger march speeches with Hauser's narrative. How do their perspectives differ? What differences might that lead to in their approach to the problems of the depression?

27

Dictatorships and the Second World War

1919–1945

The period of anxiety and depression that followed the Great War led many to question whether democracy and capitalism could meet the challenges of modern society. In this context, radical political parties gained new prominence in every European nation. In Italy, Benito Mussolini and the Fascists seized power in the early 1920s, providing a model and an ideology for the right-wing dictatorships of the 1930s. In the Soviet Union after 1928, Joseph Stalin led his nation through a brutal and repressive "second revolution" that used the tools of totalitarianism to establish Stalin's absolute power and to force the rapid industrialization of the Soviet Union. In 1933, Germany's new chancellor and Nazi Party leader, Adolf Hitler, began plans to create a German Nazi empire based on the ideology of Aryan supremacy. Hampered by their own worries, other nations, including Great Britain, seemed powerless to stop Germany's remilitarization or to check Hitler's aggressive expansion. The invasion of Poland in 1939 by Germany and the Soviet Union demonstrated beyond the shadow of a doubt that negotiation with Hitler was futile, and France and Great Britain declared war, marking the start of World War II. Even as the Germans carried out their plans for the conquest and domination of Europe, they pursued another of Hitler's key objectives, the extermination of all European Jews.

27-1 | A Culture of Paranoia and Coercion

VLADIMIR TCHERNAVIN, *I Speak for the Silent* (1930)

To maintain his power and Communist rule in the Soviet Union, Joseph Stalin instituted a massive security apparatus that pervaded most aspects of Soviet life. Vladimir Tchernavin was a scientist in the northwestern port city of Murmansk, working to transform the Soviet Union from an agrarian to an industrial state. Such an ambitious project was bound to have its share of failures, but in the climate of paranoia that pervaded Stalinist society, such failures were attributed to sabotage, and sabotage was brutally punished.

It was my second day in prison — my second cross-examination. I was called before the tea ration was given out and had only time to eat an apple.

"How do you do?" the examining officer asked, scanning me attentively to see if I showed signs of a sleepless night.

"All right."

"It isn't so good in your cell. You are in 22?"

"A cell like any other."

"Well, did you do any thinking? Are you going to tell the truth today?"

"Yesterday I told only the truth."

He laughed. "What will it be today — not the truth?"

Then he returned to the subject of the cell.

"I tried to choose a better cell for you, but we are so crowded. I hope we will come to an understanding and that I will not be forced to change the regime I have ordered for you. The third category is the mildest: exercise in the yard, permission to receive food parcels from outside, a newspaper and books. The first two categories are much stricter. Remember, however, that it depends entirely on me; any minute you may be deprived of everything and transferred to solitary confinement. Or rather, this depends not on me but on your own behavior, your sincerity. The more frank your testimony, the better will be the conditions of your imprisonment. . . ."

He spoke slowly, looking me straight in the eye, emphasizing his words with evident pleasure and relish, watching for their effect.

"Did you know Scherbakoff? He was a strong man, but I broke him and forced him to confess."

With great difficulty I controlled myself before replying.

"I don't doubt for a minute that you use torture, and if you believe that this assists in discovering the truth and speeding up the investigation, and since Soviet laws permit its use, I would suggest that you don't give up medieval methods: a little fire is a wonderful measure. Try it! I am not afraid of you. Even with that you can't get anything out of me."

From Vladimir Tchernavin, *I Speak for the Silent* (Newton Centre, Mass.: Charles T. Branford, 1935), pp. 116–120.

"Well, we will see about that later. Now let's get down to business. Let's talk about your acquaintances. Did you know V. K. Tolstoy, the wrecker, executed in connection with the case of the '48'?"[1]

"Yes, I knew him. How could I not know him when he was the director of the fishing industry in the north?" I replied in frank astonishment. "We both worked in it for more than twenty years."

"And did you (know) him well?"

"Very well."

"How long did you know him?"

"From childhood."

His manner changed completely; he hurriedly picked up a statement sheet and placed it in front of me. "Write down your confession."

"What confession?"

"That you knew Tolstoy, that you were in friendly relation with him from such and such a time. I see that we will come to an understanding with you; your frankness will be appreciated. Write."

He evidently was in a hurry, did not quite know what he was saying, afraid that I might reverse my statements.

I took the sheet and wrote down what I had said.

"Excellent. Let's continue."

Then followed a barrage of questions about Tolstoy, about Scherbakoff and other people that I had known. He did not find me quite so tractable and we launched into a battle of wits that kept up hour after hour. He questioned me with insistence and in great detail, trying without success to make me give dates.

"You'll not succeed in outwitting me," he snapped sharply. "I advise you not to try. I am going home to dinner now and you will stay here till evening. This examination will continue—not for a day or two, but for months and, if necessary, for years. Your strength is not equal to mine. I will force you to tell us what we need."

After threatening me still further he handed me some sheets of paper.

"You are going to state in writing your opinion regarding the building of a fertilization factory in Murmansk, its equipment and work in the future. I'll soon be back; when I return, your comments on these questions must be completed."

He put on his overcoat and left. His assistant took his place, and I busied myself with my writing. It was three or four hours before he returned, already evening.

Although I had eaten almost nothing for three days, I was still in good fighting form. He questioned me about the buying of a ship from abroad, trying to make me say that here was "wrecking," because the price had been exorbitant and the ship itself had proved unsatisfactory. It was most confusing and his questions far-fetched. We talked and we argued, but I would not give the answers he wanted.

He began on another tack. . . .

"All right," he said. "And what is your attitude regarding the subject of the fish supply in the Sea of Barents in connection with the construction of trawlers as provided for by the Five-Year Plan?"

---

[1]**the case of the '48'**: Tchernavin refers to the accusation and subsequent execution of forty-eight prominent Russian scientists accused of sabotaging the food supply in 1930.

Now he had broached a subject with which I could have a direct connection. The evening was already changing into night, but I was still sitting in the same chair. I was becoming unconscious of time: was it my second day in prison or my tenth? In spite of the depressing weariness, mental and physical, which was taking hold of me, I told him that I thought the fresh fish supply should be minutely and thoroughly investigated. I tried to make him see the hazards of the fishing industry in Murmansk and the enormous equipment that would be necessary to meet the proposals of the Five-Year Plan.

"And thus you confess that you doubted the practicability of the Five-Year Plan?" he said with a smile of smug satisfaction.

What could one say? I believed, as did everybody, that the plan was absurd, that it could not be fulfilled. For exactly such statements—no, for only a suspicion of having such thoughts—forty-eight men had been shot.

READING QUESTIONS

1. From the perspective of the state, what purposes would be served by arresting and torturing Vladimir Tchernavin?

2. What incentives could Tchernavin have for resisting, and what might convince him to comply with the interrogator?

3. Based on your reading of this account, what relationship did truth and guilt have in the Stalinist justice system?

27-2 | Stalin Touts the Successes of the Five-Year Plans

JOSEPH STALIN, *Speech Given to the Voters of the Stalin Electoral District, Moscow* (1946)

Between 1922 and 1927, Joseph Stalin brilliantly moved against his political foes in the Soviet Union to consolidate his complete power over the Communist Party, and effectively the country. He then unleashed a series of aggressively ambitious five-year plans to quickly industrialize the USSR and collectivize agriculture in order to secure the socialist government and economic structure of the new state and to also consolidate political power. While the industrial reforms boosted output incredibly fast, the agricultural reforms were much less successful, and the growth that occurred was built upon substantial suffering experienced by the Soviet people. Along with economic growth, the second five-year plan sought to close churches and eliminate Russian Orthodox clergy. Stalin's third five-year plan was interrupted after three years by Germany's invasion of the U.S.S.R., but once the war was over, he restarted the plans, and in this 1946 speech, he boasted about the successes of the previous plans and promised industrial supremacy for the Soviet Union.

Comrades!

Eight years have passed since the last elections to the Supreme Soviet. This has been a period replete with events of a decisive nature. The first four years were years of intense labour on the part of Soviet people in carrying out

From Joseph Stalin, "Speech Delivered by Stalin at a Meeting of Voters of the Stalin Electoral District, Moscow," February 9, 1946, History and Public Policy Program Digital Archive, Gospolitizdat, Moscow, 1946, http://digitalarchive.wilsoncenter.org/document/116179.

the Third Five-Year Plan. The second four years covered the events of the war against the German and Japanese aggressors—the events of the Second World War. Undoubtedly, the war was the main event during the past period.

It would be wrong to think that the Second World War broke out accidentally, or as a result of blunders committed by certain statesmen, although blunders were certainly committed. As a matter of fact, the war broke out as the inevitable result of the development of world economic and political forces on the basis of present-day monopolistic capitalism. Marxists have more than once stated that the capitalist system of world economy contains the elements of a general crisis and military conflicts, that, in view of that, the development of world capitalism in our times does not proceed smoothly and evenly, but through crises and catastrophic wars. The point is that the uneven development of capitalist countries usually leads, in the course of time, to a sharp disturbance of the equilibrium within the world system of capitalism, and that group of capitalist countries regards itself as being less securely provided with raw materials and markets usually attempts to change the situation and to redistribute "spheres of influence" in its own favour—by employing armed force. As a result of this, the capitalist world is split into two hostile camps, and war breaks out between them. . . .

Thus, as a result of the first crisis of the capitalist system of world economy, the First World War broke out, and as a result of the second crisis, the Second World War broke out.

. . .

There is one principal summation upon which all the others rest. This summation is, that towards the end of the war the enemies sustained defeat and we and our Allies proved to be the victors.

. . .

Our victory signifies, first of all, that our Soviet social system was victorious, that the Soviet social system successfully passed the test of fire in the war and proved that it is fully viable.

As we know, the foreign press on more than one occasion asserted that the Soviet social system was a "dangerous experiment" that was doomed to failure. . . .

Now we can say that the war has refuted all these assertions of the foreign press and has proved them to be groundless. The war proved that the Soviet social system is a genuinely people's system, which grew up from the ranks of the people and enjoys their powerful support; that the Soviet social system is fully viable and stable form of organization in society.

. . .

It would be wrong to think that such a historical victory could have been achieved without preliminary preparation by the whole country for active defence. It would be no less wrong to assume that such preparation could have been made in a short space of time, in a matter of three or four years. . . . To withstand the blow of such an enemy, to resist him and then to inflict utter defeat upon him it was necessary to have, in addition to the unexampled bravery of our troops, fully up-to-date armaments, and in sufficient quantities, and well-organized supplies, also in sufficient quantities. But for this it was necessary to have, and in sufficient quantities, elementary things such as: *metals* — for the production of armaments, equipment and industrial machinery, *fuel* — to ensure the operation of industry and transport; *cotton* — to manufacture army clothing; *grain* — to supply the army with food.

Can it be said that before entering the Second World War our country already possessed the necessary minimum of the material potentialities needed to satisfy these main requirements? I think it can. To prepare for this immense task we had to carry out three five-year plans of national-economic development. It was these three five-year plans that enabled us to create these material potentialities. At all events, the situation in our country in this respect was ever so much better before the Second World War, in 1940, than it was before the First World War, in 1913.

. . .

If we take the data for 1940 the eve of the Second World War — and compare it with the data for 1913 — the eve of the First World War — we shall get the following picture.

. . .

As regards 1940, in that year the following was produced in our country: 15,000,000 tons of *pig iron*, i.e., nearly four times as much as in 1913; 18,300,000 tons of *steel*, i.e., four and a half times as much as in 1913; 31,000,000 tons of *oil*, i.e., three and a half times as much as in 1913; 38,300,000 tons of *market grain*, i.e., 17,000,000 tons more than in 1913; 2,700,000 tons of *raw cotton*, i.e., three and a half times as much as in 1913.

. . .

Now a few words about the Communist Party's plans of work for the imme-diate future. As you know, these plans are formulated in the new five-year plan, which is to be adopted in the very near future. The main tasks of the new five-year plan are to rehabilitate the devastated regions of our country, to restore industry and agriculture to the prewar level, and then to exceed that level to a more or less considerable extent. Apart from the fact that the rationing system is to be abolished in the very near future, special attention will be devoted to the expansion of the production of consumer's goods, to raising the standard of living of the working people by steadily reducing the prices of all commodities, and to the extensive organization of scientific research institutes of every kind capable of giving the fullest scope to our scientific forces.

. . .

As regards long-term plans, our Party intends to organize another powerful upswing of our national economy that will enable us to raise our industry to a level, say, three times as high as that of prewar industry. We must see to it that our industry shall be able to produce annually up to 50,000,000 tons of pig iron, up to 60,000,000 tons of steel, up to 500,000,000 tons of coal, and up to 60,000,000 tons of oil. Only when we succeed in doing that can we be sure that our Motherland will be insured against all contingencies. This will need, perhaps, another three five-year plans, if not more. But it can be done, and we must do it.

. . .

In this election contest the Communist Party does not stand alone. It is going to the polls in a bloc with the non-Party people. In the past Communists were rather distrustful of non-Party people and of non-Partyism. This was due to the fact that various bourgeois groups, who thought it was not to their advantage to come before the voters without a mask, not infrequently used the non-Party flag as a screen. . . . Times are different now. Non-Party people are now separated from the bourgeoisie by a barrier called the Soviet social system. But on the other side of the barrier the non-Party people are united with the Communists in one, common, collective body of *Soviet people*. Within this collective body they fought side by side to consolidate the might of our country, they fought side by side and shed their blood on the various fronts for the sake of freedom and greatness of our Motherland, and side by side they hammered out and forged our country's victory over her enemies. The only difference between them is that some belong to the Party and some don't. But this difference is only a formal one. The important thing is that all are engaged in one common cause. That is why the bloc of Communists and non-Party people is a natural and vital thing.

READING QUESTIONS

1. How does Stalin support his argument about the success of the prewar five-year plans?

2. How does he demonstrate the success and stability of the Soviet social system, thus refuting accounts of the Western press?

3. How does he intend to unite the people to achieve a favorable result in the upcoming election?

4. Considering the negative impacts of the five-year plans that Stalin does not mention in this speech, how would Stalin probably respond to Western critiques that his plans stifled individual freedoms, entrepreneurship, and capitalistic market forces?

SOURCES IN CONVERSATION

Propaganda and the Totalitarian State

Totalitarian governments may have dismissed liberal democracy as a failed system of government whose time had passed, but that did not mean that totalitarian leaders could ignore the power of public opinion, or that they did not need to communicate with their people. If such leaders were to remake their societies, defeat their enemies, and "change history," they would need the cooperation of the masses, and one of the most important tools for acquiring that cooperation was propaganda. In the first document included below, Adolf Hitler explains the essential elements of effective propaganda. In the second, two Soviet posters from the early days of World War II illustrate the way Soviet propagandists adjusted their messages to mesh with the values and beliefs of their intended audience.

READ AND COMPARE

1. How do the Soviet propaganda posters reflect the tactics that Hitler describes?

2. Are there any differences you can detect between Soviet and Nazi tactics of propaganda?

27-3 | ADOLF HITLER, *Mein Kampf: The Art of Propaganda* (1924)

While in prison for a failed 1923 coup attempt, Hitler dictated his autobiography, *Mein Kampf (My Struggle)*, detailing his views on politics and society. Based on his interpretation of the end of the Great War, Hitler argued that Germany had been defeated not by Allied armies, but by the failure of German propaganda to effectively counter Allied propaganda, something he proposed to change when he came to power. At the time of its publication, *Mein Kampf* was not popular, but it proved prophetic: one of Hitler's first acts as chancellor was to establish the Ministry for Enlightenment and Propaganda in March 1933.

The psyche of the great masses is not receptive to anything that is halfhearted and weak. . . .

To whom should propaganda be addressed? To the scientifically trained intelligentsia or to the less educated masses?

It must be addressed always and exclusively to the masses. . . .

All propaganda must be popular and its intellectual level must be adjusted to the most limited intelligence among those it is addressed to. Consequently, the greater the mass it is intended to reach, the lower its purely intellectual level will have to be. . . .

The art of propaganda lies in understanding the emotional ideas of the great masses and finding, through a psychologically correct form, the way to the attention and thence to the heart of the broad masses. The fact that our bright boys do not understand this merely shows how mentally lazy and conceited they are.

Once we understand how necessary it is for propaganda to be adjusted to the broad mass, the following rule results:

It is a mistake to make propaganda many-sided, like scientific instruction, for instance. The receptivity of the great masses is very limited, their intelligence is small, but their power of forgetting is enormous. In consequence of these facts, all effective propaganda must be limited to a very few points and must harp on these in slogans until the last member of the public understands what you want him to understand by your slogan. As soon as you sacrifice this slogan and try to be many-sided, the effect will piddle away, for the crowd can neither digest nor retain the material offered. In this way, the result is weakened and in the end entirely cancelled out. . . .

The broad mass of a nation does not consist of diplomats, or even professors of political law, or even individuals capable of forming a rational opinion; it consists of plain mortals, wavering and inclined to doubt and uncertainty. As soon as our own propaganda admits so much as a glimmer of right on the other side, the foundation for doubt in our own right has been laid. . . .

The people in their overwhelming majority are so feminine by nature and attitude that sober reasoning determines their thoughts and actions far less than emotion and feeling. . . . But the most brilliant propagandist technique will yield no success unless one fundamental principle is borne in mind constantly and with unflagging attention. It must confine itself to a few points and repeat them over and over. Here, as so often in this world, persistence is the first and most important requirement for success. . . .

The purpose of propaganda is not to provide interesting distraction for blasé young gentlemen, but to convince, and what I mean is to convince the masses. But the masses are slow-moving, and they always require a certain time before they are ready even to notice a thing, and only after the simplest ideas are repeated thousands of times will the masses finally remember them. . . .

[During World War I] at first the claims of the [enemy] propaganda were so impudent that people thought it insane; later, it got on people's nerves; and in the end, it was believed.

READING QUESTIONS

1. What are Hitler's main suggestions for the propagandist who wants to be successful?

2. In Hitler's view, what role did rational, factual argument play in propaganda? What about emotions and feelings?

3. What does Hitler's conception of who matters in society reveal about his attitudes toward both the powerful and the powerless members of his society?

27-4 | *Soviet Propaganda Posters* (1941 and 1945)

In the initial days of the German invasion of 1941, Soviet propaganda was of a piece with the messages of the 1920s and 1930s, emphasizing revolutionary and Leninist themes. Later efforts, however, reveal a dramatic shift in tactics. Instead of presenting the clash between the Soviet Union and Germany in ideological terms, Soviet propaganda focused on the essential emotional response of Soviet citizens to invasion, emphasizing nationalism and the defense of the motherland, and reviving Great Russian historical figures, even some from the tsarist era, as examples of heroic resistance to would-be conquerors. The poster featuring a massed Soviet army marching to victory under the banner of Lenin epitomizes the early approach to wartime propaganda. The poster below it, linking the fates of Hitler and Napoleon, illustrates the later approach.

[*top*] Universal History Archive/UIG/Shutterstock. [*bottom*] Historia/Shutterstock.

READING QUESTIONS

1. What are the different ways in which Soviet soldiers are portrayed in the two images? How might this reflect a changing appreciation of the nature of the war?

2. How could the use of aristocratic generals from the nineteenth century be reconciled with the official Soviet emphasis on breaking with that tradition?

3. Why might Soviet citizens have found the later poster more inspiring than the earlier one?

27-5 | Freedom's Last Line of Defense

WINSTON CHURCHILL, *Speech Before the House of Commons* (June 18, 1940)

Once World War II began in 1939, much of central and western Europe quickly fell to the German *blitzkrieg* strategy. After sending troops to aid the French against the Germans in 1940, the British army lost most of its tanks, trucks, and other heavy equipment while evacuating from Dunkirk following a decisive Nazi victory. Germany held the deep-water ports along the English Channel crucial for an invasion, and it had the most feared air force in Europe. Facing these grim prospects, Churchill addressed the House of Commons to rally a nation unenthusiastic about another war.

The military events which have happened during the past fortnight have not come to me with any sense of surprise. Indeed, I indicated a fortnight ago as clearly as I could to the House that the worst possibilities were open, and I made it perfectly clear then that whatever happened in France would make no difference to the resolve of Britain and the British Empire to fight on, "if necessary for years, if necessary alone." During the last few days we have successfully brought off the great majority of the troops we had on the lines of communication in France—a very large number, scores of thousands—and seven-eighths of the troops we have sent to France since the beginning of the war, that is to say, about 350,000 out of 400,000 men, are safely back in this country. Others are still fighting with the French, and fighting with considerable success in their local encounters with the enemy. We have also brought back a great mass of stores, rifles, and munitions of all kinds which had been accumulated in France during the last nine months.

We have, therefore, in this island to-day a very large and powerful military force. . . . This brings me, naturally, to the great question of invasion from the air and of the impending struggle between the British and German air forces. It seems quite clear that no invasion on a scale beyond the capacity of our land

---

From Winston Churchill, "June 18, 1940, Speech Before House of Commons," in *The Past Speaks*, 2d ed., ed. Walter Arnstein, vol. 2 (Lexington, Mass.: D. C. Heath, 1993), pp. 376–378.

forces to crush speedily is likely to take place from the air until our air force has been definitely overpowered. In the meantime, there may be raids by parachute troops and attempted descents of airborne soldiers. We should be able to give those gentry a warm reception both in the air and if they reach the ground in any condition to continue the dispute. But the great question is, can we break Hitler's air weapon? Now, of course, it is a very great pity that we have not got an air force at least equal to that of the most powerful enemy within striking distance of these shores. But we have a very powerful air force which has proved itself far superior in quality, both in men and in many types of machine, to what we have met so far in the numerous fierce air battles which have been fought. In France, where we were at a considerable disadvantage and lost many machines on the ground, we were accustomed to inflict losses of as much as two to two and a half to one. In the fighting over Dunkirk, which was a sort of no man's land, we undoubtedly beat the German air force, and this gave us the mastery locally in the air, and we inflicted losses of three or four to one. . . .

There remains the danger of bombing attacks, which will certainly be made very soon upon us by the bomber forces of the enemy. It is true that the German bomber force is superior in numbers to ours, but we have a very large bomber force also which we shall use to strike at military targets in Germany without intermission. I do not at all underrate the severity of the ordeal which lies before us, but I believe our countrymen will show themselves capable of standing up to it. . . .

What General Weygand[1] called the "Battle of France" is over. I expect that the battle of Britain is about to begin. Upon this battle depends the survival of Christian civilization. Upon it depends our own British life and the long continuity of our institutions and our empire. The whole fury and might of the enemy must very soon be turned on us. Hitler knows that he will have to break us in this island or lose the war. If we can stand up to him all Europe may be free, and the life of the world may move forward into broad, sunlit uplands, but if we fail then the whole world, including the United States, and all that we have known and cared for, will sink into the abyss of a new dark age made more sinister, and perhaps more prolonged, by the lights of a perverted science. Let us therefore brace ourselves to our duty and so bear ourselves that if the British Commonwealth and Empire lasts for a thousand years men will still say, "This was their finest hour."

READING QUESTIONS

1. What reasons would Churchill have for mentioning the United States specifically in the last paragraph? For what audiences might this speech have been intended?

2. What could this speech reveal about Churchill's attitude toward the British citizenry and the concept of democratic rule in general?

3. How did Churchill characterize the situation facing the British people? Do you find his assessment convincing? Why or why not?

---

[1]**General Weygand**: General Maxime Weygand took command of all French forces on May 17, 1940, and held that post until the French surrender, after which he collaborated with the German occupation.

27-6 | Legislating Racial Purity

The Nuremberg Laws: The Centerpiece of Nazi Racial Legislation (1935)

Anti-Semitism was never a mere aspect of Hitler's political ideology; it was central to his vision of a new Germany. In Hitler's view, the achievement of Germany's national potential, its historical destiny, depended on the exclusion of the Jews from German life. The Jews were responsible for all of Germany's past miseries and, if left to their own devices, would do everything in their power to sabotage and undermine the construction of the glorious National Socialist future. The 1935 Nuremburg Laws, excerpted here, were the first formal steps toward Hitler's goal of a "Jew-free" Germany.

Article 5

1. A Jew is anyone who descended from at least three grandparents who were racially full Jews. Article 2, par. 2, second sentence will apply.
2. A Jew is also one who descended from two full Jewish parents, if: (a) he belonged to the Jewish religious community at the time this law was issued, or who joined the community later; (b) he was married to a Jewish person, at the time the law was issued, or married one subsequently; (c) he is the offspring from a marriage with a Jew, in the sense of Section 1, which was contracted after the Law for the Protection of German Blood and German Honor became effective. . . . (d) he is the offspring of an extramarital relationship, with a Jew, according to Section 1, and will be born out of wedlock after July 31, 1936. . . .

Law for the Protection of German Blood and German Honor of 15 September 1935

Thoroughly convinced by the knowledge that the purity of German blood is essential for the further existence of the German people and animated by the inflexible will to safe-guard the German nation for the entire future, the Reichstag[1] has resolved upon the following law unanimously, which is promulgated herewith:

Section 1

1. Marriages between Jews and nationals of German or kindred blood are forbidden. Marriages concluded in defiance of this law are void, even if, for the purpose of evading this law, they are concluded abroad. . . .

From U.S. Chief of Counsel for the Prosecution of Axis Criminality, *Nazi Conspiracy and Aggression* (Washington, D.C.: U.S. Government Printing Office, 1946), vol. 4, doc. no. 1417-PS, pp. 8–10; vol. 4, doc. no. 2000-PS, pp. 636–638.

[1]**Reichstag**: German legislative assembly; a holdover from Bismarck's Second Empire (1871–1919) that had little real power after it granted Hitler "temporary" dictatorial powers in March 1933.

Section 2

Relation[s] outside marriage between Jews and nationals of German or kindred blood are forbidden.

Section 3

Jews will not be permitted to employ female nationals of German or kindred blood in their household.

Section 4

1. Jews are forbidden to hoist the Reich and national flag and to present the colors of the Reich. . . .

Section 5

1. A person who acts contrary to the prohibition of section 1 will be punished with hard labor.
2. A person who acts contrary to the prohibition of section 2 will be punished with imprisonment or with hard labor.
3. A person who acts contrary to the provisions of sections 3 or 4 will be punished with imprisonment up to a year and with a fine or with one of these penalties.

READING QUESTIONS

1. According to the law, what made someone a Jew? Why was it important to the Nazis to establish a legal definition of Jewish status?

2. What do the laws tell you about the importance of biological "purity" in Nazi ideology?

3. Why might Jews have been forbidden to raise the national and Reich flags? What does this provision of the law suggest about the Nazi vision of the relationship of German Jews to the German nation as a whole?

27-7 | The First Steps Toward a "Final Solution"

ALFRED ROSENBERG, *The Jewish Question as a World Problem* (1941)

German military conquests in the early years of World War II allowed the Nazis to expand the scope of their anti-Jewish policies. What began as an effort to create a "Jew-free" Germany became a global crusade to resolve, once and for all, the "Jewish question." The Nazi propagandist and party official Alfred Rosenberg gave this speech on the "world Jewish

Office of the U.S. Chief of Counsel for Prosecution of Axis Criminality, *Nazi Conspiracy and Aggression*, vol. 5 (Washington, D.C.: U.S. Government Printing Office, 1946), pp. 554–557 [Doc. 2889-PS].

problem" in a radio address in March 1941. A few months later, he was appointed Reich Minister for the Occupied Eastern Territories. In the speech, Rosenberg rejected the idea of a Jewish state, outlined Germany's plans for Europe's Jews, and argued that world peace would be possible only when these plans had been brought to fruition.

The war which is being waged today by the German armed forces under the highest command of Adolf Hitler, is therefore a war of an immense reform. It does not only overcome the world of ideas of the French revolution, but it also exterminates directly all those racially infecting germs of Jewry and its bastards, which now since over a hundred years could develop without check among the European nations. The Jew question which for 2,000 years was a problem for the European nations which was not solved, will now find its solution through the national socialistic revolution for Germany and whole Europe.

And if one asks, in which form, then we have to say the following to this: During these decades a lot has been talked about a Jewish state as solution, and Zionism appears to some harmless people perhaps even today as an honest attempt to contribute on the part of the Jews also something toward the solution of the Jewish question.

In reality there never was nor will there ever be a Jewish State.

Contrary to the other nations on this globe, Judaism is no vertical organization which comprises all professions, but has been always a horizontal class among the different nations, that class which carried on material and spiritual intermediate trade. Secondly, the space being considered in Palestine is in no way suitable for any Jewish state. It is too small to absorb what was formerly 10 and is now 15 million Jews; in other words, therefore impractical for solving the Jewish question. The purpose of Zionism, in reality, was not to solve the Jewish question in the sense of the coordination of the whole Jewish people, but lay in an entirely different direction.

It was intended to build in Palestine a purely Jewish center, a real legitimate Jewish state in order to be able, at first, to be represented at all diplomatic conferences with full rights as national Jew.

Secondly it was intended to make Palestine into a huge, economic staging area against the entire Near East. Thirdly, this Jewish state should have been an asylum for all those Jewish adventurers in the world who were evicted from the countries in which they acted. And, finally, nobody was even thinking of limiting even in the slightest, the so-called state civil rights of the Jews in Germany, England, America, and also France. The Jews therefore, would have maintained the rights of the Germans, Englishmen, Frenchmen etc., and the spaceless Jewish world state would have come constantly closer toward its realization, that is, an all-Jewish center without any interference of non-Jews and the Jewish high finance at the state rudder in all other countries of the world.

This dream is now finished. Now, just the reverse, we have to think of how and where to put the Jews. This can, as mentioned, not be done in a Jewish state, but only in a way which I shall call the Jewish reservation.

It is to be hoped that future statesmen will get together in order to gradually institute a settlement of Jews who, under experienced police supervision, now should do such useful work as they wanted to see done until now by non-Jews.

From an almost unlimited Jewish rule in all European countries to such a radical reverse, to an evacuation of this same Jewish race after 2,000 years of parasitism on the European continent, then only can one conceive through this an idea what an enormous philosophical and political revolution is in the making in Europe today.

Today the Jewish question is somewhat clear before our eyes. It is the problem of a simple national purity. It means the necessity for defense of inherent national tradition for all nations which still value culture and future. It is still a problem of economy for all those who cannot solve the social questions under the Jewish financial dictatorship. It is a political problem of power, because in many states the will has not yet been found to break this financial dictatorship of the Jewry. And, lastly, it is a historically ideological problem, given to the Europeans since the days when the first Jews immigrated to Rome. The totality of this as national socialist, have but one clear answer for all these questions:

For Germany the Jewish Question is only then solved, when the Last Jew has left the Greater German space.

Since Germany with its blood and its nationalism has now broken for always this Jewish dictatorship for all Europe, and has seen to it that Europe as a whole will become free from the Jewish parasitism once more, we may, I believe, also say for all Europeans: For Europe the Jewish question is only then solved, when the last Jew has left the European continent.

At that, it does not matter whether such a program can be realized in five, ten or twenty years. The transportation facilities in our time, if all nations join, would be strong enough to institute and to execute such a resettlement to a great extent. But the problem must and will one day be solved as we have visualized it from the first day of our fight — then accused utopists — and now proclaim it as strict realistic politicians. All nations are interested in the solution of this question, and we must declare here with all passion:

In this cleaning-up even Mr. Roosevelt with his Baruchs and his trophy film Jews will not be able to hamper us, but wholly to the contrary, just this proclamation that the Jewish parasitical spirit shall represent today the freedom of the world, will especially awaken all resistance of the German character, and the strongest military instrument which history has seen, the German Armed forces of Adolf Hitler, will take care of it that this last furious attempt to let the white race once more march against Europe for the benefit of the Jewish financial dominion, will find an end for all times.

We are of the opinion that this great war constitutes also a cleansing biological world revolution and that also those nations which are still opposed to us, will recognize at the end of the war, that Germany's business is today the business of the whole European continent, the business of the whole Jewish race, but also the business of all other cultured races on this globe who fight for a safe national cultural and state life. Thus we hope that one day, in a reasonable distribution of the great living spaces of this globe the nations will find that peace, that work and that prosperity which for decades have been harassed by never-tiring parasitical activity. Thus, we consider today the Jewish question as one of the most important problems among the total politics of Europe, as a problem which must be solved and will be solved, and we hope, yes, we know already today, that all nations of Europe will march behind this cleansing at the end.

READING QUESTIONS

1. Why did Rosenberg reject the idea of a Jewish state in Palestine?

2. What solution did Rosenberg put forward for the "Jewish question"? Does it seem practical to you? Why or why not?

3. How did Rosenberg justify the expulsion of Europe's Jews and their confinement in a Jewish "reservation"?

4. In what ways did Rosenberg's speech foreshadow the Nazis' eventual efforts to exterminate Europe's Jews? In your opinion, were schemes such as the one Rosenberg outlined ever truly entertained, or did Nazi leaders have extermination in mind from the beginning?

■ COMPARATIVE AND DISCUSSION QUESTIONS ■

1. What similarities can you see between German and Soviet attitudes toward their citizens, and how might these attitudes contrast with the British attitude expressed by Churchill?

2. Apply Hitler's definition of effective propaganda to Churchill's speech. Where does it seem Churchill agrees with Hitler's principles, and where does it seem he departs from them?

3. What connections can you make between the Nuremburg Laws and Rosenberg's speech on the "Jewish question"? In what ways was Rosenberg's plan a logical extension of the laws?

4. How might Stalin have responded to Churchill's speech? How did his characterization of the war differ from Churchill's?

28

Cold War Conflict and Consensus
1945–1965

Even before the war ended, tensions had emerged between the Allies — the United States, the Soviet Union, and Great Britain. Each looked ahead to a postwar world that would be very different from the world of the 1920s and 1930s. Within five years, the Soviet Union and the United States had organized competing alliances, each aimed at thwarting the other's perceived efforts at expansion and global domination. The development of nuclear weapons brought a terrifying new dimension to Cold War conflict. Ironically, despite the ever-present threat of nuclear war between 1949 and 1991, these years were among the most peaceful of Europe's long history. American aid gave the western European economies the means to recover and the means to develop a consumer-oriented society, where the good life was measured in access to modern conveniences for everyday life. Meanwhile, those excluded in Western society, from women to the colonized, began to press, sometimes violently, for cultural and economic equality.

28-1 | The United States Rebuilds Europe

GEORGE C. MARSHALL, *An American Plan to Rebuild a Shattered Europe* (June 5, 1947)

At the conclusion of World War II, American policymakers were determined to avoid the mistake of withdrawing into neutrality as they had in 1919. George Marshall was the highest-ranking American officer in World War II and served as secretary of state for the Truman administration. When Communist parties began to win elections in France and Italy, Marshall

---

"The Address of Secretary Marshall at Harvard," *New York Times*, June 6, 1947.

used a speech to Harvard University's graduating class to propose spending billions to rebuild Europe, an initiative he believed would curtail the appeal of Communist parties, reduce tensions within European societies, and advance American interests by creating strong allies and viable trade partners.

I need not tell you, gentlemen, that the world situation is very serious. That must be apparent to all intelligent people. I think one difficulty is that the problem is one of such enormous complexity that the very mass of facts presented to the public by press and radio make it exceedingly difficult for the man in the street to reach a clear appraisement of the situation. Furthermore, the people of this country are distant from the troubled areas of the earth and it is hard for them to comprehend the plight and consequent reactions of the long-suffering peoples, and the effect of those reactions on their governments in connection with our efforts to promote peace in the world.

In considering the requirements for the rehabilitation of Europe the physical loss of life, the visible destruction of cities, factories, mines, and railroads was correctly estimated, but it has become obvious during recent months that this visible destruction was probably less serious than the dislocation of the entire fabric of European economy. For the past ten years conditions have been highly abnormal.

The feverish preparation for war and the more feverish maintenance of the war effort engulfed all aspects of national economies. Machinery has fallen into disrepair or is entirely obsolete. Under the arbitrary and destructive Nazi rule, virtually every possible enterprise was geared into the German war machine. Long-standing commercial ties, private institutions, banks, insurance companies, and shipping companies disappeared, through loss of capital, absorption through nationalization, or by simple destruction.

In many countries, confidence in the local currency has been severely shaken. The breakdown of the business structure of Europe during the war was complete. Recovery has been seriously retarded by the fact that two years after the close of hostilities a peace settlement with Germany and Austria has not been agreed upon. But even given a more prompt solution of these difficult problems, the rehabilitation of the economic structure of Europe quite evidently will require a much longer time and greater effort than had been foreseen.

There is a phase of this matter which is both interesting and serious. The farmer has always produced the foodstuffs to exchange with the city dweller for the other necessities of life. This division of labor is the basis of modern civilization. At the present time it is threatened with breakdown. The town and city industries are not producing adequate goods to exchange with the food-producing farmer. Raw materials and fuel are in short supply. Machinery is lacking or worn out.

The farmer or the peasant cannot find the goods for sale which he desires to purchase. So the sale of his farm produce for money which he cannot use seems to him an unprofitable transaction. He, therefore, has withdrawn many fields from crop cultivation and is using them for grazing. He feeds more grain to stock and finds for himself and his family an ample supply of food, however short he may be on clothing and the other ordinary gadgets of civilization. Meanwhile, people in the cities are short of food and fuel. So the governments are forced to use their foreign money and credits to procure these necessities abroad. This process exhausts funds which are urgently needed for reconstruction. Thus a very serious situation is rapidly developing which bodes no good for the world. The modern system of the division of labor upon which the exchange of products is based is in danger of breaking down.

The truth of the matter is that Europe's requirements for the next three or four years of foreign food and other essential products—principally from America—are so much greater than her present ability to pay that she must have substantial additional help, or face economic, social, and political deterioration of a very grave character.

The remedy lies in breaking the vicious circle and restoring the confidence of the European people in the economic future of their own countries and of Europe as a whole. The manufacturer and the farmer throughout wide areas must be able and willing to exchange their products for currencies, the continuing value of which is not open to question.

Aside from the demoralizing effect on the world at large and the possibilities of disturbances arising as a result of the desperation of the people concerned, the consequences to the economy of the United States should be apparent to all. It is logical that the United States should do whatever it is able to do to assist in the return of normal economic health in the world, without which there can be no political stability and no assured peace.

Our policy is directed not against any country or doctrine but against hunger, poverty, desperation, and chaos. Its purpose should be the revival of a working economy in the world so as to permit the emergence of political and social conditions in which free institutions can exist. Such assistance, I am convinced, must not be on a piecemeal basis as various crises develop. Any assistance that this Government may render in the future should provide a cure rather than a mere palliative.

Any government that is willing to assist in the task of recovery will find full cooperation, I am sure, on the part of the United States Government. Any government which maneuvers to block the recovery of other countries cannot expect help from us. Furthermore, governments, political parties, or groups which seek to perpetuate human misery in order to profit therefrom politically or otherwise will encounter the opposition of the United States.

It is already evident that, before the United States Government can proceed much further in its efforts to alleviate the situation and help start the European world on its way to recovery, there must be some agreement among the countries of Europe as to the requirements of the situation and the part those countries themselves will take in order to give proper effect to whatever action might be undertaken by this Government. It would be neither fitting nor efficacious for this Government to undertake to draw up unilaterally a program designed to place Europe on its feet economically. This is the business of the Europeans. The initiative, I think, must come from Europe. The role of this country should consist of friendly aid in the drafting of a European program and of later support of such a program so far as it may be practical for us to do so. The program should be a joint one, agreed to by a number of, if not all, European nations.

An essential part of any successful action on the part of the United States is an understanding on the part of the people of America of the character of the problem and the remedies to be applied. Political passion and prejudice should have no part. With foresight, and a willingness on the part of our people to face up to the vast responsibility which history has clearly placed upon our country, the difficulties I have outlined can and will be overcome.

READING QUESTIONS

1. According to Marshall, what problems did Europe face after World War II? What solutions does he propose?

2. What light does the speech shed on the changed place of both Europe and the United States in the global economy?

3. In what ways does Marshall's speech hint at the growing tensions between the United States and the Soviet Union?

4. How did the Marshall Plan serve American national interests? What might explain the fact that the Soviets saw the plan as a hostile action?

28-2 | The Stalinist Gulag

ALEXANDER SOLZHENITSYN, *One Day in the Life of Ivan Denisovich* (1962)

After Joseph Stalin died in 1953, the Soviet Union backed away from many of his policies. The next Soviet leader, Nikita Khrushchev (r. 1953–1964), denounced the gulag—the terror and labor camps Stalin had created—and considerably relaxed censorship. In this new period of increased critical freedom, Alexander Solzhenitsyn was permitted to publish an account of his life in the camps, to which he had been sentenced in 1945 for criticizing Stalin's conduct of the war. His continued criticism of the Soviet regime led to his deportation to the West in 1974. Once in exile, Solzhenitsyn condemned both the repression of the Soviets and the materialism of the capitalist world.

At five o'clock that morning reveille was sounded, as usual, by the blows of a hammer on a length of rail hanging up near the staff quarters. The intermittent sounds barely penetrated the windowpanes on which the frost lay two fingers thick, and they ended almost as soon as they'd begun. It was cold outside, and campguard was reluctant to go on beating out the reveille for long.

The clanging ceased, but everything outside still looked like the middle of the night when Ivan Denisovich Shukhov got up to go to the bucket. It was pitch dark except for the yellow light cast on the window by three lamps—two in the outer zone, one inside the camp itself.

And no one came to unbolt the barracks door; there was no sound of the barrack orderlies pushing a pole into place to lift the barrel of excrement and carry it out.

Shukhov never overslept reveille. He always got up at once, for the next ninety minutes, until they assembled for work, belonged to him, not to the authorities, and any old-timer could always earn a bit—by sewing a pair of mittens for someone out of his old sleeve lining; or bringing some rich loafer in the squad his dry valenki[1]—right up to his bunk, so that he wouldn't have to stumble barefoot round the heap of boots looking for his own pair; or going the rounds to the warehouses, offering to be of service, sweeping up this or fetching that; or going to the mess hall to collect bowls from the tables and bring them stacked to the dishwashers—you're sure to be given something to eat there, though there were plenty of others at that game, more than plenty—and, what's worse, if you found a bowl with something left in it you could hardly resist licking it out. But Shukhov had never forgotten the words of his first squad leader, Kuziomin—a hard-bitten prisoner who had already been in for twelve years by 1943—who told the newcomers, just in from the front, as they sat beside a fire in a desolate cutting in the forest:

"Here, men, we live by the law of the taiga.[2] But even here people manage to live. The ones that don't make it are those who lick other men's leftovers, those who count on the doctors to pull them through, and those that squeal on their buddies."

As for squealers, he was wrong there. Those people were sure to get through the camp alright. Only, they were saving their own skin at the expense of other people's blood.

Shukhov always arose at reveille. But this day he didn't. He had felt strange the evening before, feverish, with pains all over his body. He hadn't been able to get warm all through the night. Even in his sleep he had felt at one moment that he was getting seriously ill, at another that he was getting better. He had wished morning would never come.

But morning came as usual.

Anyway, where would you get warm in a place like this, with the windows iced over and the white cobwebs of frost all along the huge barracks where the walls joined the ceiling!

He didn't get up. He lay there in his bunk on the top tier, his head buried in a blanket and a coat, both feet stuffed into one tucked-up sleeve of his wadded jacket.

He couldn't see, but his ears told him everything going on in the barrack room and especially in the corner his squad occupied. He heard the heavy tread of the orderlies carrying one of the big barrels of excrement along the passage

---

[1]**valenki:** Knee-high felt boots worn in winter.
[2]**taiga:** Cold, coniferous forestland. The taiga comprises a large portion of Siberia, where the camps were located.

outside. A light job, that was considered, a job for the infirm, but just you try and carry out the muck without spilling any. He heard some of the 75th slamming bunches of boots onto the floor from the drying shed. Now their own men were doing it (it was their own squad's turn, too, to dry valenki). Tiurin, the squad leader, and his deputy Pavlo put on their valenki without a word but he heard their bunks creaking. Now Pavlo would be going off to the bread-storage and Tiurin to the staff quarters to see the P.P.D.[3]

Ah, but not simply to report as usual to the authorities for the daily assignment. Shukhov remembered that this morning his fate hung in the balance: they wanted to shift the 104th from the building shops to a new site, the "Socialist Way of Life" settlement. It lay in open country covered with snowdrifts, and before anything else could be done there they would have to dig holes and put up posts and attach barbed wire to them. Wire themselves in, so that they wouldn't run away. Only then would they start building.

There wouldn't be a warm corner for a whole month. Not even a doghouse. And fires were out of the question. There was nothing to build them with. Let your work warm you up, that was your only salvation.

No wonder the squad leader looked so worried, that was his job—to elbow some other squad, some bunch of suckers, into the assignment of the 104th. Of course with empty hands you got nowhere. He'd have to take a pound of salt pork to the senior official there, if not a couple of pounds.

There's never any harm in trying, so why not have a go at the dispensary and get a few days off if you can? After all, he did feel as though every limb was out of joint.

Then Shukhov wondered which of the campguards was on duty that morning. It was "One-and-a-half" Ivan's turn, he recalled. Ivan was a thin, weedy, dark-eyed sergeant. At first sight he looked like a real bastard, but when you got to know him he turned out to be the most good-natured of the guards on duty; he didn't put you in the guardhouse, he didn't haul you off before the authorities. So Shukhov decided he could lie in his bunk a little longer, at least while Barracks 9 was at the mess hall.

The whole four-bunk frame began to shake and sway. Two of its occupants were getting up at the same time: Shukhov's top-tier neighbor, Alyosha the Baptist, and Buinovsky, the ex-naval captain down below.

The orderlies, after removing both barrels of excrement, began to quarrel about which of them should go for hot water. They quarreled naggingly, like old women.

"Hey you, cackling like a couple of hens!" bellowed the electric welder in the 20th squad. "Get going." He flung a boot at them.

The boot thudded against a post. The squabbling stopped.

In the next squad the deputy squad leader growled quietly: "Vasily Fyodorovich, they've cheated us again at the supply depot, the dirty rats. They should have given us four twenty-five ounce loaves and I've only got three. Who's going to go short?"

---

[3]**P.P.D.:** Production Planning Department.

He kept his voice down, but of course everyone in the squad heard him and waited fearfully to learn who would be losing a slice of bread that evening.

Shukhov went on lying on his sawdust mattress, as hard as a board from long wear. If only it could be one thing or the other — let him fall into a real fever or let his aching joints ease up.

Meanwhile Alyosha was murmuring his prayers and Buinovsky had returned from the latrines, announcing to no one in particular but with a sort of malicious glee: "Well, sailors, grit your teeth. It's twenty below, for sure."

Shukhov decided to report sick.

At that very moment his blanket and jacket were imperiously jerked off him. He flung his coat away from his face and sat up. Looking up at him, his head level with the top bunk, was the lean figure of The Tartar.

So the fellow was on duty out of turn and had stolen up.

"S 854," The Tartar read from the white strip that had been stitched to the back of his black jacket. "Three days' penalty with work."

The moment they heard that peculiar choking voice of his, everyone who wasn't up yet in the whole dimly lit barracks, where two hundred men slept in bug-ridden bunks, stirred to life and began dressing in a hurry.

"What for, citizen chief?" asked Shukhov with more chagrin than he felt in his voice.

With work — that wasn't half so bad. They gave you hot food and you had no time to start thinking. Real jail was when you were kept back from work.

"Failing to get up at reveille. Follow me to the camp commandant's office," said The Tartar lazily.

His crumpled, hairless face was imperturbable. He turned, looking around for another victim, but now everybody, in dim corners and under the lights, in upper bunks and in lower, had thrust their legs into their black wadded trousers or, already dressed, had wrapped their coats around themselves and hurried to the door to get out of the way until The Tartar had left.

Had Shukhov been punished for something he deserved he wouldn't have felt so resentful. What hurt him was that he was always one of the first to be up. But he knew he couldn't plead with The Tartar. And, protesting merely for the sake of form, he hitched up his trousers (a bedraggled scrap of cloth had been sewn on them, just above the left knee, with a faded black number), slipped on his jacket (here the same digits appeared twice — on the chest and on the back), fished his valenki from the heap on the floor, put his hat on (with his number on a patch of cloth at the front), and followed The Tartar out of the barrack room.

The whole 104th saw him go, but no one said a word — what was the use, and anyway what could they say? The squad leader might have tried to do something, but he wasn't there. And Shukhov said nothing to anyone. He didn't want to irritate The Tartar. Anyway he could rely on the others in his squad to keep his breakfast for him.

The two men left the barracks. The cold made Shukhov gasp.

Two powerful searchlights swept the camp from the farthest watchtowers. The border lights, as well as those inside the camp, were on. There were so many of them that they outshone the stars.

With the snow creaking under their boots, the prisoners hurried away, each on his own business, some to the parcels office, some to hand in cereals to be cooked in the "individual" kitchen. All kept their heads down, buried in their buttoned-up coats, and all were chilled to the bone, not so much from the actual cold as from the prospect of having to spend the whole day in it. But The Tartar in his old army coat with the greasy blue tabs walked at a steady pace, as though the cold meant nothing to him.

They walked past the high wooden fence around the guardhouse, the only brick building in the camp; past the barbed wire that protected the camp bakery from the prisoners; past the corner of the staff quarters where the length of frosted rail hung on thick strands of wire; past another pole with a thermometer hanging on it (in a sheltered spot, so that the registered temperature shouldn't drop too low). Shukhov looked hopefully out of the corner of an eye at the milk-white tube—if it had shown −41° they ought not to be sent out to work. But today it was nowhere near −41°.

They walked into the staff quarters and The Tartar led him straight to the guardroom; and Shukhov realized, as he had guessed on the way there, that he wasn't being sent to the guardhouse at all—it was simply that the guardroom floor needed scrubbing. The Tartar told him he was going to let him off, and ordered him to scrub the floor.

Scrubbing the guardroom floor had been the job of a special prisoner who wasn't sent to work outside the camp—a staff orderly. The fellow had long ago made himself at home in the staff quarters; he had access to the offices of the camp commandant, the man in charge of discipline, and the security officer (the Father Confessor, they called him). When working for them he sometimes heard things that even the guards didn't know, and after a time he got a big head and came to consider scrubbing the floor for rank-and-file campguards a bit beneath him. Having sent for him once or twice, the guards discovered what was in the wind and began to pick on other prisoners for floor-scrubbing.

In the guardroom the stove was throwing out a fierce heat. Two guards in grubby tunics were playing checkers, and a third, who had not bothered to remove his sheepskin and valenki, lay snoring on a narrow bench. In one corner of the room stood an empty pail with a rag inside.

Shukhov was delighted. He thanked The Tartar for letting him off and said: "From now on I'll never get up late again."

The rule in this place was a simple one: when you'd finished you left. And now that he'd been given work to do, Shukhov's aches and pains seemed to have gone. He picked up the pail and, bare-handed—in his hurry he'd forgotten to take his mittens from under his pillow—went to the well.

Several of the squad leaders who were on their way to the P.P.D. had gathered near the pole with the thermometer, and one of the younger ones, a former Hero of the Soviet Union, shinnied up it and wiped off the instrument.

The others shouted advice from below:

"See you don't breathe on it. It'll push up the temperature."

"Push it up? Not fucking likely. *My* breath won't have any effect."

Tiurin of the 104th—Shukhov's squad—was not among them. Shukhov put down the pail, tucked his hands into his sleeves, and watched with interest.

The man up the pole shouted hoarsely: "Seventeen and a half. Not a damn bit more."

And, taking another look for sure, slid down.

"Oh, it's cockeyed. It always lies," someone said. "Do you think they'd ever hang one up that gave the true temperature?"

The squad leaders scattered. Shukhov ran to the well. The frost was trying to nip his ears under his earflaps, which he had lowered but not tied.

The top of the well was so thickly coated with ice that he only just managed to slip the bucket into the hole. The rope hung stiff as a ramrod.

With numb hands he carried the dripping bucket back to the guardroom and plunged his hands into the water. It felt warm.

The Tartar was no longer there. The guards—there were four now—stood in a group. They'd given up their checkers and their nap and were arguing about how much cereal they were going to get in January (food was in short supply at the settlement, and although rationing had long since come to an end, certain articles were sold to them, at a discount, which were not available to the civilian inhabitants).

"Shut that door, you scum. There's a draft," said one of the guards.

No sense in getting your boots wet in the morning. Even if Shukhov had dashed back to his barracks he wouldn't have found another pair to change into. During eight years' imprisonment he had known various systems for allocating footwear: there'd been times when he'd gone through the winter without valenki at all, or leather boots either, and had had to make shift with rope sandals or a sort of galoshes made of scraps of motor tires—"Chetezes" they called them, after the Cheliabinsk tractor works. Now the footwear situation seemed better; in October Shukhov had received (thanks to Pavlo, whom he trailed to the warehouse) a pair of ordinary, hard-wearing leather boots, big enough for a double thickness of rags inside. For a week he went about as though he'd been given a birthday present, kicking his new heels. Then in December the valenki arrived, and, oh, wasn't life wonderful?

But some devil in the bookkeeper's office had whispered in the commandant's ear that valenki should be issued only to those who surrendered their boots. It was against the rules for a prisoner to possess two pairs of footwear at the same time. So Shukhov had to choose. Either he'd have to wear leather throughout the winter, or surrender the boots and wear valenki even in the thaw. He'd taken such good care of his new boots, softening the leather with grease! Ah, nothing had been so hard to part with in all his eight years in camps as that pair of boots! They were tossed into a common heap. Not a hope of finding your own pair in the spring.

READING QUESTIONS

1. What motivations does Solzhenitsyn ascribe to the inhabitants of the gulags? Do they seem particularly criminal to you? Why or why not?

2. In what ways could this passage contradict the official Soviet image of the U.S.S.R. as a "worker's paradise"?

3. What motivations might the Soviet leadership have had for allowing this publication?

SOURCES IN CONVERSATION

Debating the "Iron Curtain"

The end of World War II saw the most powerful members of the Allies, particularly the new superpowers, the United States and the Soviet Union, fighting over the spoils of the power vacuum that resulted from the peace treaties ending the war. Military occupation at the end of the war determined the western and eastern spheres of influence in Europe, with the agreement at the Yalta conference in February 1945 determining that free elections would occur in Soviet-occupied eastern Europe. Despite this agreement, governments in eastern European countries would come to be effectively dominated by Communist parties, eventually as one-party dictatorships. After the mayhem the two world wars had caused for Russia and the U.S.S.R., Stalin wanted buffer states to protect his borders, so he resisted the British and U.S. demands for free elections and actively supported the rise of Communist dictatorships after the war ended, while the United States for its part attempted to contain communism using diplomacy, financial support, and eventually military force as well. The following two documents present British prime minister Winston Churchill's description of the "iron curtain" that divided eastern and western Europe, and Stalin's response to that characterization.

READ AND COMPARE

1. How did these politicians craft their speeches to address their chosen audience?

2. In the tone of each speech, what makes it clear that one speaker is coming from a position of relative strength, and one from a position of relative weakness?

28-3 | WINSTON CHURCHILL, *"Sinews of Peace"* Speech (March 5, 1946)

In 1946, despite his recent defeat in an election in the United Kingdom, Winston Churchill traveled to America to deliver his most famous postwar speech, meant to foment support for cooperation between the United States and Britain against their perceived mutual enemy, the Soviet Union. The term *iron curtain* had been used previously to describe the wall of Soviet buffer states in eastern Europe, but this speech made it a household term and made a powerful case for a joint U.S.-U.K. effort to resist what Churchill called "tyranny."

The United States stands at this time at the pinnacle of world power. It is a solemn moment for the American Democracy. For with primacy in power is also joined an awe inspiring accountability to the future. If you look around you, you must feel not only the sense of duty done but also you must feel anxiety lest you fall below the level of achievement. Opportunity is here now, clear and shining for both our countries. To reject it or ignore it or fritter it away will bring upon us all the long reproaches of the after-time. It is necessary that constancy of mind, persistency of purpose, and the grand simplicity of decision shall guide and rule the conduct of the English-speaking peoples in peace as they did in war. We must, and I believe we shall, prove ourselves equal to this severe requirement.

. . .

All this means that the people of any country have the right, and should have the power by constitutional action, by free unfettered elections, with secret ballot, to choose or change the character or form of government under which they dwell; that freedom of speech and thought should reign; that courts of justice, independent of the executive, unbiased by any party, should administer laws which have received the broad assent of large majorities or are consecrated by time and custom. Here are the title deeds of freedom which should lie in every cottage home. Here is the message of the British and American peoples to mankind. Let us preach what we practise—let us practise what we preach.

. . .

Now, while still pursuing the method of realising our overall strategic concept, I come to the crux of what I have travelled here to Say. Neither the sure prevention of war, nor the continuous rise of world organisation will be gained without what I have called the fraternal association of the English-speaking peoples. This means a special relationship between the British Commonwealth and Empire and the United States. This is no time for generalities, and I will venture to be precise. Fraternal association requires not only the growing friendship and mutual understanding between our two vast but kindred Systems of society, but the continuance of the intimate relationship between our military advisers, leading to common study of potential dangers, the similarity of weapons and manuals of instructions, and to the interchange of officers and cadets at technical colleges. It should carry with it the continuance of the present facilities for mutual security by the joint use of all Naval and Air Force bases in the possession of either country all over the world. This would perhaps double the mobility of the American Navy and Air Force. It would greatly expand that of the British Empire Forces and it might well lead, if and as the world calms down, to important financial savings. Already we use together a large number of islands; more may well be entrusted to our joint care in the near future.

. . .

A shadow has fallen upon the scenes so lately lighted by the Allied victory. Nobody knows what Soviet Russia and its Communist international organisation intends to do in the immediate future, or what are the limits, if any, to their expansive and proselytising tendencies. I have a strong admiration and regard for the valiant Russian people and for my wartime comrade, Marshal Stalin. There is deep sympathy and goodwill in Britain—and I doubt not here also—towards the peoples of all the Russias and a resolve to persevere through many differences and rebuffs in establishing lasting friendships. We understand the Russian need to be secure on her western frontiers by the removal of all possibility of German aggression. We welcome Russia to her rightful place among the leading nations of the world. We welcome her flag upon the seas. Above all, we welcome constant, frequent and growing contacts between the Russian people and our own people on both sides of the Atlantic. It is my duty however, for I am sure you would wish me to state the facts as I see them to you, to place before you certain facts about the present position in Europe.

From Stettin in the Baltic to Trieste in the Adriatic, an iron curtain has descended across the Continent. Behind that line lie all the capitals of the ancient states of Central and Eastern Europe. Warsaw, Berlin, Prague, Vienna, Budapest, Belgrade, Bucharest and Sofia, all these famous cities and the populations around them lie in what I must call the Soviet sphere, and all are subject in one form or another, not only to Soviet influence but to a very high and, in many cases, increasing measure of control from Moscow. Athens alone—Greece with its immortal glories—is free to decide its future at an election under British, American and French observation. The Russian-dominated Polish Government has been encouraged to make enormous and wrongful inroads upon Germany, and mass expulsions of millions of Germans on a scale grievous and undreamed-of are now taking place. The Communist parties, which were very small in all these Eastern States of Europe, have been raised to pre-eminence and power far beyond their numbers and are seeking everywhere to obtain totalitarian control. Police governments are prevailing in nearly every case, and so far, except in Czechoslovakia, there is no true democracy.

Turkey and Persia are both profoundly alarmed and disturbed at the claims which are being made upon them and at the pressure being exerted by the Moscow Government. An attempt is being made by the Russians in Berlin to build up a quasi-Communist party in their zone of Occupied Germany by showing special favours to groups of left-wing German leaders. At the end of the fighting last June, the American and British Armies withdrew westwards, in accordance with an earlier agreement, to a depth at some points of 150 miles upon a front of nearly four hundred miles, in order to allow our Russian allies to occupy this vast expanse of territory which the Western Democracies had conquered.

If now the Soviet Government tries, by separate action, to build up a pro-Communist Germany in their areas, this will cause new serious difficulties in the British and American zones, and will give the defeated Germans the power of putting themselves up to auction between the Soviets and the Western Democracies. Whatever conclusions may be drawn from these facts—and facts they are—this is certainly not the Liberated Europe we fought to build up. Nor is it one which contains the essentials of permanent peace.

. . .

In front of the iron curtain which lies across Europe are other causes for anxiety. In Italy the Communist Party is seriously hampered by having to Support the Communist-trained Marshal Tito's claims to former Italian territory at the head of the Adriatic. Nevertheless the future of Italy hangs in the balance. Again one cannot imagine a regenerated Europe without a strong France. All my public life I have worked for a Strong France and I never lost faith in her destiny, even in the darkest hours. I will not lose faith now. However, in a great number of countries, far from the Russian frontiers and throughout the world, Communist fifth columns are established and work in complete unity and absolute obedience to the directions they receive from the Communist centre. Except in the British Commonwealth and in the United States where Communism is in its infancy, the Communist parties or fifth columns constitute a growing challenge and peril to Christian civilisation. These are sombre facts for anyone to have to recite on the morrow of a victory gained by so much splendid comradeship in arms and in the cause of freedom and democracy; but we should be most unwise not to face them squarely while time remains.

The outlook is also anxious in the Far East and especially in Manchuria. The Agreement which was made at Yalta, to which I was a party, was extremely favourable to Soviet Russia, but it was made at a time when no one could say that the German war might not extend all through the summer and autumn of 1945 and when the Japanese war was expected to last for a further 18 months from the end of the German war. In this country you are all so well-informed about the Far East, and such devoted friends of China, that I do not need to expatiate on the situation there.

I have felt bound to portray the shadow which, alike in the west and in the east, falls upon the world. I was a high minister at the time of the Versailles Treaty and a close friend of Mr. Lloyd-George, who was the head of the British delegation at Versailles. I did not myself agree with many things that were done, but I have a very Strong impression in my mind of that situation, and I find it painful to contrast it with that which prevails now. In those days there were high hopes and unbounded confidence that the wars were over, and that the League of Nations would become all-powerful. I do not see or feel that same confidence or even the same hopes in the haggard world at the present time.

On the other hand I repulse the idea that a new war is inevitable; still more that it is imminent. It is because I am sure that our fortunes are still in our own hands and that we hold the power to save the future, that I feel the duty to speak out now that I have the occasion and the opportunity to do so. I do not believe that Soviet Russia desires war. What they desire is the fruits of war and the indefinite expansion of their power and doctrines. But what we have to consider here to-day while time remains, is the permanent prevention of war and the establishment of conditions of freedom and democracy as rapidly as possible in all countries. Our difficulties and dangers will not be removed by closing our eyes to them. They will not be removed by mere waiting to see what happens; nor will they be removed by a policy of appeasement. What is needed is a settlement, and the longer this is delayed, the more difficult it will be and the greater our dangers will become.

From what I have seen of our Russian friends and Allies during the war, I am convinced that there is nothing they admire so much as strength, and there is nothing for which they have less respect than for weakness, especially military weakness. For that reason the old doctrine of a balance of power is unsound. We cannot afford, if we can help it, to work on narrow margins, offering temptations to a trial of strength. If the Western Democracies stand together in strict adherence to the principles of the United Nations Charter, their influence for furthering those principles will be immense and no one is likely to molest them. If however they become divided or falter in their duty and if these all-important years are allowed to slip away then indeed catastrophe may overwhelm us all. Last time I saw it all coming and cried aloud to my own fellow-countrymen and to the world, but no one paid any attention. Up till the year 1933 or even 1935, Germany might have been saved from the awful fate which has overtaken her and we might all have been spared the miseries Hitler let loose upon mankind. There never was a war in all history easier to prevent by timely action than the one which has just desolated such great areas of the globe. It could have been prevented in my belief without the firing of a single shot, and Germany might be powerful, prosperous and honoured to-day; but no one would listen and one by one we were all sucked into the awful whirlpool. We surely must not let that happen again. This can only be achieved by reaching now, in 1946, a good understanding on all points with Russia under the general authority of the United Nations Organisation and by the maintenance of that good understanding through many peaceful years, by the world instrument, supported by the whole strength of the English-speaking world and all its connections. There is the solution which I respectfully offer to you in this Address to which I have given the title "The Sinews of Peace."

READING QUESTIONS

1. What does Churchill identify as the main shared problems facing the United States, Britain, and Europe, along with other non-Soviet nations?

2. What are his proposed solutions to those problems?

3. Is there anything limiting or distorting about his interpretation of the situation? If so, what is it?

4. Do you think his speech would have been different if he were making it to a British audience? If so, how might it be different?

28-4 | JOSEPH STALIN, *Interview Regarding Winston Churchill's Iron Curtain Speech* (March 14, 1946)

Days after Winston Churchill delivered his "Sinews of Peace" speech, Joseph Stalin responded to it in an interview with the Soviet newspaper *Pravda*. As you read the interview, ask yourself who Stalin's intended audience might have been. Whom did he want to influence, and how did he go about doing so?

Question: How do you appraise Mr. Churchill's latest speech in the United States of America? . . . Can it be considered that Mr. Churchill's speech is prejudicial to the cause of peace and security?

Answer: [Stalin says] Yes, unquestionably. As a matter of fact, Mr. Churchill now takes the stand of the warmongers, and in this Mr. Churchill is not alone. He has friends not only in Britain but in the United States of America as well.

A point to be noted is that in this respect Mr. Churchill and his friends bear a striking resemblance to Hitler and his friends. Hitler began his work of unleashing war by proclaiming a race theory, declaring that only German-speaking people constituted a superior nation. Mr. Churchill sets out to unleash war with a race theory, asserting that only English-speaking nations are superior nations, who are called upon to decide the destinies of the entire world. . . .

Actually, Mr. Churchill, and his friends in Britain and the United States, present to the non-English speaking nations something in the nature of an ultimatum: "Accept our rule voluntarily, and then all will be well; otherwise war is inevitable." . . . There can be no doubt that Mr. Churchill's position is a war position, a call for war on the U.S.S.R. . . .

Question: How do you appraise the part of Mr. Churchill's speech in which he attacks the democratic systems in the European states bordering upon us, and criticizes the good-neighbourly relations established between these States and the Soviet Union.

Answer: [Stalin says] . . . Mr. Churchill asserts that "Warsaw, Berlin, Prague, Vienna, Budapest, Belgrade, Bucharest, Sofia—all these famous cities and the populations around them lie within the Soviet sphere and are all subject in one form or another not only to Soviet influence, but to a very high and increasing measure of control from Moscow." . . .

In the first place it is quite absurd to speak of exclusive control by the U.S.S.R. in Vienna and Berlin, where there are Allied Control Councils made up of the representatives of four States and where the U.S.S.R. has only one-quarter of the votes. . . .

Secondly, the following circumstance should not be forgotten. The Germans made their invasion of the U.S.S.R. through Finland, Poland, Rumania, Bulgaria and Hungary. The Germans were able to make their invasion through these countries because, at the time, governments hostile to the Soviet Union existed in these countries. As a result of the German invasion the Soviet Union has lost irretrievably in the fighting against the Germans, and also through the German occupation

"J. V. Stalin on Post-War International Relations" (interview with *Pravda*), Marxists Internet Archive.

and the deportation of Soviet citizens to German servitude, a total of about seven million people. In other words, the Soviet Union's loss of life has been several times greater than that of Britain and the United States of America put together. . . .

READING QUESTIONS

1. What aspects of the interview might have been seen as most provocative in the West? Why?

2. How does Stalin justify Soviet intervention in eastern Europe? Do you find his position convincing? Why or why not?

3. How might this interview have been received outside of Europe? How might readers in Asia and Africa have responded to Stalin's characterization of American and British policy?

28-5 | An Argument for Women's Equality

SIMONE DE BEAUVOIR, *The Second Sex* (1949)

In twentieth-century Europe, women achieved many goals of the nineteenth century's feminists, notably the rights to vote and to own property. Simone de Beauvoir (1908–1986) — a French writer and companion of the existentialist philosopher Jean-Paul Sartre — was part of the generation of women who wanted full inclusion in society but who realized that suffrage and property rights did not always translate to social equality. De Beauvoir's writing took up the complex issues of attitudes and values and was particularly concerned with the persistence of traditional attitudes long after the circumstances that had created them no longer existed.

French law no longer includes obedience among a wife's duties, and every woman citizen has become a voter; these civic liberties remain abstract if there is no corresponding economic autonomy; the kept woman — wife or mistress — is not freed from the male just because she has a ballot paper in her hands; while today's customs impose fewer constraints on her than in the past, such negative licenses have not fundamentally changed her situation; she remains a vassal, imprisoned in her condition. It is through work that woman has been able, to a large extent, to close the gap separating her from the male; work alone can guarantee her concrete freedom. The system based on her dependence collapses as soon as she ceases to be a parasite; there is no longer need for a masculine mediator between her and the universe. The curse on the woman vassal is that she is not allowed to do anything; so she stubbornly pursues the impossible quest for being through narcissism, love, or religion; when she is productive and active,

---

she regains her transcendence; she affirms herself concretely as subject in her projects; she senses her responsibility relative to the goals she pursues and to the money and rights she appropriates. Many women are conscious of these advantages, even those with the lowest-level jobs. I heard a cleaning woman as she was washing a hotel lobby floor say, "I never asked anyone for anything. I made it on my own." She was as proud of being self-sufficient as a Rockefeller. However, one must not think that the simple juxtaposition of the right to vote and a job amounts to total liberation; work today is not freedom. Only in a socialist world would the woman who has one be sure of the other. Today, the majority of workers are exploited. Moreover, social structures have not been deeply modified by the changes in women's condition. This world has always belonged to men and still retains the form they have imprinted on it. It is important not to lose sight of these facts that make the question of women's work complex. An important and self-righteous woman recently carried out a study on women workers at a Renault factory: she asserts that they would rather stay at home than work in a factory. Without a doubt, they are economically independent only within an economically oppressed class; and besides, tasks carried out in a factory do not free them from household chores. If they had been able to choose between forty hours of weekly work in a factory *or* at home, they would undoubtedly have responded quite differently; and they might even accept both jobs eagerly if, as women workers, they would become part of the world that would be their world, that they would proudly and happily participate in building. In today's work, without even mentioning women who work on the land, most working women do not escape the traditional feminine world; neither society nor their husbands give them the help needed to become, in concrete terms, the equals of men. Only those women with political convictions, active in trade unions, who are confident in the future, can give an ethical meaning to the thankless daily labor; but as women deprived of leisure time and inheriting a tradition of submissiveness, it is understandable that they are just beginning to develop their political and social awareness. It is understandable that since they do not receive the moral and social benefits they could legitimately expect in exchange for their work, they simply resign themselves to its constraints. It is also understandable that a shop-girl, an office worker, or a secretary should not want to give up the advantages of having a male to lean on. I have already said that it is an almost irresistible temptation for a young woman to be part of a privileged caste when she can do so simply by surrendering her body; she is doomed to have love affairs because her wages are minimal for the very high standard of living society demands of her; if she settles for what she earns, she will be no more than a pariah: without decent living accommodations or clothes, all amusement and even love will be refused her. Virtuous people preach asceticism to her; in fact, her diet is often as austere as a Carmelite's; but not everyone can have God as a lover: she needs to please men to succeed in her life as a woman. So she will accept help: her employer cynically counts on this when he pays her a pittance. Sometimes this help will enable her to improve her situation and achieve real independence; but sometimes she will give up her job to become a kept woman. She often does both: she frees herself from her lover through work, and she escapes work thanks to her lover; but then she experiences the double servitude of a job and masculine protection. For the married woman, her salary usually only means extra income; for the "woman who is helped," it is the man's protection that seems inessential; but neither woman buys total independence through her own efforts.

However, there are quite a lot of privileged women today who have gained economic and social autonomy in their professions. They are the ones who are at issue when the question of women's possibilities and their future is raised. While they are still only a minority, it is particularly interesting to study their situation closely; they are the subject of continuing debate between feminists and antifeminists. The latter maintain that today's emancipated women do not accomplish anything important, and that besides they have trouble finding their inner balance. The former exaggerate the emancipated women's achievements and are blind to their frustrations. In fact, there is no reason to assume that they are on the wrong track; and yet it is obvious that they are not comfortably settled in their new condition: they have come only halfway as of yet. Even the woman who has emancipated herself economically from man is still not in a moral, social, or psychological situation identical to his. Her commitment to and focus on her profession depend on the context of her life as a whole. And, when she starts her adult life, she does not have the same past as a boy; society does not see her with the same eyes; she has a different perspective on the universe. Being a woman poses unique problems to an autonomous human being today.

READING QUESTIONS

1. Based on this excerpt, what does "equality" mean to Simone de Beauvoir?

2. What problems does de Beauvoir anticipate for women attempting to achieve her definition of equality?

3. What reasons could women have for not wanting to achieve the sort of liberation de Beauvoir promotes?

4. Based on your reading, what would de Beauvoir like to see change?

▪ COMPARATIVE AND DISCUSSION QUESTIONS ▪

1. Given his response to Churchill's "iron curtain" speech, how might Stalin have characterized the Marshall Plan? How might Marshall have responded to Stalin's position?

2. Compare Beauvoir's perspective to those of Pankhurst (Document 22-5) and Swanwick (Document 25-4). How does her vision of women's societal roles compare to the ones found there?

3. How did ideas about feminism and women's rights change from the time that Mary Wollstonecraft wrote her *Vindication of the Rights of Woman* (Document 19-5) to when de Beauvoir wrote *The Second Sex*? What continuities in thinking can you discern?

4. How might Churchill have used accounts like that of Solzhenitsyn to bolster his argument about division of the world?

29

Challenging the Postwar Order
1960–1991

The West and the Soviets both faced identity crises in the 1970s and 1980s. Economic difficulties in the seventies, West and East, underscored the tensions and conflicts within both capitalist and communist systems. As western European economies slowed and then contracted, discontent grew with the American-style consumer society that had emerged after World War II. Increasingly resentful of American influence on European economics, foreign policy, and culture, many Europeans came to believe that it was time to make a sharper distinction between American and European interests. In the East, workers began to grow restless, as the widening gap between Communist ideals and realities became ever more difficult to disguise or ignore. In the Communist world the growing tide of protest proved difficult to stop, and by the early 1990s Communist regimes across eastern Europe had been toppled and the Soviet Union had collapsed.

Reforming Socialist Societies

The Soviet decision to allow limited, cautious reform in the Eastern bloc in the 1960s encouraged reformers in Czechoslovakia to initiate much more dramatic changes in 1968. Frightened by the possibility of similar movements erupting elsewhere in eastern Europe, the Soviets moved in and forcefully reasserted their control. Soviet leaders took a stark lesson away from the events of 1968. Communist rule was to be maintained at any cost. There would be no more "reform from within." Pressure for change, however, continued to build, and the 1980s would see dramatic challenges to Soviet rule, challenges that would culminate in the collapse of communism.

READ AND COMPARE

1. What is similar in the messages and arguments of these two documents, and what is different?
2. Who are the intended audiences for each document, and how do Gorbachev and Havel specifically appeal to them?

29-1 | MIKHAIL GORBACHEV, *Perestroika: A Soviet Leader Calls for Change* (1987)

Throughout the 1970s, Soviet leaders resisted pressure for political and economic reform, refusing to acknowledge the inequities, inefficiencies, and injustices of the Soviet system. The party leaders that controlled the government were insulated and inflexible. Years of focus on military production and heavy industry had created a shortage of consumer goods, a situation that led the West German chancellor to liken the Soviet Union to an abysmally poor African country, but with rockets. Soviet leaders could not, however, ignore reality forever. In 1985 Mikhail Gorbachev became head of the Communist Party. Convinced that the survival of the Soviet Union was at stake, Gorbachev committed himself to the reform of the Soviet economy and the apparatus by which the party controlled information. These changes were referred to, respectively, as *perestroika*— "restructuring" —and *glasnost*— "openness."

Perestroika is an urgent necessity arising from the profound processes of development in our socialist society. This society is ripe for change. It has long been yearning for it. Any delay in beginning perestroika could have led to an exacerbated internal situation in the near future, which, to put it bluntly, would have been fraught with serious social, economic and political crises. . . .

In the latter half of the seventies — something happened that was at first sight inexplicable. The country began to lose momentum. Economic failures became more frequent. Difficulties began to accumulate and deteriorate, and unresolved problems to multiply. Elements of what we call stagnation and other phenomena alien to socialism began to appear in the life of society. A kind of "braking mechanism" affecting social and economic development formed. And all this happened at a time when scientific and technological revolution opened up new prospects for economic and social progress. . . .

An absurd situation was developing. The Soviet Union, the world's biggest producer of steel, raw materials, fuel and energy, has shortfalls in them due to wasteful or inefficient use. One of the biggest producers of grain for food, it nevertheless has to buy millions of tons of grain a year for fodder. We have the largest number of doctors and hospital beds per thousand of the population and, at the same time, there are glaring shortcomings in our health services. Our rockets can find Halley's comet and fly to Venus with amazing accuracy, but side by side with these scientific and technological triumphs is an obvious lack of efficiency in using scientific achievements for economic needs, and many Soviet household appliances are of poor quality.

This, unfortunately, is not all. A gradual erosion of the ideological and moral values of our people began.

It was obvious to everyone that the growth rates were sharply dropping and that the entire mechanism of quality control was not working properly; there was a lack of receptivity to the advances in science and technology; the improvement in living standards was slowing down and there were difficulties in the supply of foodstuffs, housing, consumer goods and services.

On the ideological plane as well, the braking mechanism brought about ever greater resistance to the attempts to constructively scrutinize the problems that were emerging and to the new ideas. Propaganda of success—real or imagined—was gaining the upper hand. Eulogizing and servility were encouraged; the needs and opinions of ordinary working people, of the public at large, were ignored. . . .

The presentation of a "problem-free" reality backfired: a breach had formed between word and deed, which bred public passivity and disbelief in the slogans being proclaimed. It was only natural that this situation resulted in a credibility gap: everything that was proclaimed from the rostrums and printed in newspapers and textbooks was put in question. Decay began in public morals; the great feeling of solidarity with each other that was forged during the heroic times of the Revolution [1917], the first five-year plans,[1] the Great Patriotic War[2] and postwar rehabilitation was weakening; alcoholism, drug addiction and crime were growing; and the penetration of the stereotypes of mass culture alien to us, which bred vulgarity and low tastes and brought about ideological barrenness increased. . . .

An unbiased and honest approach led us to the only logical conclusion that the country was verging on crisis. . . .

I would like to emphasize here that this analysis began a long time before the April Plenary Meeting[3] and that therefore its conclusions were well thought out. It was not something out of the blue, but a balanced judgment. It would be

---

[1]**five-year plans**: Stalin's attempts to transform the rural, agrarian Soviet Union into an industrial state. The first plan began in 1928, the second in 1932 (a year early), and they succeeded but at tremendous human cost.

[2]**Great Patriotic War**: Soviet name for World War II, in which the Soviets lost at least 20 million people.

[3]**April Plenary Meeting**: Regular meeting of the Communist Party's officials.

a mistake to think that a month after the Central Committee Plenary Meeting in March 1985, which elected me General Secretary, there suddenly appeared a group of people who understood everything and knew everything, and that these people gave clear-cut answers to all questions. Such miracles do not exist.

The need for change was brewing not only in the material sphere of life but also in public consciousness. People who had practical experience, a sense of justice and commitment to the ideals of Bolshevism[4] criticized the established practice of doing things and noted with anxiety the symptoms of moral degradation and erosion of revolutionary ideals and socialist values. . . .

Perestroika is closely connected with socialism as a system. That side of the matter is being widely discussed, especially abroad, and our talk about perestroika won't be entirely clear if we don't touch upon that aspect.

Does perestroika mean that we are giving up socialism or at least some of its foundations? Some ask this question with hope, others with misgiving.

There are people in the West who would like to tell us that socialism is in a deep crisis and has brought our society to a dead end. That's how they interpret our critical analysis of the situation at the end of the seventies and beginning of the eighties. We have only one way out, they say: to adopt capitalist methods of economic management and social patterns, to drift toward capitalism.

They tell us that nothing will come of perestroika within the framework of our system. They say we should change this system and borrow from the experience of another socio-political system. To this they add that, if the Soviet Union takes this path and gives up its socialist choice, close links with the West will supposedly become possible. They go so far as to claim that the October 1917 Revolution was a mistake which almost completely cut off our country from world social progress.

To put an end to all the rumors and speculations that abound in the West about this, I would like to point out once again that we are conducting all our reforms in accordance with the socialist choice. We are looking within socialism, rather than outside it, for the answers to all the questions that arise. We assess our successes and errors alike by socialist standards. Those who hope that we shall move away from the socialist path will be greatly disappointed. Every part of our program of perestroika — and the program as a whole, for that matter — is fully based on the principle of more socialism and more democracy. . . .

We will proceed toward better socialism rather than away from it. We are saying this honestly, without trying to fool our own people or the world. Any hopes that we will begin to build a different, nonsocialist society and go over to the other camp are unrealistic and futile. Those in the West who expect us to give up socialism will be disappointed. It is high time they understood this, and, even more importantly, proceeded from that understanding in practical relations with the Soviet Union. . . .

We want more socialism and, therefore, more democracy.

---

[4]**Bolshevism**: Vladimir Lenin's — the first Soviet leader — interpretation of Marx's ideas; named after the Bolshevik faction of the prerevolutionary Social Democratic Party.

READING QUESTIONS

1. What attitudes does Gorbachev seem to hold toward the West, particularly Western culture, as gleaned from this document?

2. In what ways might this document be seen as a refutation of the policies of former Soviet leaders? In what ways does it seek to continue them?

3. Based on this document, what is Mikhail Gorbachev's relationship with Western free-market ideology?

4. To whom does Gorbachev ascribe the blame for the Soviet Union's recent economic failures? What solutions does he propose?

29-2 | VÁCLAV HAVEL, *New Year's Address to the Nation* (1990)

One of the last countries to fall under Soviet influence after the World War II was Czechoslovakia. In 1968 an attempt to escape that influence led to Soviet tanks on the streets of Prague. After Gorbachev announced in 1989 that he would no longer enforce membership in the Soviet bloc, the Czechs and Slovaks retreated from one-party rule in a revolution so bloodless it became known as the "Velvet Revolution." Simply escaping from communism did not solve all their problems, however, and here the newly elected president, playwright Václav Havel (VAH-slav HAH-vel), muses on the nature of the past and the potential of the future.

My dear fellow citizens,

For forty years you heard from my predecessors on this day different variations on the same theme: how our country was flourishing, how many million tons of steel we produced, how happy we all were, how we trusted our government, and what bright perspectives were unfolding in front of us.

I assume you did not propose me for this office so that I, too, would lie to you.

Our country is not flourishing. The enormous creative and spiritual potential of our nation is not being used sensibly. Entire branches of industry are producing goods that are of no interest to anyone, while we are lacking the things we need. A state which calls itself a workers' state humiliates and exploits workers. Our obsolete economy is wasting the little energy we have available. A country that once could be proud of the educational level of its citizens spends so little on education that it ranks today as seventy-second in the world. We have polluted the soil, rivers, and forests bequeathed to us by our ancestors, and we have today the most contaminated environment in Europe. Adults in our country die earlier than in most other European countries.

Allow me a small personal observation. When I flew recently to Bratislava, I found some time during discussions to look out of the plane window. I saw the industrial complex of Slovnaft chemical factory and the giant Petr'alka

---

Václav Havel, New Year's Address to the Nation (1990). Reprinted by permission of Dilia Agency on behalf of the estate of Václav Havel.

housing estate right behind it. The view was enough for me to understand that for decades our statesmen and political leaders did not look or did not want to look out of the windows of their planes. No study of statistics available to me would enable me to understand faster and better the situation in which we find ourselves.

But all this is still not the main problem. The worst thing is that we live in a contaminated moral environment. We fell morally ill because we became used to saying something different from what we thought. We learned not to believe in anything, to ignore one another, to care only about ourselves. Concepts such as love, friendship, compassion, humility, or forgiveness lost their depth and dimension, and for many of us they represented only psychological peculiarities, or they resembled gone-astray greetings from ancient times, a little ridiculous in the era of computers and spaceships. Only a few of us were able to cry out loudly that the powers that be should not be all-powerful and that the special farms, which produced ecologically pure and top-quality food just for them, should send their produce to schools, children's homes, and hospitals if our agriculture was unable to offer them to all.

The previous regime—armed with its arrogant and intolerant ideology— reduced man to a force of production, and nature to a tool of production. In this it attacked both their very substance and their mutual relationship. It reduced gifted and autonomous people, skillfully working in their own country, to the nuts and bolts of some monstrously huge, noisy, and stinking machine, whose real meaning was not clear to anyone. It could not do more than slowly but inexorably wear out itself and all its nuts and bolts.

When I talk about the contaminated moral atmosphere, I am not talking just about the gentlemen who eat organic vegetables and do not look out of the plane windows. I am talking about all of us. We had all become used to the totalitarian system and accepted it as an unchangeable fact and thus helped to perpetuate it. In other words, we are all—though naturally to differing extents—responsible for the operation of the totalitarian machinery. None of us is just its victim. We are all also its co-creators.

Why do I say this? It would be very unreasonable to understand the sad legacy of the last forty years as something alien, which some distant relative bequeathed to us. On the contrary, we have to accept this legacy as a sin we committed against ourselves. If we accept it as such, we will understand that it is up to us all, and up to us alone to do something about it. We cannot blame the previous rulers for everything, not only because it would be untrue, but also because it would blunt the duty that each of us faces today: namely, the obligation to act independently, freely, reasonably, and quickly. Let us not be mistaken: the best government in the world, the best parliament and the best president, cannot achieve much on their own. And it would be wrong to expect a general remedy from them alone. Freedom and democracy include participation and therefore responsibility from us all.

If we realize this, then all the horrors that the new Czechoslovak democracy inherited will cease to appear so terrible. If we realize this, hope will return to our hearts.

In the effort to rectify matters of common concern, we have something to lean on. The recent period — and in particular the last six weeks of our peaceful revolution — has shown the enormous human, moral and spiritual potential, and the civic culture that slumbered in our society under the enforced mask of apathy. Whenever someone categorically claimed that we were this or that, I always objected that society is a very mysterious creature and that it is unwise to trust only the face it presents to you. I am happy that I was not mistaken. Everywhere in the world people wonder where those meek, humiliated, skeptical, and seemingly cynical citizens of Czechoslovakia found the marvelous strength to shake the totalitarian yoke from their shoulders in several weeks, and in a decent and peaceful way. And let us ask: Where did the young people who never knew another system get their desire for truth, their love of free thought, their political ideas, their civic courage and civic prudence? How did it happen that their parents — the very generation that had been considered lost — joined them? How is it that so many people immediately knew what to do and none needed any advice or instruction?

I think there are two main reasons for the hopeful face of our present situation. First of all, people are never just a product of the external world; they are also able to relate themselves to something superior, however systematically the external world tries to kill that ability in them. Secondly, the humanistic and democratic traditions, about which there had been so much idle talk, did after all slumber in the unconsciousness of our nations and ethnic minorities, and were inconspicuously passed from one generation to another, so that each of us could discover them at the right time and transform them into deeds.

We had to pay, however, for our present freedom. Many citizens perished in jails in the 1950s, many were executed, thousands of human lives were destroyed, hundreds of thousands of talented people were forced to leave the country. Those who defended the honor of our nations during the Second World War, those who rebelled against totalitarian rule and those who simply managed to remain themselves and think freely, were all persecuted. We should not forget any of those who paid for our present freedom in one way or another. Independent courts should impartially consider the possible guilt of those who were responsible for the persecutions, so that the truth about our recent past might be fully revealed.

We must also bear in mind that other nations have paid even more dearly for their present freedom, and that indirectly they have also paid for ours. The rivers of blood that have flowed in Hungary, Poland, Germany, and recently in such a horrific manner in Romania, as well as the sea of blood shed by the nations of the Soviet Union, must not be forgotten. First of all because all human suffering concerns every other human being. But more than this, they must also not be forgotten because it is these great sacrifices that form the tragic background of today's freedom or the gradual emancipation of the nations of the Soviet Bloc, and thus the background of our own newfound freedom. Without the changes in the Soviet Union, Poland, Hungary, and the German Democratic Republic, what has happened in our country would have scarcely happened. And if it did, it certainly would not have followed such a peaceful course.

The fact that we enjoyed optimal international conditions does not mean that anyone else has directly helped us during the recent weeks. In fact, after hundreds of years, both our nations have raised their heads high of their own initiative without relying on the help of stronger nations or powers. It seems to me that this constitutes the great moral asset of the present moment. This moment holds within itself the hope that in the future we will no longer suffer from the complex of those who must always express their gratitude to somebody. It now depends only on us whether this hope will be realized and whether our civic, national, and political self-confidence will be awakened in a historically new way.

Self-confidence is not pride. Just the contrary: only a person or a nation that is self-confident, in the best sense of the word, is capable of listening to others, accepting them as equals, forgiving its enemies and regretting its own guilt. Let us try to introduce this kind of self-confidence into the life of our community and, as nations, into our behavior on the international stage. Only thus can we restore our self-respect and our respect for one another as well as the respect of other nations.

Our state should never again be an appendage or a poor relative of anyone else. It is true that we must accept and learn many things from others, but we must do this in the future as their equal partners, who also have something to offer.

Our first president[1] wrote: "Jesus, not Caesar." In this he followed our philosophers Chelick[2] and Komensk.[3] I dare to say that we may even have an opportunity to spread this idea further and introduce a new element into European and global politics. Our country, if that is what we want, can now permanently radiate love, understanding, the power of the spirit and of ideas. It is precisely this glow that we can offer as our specific contribution to international politics.

Masaryk based his politics on morality. Let us try, in a new time and in a new way, to restore this concept of politics. Let us teach ourselves and others that politics should be an expression of a desire to contribute to the happiness of the community rather than of a need to cheat or rape the community. Let us teach ourselves and others that politics can be not simply the art of the possible, especially if this means the art of speculation, calculation, intrigue, secret deals, and pragmatic maneuvering, but that it can also be the art of the impossible, that is, the art of improving ourselves and the world.

We are a small country, yet at one time we were the spiritual crossroads of Europe. Is there a reason why we could not again become one? Would it not be another asset with which to repay the help of others that we are going to need?

---

[1]**our first president**: Thomas Garrigue Masaryk, the first president of Czechoslovakia (1918–1935); a humanist and democrat.

[2]**Chelick**: Petr Chelčický; Bohemian author who lived roughly between 1390 and 1460 and who decried secular power and war as being in opposition to Christianity.

[3]**Komensk**: J. A. Komensky (1592–1670); Bohemian (Czech) religious reformer who valued education as a way to universal humanity and who became a Czech national symbol in the nineteenth century.

Our homegrown Mafia, those who do not look out of the plane windows and who eat specially fed pigs, may still be around and at times may muddy the waters, but they are no longer our main enemy. Even less so is our main enemy any kind of international Mafia. Our main enemy today is our own bad traits: indifference to the common good, vanity, personal ambition, selfishness, and rivalry. The main struggle will have to be fought on this field.

There are free elections and an election campaign ahead of us. Let us not allow this struggle to dirty the so-far clean face of our gentle revolution. Let us not allow the sympathies of the world, which we have won so fast, to be equally rapidly lost through our becoming entangled in the jungle of skirmishes for power. Let us not allow the desire to serve oneself to bloom once again under the stately garb of the desire to serve the common good. It is not really important now which party, club or group prevails in the elections. The important thing is that the winners will be the best of us, in the moral, civic, political and professional sense, regardless of their political affiliations. The future policies and prestige of our state will depend on the personalities we select, and later, elect to our representative bodies.

My dear fellow citizens!

Three days ago I became the president of the republic as a consequence of your will, expressed through the deputies of the Federal Assembly. You have a right to expect me to mention the tasks I see before me as president.

The first of these is to use all my power and influence to ensure that we soon step up to the ballot boxes in a free election, and that our path toward this historic milestone will be dignified and peaceful.

My second task is to guarantee that we approach these elections as two self-governing nations who respect each other's interests, national identity, religious traditions, and symbols. As a Czech who has given his presidential oath to an important Slovak who is personally close to him, I feel a special obligation — after the bitter experiences that Slovaks had in the past — to see that all the interests of the Slovak nation are respected and that no state office, including the highest one, will ever be barred to it in the future.

My third task is to support everything that will lead to better circumstances for our children, the elderly, women, the sick, the hardworking laborers, the national minorities, and all citizens who are for any reason worse off than others. High-quality food or hospitals must no longer be a prerogative of the powerful; they must be available to those who need them the most.

As supreme commander of the armed forces I want to guarantee that the defensive capability of our country will no longer be used as a pretext for anyone to stand in the way of courageous peace initiatives, the reduction of military service, the establishment of alternative military service, and the overall humanization of military life.

In our country there are many prisoners who, though they may have committed serious crimes and have been punished for them, have had to submit — despite the goodwill of some investigators, judges, and above all defense lawyers — to a debased judiciary process that curtailed their rights. They now have to live in prisons that do not strive to awaken the better qualities contained in every person, but rather humiliate them and destroy them physically and mentally. In a view [*sic*] of this fact, I have decided to declare a relatively extensive amnesty. At the same time I call on the prisoners to understand that forty years of unjust investigations, trials, and imprisonments cannot be put right overnight, and to understand that the changes that are being speedily prepared still require time to implement. By rebelling, the prisoners would help neither society nor themselves. I also call on the public not to fear the prisoners once they are released, not to make their lives difficult, to help them, in the Christian spirit, after their return among us to find within themselves that which jails could not find in them: the capacity to repent and the desire to live a respectable life.

My honorable task is to strengthen the authority of our country in the world. I would be glad if other states respected us for showing understanding, tolerance, and love for peace. I would be happy if Pope John Paul II and the Dalai Lama of Tibet could visit our country before the elections, if only for a day. I would be happy if our friendly relations with all nations were strengthened. I would be happy if we succeeded before the elections in establishing diplomatic relations with the Vatican and Israel. I would also like to contribute to peace by briefly visiting our close neighbors, the German Democratic Republic and the Federal Republic of Germany. Neither shall I forget our other neighbors — fraternal Poland and the ever-closer countries of Hungary and Austria.

In conclusion, I would like to say that I want to be a president who will speak less and work more. To be a president who will not only look out of the windows of his airplane but who, first and foremost, will always be present among his fellow citizens and listen to them well.

You may ask what kind of republic I dream of. Let me reply: I dream of a republic independent, free, and democratic, of a republic economically prosperous and yet socially just; in short, of a humane republic that serves the individual and that therefore holds the hope that the individual will serve it in turn. Of a republic of well-rounded people, because without such people it is impossible to solve any of our problems — human, economic, ecological, social, or political.

The most distinguished of my predecessors opened his first speech with a quotation from the great Czech educator Komensk. Allow me to conclude my first speech with my own paraphrase of the same statement:

People, your government has returned to you!

READING QUESTIONS

1. What were the successes and failures of the Communist system as Havel describes them?

2. How does Havel appear to apportion responsibility for the system he has inherited? Are the average citizens exempt from these criticisms?

3. What are the problems Havel sees for the future? How does he approach solving them?

29-3 | Tiananmen Square: Resistance to the Power of the State

JEFF WIDENER, *Tank Man* (1989)

In 1989 prodemocracy demonstrations were not confined to Europe. Chinese students camped out in Tiananmen Square for weeks in the same sort of protests that seemed to have worked in Czechoslovakia and Poland. Unlike the Communist governments of eastern Europe, however, the Chinese government proved willing to use force to maintain itself, and the Chinese army proved willing to obey orders to suppress the demonstrations. As the tanks rolled toward the square, they were held up by a single man, apparently with his shopping purchases, who blocked their path. Photojournalist Jeff Widener snapped this picture of the scene, which came to symbolize resistance—albeit ultimately futile—to state power.

JEFF WIDENER/AP Images.

READING QUESTIONS

1. To what use might this image be put by advocates of nonviolent revolution? How effective would those uses be, given the ultimate fate of the Tiananmen Square demonstrators?

2. What sort of reaction might this image provoke in a supporter of strong state power?

3. What reasons might the tank commander have for not running down the man in his way? What could this suggest about the limits of military power?

29-4 | Women Demand Fundamental Change

BETTY FRIEDAN, *Statement of Purpose of the National Organization for Women: Defining Full Equality* (1966)

Women's rights activists of the late nineteenth and early twentieth centuries focused their attention on the right to vote. The "second-wave" feminists of the 1960s and 1970s pursued a much broader agenda. Rejecting biological determinism, second-wave feminists attacked both discrimination against women and the social structures and patterns that established and reinforced male dominance. This statement of purpose, written in 1966 for the National Organization for Women by Betty Friedan, one of the organization's founders, captures much of the outlook and objectives of this new generation of activists. As you read it, think about how it differs from earlier efforts to define and defend women's rights.

We, men and women who hereby constitute ourselves as the National Organization for Women, believe that the time has come for a new movement toward true equality for all women in America, and toward a fully equal partnership of the sexes, as part of the world-wide revolution of human rights now taking place within and beyond our national borders.

The purpose of NOW is to take action to bring women into full participation in the mainstream of American society now, exercising all the privileges and responsibilities thereof in truly equal partnership with men. . . .

NOW is dedicated to the proposition that women, first and foremost, are human beings, who, like all other people in our society, must have the chance to develop their fullest human potential. We believe that women can achieve such equality only by accepting to the full the challenges and responsibilities they share with all other people in our society, as part of the decision-making mainstream of American political, economic and social life. . . .

Enormous changes taking place in our society make it both possible and urgently necessary to advance the unfinished revolution of women toward true equality, now. With a life span lengthened to nearly 75 years it is no longer either necessary or possible for women to devote the greater part of their lives to child-rearing; yet childbearing and rearing which continues to be a most important part of most women's lives — still is used to justify barring women from equal professional and economic participation and advance.

Today's technology has reduced most of the productive chores which women once performed in the home and in mass-production industries based upon routine unskilled labor. This same technology has virtually eliminated the quality of muscular strength as a criterion for filling most jobs, while intensifying American industry's need for creative intelligence. In view of this new industrial revolution created by automation in the mid-twentieth century, women can and must participate in old and new fields of society in full equality — or become permanent outsiders.

Betty Friedan, *The National Organization for Women's 1966 Statement of Purpose*. From *The National Organization for Women*, https://now.org/about/history/statement-of-purpose/.

Despite all the talk about the status of American women in recent years, the actual position of women in the United States has declined, and is declining, to an alarming degree throughout the 1950s and 60s. Although 46.4% of all American women between the ages of 18 and 65 now work outside the home, the overwhelming majority — 75% — are in routine clerical, sales, or factory jobs, or they are household workers, cleaning women, hospital attendants. About two-thirds of Negro women workers are in the lowest paid service occupations. Working women are becoming increasingly — not less — concentrated on the bottom of the job ladder. As a consequence full-time women workers today earn on the average only 60% of what men earn, and that wage gap has been increasing over the past twenty-five years in every major industry group. In 1964, of all women with a yearly income, 89% earned under $5,000 a year; half of all full-time year round women workers earned less than $3,690; only 1.4% of full-time year round women workers had an annual income of $10,000 or more.

Further, with higher education increasingly essential in today's society, too few women are entering and finishing college or going on to graduate or professional school. Today, women earn only one in three of the B.A.'s and M.A.'s granted, and one in ten of the Ph.D.'s.

In all the professions considered of importance to society, and in the executive ranks of industry and government, women are losing ground. Where they are present it is only a token handful. Women comprise less than 1% of federal judges; less than 4% of all lawyers; 7% of doctors. Yet women represent 51% of the U.S. population. And, increasingly, men are replacing women in the top positions in secondary and elementary schools, in social work, and in libraries — once thought to be women's fields. . . .

WE BELIEVE that the power of American law, and the protection guaranteed by the U.S. Constitution to the civil rights of all individuals, must be effectively applied and enforced to isolate and remove patterns of sex discrimination, to ensure equality of opportunity in employment and education, and equality of civil and political rights and responsibilities on behalf of women, as well as for Negroes and other deprived groups.

We realize that women's problems are linked to many broader questions of social justice; their solution will require concerted action by many groups. Therefore, convinced that human rights for all are indivisible, we expect to give active support to the common cause of equal rights for all those who suffer discrimination and deprivation, and we call upon other organizations committed to such goals to support our efforts toward equality for women. . . .

WE BELIEVE that this nation has a capacity at least as great as other nations, to innovate new social institutions which will enable women to enjoy the true equality of opportunity and responsibility in society, without conflict with their responsibilities as mothers and homemakers. In such innovations, America does not lead the Western world, but lags by decades behind many European countries. We do not accept the traditional assumption that a woman has to choose between marriage and motherhood, on the one hand, and serious participation in industry or the professions on the other. We question the present expectation that all normal women will retire from job or profession for 10 or 15 years, to devote their full time to raising children, only to reenter the job market at a relatively minor level. This, in itself, is a deterrent to the aspirations of women, to their acceptance into management or professional training courses, and to the very possibility of equality of opportunity or real choice, for all but a few women. Above all, we reject the assumption that these problems are the unique responsibility of each individual woman, rather than a basic social dilemma which society must solve. True equality of opportunity and freedom of choice for women requires such practical, and possible innovations as a nationwide network of child-care centers, which will make it unnecessary for women to retire completely from society until their children are grown, and national programs to provide retraining for women who have chosen to care for their children full-time.

WE BELIEVE that it is as essential for every girl to be educated to her full potential of human ability as it is for every boy—with the knowledge that such education is the key to effective participation in today's economy and that, for a girl as for a boy, education can only be serious where there is expectation that it will be used in society. We believe that American educators are capable of devising means of imparting such expectations to girl students. Moreover, we consider the decline in the proportion of women receiving higher and professional education to be evidence of discrimination. This discrimination may take the form of quotas against the admission of women to colleges, and professional schools; lack of encouragement by parents, counselors and educators; denial of loans or fellowships; or the traditional or arbitrary procedures in graduate and professional training geared in terms of men, which inadvertently discriminate against women. We believe that the same serious attention must be given to high school dropouts who are girls as to boys.

WE REJECT the current assumptions that a man must carry the sole burden of supporting himself, his wife, and family, and that a woman is automatically entitled to lifelong support by a man upon her marriage, or that marriage, home and family are primarily woman's world and responsibility—hers, to dominate—his to support. We believe that a true partnership between the sexes demands a different concept of marriage, an equitable sharing of the responsibilities of home and children and of the economic burdens of their support. We believe that proper recognition should be given to the economic and social value of homemaking and child-care. To these ends, we will seek to open a reexamination of laws and mores governing marriage and divorce, for we believe that the current state of "half-equity" between the sexes discriminates against both men and women, and is the cause of much unnecessary hostility between the sexes.

WE BELIEVE that women must now exercise their political rights and responsibilities as American citizens. They must refuse to be segregated on the basis of sex into separate-and-not-equal ladies' auxiliaries in the political parties, and they must demand representation according to their numbers in the regularly constituted party committees — at local, state, and national levels — and in the informal power structure, participating fully in the selection of candidates and political decision-making, and running for office themselves.

IN THE INTERESTS OF THE HUMAN DIGNITY OF WOMEN, we will protest, and endeavor to change, the false image of women now prevalent in the mass media, and in the texts, ceremonies, laws, and practices of our major social institutions. Such images perpetuate contempt for women by society and by women for themselves. We are similarly opposed to all policies and practices — in church, state, college, factory, or office — which, in the guise of protectiveness, not only deny opportunities but also foster in women self-denigration, dependence, and evasion of responsibility, undermine their confidence in their own abilities and foster contempt for women. . . .

WE BELIEVE THAT women will do most to create a new image of women by acting now, and by speaking out in behalf of their own equality, freedom, and human dignity — not in pleas for special privilege, nor in enmity toward men, who are also victims of the current, half-equality between the sexes — but in an active, self-respecting partnership with men. By so doing, women will develop confidence in their own ability to determine actively, in partnership with men, the conditions of their life, their choices, their future and their society.

READING QUESTIONS

1.   What was the purpose of NOW? How did its agenda differ from that of earlier women's rights organizations?

2.   Why did NOW believe that a push for full equality was particularly urgent in 1966?

3.   How was the statement of purpose shaped by the larger context of social and political change in the mid-1960s?

29-5 | Resisting through Unionization

LECH WAŁĘSA, *Letter to the Council of State* (1986)

Poland was one of the eastern European countries that resisted Soviet influence in the 1980s, largely thanks to the tireless efforts of Lech Wałęsa. Wałęsa was a Polish electrician who founded Solidarity, the first independent trade union to be formed in the Soviet satellite states. He was arrested in the 1970s for union activities, and again during the period of martial law when Solidarity was banned. He received the Nobel Peace Prize in 1983 for his actions, was elected president of Poland in the 1990s, and helped Poland develop a new government outside the Soviet sphere. In this letter, he makes a case for the government to end martial law and make trade unions legal again.

From Lech Wałęsa, "Letter of Lech Wałęsa to the Council of State," Wilson Center Digital Archive website, https://digitalarchive.wilsoncenter.org/document/113097.

Acting on the basis of a mandate given to me in democratic elections at the First Congress of delegates of the NSZZ [National Commission of the Independent Sovereign Trade Union] "Solidarity" in 1981, as chairman of that Union, led by an opinion expressed by the leaders of national and regional authorities:

- taking into consideration an unusually important decision of the PRL [Polish People's Republic] authorities relating to the release of political prisoners,[1] including a group of NSZZ "Solidarity" activists, which creates a new socio-political situation, allowing for an honest dialogue of all important social forces in Poland;
- motivated by my concern about further economic development of our country and having in mind the concentration of all Poles around the task of economic reform as a task of particular importance, in the absence of which we are faced with economic regression and backwardness, particularly in relation to the developed countries;
- drawing conclusions from the attitude of millions of working people, who over the last four years didn't find a place for themselves in the present trade unions, remained faithful to the ideals of "Solidarity" and wished to get involved together with them in active work for the good of the Motherland within the framework of a socio-trade union organization, which they could recognize on their own;

I am calling on the Council of State to take measures, which—consistent with binding legislation—would enable the realization of the principle of union pluralism, finally putting an end to the martial law legislation which constrains the development of trade unionism.

At the same time—for the sake of social peace and the need to concentrate all social forces on [the task of] getting out of the crisis—I declare readiness to respect the constitutional order, as well as the law of 8 October 1982 on trade unions.[2] True, the provisions of this law are far from our expectations, but they nevertheless create possibilities of working and respecting the principles of freedom of trade unions and union pluralism, and only temporary regulations are blocking the realization of those principles. It is high time to put an end to those temporary regulations and to lead to the normalization of social relations in the area of trade unionism. This is [within] the competence of the Council of State.

I trust that the Council of State will wish to take advantage of that competence and use—perhaps this unique chance—to strengthen social peace and activization of all social forces for the good of our country.

---

[1]**relating to the release of political prisoners**: On September 11, 1986, the Polish government freed all political prisoners.

[2]**the law of 8 October 1982 on trade unions**: In 1982 the Polish legislature passed a law that dissolved the trade union Solidarity.

READING QUESTIONS

1. What does Wałęsa ask of the government, and what does he offer in return?

2. What does he tout as the benefits of the government complying with his request?

3. How do you suppose the government would respond to his request, given the changes that were going on in the 1980s in eastern Europe? How would it have responded ten years earlier?

▪ COMPARATIVE AND DISCUSSION QUESTIONS ▪

1. How do Gorbachev's and Havel's descriptions of the shortcomings of socialism differ, and how do their prescribed solutions differ? Why do you suppose they are different? What political, economic, and/or cultural problems would each leader have to face in the process of reforming their country?

2. How do Havel's thoughts on the nature of unfree society compare with the photograph from China of a single man holding up four tanks? Based on what happened to the Tiananmen demonstrators, are Havel's beliefs about the future justified?

3. What do you notice as similarities or differences between the approaches toward resisting oppression in the Friedan and Wałęsa sources, and the photo of Tiananmen Square? Why did the approaches differ, and given the context of each source, which approach has the most potential to achieve real change, and why?

4. Compare and contrast NOW's statement of purpose with the excerpt from Simone de Beauvoir's *The Second Sex* (Document 28-5). What similarities do you see in Friedan's and de Beauvoir's analyses of the place of women in modern society? What differences do you note?

30

Life in an Age of Globalization

1990 to the Present

Although global relationships have impacted the world's economy at least since the time of the Crusades, in the years after the collapse of the Soviet Union triumphal narratives of the expansion of Western ideals of democracy and capitalism began to speak of globalization. Europe's economy was unified as it had never been before, and the interchange of peoples, products, and ideas seemed to be proceeding on Western terms. But in the late 1990s opposition to the cultural and economic domination of the West emerged among both activists in the West and traditionalists in other parts of the world. The skeptical rationalist world that the Enlightenment had created was not welcoming for everyone, and some discontented groups began to return to and reinterpret their traditional identities in opposition to the West. Then in 2008 a new dimension was added to the opposition to economic globalization when an economic crisis in the United States triggered a global economic downturn. The resulting economic upheaval in Europe threatened to reverse the decades-long trend toward European unity.

SOURCES IN CONVERSATION

Islam Versus the West?

The end of the Cold War gave rise to the hope that a new era of international cooperation was about to begin. With the world no longer divided into rival camps along ideological lines, nations would be free to find common interests and to work together to achieve common objectives. However, little more than a decade after the end of the Cold War, many observers were convinced that a new global dividing line had emerged, this time with the West pitted against militant Islam. The two documents included here challenged the validity of this claim. In the first, Amartya Sen examines the proposition that the terrorist attacks of September 11, 2001, were part of a larger "clash of civilizations." In the second, Abdolkarim Soroush argues that secularism, as it has recently evolved in parts of Europe and the United States, can potentially promote discrimination against people who are non-secular and restrict their religious freedom.

READ AND COMPARE

1. How does each of these documents challenge Western concepts about the relationship between the Western world and Islam?

2. How might each of these scholars respond to the arguments of the other? Would they agree with each other's ideas? Why or why not?

30-1 | AMARTYA SEN, *A World Not Neatly Divided* (November 23, 2001)

The widely held assumption that the fall of the Soviet Union had made the world safer was shattered by the terrorist attacks of September 11, 2001. In the wake of the al-Qaeda terrorist attack on the Pentagon and World Trade Center towers, leaders and ordinary individuals alike cast about for an explanation of the horror they had witnessed. Many focused on the fact that the plane hijackers were Muslim, positing a connection between the tenets of Islam and terrorism and suggesting that Islam and the West were locked in a battle for cultural and ideological supremacy. Amartya Sen, an Indian academic then at Cambridge University, argued six weeks after the attacks that this rhetoric of "clashing civilizations" was ill-equipped to capture the complexity of a diverse world.

When people talk about clashing civilizations, as so many politicians and academics do now, they can sometimes miss the central issue. The inadequacy of this thesis begins well before we get to the question of whether civilizations must clash. The basic weakness of the theory lies in its program of categorizing people of the world according to a unique, allegedly commanding system of classification. This is problematic because civilizational categories are crude and inconsistent and also because there are other ways of seeing people (linked to politics, language, literature, class, occupation, or other affiliations).

The befuddling influence of a singular classification also traps those who dispute the thesis of a clash: To talk about "the Islamic world" or "the Western

---

world" is already to adopt an impoverished vision of humanity as unalterably divided. In fact, civilizations are hard to partition in this way, given the diversities within each society as well as the linkages among different countries and cultures. For example, describing India as a "Hindu civilization" misses the fact that India has more Muslims than any other country except Indonesia and possibly Pakistan. It is futile to try to understand Indian art, literature, music, food, or politics without seeing the extensive interactions across barriers of religious communities. These include Hindus and Muslims, Buddhists, Jains,[1] Sikhs,[2] Parsees,[3] Christians (who have been in India since at least the fourth century, well before England's conversion to Christianity [sixth century C.E.]), Jews (present since the fall of Jerusalem [70 C.E.]), and even atheists and agnostics. Sanskrit has a larger atheistic literature than exists in any other classical language. Speaking of India as a Hindu civilization may be comforting to the Hindu fundamentalist, but it is an odd reading of India.

A similar coarseness can be seen in the other categories invoked, like "the Islamic world." Consider Akbar and Aurangzeb, two Muslim emperors of the Mogul[4] dynasty in India. Aurangzeb tried hard to convert Hindus into Muslims and instituted various policies in that direction, of which taxing the non-Muslims was only one example. In contrast, Akbar reveled in his multiethnic court and pluralist laws, and issued official proclamations insisting that no one "should be interfered with on account of religion" and that "anyone is to be allowed to go over to a religion that pleases him."

If a homogeneous view of Islam were to be taken, then only one of these emperors could count as a true Muslim. The Islamic fundamentalist would have no time for Akbar; Prime Minister Tony Blair, given his insistence that tolerance is a defining characteristic of Islam, would have to consider excommunicating Aurangzeb. I expect both Akbar and Aurangzeb would protest, and so would I. A similar crudity is present in the characterization of what is called "Western civilization." Tolerance and individual freedom have certainly been present in European history. But there is no dearth of diversity here, either. When Akbar was making his pronouncements on religious tolerance in Agra [in northern India, near Nepal], in the 1590s, the Inquisitions were still going on; in 1600, Giordano Bruno[5] was burned at the stake, for heresy, in Campo dei Fiori in Rome.

Dividing the world into discrete civilizations is not just crude. It propels us into the absurd belief that this partitioning is natural and necessary and must

---

[1]**Jains:** Followers of one of the oldest religions in India, who believe in the potential of each individual soul. Jains have many beliefs similar to Hindus.

[2]**Sikhs:** Followers of another Indian religion, founded in the fifteenth century but only becoming prominent in the seventeenth. Sikhs were once persecuted by both Hindus and Muslims.

[3]**Parsees:** Members of a branch of Zoroastrianism, the religion of the ancient Persians, believed to have been in India for at least a thousand years.

[4]**Mogul:** Descendants of the Mongols in central India who converted to Islam. Akbar ruled from 1556 to 1605, and Aurangzeb from 1658 to 1707.

[5]**Giordano Bruno:** An Italian who argued that the earth went around the sun, though some of his unusual theological beliefs were the reason why he was burned in a Roman plaza.

overwhelm all other ways of identifying people. That imperious view goes not only against the sentiment that "we human beings are all much the same," but also against the more plausible understanding that we are diversely different. For example, Bangladesh's split from Pakistan was not connected with religion, but with language and politics.

Each of us has many features in our self-conception. Our religion, important as it may be, cannot be an all-engulfing identity. Even a shared poverty can be a source of solidarity across the borders. The kind of division highlighted by, say, the so-called "antiglobalization" protesters—whose movement is, incidentally, one of the most globalized in the world—tries to unite the underdogs of the world economy and goes firmly against religious, national or "civilizational" lines of division.

The main hope of harmony lies not in any imagined uniformity, but in the plurality of our identities, which cut across each other and work against sharp divisions into impenetrable civilizational camps. Political leaders who think and act in terms of sectioning off humanity into various "worlds" stand to make the world more flammable—even when their intentions are very different. They also end up, in the case of civilizations defined by religion, lending authority to religious leaders seen as spokesmen for their "worlds." In the process, other voices are muffled and other concerns silenced. The robbing of our plural identities not only reduces us; it impoverishes the world.

READING QUESTIONS

1. According to Sen, when are generalizations about the world possible? In what ways are they necessary in talking about a complex world?

2. Why might Sen's argument challenge the worldview of both the extremists behind the September 11 attacks and the leaders of the governments who oppose them?

3. What advantages did Sen believe would result from embracing the "plurality of our identities"?

30-2 | ABDOLKARIM SOROUSH, *Militant Secularism* (2007)

Traditional Western narratives of the evolution of secularism, or the movement away from religious institutions and influences in society, tie the origins of secularism in Europe to the Scientific Revolution and the Protestant Reformation beginning in the sixteenth century. The rise of secularism was accompanied by the growth of religious tolerance in European countries and the United States. Recently there have been critiques of the resurgence of Islam, as there are now over 20 million Muslims living in Europe and over 2 million in the United States. Westerners sometimes perceive Muslims to be intolerant of other religions and to be a threat to representative democracy and the rights of women and people with diverse

From Abdolkarim Soroush, "Militant Secularism," lecture at Cite Universaire, Paris, August 2, 2007, Abdolkarim Soroush website, http://drsoroush.com/en/militant-secularism/.

sexual identities. In this document, Abdolkarim Soroush, who is considered the premier Iranian Muslim reformist scholar, pushes back against such critiques, arguing that secularism itself has become intolerant of some religions.

We have at least two types of secularism: political secularism and philosophical secularism. The meaning of political secularism is clear; it means the separation of religion and the State. It means governing this world without concern for the two other worlds, as if this is the only world and we, human beings, are its rulers and our self-justifying reason is the judge of all things. It means that the State's legitimacy is not pegged on religion. It means that the State is neutral towards religions. It means that society's laws are not obtained from religion. But we also have philosophical secularism. Philosophical secularism means that there is no God. There is no supernatural world. There is no hereafter. It is akin to naturalism and materialism. In political secularism, you don't necessarily reject God, but, in politics, you don't concern yourself with God and religion. You don't need to reject the hereafter, but you don't concern yourself with it. But in philosophical secularism, you make judgments and your judgments are negative, you consider religions to be without truth. When Max Weber said that modernity meant the demystification of the world, this is what he meant.

Now, why is it that secularism came into being in the West from the 16th century onwards, whereas it did not develop in the world of Islam and in the East as a whole? What was the factor behind secularism's growth in the West? First and foremost, I have to say in this connection that secularism had a natural birth in the West. In other words, it was an infant that spent the appropriate length of time in the womb of the West's history and, when it had reached its full term, it came into this world; its birth was not accompanied by a Caesarean section and bleeding. We can attribute this to two causes. The first cause was the confrontation and clash between science and religion. The quarrel between science and religion was a very fateful quarrel in the history of Europe. And it was not a product of a conspiracy, ill will, malice or irreligiosity. In fact, it was a very natural quarrel: there was growth in the natural sciences, in geology, biology, astronomy. And new information came to light that was in conflict with the contents of Scripture and the conflict intensified to the point where it became impossible to hide or deny. There was Copernicus, Kepler, Galileo and Newton and, later, Buffon and Darwin. Some of these people were religious themselves. As it happens, Galileo was a religious man. Copernicus was once a priest. Kepler was someone who had gone several steps beyond the common religion of the masses to the point of being superstitious. But the product of these people's work was something that was not in any way in keeping with the contents of Scripture, especially on the subject of the motion of the earth and the sun and the planets. The Church tolerated these ideas for a while but, then, the quarrel flared up. The status that the Church and Scripture acquired thereafter never went back to what it had been before the quarrel. In all fairness, despite all its hostility towards science, the Church did not go down the path of fanaticism. The Church allowed the publication of Copernicus's book. In *The Revolutions of the Heavenly Spheres,* Copernicus explicitly stated that the earth was in motion and that the sun was still, whereas, according to Scripture, it was the sun that moved and the earth that was still. From the 400 copies of the book that were published in the 16th century, 200 still exist today. The tales about Galileo having been put to death are all untrue. Of course, they did put Galileo under house arrest. The Church allowed the publication of Copernicus's book but wrote an introduction to it. And the important point that was made in this introduction was "what is stated in this book is a theory and not the absolute truth." This was a laudable and sensible solution.

The big and small discoveries that were being made here and there gradually robbed Scripture of the status that it had had heretofore. Religion lost its former power and status and, from then on, it was no longer the actor on the social and political stage that it had been before. As long as religion was strong, it was in the political arena. When faith diminished and religion's status declined, this actor ended up playing a smaller role. It was not as if anyone evicted religion from the political stage; it just grew weaker and moved to the sidelines. This is why I said it was a natural birth. The political stage is for powerful players. When religion was strong, there was no need for anyone to invite religion onto the political stage. And, when it grew weak, it inevitably left the stage; there was no need for anyone to evict it.

The second cause was the rupture that occurred in Christianity; that is to say, the birth of Protestantism from the ribs of Catholicism. This Protestantism reduced the Church's strength; in fact, it stood exactly opposite the Church. Martin Luther was the first person to translate the Bible into German. And he said that everyone was their own priest and he rejected the authority of the Church.

These two events together weakened the Christian Church so that it departed from the game of power, and this departure meant that there was now a separation between religion and the State. Some people imagine that, in European countries, some people drew up Constitutions stating that, henceforth, there must be a separation between religion and politics. This was not at all the case. The fact that this has been stated in European Constitutions was the effect of this development, not its cause. At any rate, the secularism that was born was a tolerant secularism. It was not militant. Since it knew that religion was weak, it felt no need to attack it. As recently as about 30 or 40 years ago, many sociologists were of the view that not just Christianity but all religions were on the decline. They believed that history was moving in the direction of political secularism. So, what do you do when faced with weaklings? You are tolerant and you tell yourself that they pose no danger, they are doing no harm, let them have their mosque or church, let them observe their rituals. Secularism proceeded on the assumption that it should be neutral towards religions and view them all in the same light. As far as secularism is concerned, it makes no difference that there are Bahais, Christians, Muslims, Jews and/or Zoroastrians in society, because it assumed that they were all being left behind by history.

Secularism in this sense both led to the separation of religion and the State and adopted a neutral approach to religions. Former US Secretary of State Colin Powell said with pride: "In the US now, you can see mosques and synagogues alongside churches, and they are all coexisting peacefully." And, in fact, this is something to be proud of and it is a very laudable situation.

But gradually secularism enters a new era which I call the era of militant secularism; a secularism that has lost its capacity for tolerance, that does not view all religions in the same light. A secularism that loses its previous, strong digestion system, as if surrendering to secularism's enemies. One example of this is the question of schoolgirls and the *hijab* in France. Or Tony Blair, when he said: "If they don't like our values, they can leave Britain." Turkey's position is the clearest of all in this respect. It officially baulks at the idea of having a Muslim president. Some people come out into the streets in the name of defending secularism and Western media fuel the flames.

First, one of the underlying assumptions of secularism has now been falsified. Political secularism bore one meaning, which is the separation of religion and the State, and one historical prediction, which is that religion will become increasingly weak. Hence, secularism would become easier with every passing day. Today, the prediction has turned out false and this is something that you've been hearing from major sociologists over the past 20 or 30 years, that religions are gaining in strength. We won't go into why this is happening now, but it is happening. In sociology, they were always speaking about the USA as an exception, because religiosity is strong in the US. But now, this is happening everywhere. People like Peter Berger and Jose Casanova are openly saying that secularism is not history's destination; just as they used to say in Marxism that socialism was historically inevitable, but it became clear that this wasn't necessarily the case.

Now, when religions grow stronger, it is not clear whether they will be tolerant towards them. This is a flaw that applies to both liberalism and secularism. Secularism's digestion system was good for swallowing weak religions, but it can't swallow strong religions. They get stuck in its throat so it turns militant. A new theory is needed. Don't look at Al-Qaeda and the like, which the gentlemen like to emphasize. First of all, it is not a broad-based movement and, secondly, it is a minor exception that will not last. This is not what people mean when they say religions are growing stronger.

As to why religion is springing back to life, American sociologists say that it is because there is a crisis of identity. Some others say that there is a crisis of meaning and spirituality. Whatever it may be, there are obviously some causes and, whatever these causes, the effect is what we're seeing. The US attacked Afghanistan and Iraq. Then, both countries stipulated in their new Constitutions that they must derive their laws from the *shariah*. This is something that the Americans couldn't have imagined. In other words, Saddam's secularism has been transformed into the current anti-secularism in Iraq. In Afghanistan, too, they've stated officially that their laws must not contravene the *shariah*. The second time when Mr Bush was elected president, it was because some people thought that he's a very religious man. They made a pact with God and voted for him.

Religious minorities now have a stronger sense of identity. Because of the way they behaved over the *hijab*, the *hijab* has turned into a matter of identity. Before, it used to be a religious matter, like the prayer and fasting that Muslims consider themselves duty-bound to perform without making any claims about it and without making a show of it. They were simply performing their duty. The *hijab* has turned into a matter of identity. Religion has two aspects: identity and truth. And militant secularism unfortunately intensifies the identity aspect of religion. And this is to the detriment of both religion and secularism.

The second point is that, in countries such as Turkey, where religion is strong, secularism cannot be imposed from above, with militancy and high-handedness. As I said, secularism had a natural birth in Europe. Religion grew weak, it left the game of politics. But in Turkey religion isn't weak; more people go to mosques there than they do in Iran. Thirty years ago, when I went to Turkey, I saw big crowds of worshippers in Istanbul's mosques. When I returned to Iran, I said: "I'm sure something is going to happen in Turkey." In Turkey, no one receives rewards for being a Muslim; unlike Iran, where if you make a show of going to the mosque for the ritual prayers a couple of times, it has an impact on your promotion in your university post! There, you can see crowds eagerly going to Friday prayers and the daily congregational prayers which shows that religion is alive. And in a place where religion is alive and strong, it will definitely play a role in politics. If you want to harp on secularism in such a place, then it's clear that it can only be militant secularism; that is to say, a secularism that wants to quarrel, not a secularism that favours tolerance.

In European countries, States are slowly losing their tolerance towards religious minorities and their tolerant secularism is turning into militant secularism, which means that it is no different from religions. Because Secularism was supposed to have been capable of digesting religions; not to turn into a religion in its own right that banishes some other religions. Was this not the objection to religions after all? That an Islamic State, for example, does not treat Jews or Christians well, that it does not view them as equals, that it gives Muslims special rights which it denies to others? Well, if secularism starts behaving in this same way and does not treat non-secular people well and withholds some rights from them, we will have returned to where we began.

I believe that neither liberalism nor secularism will remain in their current form. However — and a thousand howevers — I don't want to conclude, on the basis of what I've said, that we should move towards intolerance. Tolerance is a great human value and virtue, and this isn't even something that we need to learn from foreigners. Hafez, our great poet, said: "In these two phrases lies peace in this world and the next / With friends magnanimity; with enemies, tolerance." From now on, the West must formulate theories on how they intend to be tolerant towards the strong. So far, their theories were directed at being tolerant towards the weak, but now the challenge is greater. Muslims can contribute to the formulation of these theories and offer a civilized response to this challenge.

READING QUESTIONS

1. How does Soroush argue that secularism developed in the West, and how has it evolved recently to become "militant secularism"?

2. How might Westerners who saw the relationship with Islam as a "clash of civilizations" disagree with Soroush's characterization of "militant secularism"?

3. How might Soroush critique the separation of church and state in the United States? Would he argue that religion continues to weaken, and thus secularism continues to rise, or would he argue the opposite?

30-3 | Protesting Globalization

A Greenpeace Activist at the G8 Summit (2001)

The creation of the global economy sped up in the 1990s with the development of the Internet and the accompanying economic boom. As triumphal narratives of a global West emerged, a counternarrative of exploitation of the developing world for the comfort of the world's wealthiest nations emerged as well. Since 2001, every gathering of the G8 (the

Stefano Rellandini/Reuters/Newscom.

leaders of the eight largest economies in the world: France, Germany, Italy, Japan, the United Kingdom, the United States, Canada, and Russia) has been met with organized, sometimes violent, protests. The marchers decry the consumerism and materialism of the West and the use of poorly paid labor in Africa and Asia to sustain Western economies, as suggested by this Greenpeace protester at the 2001 G8 summit in Genoa, Italy.

READING QUESTIONS

1. What criticism is the protester making of American policy? How might the people who benefit from those policies respond?

2. Is there any irony in the ability of the protesters to use the products of the globalized society to protest it? Does that compromise their message or strengthen it?

30-4 | Arab Spring

A Tunisian Woman Casts Her Vote (2011)

In 2011, revolution in Tunisia triggered a chain reaction that led to the fall of the Mubarak regime in Egypt and the outbreak of civil war in Syria. Dubbed the "Arab Spring," a term that recalled prodemocracy uprisings in eastern Europe decades earlier, the events gave hope to many that the era of authoritarian government in North Africa and the Middle East would someday come to an end. In this photograph taken in October 2011, a Tunisian woman casts her vote in the elections that followed the overthrow of the Tunisian dictatorship.

Ezequiel Scagnetti/fotogloria/LUZ/ReduxPictures.

READING QUESTIONS

1. Why might the photographer have chosen to represent the Tunisian election with an image of a woman voting? What implications might this image have had for Western viewers?

2. In your opinion, what are the long-term implications of the Arab Spring for the political development of the Islamic world?

30-5 | Rising Nationalism: Britain Votes to Leave the European Union

NIGEL FARAGE AND OTHERS, *Outcome of the Referendum in the United Kingdom* (2016)

As the world has continued to globalize, migrants have streamed into Europe and the United States in the twenty-first century. Many of them come from the Muslim world or from developing countries that provide bleak economic prospects or that are reeling from the ravages of war, political corruption, or violence because of organized crime. Their arrival is not always welcomed by Europeans and Americans. Coupled with global migration, the rapidly transforming global economy has also caused job losses and economic distress for many people, leading to the rise of nationalism, xenophobia, and insularity in contemporary politics in Europe and the United States. Such trends contributed in 2016 to the election of President Donald Trump in the United States and also to the referendum known as Brexit, where British people voted to leave the European Union. In this document, the chief political architect of Brexit, Nigel Farage, lauds the result of the vote as he addresses the European Parliament.

Mr President, isn't it funny? When I came here 17 years ago and said that I wanted to lead a campaign to get Britain to leave the European Union, you all laughed at me. Well I have to say, you're not laughing now, are you? And the reason you are so upset, the reason you are so angry, has been perfectly clear from all the angry exchanges this morning: you, as a political project, are in denial. You are in denial that your currency is failing. You are in denial. . . .

Well, just look at the Mediterranean. No, no, as a policy to impose poverty on Greece and the rest of the Mediterranean you have done very well, and you are in denial over Ms Merkel's[1] call last year for as many people as possible to cross the Mediterranean into the European Union, which has led to massive divisions between countries and within countries. But the biggest problem you have got, and the main reason the United Kingdom voted the way that it did, is that you have, by stealth, by deception, without ever telling the truth to the British or the rest of the peoples of Europe, imposed upon them a political union. You

---

From Nigel Farage, "Outcome of the Referendum in the United Kingdom (debate)," Tuesday, June 28, 2016, Brussels, European Parliament website, http://www.europarl.europa.eu /sides/getDoc.do?pubRef=-//EP//TEXT+CRE+20160628+ITEM-004+DOC+XML+V0 //EN&language=EN.

[1]**Ms. Merkel:** Angela Merkel, chancellor of Germany since 2005.

have imposed upon them a political union, and when the people in 2005 in the Netherlands and France voted against that political union, when they rejected the Constitution, you simply ignored them and brought the Lisbon Treaty[2] in through the back door.

What happened last Thursday was a remarkable result. It was indeed a seismic result, not just for British politics, for European politics, but perhaps even for global politics, too, because what the little people did, what the ordinary people did, the people who have been oppressed over the last few years and seen their living standards go down, they rejected the multinationals. They rejected the merchant banks, they rejected big politics, and they said, actually, we want our country back. We want our fishing waters back, we want our borders back, we want to be an independent, self-governing normal nation, and that is what we have done and that is what must happen. And in doing so, we now offer a beacon of hope to democrats across the rest of the European continent. I will make one prediction this morning: the United Kingdom will not be the last Member State to leave the European Union.

So the question is: what we do next? Now it is up to the British Government to invoke Article 50 and I have to say that I do not think we should spend too long in doing it. I totally agree, Mr Juncker,[3] that the British people have voted. We need to make sure that it happens. But what I would like to see is a grown-up and sensible attitude to how we negotiate a different relationship.

Now I know that virtually none of you have ever done a proper job in your lives . . . or worked in business, or worked in trade, or indeed ever created a job. But listen. Just listen. . . . UKIP[4] used to protest against the establishment, and now the establishment protests against UKIP, so something has happened here. Let us listen to some simple pragmatic economics. We, between us, between your countries and my country, do an enormous amount of business in goods and services. That trade is mutually beneficial to both of us. That trade matters. If you were to decide to cut off your noses to spite your faces and to reject any idea of a sensible trade deal, the consequences would be far worse for you than it would be for us.

Even no deal is better for the United Kingdom than the current rotten deal that we have got. But if we were to move to a position where tariffs were reintroduced on products like motor cars, then hundreds of thousands of German workers would risk losing their jobs. So why don't we just be pragmatic, sensible, grown-up, realistic and let's cut between us a sensible tariff-free deal, and thereafter recognise that the United Kingdom will be your friend, that we will trade with you, we will cooperate with you, we will be your best friends in the world, but do it sensibly and allow us to go off and pursue our global ambitions and future.

. . .

---

[2] **Lisbon Treaty:** Treaty that took effect in 2009 that reorganized the political structure of the European Union, giving more power to the European Parliament.

[3] **Mr Juncker:** Luxembourg politician serving as the president of the European Parliament.

[4] **UKIP:** UK Independence Party, which pushed for Britain to leave the European Union.

Mr President, the London stock market is rallying strongly this morning. It is now 12% up since its February lows. Sterling is weak, but then it started declining from July 2014, and the Prime Ministers of Australia and New Zealand are now vying for who can be the first country from outside the EU to do a trade deal with the United Kingdom. Things are looking pretty good.

The only upheaval is political upheaval, where we have seen a Prime Minister resign and indeed the British Commissioner, Lord Hill resign. I think they have both done so for the right reasons. You never know, we may be getting rid of a Labour Party leader as well. But upheavals in politics can actually be a very healthy and a very good thing. I got into politics because our political class in Britain led us towards a European political project. So, if that result last week sweeps a few of them away, so be it. But I am looking forward next year to celebrating our independence day on 23 June.

READING QUESTIONS

1. What tone does Farage use in addressing the members of the Parliament? Why is he using that tone?

2. What does Farage argue are the benefits of Britain leaving the European Union? How did membership in the union impact Britain, and how does it impact other European countries, according to him?

3. What does Farage need to happen for Brexit to be a success for Britain? How likely do you think it will be for those things to happen?

4. How does Farage's speech reflect British nationalism, xenophobia, and distrust of global financial elites?

■ COMPARATIVE AND DISCUSSION QUESTIONS ■

1. How might Sen and Soroush disagree about the basis of personal identity in the globalized society? On what points might they agree? How might they disagree with Farage?

2. Would Sen and Soroush support the process of globalization? What reaction do you think they would have to the protesters against the G8?

3. Based on the documents in this chapter, what are the bases for individual and group identity in the globalizing world?

4. How would Sen and Soroush respond to the arguments of Farage, and vice versa? How would each of them respond to the events of the Arab Spring?

5. In your opinion, can an appropriate analogy be made between the Cold War (see Chapter 28) and current relations between the West and the Islamic world? How do recent events in Tunisia, Egypt, and Syria fit into your analysis?

Acknowledgments (*continued from page iv*)

Chapter 11

11-6 Republished with permission of Manchester University Press from Craig Taylor, trans. and ed., *Joan of Arc: La Pucelle* (Manchester, U.K.: Manchester University Press, 2006), pp. 82–83, 125–127; permission conveyed through Copyright Clearance Center, Inc.

Chapter 12

12-4 From Desiderius Erasmus, *The Education of a Christian Prince*, translated by Lester K. Born. Copyright © 1936 by Columbia University Press. Reprinted with permission of Columbia University Press.

12-5 Christine de Pizan, excerpts from *The Book of the City of Ladies*, translated by Earl J. Richards, pp. 153–155. Copyright © 1982, 1998 by Persea Books, Inc. Reprinted with the permission of Persea Books, Inc. (New York), www.perseabooks.com. All rights reserved.

Chapter 13

13-4 Excerpt (pp. 208–213) from Jean Bodin, *On the Demon-Mania of Witches*, translated by Randy A. Scott, with an introduction by Jonathan L. Pearl. Reprinted by permission of the Centre for Reformation & Renaissance Studies, Victoria University.

Chapter 14

14-1 Material originally published in *The Diario of Christopher Columbus's First Voyage to America, 1942–1943*, trans. by Oliver Dunn and James E. Kelly, Jr. Copyright © 1989 by Oliver Dunn and James E. Kelly, Jr. Reprinted by permission of the publisher, University of Oklahoma Press.

14-4 From Basil Davidson, *The African Past: Chronicles from Antiquity to Modern Times* (Boston: Little, Brown and Company, 1964), pp. 191–193; reissued by Africa World Press in 1990 as African Civilization Revisited: From Antiquity to Modern Times. Reproduced with permission of Curtis Brown Ltd., on behalf of the Beneficiaries of the Estate of Basil Davidson.

Chapter 16

16-3 Galileo Galilei, "Letter to the Grand Duchess Christina," in *The Galileo Affair: A Documentary History*, translated by Maurice A. Finocchiaro. Copyright © 1989 by The Regents of the University of California. Reprinted by permission of the University of California Press.

Chapter 19

19-3 The Law of Prairial and the Great Terror (Fall, year IV), from *Histoire Socialiste de la Revolution*, Editions Sociales, 1968, translated for marxists.org, Marxists Internet Archive by Mitchell Abidor.

19-4 From E. A. Arnold, ed. and trans., *A Documentary Survey of Napoleonic France* (Lanham, Md.: University Press of America, 1993), pp. 151–164. Reprinted by permission of Rowman & Littlefield.

19-6 From François Dominique Toussaint L'Ouverture, Letter, in *The Black Jacobins*, 2nd Edition, edited by C. L. R. James. Reproduced by permission of Curtis Brown Group Ltd., London on behalf of the Estate of C L R James. Copyright © C L R James, 1938.

Chapter 23

23-2 Otto von Bismarck, Speech Before the Reichstag: On the Law for Workers' Compensation (1884). Republished with permission of University of Chicago Press, from *Readings in Western Civilization, Volume 8, Nineteenth-Century Europe: Liberalism and Its Critics*, edited and translated by John W. Boyer. Copyright © 1988 University of Chicago Press; permission conveyed through Copyright Clearance Center, Inc.

Chapter 26

26-1 From *The Interpretation of Dreams* by Sigmund Freud and edited and translated by James Strachey, copyright © 1955, 2010. Reprinted by permission of Basic Books, an imprint of Hachette Book Group, Inc., The Random House Group Limited, and The Marsh Agency Ltd. on behalf of The Estate of Sigmund Freud.

Chapter 27

27-2 From Joseph Stalin, "Speech Delivered by Stalin at a Meeting of Voters of the Stalin Electoral District, Moscow," February 09, 1946, History and Public Policy Program Digital Archive, Gospolitizdat, Moscow, 1946. http://digitalarchive.wilsoncenter.org/document/116179. Reprinted by permission of the Woodrow Wilson International Center for Scholars.

27-3 Excerpt from *Mein Kampf* by Adolf Hitler, translated by Ralph Mannheim. Copyright © 1943, renewed 1971 by Houghton Mifflin Harcourt Publishing Company. Reprinted by permission of Houghton Mifflin Harcourt Publishing Company. All rights reserved.

Chapter 28

28-2 From *One Day in the Life of Ivan Denisovich*, by Alexander Solzhenitsyn, translated by Ralph Parker. English translation copyright © 1963, renewed © 1991 by Penguin Random House LLC and Victor Gollancz Ltd. Used by permission of Dutton, an imprint of Penguin Publishing Group, a division of Penguin Random House LLC. All rights reserved.

28-3 From Winston Churchill, "Sinews of Peace" speech, March 5, 1946. Reproduced with permission of Curtis Brown, London, on behalf of The Estate of Winston S. Churchill. Copyright © The Estate of Winston S. Churchill.

28-5 Simone de Beauvoir, from *The Second Sex* by Simone de Beauvoir and translated by Constance Borde and Sheila Malovany-Chevallier, translation copyright © 2009 by Constance Borde and Sheila Malovany-Chevallier. Used by permission of Alfred A. Knopf, an imprint of the Knopf Doubleday Publishing Group, a division of Penguin Random House LLC. All rights reserved.

Chapter 29

29-1 pp. 3–5, 7–8, 10, 22–24 from *Perestroika* by Mikhail Gorbachev. Copyright © 1987 by Mikhail Gorbachev. Reprinted by permission of HarperCollins Publishers.

29-2 Václav Havel, New Year's Address to the Nation (1990). Reprinted by permission of the Dilia Agency on behalf of the Estate of Václav Havel.

29-4 The National Organization for Women's 1966 Statement of Purpose, adopted October 29, 1966. https://now.org/about/history/statement-of-purpose/. Reprinted by permission.

29-5 From Lech Wałęsa, "Letter of Lech Wałęsa to the Council of State," Wilson Center Digital Archive website, https://digitalarchive.wilsoncenter.org/document/113097. Reprinted by permission of the Woodrow Wilson International Center for Scholars.

Chapter 30

30-1 Amartya Sen, "A World Not Neatly Divided," *The New York Times*, November 23, 2001. Copyright © 2001 The New York Times. All rights reserved. Used under license.

30-2 From AbdolKarim Soroush, "Militant Secularism," lecture at Cite Universaire, Paris, August 2, 2007, AbdolKarim Soroush website, http://drsoroush.com/en/militant-secularism/. Reprinted by permission of AbdolKarim Soroush.

30-5 From Nigel Farage, "Outcome of the Referendum in the United Kingdom (debate)," Tuesday, June 28, 2016, Brussels. Reprinted by permission.